Human-Computer Interaction Series

Human-Computer Interaction is a multidisciplinary field focused on human aspects of the development of computer technology. As computer-based technology becomes increasingly pervasive - not just in developed countries, but worldwide - the need to take a human-centered approach in the design and development of this technology becomes ever more important. For roughly 30 years now, researchers and practitioners in computational and behavioral sciences have worked to identify theory and practice that influences the direction of these technologies, and this diverse work makes up the field of human-computer interaction. Broadly speaking it includes the study of what technology might be able to do for people and how people might interact with the technology.

In this series, we present work which advances the science and technology of developing systems which are both effective and satisfying for people in a wide variety of contexts. The human-computer interaction series will focus on theoretical perspectives (such as formal approaches drawn from a variety of behavioral sciences), practical approaches (such as the techniques for effectively integrating user needs in system development), and social issues (such as the determinants of utility, usability and acceptability).

Author guidelines: www.springer.com/authors/book+authors > Author Guidelines

For other titles published in this series, go to
http://www.springer.com/series/6033

John M. Carroll
Editor

Learning in Communities

Interdisciplinary Perspectives on Human Centered Information Technology

Springer

Editor
John M. Carroll
The Pennsylvania State University
College of Information Sciences and Technology
307H IST Building
University Park, PA 16802-6823, USA
jcarroll@ist.psu.edu

Human-Computer Interaction Series ISSN: 1571-5035
ISBN: 978-1-84996-786-0 e-ISBN: 978-1-84800-332-3
DOI 10.1007/978-1-84800-332-3

British Library Cataloguing in Publication Data
A catalogue record for this book is available from the British Library

Printed on acid-free paper

Springer Science+Business Media
springer.com

Preface

Most learning takes place in communities. People continually learn through their participation with others in everyday activities. Such learning is important in contemporary society because formal education cannot prepare people for a world that changes rapidly and continually. We need to live in learning communities.

A discourse on learning in communities encompasses (at least) communities of practice, learning communities, community networks, communities of interest, learning organizations, learning-by-doing, cognitive apprenticeship, subjugated learning, collaborative/cooperative learning, situated cognition, design as inquiry, knowledge management, lifelong learning, informal learning, case-based learning, and learning cultures. Although it is difficult to find any contemporary technical work in the multidisciplinary space of informal learning and collaborative activity that does not appeal to at least one of these touchstone concepts, it is also difficult to find work that tries to confront or to systematize the full range of these concepts.

Existing conferences tend to "stovepipe" such discussions: Thus, meetings of the Cognitive Science Society and the Journal of the Learning Sciences focus much attention on the concepts of cognitive apprenticeship, situated cognition, collaborative/cooperative learning, and even classroom-based learning communities, but ignore informal and collective learning, such as learning organizations, community networks, and learning cultures. Information systems conference and journals focus much attention on knowledge management and learning organizations, but do not focus on community networks and informal learning. The Computer-Support Cooperative Work Conference and Journal address knowledge management, communities of practice, and to a limited extent on community networks, but do not consider case-based learning, learning cultures, lifelong learning, or subjugated learning. The Communities and Technology Conferences and journals like Community Informatics focus on communities of practice, community networks, and subjugated learning, but do not address issues such as cognitive apprenticeship, situated cognition, and learning communities.

The Meeting

On August 14–17, 2005, a multidisciplinary group of scholars met at Penn State's College of Information Sciences and Technology to discuss "learning in communities." The goals of this workshop were to bring together a wide range of perspectives and approaches to learning in communities, to articulate the state of the art, and to define agendas for research and technology infrastructures and initiatives. The group included the following:

- **Ann Bishop**, Graduate School of Library and Information Science, University of Illinois, Champaign: Bishop is interested in community information systems for traditionally marginalized groups; she was a founder of the PrairieNet community network.
- **John M. Carroll**, College of Information Sciences and Technology and Center for Human-Computer Interaction, Penn State, University Park: Carroll investigates social and computational infrastructures for community-based learning, and is Principal Investigator for the National Science Foundation's Civic Nexus project in sustainable information technology learning.
- **Andrew Clement**, Faculty of Information Studies, University of Toronto: Clement has worked in community informatics for 30 years, and is currently Principal Investigator for the Canadian Research Alliance for Community Innovation and Networking.
- **Nancy Kranich**, Library Consultant and Past President of the American Library Association: Kranich is interested in the role of libraries in providing an information commons, facilitating community-building and democracy, and in enhancing civic literacy.
- **Gerhard Fischer**, Department of Computer Science and Institute for Cognitive Science, University of Colorado, Boulder: Fischer investigates reflective communities, tools, and environments to support lifelong learning, and in facilitating creativity.
- **Christopher Hoadley**, Department of Instructional Systems and School of Information Sciences and Technology, Penn State, University Park: Hoadley is interested in knowledge-building communities, and in techniques for measuring community achievements.
- **Andrea Kavanaugh**, Center for Human-Computer Interaction, Virginia Tech, Blacksburg, VA: Kavanaugh investigates communication behavior and effects in the context of community networks; she made a decade-long study of the Blacksburg Electronic Village, and is now evaluating Internet services in local government.
- **Lynette Kvasney**, School of Information Sciences and Technology and Center for the Information Society, Penn State, University Park: Kvasney is interested in how inner-city and third-world women understand and recruit information technology to build social, cultural, and economic capital.
- **Jenny Preece**, University of Maryland, College Park, MD: Preece has studied behavior in health-related communities, contrasting face-to-face and online interactions; she is currently investigating community development in the context of the International Children's Digital Library.

- **Paul Resnick**, School of Information, University of Michigan, Ann Arbor: Resnick is interested in the role universities could play in information technology cooperative extension, and in how to cultivate information technology careers in the civic sector.
- **Mary Beth Rosson**, School of Information Sciences and Technology and Center for Human-Computer Interaction, Penn State, University Park: Rosson investigates end-user programming and design, particularly in community computing contexts.
- **Jorge Schement**, Department of Telecommunications and Institute for Information Policy, Penn State, University Park: Schement investigates telecommunication policy implications for Hispanic-American communities, rural areas, and evolving conceptions of democracy.
- **Mark Schlager**, Center for Technology in Learning, SRI, Menlo Park, CA: Schlager is interested in community infrastructures, and has investigated community-based approaches to teacher professional development in TappedIn through the past decade.
- **Murali Venkatesh**, School of Information Studies, Syracuse University, NY: Venkatesh investigates power and progressive social action in the context of broadband civic network planning.
- **Volker Wulf**, University of Siegen and Fraunhofer Institute of Applied Information Technology, Germany: Wulf is interested in supporting knowledge management in communities and social networks, especially in the context of multicultural communities.

Also participating were **Umer Farooq**, **Roderick Lee**, **Cecelia Merkel**, and **Lu Xiao** who were then doctoral and postdoctoral students at Penn State.

Orienting Themes and Questions

We developed a set of orienting questions, as part of the planning process for the workshop and successively elaborated through the course of the workshop itself.

- *Design:* What are effective strategies and methods for initiating (designing) and sustaining communities of various types? How do and how can communities evolve over time?
- *Learning:* Is learning, in the sense of human development, constitutive of healthy communities? How can communities facilitate various educational objectives, such as lifelong learning, cross-generational learning, knowledge building, and universal technology literacy? What is the role of the university in facilitating communities, with respect to service learning, better integration of community action and research, and support for careers in civic information technology?
- *Context:* How can communities cultivate and leverage indigenous/subjugated knowledge? How do communities cope with power structures of the cultures and institutions in which they are embedded?
- *Agency:* How can communities facilitate innovation and collective action?

- *Measurement and evaluation:* How can we know when a community project or a community succeeds/fails? What are effective strategies and methods for assessing the impacts (e.g., learning, knowledge sharing) of communities on their participants individually and collectively? What are current success stories?
- *Infrastructure:* What are useful information technology tools and techniques for promoting community objectives (end-user programming, participatory design)? How can information technology support community building (e.g., by increasing opportunities for civic discourse and by visualizing the community to itself)?
- *Theory:* What are useful models, theories, and frameworks for understanding community dynamics (activity theory, distributed cognition)?
- *Diversity:* How can different audiences' needs be met? What power issues relate to different participants' roles and backgrounds? Are there ways that communities can be designed to enhance interconnection between different types of people? How can communities facilitate communication and cooperation across international, cultural, and social boundaries?

Our discussion wound up focusing on three theme clusters: (1) learning in the context of community informatics, (2) paradigms of research and action for studies of learning in community, and (3) community infrastructures that facilitate learning.

Learning in the Context of Community Informatics

We distinguished "learning in communities," in which learning is often informal, incidental, and integrated with participation in community activity, from "learning communities," which exist for and are all about learning. Learning in communities is not just reciprocal or mutual learning; it is the collaborative construction of ideas in practice.

This concept of learning in communities is implicit in democracy, and discovering how to facilitate such learning is a challenge in the future trajectory of democracy in an age when face-to-face learning may become less important. A key issue for community informatics is how to construct environments that encourage sharing of knowledge, particularly about content and perspectives that are not mainstream.

Paradigms of Research and Action for Studies of Learning in Communities

There is a tension between research and action in studies of learning in communities. Many of the workshop participants engage in some form of participatory action research. These methods are appropriate, but they are very costly with respect to the time and effort of faculty and students. Standard promotion and tenure values do not weigh community outreach highly.

In US land grant universities, there is a well-developed concept of cooperative extension, although its history is primarily agricultural outreach. Perhaps, a concept of information technology cooperative extension could be developed as a more standard model. One issue to consider is that, within universities, there often is a clear distinction between cooperative extension faculty and "regular" research and teaching faculty. Perhaps, the extension model would just institutionalize the tension between research and action.

One approach to this tension is to clearly divide consultancy and research engagement. For example, school systems and commercial organizations have well-articulated concepts of consultant. In such a role, one can efficiently provide guidance for a client's problem. But successful consulting often requires focusing totally on solving a specific problem at hand, and not abstracting or generalizing that problem, or on enrolling practitioners as research collaborators.

Consultancy as an action research paradigm produces case studies that can subsequently be reflected on and developed as research activities. (Donald Schon might be a good example of this.)

Community Infrastructures that Facilitate Learning

Infrastructure is the sociotechnical background that allows work activity to move smoothly. It includes hardware and software, processes of governance, social facilitation of learning, and cultural and cognitive models.

Infrastructure is often invisible, but invisibility can entail neglect and breakdown, and can replicate existing power structures. Different segments of society are differentially able to shape infrastructures.

One strategy for managing infrastructures is to make them more visible and participatory, especially during periods of transition when infrastructures are changing. A related strategy is to slow down adoption through collective resistance. One tool for this is raising questions about infrastructures.

We are in a period now of rapid development and adoption of new information technology infrastructures. Several workshop participants are exploring alternative infrastructure initiatives that attempted to deliberately strengthen specific aspects of community-oriented activity, such as discussion and debate or visualization of the community.

This Book

This volume gathers together all of the scholarly materials directly emanating from the workshop. The participants used the workshop as a catalyst for three multidisciplinary discussions of learning in communities. Initially, a sectioned report on the workshop, incorporating ten short papers, was published as a special section in the *Journal of Community Informatics,* volume 2, number 2, in 2006 (www.ci-journal.net/). Subsequently, a special issue of five full papers was published in the *Journal of Computer-Supported Cooperative Work*, volume 16, 2007, and a special section of two full papers was published in the *International Journal of Computer-Supported Collaborative Learning*, volume 2, in 2007.

Part I presents the ten short papers from the special section of the *Journal of Community Informatics*. In Chap. 1, Ann Peterson Bishop, Bertrum C. Bruce, and Cameron Jones argue that community inquiry is a core mechanism of effective collaborative learning. In Chap. 2, John Carroll argues that, in participatory approaches to community-based learning, the designer/researcher must act in the periphery to be effective. In Chap. 3, Gerhard Fischer describes how learning in community transcends individual learning by better exploiting human diversity and social sources of creativity. In Chap. 4, Fischer, along with Markus Rohde and Volker Wulf, argues that traditional universities can incorporate community-based learning models – an idea they subsequently developed more fully in a full paper (see below).

In Chap. 5, Andrea Kavanaugh and Philip Isenhour describe a planning process for developing specialized wiki/weblog applications to support civic and political deliberation among community members. In Chap. 6, Volmar Pipek, Mary Beth Rosson, Gunnar Stevens, and Volker Wulf argue that technology appropriation by communities of citizens requires many specific kinds of support. In Chap. 7, Rosson, with John Carroll, describes a community-based learning project involving women at various levels of development as information technology professionals. In Chap. 8, Lynette Kvasney describes how digital divides tend to reproduce larger patterns of inequity, and what strategies might interrupt such a status quo. In Chap. 9, Kvasney, with Nancy Kranich and Jorge Reina Schement, reminds us that effective digital access requires far more than the mere possibility of transmitting bits. In Chap. 10, Murali Venkatesh and Jeffrey Owens continue this line of analysis, viewing design, and the design of civic networks in particular, as inherently a battleground in the social construction of technology between entrenched cultural practices and alternatives.

Part II presents the seven full papers from the *Journal of Computer-Supported Cooperative Work* and the *International Journal of Computer-Supported Collaborative Learning*. Chapter 11, by Andrea Kavanaugh, Than Than Zin, Mary Beth Rosson, John M. Carroll, Joseph Schmitz, and B. Joon Kim, presents results from a longitudinal survey study of the Blacksburg Electronic Village community. The chapter investigates how affiliation with community-oriented groups affects political participation in the community. For example, as members' uses of information technology within local groups increase over time, so do their levels and types of involvement in community groups. Further, these increases most often appear among people who serve as opinion leaders and maintain weak social ties within their communities.

In Chap. 12, Gerhard Fischer, Markus Rohde, and Volker Wulf argue that learning in communities – in a variety of specific senses – provides a more effective alternative to what they call traditional "instructionist teaching." They describe their own experiences from the University of Colorado and the University of Siegen demonstrating how community-based learning can be integrated into a computer science curriculum.

In Chap. 13, Umer Farooq, Patricia Schank, Alexandra Harris, Judith Fusco, and Mark Schlager report on a decade-long design research investigation of an online community environment supporting thousands of geographically dispersed educators across many communities of practice. Many online community projects are initially interesting, but not sustainable. The authors discuss four design strategies they believe are critical to developing sustainable online environments for professional communities of practice.

In Chap. 14, Tim Reichling, Michael Veith, and Volker Wulf describe recommender system support for expertise sharing within communities of practice. They describe a 3-year case study involving a requirements gathering field study and design of an expert recommender system in a European industrial association. The recommender system took document collections as an indicator of an actor's expertise. The practices and politics of expertise sharing in this organization and the fit with existing software infrastructures were determining factors in this case.

In Chap. 15, John M. Carroll and Umer Farooq develop and illustrate the proposal that design patterns, in the sense that term is used by Christopher Alexander, provide a useful level of description for design solutions for addressing problems in community-based learning. They draw on a decade of experience working collaborative with local nonprofit groups to address learning challenges regarding the use of information technology.

In Chap. 16, Murali Venkatesh and Mawaki Chango consider how cultural values shape the basic telecommunications and Internet access services upon which software applications depend. The politics of infrastructure design are investigated in a case study of the development of a reference architecture for broadband civic networking and its impacts in a particular urban community.

The final chapter is "Supporting Community Emergency Management Planning Through a Geocollaboration Software Architecture," by Wendy A. Schafer, Craig H. Ganoe, and John M. Carroll. Community emergency management planning involves many stakeholders throughout a community. Geocollaboration is critical: Emergency managers, public works directors, first responders, and local transportation managers need to exchange information relating to possible emergency event locations and their surrounding areas. The software architecture was developed through a case study of planning for emergency management applications in a community in central Pennsylvania.

This collection of chapters is not the definitive summary of learning in communities. It is assuredly more prolegomena than coda. Learning is increasingly recognized as a critical facet of lifetime activity, one that must be become better integrated with all that people do. At the same time, community structures are increasingly recognized as a critical category of social organization – flexible and adaptable, capable of innovation and development, and yet just as strongly nurturing and supportive. The promise of learning in communities lies ahead of us. Hopefully, this set of essays will propel us all along that path.

Acknowledgments The Learning in Communities workshop was partially supported by the US National Science Foundation (IIS-0511198). I especially thank Dr. Suzi Iacono of NSF who supported this workshop through her now-legendary "Digital Society and Technology" program. I thank the editors-in-chief of the three journals that originally published the workshop papers that are gathered and re-presented here: Dr. Michael Gurstein, editor-in-chief of the *Journal of Community Informatics*, Dr. Kjeld Schmidt, editor-in-chief of the *Journal of Computer-Supported Cooperative Work*, and Dr. Gerry Stahl, editor-in-chief of the *International Journal of Computer-Supported Collaborative Learning.* I also thank Dr. Ann Bishop for her guidance and assistance in preparing the special section of short papers for the *Journal of Community Informatics*.

University Park, PA, USA John M. Carroll

Contents

Part I

Chapter 1
Community Inquiry and Informatics: Collaborative Learning Through ICT

Ann Peterson Bishop, Bertram C. Bruce, and M. Cameron Jones

Studies of learning and human-computer interaction have often focused on settings and practices that are relatively fixed and well- defined, such as a college-level course, a workgroup in a company, or a museum exploration. These studies have contributed much to our understanding of the potential and the problems associated with incorporating computers into collaborative practice. They have also contributed to the analysis of how learning happens in a wide range of settings. However, such well-defined situations represent but a small portion of realities that are relevant to the field of community informatics (CI), which aims to understand how information and communication technologies (ICTs) are employed to help communities achieve their goals (Gurstein, 2004; Keeble & Loader, 2001). When viewed from the perspective of learning in communities, we see the challenge facing CI in the form of four research questions:

- How do people learn within communities?
- How do communities themselves learn?
- What tools facilitate learning within communities?
- How can communities develop shared capacity in the form of knowledge, skills, and tools?

Our work is grounded in the philosophy of American pragmatism, which rose to prominence at the end of the nineteenth century and introduced the theory and practice of what we call *community inquiry* into a range of fields, including aesthetics, education, social work, law, and public citizenship (Menand, 2001). Developed most fully in the work of John Dewey, community inquiry is based on the premise that if individuals are to understand and create solutions for problems in complex systems, they need opportunities to engage with challenging questions, to learn through participative investigations situated in everyday experiences, to articulate their ideas to others, and to make use of a variety of resources in multiple media. These processes of inquiry form an attitude toward work and life that consists of eager and alert observations, a constant questioning of old procedure in light of new observations, and a use of grounded experience as well as recorded knowledge. The ultimate aim of community inquiry is to develop a "critical, socially engaged intelligence, which enables individuals to understand and participate effectively in the

J.M. Carroll (ed.), *Learning in Communities*,

affairs of their community in a collaborative effort to achieve a common good" (John Dewey Project on Progressive Education, 2002).

Community inquiry and informatics combine in the "pragmatic technology" (Hickman, 1990) approach to community-based ICT creation and use. Pragmatic technology encompasses the common language notion of how to design tools to meet real human needs and accommodate to users in their lived situations. It also sees ICTs as developed within a community of inquiry and embodying both means of action and forms of understanding; ICTs are an end result of, as well as a means to accomplish, community learning. Schuler and Day (2004) clearly resonate with the ideas and practice of pragmatic technology in declaring the "subordination of ICTs to building healthy, empowered, active communities" (p. 15) and noting simply that "researchers are part of the world in which they live" (p. 219).

Our Community Informatics Initiative (http://www.cii.uiuc.edu) is an effort to learn how pragmatic, community-based technology can support learning across institutional and social boundaries. The CII provides training and education, consulting, and action research in community inquiry and informatics in collaboration with nonprofit organizations and individuals worldwide. It has produced Community Inquiry Laboratories (iLabs) (http://ilabs.inquiry.uiuc.edu), a suite of free, open-source, web-based software that is developed in an open and ongoing fashion by people from all walks of life who represent different countries and a wide range of ages. iLabs have been used to create hundreds of interactive Web sites that support the communication and collaboration needed to pursue inquiry in classrooms, community centers, libraries, professional associations, research groups, and other settings—without having to download and install software or have your own server (Bishop et. al, 2004). iLabs includes software for producing library catalogs, syllabi, document sharing, online inquiry units, discussion forums, blogs, calendars, and image galleries.

iLabs represents experimentation in the integration of community inquiry and informatics. Through collaborative effort (both implicit and explicit, purposive and unknowing) in the creation of content, contribution to interactive elements, incorporation into practice, suggestions and questions, reports of what works and what doesn't, and ongoing discussion, community members are not merely recipients of these technologies, but participate actively in their ongoing development, yielding enhancements which are then available to all users while, at the same time, they learn more about ICT. We have referred to his process of end user software development as "design through use" or "participatory inquiry." To cite just a few examples:

- Members of SisterNet (a local grassroots organization of Black women devoted to nurturing a healthier lifestyle and community activism) created new templates for web-based Inquiry Units that were better suited for the personal health plans they wanted to make;
- Youth in the Paseo Boricua community in Chicago helped develop a web-based catalog for the library in the Puerto Rican Cultural Center, a tool that other iLab users can now adapt for their own purposes;

- A doctoral student in Finland, high school students in France, and others helped develop a system for translating the iLabs interface into multiple languages;
- A local environmental group figured out a way to use iLabs for polling citizens.

Collaborative inquiry has helped us investigate community interactions in many ways, come to a better understanding of "community" as a unit of analysis in multiple endeavors, and experiment with modes of open and mutual learning as a primary process for a range of disparate activities, from software development to the installation of art exhibits.

Acknowledgments We wish to thank the Institute for Museum and Library Services and National Science Foundation, whose support helped create the iLabs software. We are grateful for the creativity and hard work of all members of the iLabs collaborative, who have contributed their considerable energy and expertise to community learning.

References

Bishop, A. P., Bruce, B. C., Lunsford, K. J., Jones, M. C., Nazarova, M., Linderman, D., Won, M., Heidorn, P. B., Ramprakash, R., & Brock, A. (2004). Supporting community inquiry with digital resources. *Journal of Digital Information,* 5(3), Article No. 308. Available at: http://jodi.ecs.soton.ac.uk/Articles/v05/i03/Bishop/

Gurstein, M. B. (2004). Editorial: Welcome to the Journal of Community Informatics. *Journal of Community Informatics, 1*(1). Available at: http://ci-journal.net/viewarticle.php? id=29&layout=html

Hickman, L. A. (1990). *John Dewey's pragmatic technology*. Bloomington, IN: Indiana University Press.

John Dewey Project on Progressive Education. (2002). *A brief overview of progressive education.* Available at: http://www.uvm.edu/~dewey/articles/proged.html

Keeble, L., & Loader, B. D. (Eds.). (2001). *Community informatics: Shaping computer-mediated social relations*. London: Routledge.

Menand, L. (2001). *The metaphysical club*. NY: Farrar, Straus and Giroux.

Schuler, D., & Day, P. (2004). *Community practice in the network society: Local action/global interaction*. London: Routledge.

Chapter 2
The Participant-Observer in Community-Based Learning as Community Bard

John M. Carroll

During the past three years our Civic Nexus research group (http://cscl.ist.psu.edu) has been involved in a collection of community learning projects with groups in Centre County, Pennsylvania, a rural area of about 1,000 square miles with a population of 140,000, including the fairly cosmopolitan college town of State College (population 75,000) and the main campus of the Pennsylvania State University. The focus of the project is to investigate, develop, and assess sustainable strategies to help these groups better control their own information technology. We have worked with the county historical society, the regional emergency management coordinator, a sustainable development group, the enrichment program at the local high school, the local chapter of Habitat for Humanity, the symphony orchestra, the local food bank, an environmental preservation group, a local emergency medical services council, a group that works with at-risk youth, and with a group that trains leaders for community groups.

Our original project concept was to form participatory action research (PAR) relationships with these groups, to jointly undertake technology development projects through which our partners would learn by doing, and we could observe how the learning occurred, and how it could be facilitated and sustained (Merkel et al., 2004). We found that, in general, groups in our community already use Internet technologies, like email and the Web, to carry out their missions, but, also in general, the groups are not satisfied, often feel like they are slipping behind some norm, and do want to consider learning more and doing more. For example, many of the groups are interested in attaining more direct control of their overall Web site design, others are interested in better integrating their information technology (for example, integrating databases with their Web sites), some are interested in adding special functionalities to their Web sites (such as interactive maps), and some are interested in supporting collaborative interactions like discussion forums.

Our PAR projects have several distinctive characteristics relative to standard conceptions of participatory technology projects (Clement & Van den Besselaar, 1993): (1) The *owners* of the project are the community partners. They control the work activity being supported. They authorize the project and the approach taken. (2) The scope of the design concern is fairly broad. It is not limited to a user interface or even an application program; it generally involves adaptations in the work itself, especially including approaches to managing technology and technology training. (3) The scope of the

J.M. Carroll (ed.), *Learning in Communities,*

collaboration is also quite broad. These groups are not organized for efficient decision-making and policy implementation, rather they work through consensus building. Thus, decisions develop through considerable spans of time and involve mutual trust. (4) Finally, these groups are more responsible for their own technology than the workers typically studied in classic participatory technology projects. For example, participatory projects with office workers hinge on accurately codifying the work that is to be supported. The office workers will not have to maintain the new systems any more than had to personally maintain the old ones. For community groups, this is different. The only sustainable innovations they can make are those they can either pay for or carry out. There is no corporate infrastructure underwriting their activities; no IT Support department. Thus, their expectations about learning and development are that they will assume responsibility for maintenance and further design (Merkel et al., 2005).

Indeed, the community volunteer groups we are working with are quite unlike those in the classic participatory technology projects. In those projects, participation is conceived of as a strategy for mediating and integrating the interests of workers and managers. These different interests were often themselves conceived of as fundamentally adversarial. In the civic sector, the issues manifest differently. Most of the activity in a community group occurs through minimally coordinated and highly localized initiatives. The community groups we have worked with have few paid staff members. Most of the work activity is carried out by volunteers, who participate how and to the extent that they wish.

The characteristics of PAR projects, and our interest in investigating and developing sustainable community-based learning, impel a different sort of role for us as participant-observers. Specifically, we have learned that effective participation requires a substantial and long-term involvement in the community group, but at the same time, relegates us to the active periphery of the community. This may sound contradictory. On the one hand, the fact that the groups are constituted by loose networks of volunteers and managed by a mixture of self-initiative and consensus-building, makes it difficult to quickly understand the groups and earn sufficient trust to work with them. On the other hand, we are ultimately concerned with helping to implement sustainable learning strategies in these groups. But if we have to actually become members in order to do that, it becomes impossible to differentiate the "models" we are developing and investigating, from our own personal identities. (See Carroll et al., 2000, for a broader version of this argument.)

We call this role in the active periphery "the bard": those fellows with lutes and plumed hats, roaming about, singing ballads in medieval courts. Bards were not knights, chancellors, or bishops; they were not even blacksmiths, tailors, or farmers. They were not core members of the medieval community at any stratum. However, their songs reminded all the members of the community of their collective exploits, of the folkways, mores, and values that regulate and sustain their practices, and of their future objectives and visions. Their songs inspired other actors in the community to undertake great quests, to defend their comrades, or just to be a bit more creative and daring in their farming or whatever else they did. The bard's tools are themselves fairly unthreatening to the interests and practices of others, and at the same time participatory in the sense that a familiar or rousing ballad asks for sing-along (Carroll, 2004).

As the bards of community nonprofits in Centre County, Pennsylvania, we are much more than facilitators. We are much more than occasional visitors. We are continuously involved. We are aware of what is going on in the group, of who is doing what in the group. We understand what the group is about and what it values. We are sounding boards for the group's analysis and planning. We are on occasion direct technical resources for analysis and planning. We *represent the group to itself*, in our case from the particular perspective of technology needs and possibilities. But we are also firmly at the edge of the group. We don't have an operational role. We don't have power.

This role can be uniquely useful: Community groups are not about information technology any more than they are about plumbing. They recruit various technologies in the service of their community goals and functions. It is easy for them to lose sight of their own technology needs and goals. The peripheral participant can remind core members of their own needs and goals, and draw connections between current group issues and opportunities and technology plans. If this reminding is done creatively, it can become a vehicle for defining a zone of proximal development, in Vygotsky's (1978) sense, with respect to technology learning and mastery. The zone of proximal development is the set of concepts, skills, and other capacities that a person or an organization can undertake with help. As an individual or an organization successfully operates within the zone of proximal development, it becomes autonomously competent with a larger set of concepts, skills, and capacities. At that point, it can articulate greater ambitions and continue to push the bounds of its own development. If the peripheral participant can remind the core members of their zone of proximal development with respect to information technology, and perhaps even provide some help so that they can operate within this zone and push out its boundaries, then the peripheral participant can become an instrument of learning and development within the community. (See Carroll & Farooq, 2005, for a more specific and detailed version of this proposal.)

Acknowledgments We are grateful to the other members of the Civic Nexus project team—Cecelia Merkel, Craig Ganoe, Umer Farooq, Lu Xiao, Wendy Schafer, Michael Race, Matthew Peters, and Paula Bach. This research is supported in part by the US National Science Foundation under award IIS 03-42547.

References

Carroll, J.M. (2004). Participatory design of community information systems: The designer as bard. In F. Darses, R. Dieng, C. Simone, & M. Zacklad, (Eds.), *Cooperative Systems Design: Scenario-Based Design of Collaborative Systems, Volume 107 Frontiers in Artificial Intelligence and Applications*. Amsterdam: IOS Press, pp. 1–6.

Carroll, J.M. and Farooq, U. (2005). Community-based learning: Design patterns and frameworks. In H. Gllersen, K. Schmidt, M. Beaudouin-Lafon, and W. Mackay (Eds.), *Proceedings of the Ninth European Conference on Computer-Supported Cooperative Work* (Paris, France, September 18–22, 2005), pp. 307–324. Dordrecht, The Netherlands: Springer.

Carroll, J.M., Chin, G., Rosson, M.B., & Neale, D.C. (2000). The development of cooperation: Five years of participatory design in the virtual school. In D. Boyarski & W. Kellogg (Eds.), *DIS'2000: Designing Interactive Systems* (Brooklyn, New York, August 17–19). New York: Association for Computing Machinery, pp. 239–251.

Clement, A. & Van den Besselaar, P. (1993). A retrospective look at PD projects. *Communications of the ACM*, 36(4), 29–37.

Merkel, C.B., Xiao, L., Farooq, U., Ganoe, C.H., Lee, R., Carroll, J.M., & Rosson, M.B. (2004). Participatory design in community computing contexts: Tales from the field. *Proceedings of the Participatory Design Conference* (Toronto, Canada, July 27–31). New York: ACM Press, pp. 1–10.

Merkel, C.B., Clitherow, M., Farooq, U., Xiao, L., Ganoe, C.H., Carroll, J.M., & Rosson, M.B. (2005). Sustaining computer use and learning in community contexts: Making technology part of "Who they are and what they do". *The Journal of Community Informatics*, 1(2), 134–150. http://ci-journal.net/viewissue.php

Vygotsky, L.S. (1978). *Mind in Society*. Cambridge, MA: Harvard University Press.

Chapter 3
Learning in Communities: A Distributed Intelligence Perspective

Gerhard Fischer

Distributed Intelligence: Transcending the Individual Human Mind

The power of the unaided individual mind is highly overrated (Arias et al., 2001). In most traditional approaches, *human cognition* has been seen as existing solely "inside" a person's head, and studies on cognition have often disregarded the physical and social surroundings in which cognition takes place. *Distributed intelligence* (or *distributed cognition*) (Hollan et al., 2001; Pea, 2004; Salomon, 1993) provides an effective theoretical framework for understanding what humans can achieve and how artifacts, tools, and sociotechnical environments can be designed and evaluated to empower human beings and to change tasks. Our research efforts are focused to exploit the power of omnipotent and omniscient technology based on reliable and ubiquitous computing environments and an increasing level of technological fluency to help people to facilitate and support learning in communities.

Social Creativity

Social creativity explores computer media and technologies to help people work and learn together (Bennis & Biederman, 1997). It is specifically relevant to complex design problems because they require expertise in a wide range of domains. Software design projects, for example, typically involve designers, programmers, human-computer interaction specialists, marketing people, and end-user participants.

Information technologies have reached a level of sophistication, maturity, cost-effectiveness, and distribution such that they are not restricted only to enhancing productivity but they also open up *new creative possibilities* (National Research Council, 2003).

Our work is grounded in the basic belief that there is an "*and*" and not a "*versus*" relationship between individual and social creativity (Fischer et al., 2005). Creativity occurs in the relationship between an individual and society, and between an individual and his or her technical environment. The mind, rather than driving on solitude, is clearly dependent upon the reflection, renewal, and trust inherent in sustained human relationships (John-Steiner, 2000). We need to support this distributed fabric of interactions by integrating diversity, by making all voices heard, by increasing the back-talk of the situation, and providing systems that are open and transparent, so that people can be aware of and access each other's work, relate it to their own work, transcend the information given, and contribute the results back to the community (Fischer et al., 2004; Hippel, 2005).

In complex design projects, collaboration is crucial for success, yet it is difficult to achieve. Complexity arises from the need to synthesize different perspectives, to exploit conceptual collisions between concepts and ideas coming from different disciplines, to manage large amounts of information potentially relevant to a design task, and to understand the design decisions that have determined the long-term evolution of a designed artifact.

Exploiting Diversity and Distances by Making All Voices Heard

Social creativity thrives on the *diversity* of perspectives by making all voices heard. It requires constructive dialogs between individuals negotiating their differences while creating their shared voice and vision. We have explored different sources of creativity by exploiting four different *distances: spatial, temporal, conceptual, and technological* (Fischer, 2005).

Voices from different places: Spatial distance. Bringing spatially distributed people together with the support of computer-mediated communication allows the prominent defining feature of a group of people interacting with each other to become *shared concerns rather than shared location*. It extends the range of people to be included, thereby exploiting local knowledge. These opportunities have been successfully employed by the open source communities, collaborative content creation communities (such as Wikipedia) as well as by social networks of people who have a shared concern (such as a family member with a disability). Transcending the barrier of spatial distribution is of particular importance in *locally sparse populations*. Addressing this challenge is one of the core objectives of our research work in the CLever (Cognitive Levers: Helping People Help Themselves) project (CLever, 2005; dePaula, 2004).

Voices from the past: Temporal distance. Design processes often take place over many years, with initial design followed by extended periods of evolution and redesign. In this sense, design artifacts (including systems that support design tasks, such as reuse environments (Ye & Fischer, 2005)) are not designed once and for all, but instead evolve over long periods of time. Much of the work in ongoing design projects is done as redesign and evolution; often, the people doing this work were not members of the original design team. Long-term collaboration requires that present-day designers be aware of not only the rationale (Moran & Carroll, 1996) behind decisions that shaped the artifact, but also any information about possible alternatives that were considered but not implemented. This requires that the rationale behind decisions be recorded in the first place. A barrier to overcome is that designers are biased toward doing design but not toward putting extra effort into documentation. This creates an additional rationale-capture barrier for long-term design (Grudin, 1987).

The idea of exploiting and building on the voices of the past to enhance social creativity is important not only for software reuse but for our overall cultural heritage. In cultural evolution there are no mechanisms equivalent to genes and chromosomes (Csikszentmihalyi, 1996); therefore, new ideas or inventions are not automatically passed on to the next generation, and education becomes a critical challenge to learn from the past. Many creativity researchers have pointed out that the discoveries of many famous people (e.g., Einstein who could build on the work of Newton) would have been inconceivable without the prior knowledge, without the intellectual and social network that simulated their thinking, and without the social mechanisms that recognized and spread their innovations.

Voices from different communities: Conceptual distances. To analyze the contribution of voices from different communities, we differentiate between two types of communities: communities of practice (CoPs) and communities of interest (CoIs). This distinction will be further elaborated below.

Communities of Practice (Wenger, 1998) consist of practitioners who work as a community in a certain domain undertaking similar work. For example, copier repair personnel who work primarily in the field but meet regularly to share "war stories" about how to solve the problems they encountered in their work make up a CoP (Orr, 1996). Learning within a CoP takes the form of *legitimate peripheral participation* (LPP) (Lave & Wenger, 1991), which is a type of apprenticeship model in which newcomers enter the community from the periphery and move toward the center as they become more and more knowledgeable.

Sustained engagement and collaboration lead to boundaries that are based on shared histories of learning and that create discontinuities between participants and nonparticipants. Highly developed knowledge systems (including conceptual frameworks, technical systems, and human organizations) are biased toward efficient communication within the community at the expense of acting as barriers to communication with outsiders: boundaries that are empowering to the insider are often barriers to outsiders and newcomers to the group.

A community of practice has many possible paths and many roles (identities) within it (e.g., leader, scribe, power-user, visionary, and so forth). Over time, most members move toward the center, and their knowledge becomes part of the foundation of the community's shared background.

Communities of Interest (Fischer, 2001) bring together stakeholders from different CoPs and are defined by their collective concern with the resolution of a particular problem. CoIs can be thought of as "communities of communities" (Brown & Duguid, 1991). Examples of CoIs are (1) a team interested in software development that includes software designers, users, marketing specialists, psychologists, and programmers, or (2) a group of citizens and experts interested in urban planning. Stakeholders within CoIs are considered as informed participants who are neither experts nor novices, but rather both; they are experts when they communicate their knowledge to others, and they are novices when they learn from others who are experts in areas outside their own knowledge.

Communication in CoIs is difficult because they come from different CoPs, and therefore use different languages, different conceptual knowledge systems, and different notational systems (Snow, 1993). Members of CoIs must learn to communicate with and learn from others (Engeström, 2001) who have different perspectives and perhaps a different vocabulary for describing their ideas. In other words, this symmetry of ignorance must be exploited.

Comparing CoPs and CoIs. Learning by making all voices heard within CoIs is more complex and multifaceted than *legitimate peripheral participation* (Lave & Wenger, 1991) in CoPs. Learning in CoPs can be characterized as "learning within a single knowledge system," whereas learning in CoIs is often a consequence of the fact that there are multiple knowledge systems. CoIs have multiple centers of knowledge, with each member considered to be knowledgeable in a particular aspect of the problem and perhaps not so knowledgeable in others.

Table 3.1 characterizes and differentiates CoPs and CoIs along a number of dimensions. The point of comparing and contrasting CoPs and CoIs is not to pigeonhole groups into either category, but rather to identify patterns of practice and helpful technologies. People can participate in more than one community, or one community can exhibit attributes of both a CoI and a CoP. Our *Center for LifeLong Learning and Design (L^3D)* is an example: It has many characteristics of a CoP (having developed its own stories, terminology, and artifacts), but by actively engaging with people from outside our community (e.g., from other colleges on campus, people from industry, international visitors, and so forth), it also has many characteristics of a CoI. Design communities do not have to be strictly either CoPs or CoIs, but they can integrate aspects of both forms of communities. The community type may shift over time, according to events outside the community, the objectives of its members, and the structure of the membership.

Table 3.1 Differentiating CoPs and CoIs

Dimensions	CoPs	CoIs
Nature of problems	Different tasks in the same domain	Common task across multiple domains
Knowledge development	Refinement of one knowledge system; new ideas coming from within the practice	Synthesis and mutual learning through the integration of multiple knowledge systems
Major objectives	Codified knowledge, domain coverage	Shared understanding, making all voices heard
Weaknesses	Group-think	Lack of a shared understanding
Strengths	Shared ontologies	Social creativity; diversity; making all voices heard
People	Beginners and experts; apprentices and masters	Stakeholders (owners of problems) from different domains
Learning	Legitimate peripheral participation	Informed participation

Both forms of design communities exhibit barriers and biases. *CoPs* are biased toward communicating with the same people and taking advantage of a shared background. The existence of an accepted, well-established center (of expertise) and a clear path of learning toward this center allows the differentiation of members into novices, intermediates, and experts. It makes these attributes viable concepts associated with people and provides the foundation for legitimate peripheral participation as a workable learning strategy. The barriers imposed by CoPs are that *group-think* (Janis, 1972) can suppress exposure to, and acceptance of, outside ideas; the more someone is at home in a CoP, the more that person forgets the strange and contingent nature of its categories from the outside.

Voices from virtual stakeholders: Technological distances. The preceding subsections emphasized computer-mediated collaboration among humans to reduce the gaps created by spatial, temporal, and conceptual distances. Voices from virtual stakeholders are embedded in artifacts such as books and in more interesting and powerful ways in computational artifacts.

Design can be described as a reflective conversation between designers and the designs they create. Designers use materials to construct design situations, and then listen to the "back-talk of the situation" they have created (Schön, 1983). Unlike passive design materials, such as pen and paper, computational design materials are able to interpret the work of designers and actively talk back to them. Barriers occur when the back-talk is represented in a form that users are unable to comprehend (i.e., the back-talk is not a boundary object), or when the back-talk created by the design situation itself is insufficient, and additional mechanisms (e.g., critiquing, simulation, and visualization components) are needed. To increase the back-talk of the situation, we have developed *critiquing systems* (Fischer et al., 1998) that monitor the actions of users as they work and inform the users of potential problems. If users elect to see the information, the critiquing mechanisms find information in the repositories that is relevant to the particular problem and present this information to the user.

References

Arias, E. G., Eden, H., Fischer, G., Gorman, A., & Scharff, E. (2001). Transcending the individual human mind: Creating shared understanding through collaborative design. In J. M. Carroll (Ed.), *Human-computer interaction in the new millennium* (pp. 347–372). New York: ACM Press.

Bennis, W., & Biederman, P. W. (1997). *Organizing genius: The secrets of creative collaboration.* Cambridge, MA: Perseus Books.

Brown, J. S., & Duguid, P. (1991). Organizational learning and communities-of-practice: Toward a unified view of working, learning, and innovation. *Organization Science,* 2(1), pp. 40–57.

CLever (2005). *CLever: Cognitive Levers: Helping people help themselves.* Available at http://13d.cs.colorado.edu/clever/.

Csikszentmihalyi, M. (1996). *Creativity: Flow and the psychology of discovery and invention.* New York: Harper Collins Publishers.

dePaula, R. (2004). *The Construction of usefulness: How users and context create meaning with a social networking system,* Ph.D. Dissertation, University of Colorado at Boulder.

Engeström, Y. (2001). Expansive learning at work: Toward an activity theoretical reconceptualization. *Journal of Education and Work,* 14(1), pp. 133–156.

Fischer, G. (2001). Communities of interest: Learning through the interaction of multiple knowledge systems. *24th Annual Information Systems Research Seminar In Scandinavia (IRIS'24),* Ulvik, Norway, pp. 1–14.

Fischer, G. (2005). Distances and diversity: Sources for social creativity. *Proceedings of Creativity & Cognition,* London, April, pp. 128–136.

Fischer, G., Nakakoji, K., Ostwald, J., Stahl, G., & Sumner, T. (1998). Embedding critics in design environments. In M. T. Maybury & W. Wahlster (Eds.), *Readings in intelligent user interfaces.* San Francisco: Morgan Kaufmann, pp. 537–559.

Fischer, G., Giaccardi, E., Ye, Y., Sutcliffe, A. G., & Mehandjiev, N. (2004). Meta-design: A manifesto for end-user development. *Communications of the ACM,* 47(9), pp. 33–37.

Fischer, G., Giaccardi, E., Eden, H., Sugimoto, M., & Ye, Y. (2005). Beyond binary choices: Integrating individual and social creativity. *International Journal of Human-Computer Studies (IJHCS) Special Issue on Computer Support for Creativity (E.A. Edmonds & L. Candy, Eds.),* 63(4–5), pp. 482–512.

Grudin, J. (1987). Social evaluation of the user interface: Who does the work and who gets the benefit? In H. Bullinger & B. Shackel (Eds.). *Proceedings of INTERACT'87, 2nd IFIP Conference on Human-Computer Interaction (Stuttgart, FRG),* North-Holland, Amsterdam, pp. 805–811.

Hippel, E. v. (2005). *Democratizing innovation.* Cambridge, MA: MIT Press.

Hollan, J., Hutchins, E., & Kirsch, D. (2001). Distributed cognition: Toward a new foundation for Human-computer interaction research. In J. M. Carroll (Ed.), *Human-computer interaction in the new millennium* (pp. 75–94). New York: ACM Press.

Janis, I. (1972). *Victims of groupthink.* Boston: Houghton Mifflin.

John-Steiner, V. (2000). *Creative collaboration.* Oxford: Oxford University Press.

Lave, J., & Wenger, E. (1991). *Situated learning: Legitimate peripheral participation.* New York: Cambridge University Press.

Moran, T. P., & Carroll, J. M. (Eds.). (1996). *Design rationale: Concepts, techniques, and use.* Hillsdale, NJ: Lawrence Erlbaum Associates.

National Research Council. (2003). *Beyond productivity: Information technology, innovation, and creativity.* Washington, DC: National Academy Press.

Orr, J. (1996). *Talking about machines: An ethnography of a modern job.* Ithaca, NY: ILR Press/ Cornell University Press.

Pea, R. D. (2004). The social and technological dimensions of scaffolding and related theoretical concepts for learning, education, and human activity. *The Journal of the Learning Sciences, 13*(3), pp. 423–451.

Salomon, G. (Ed.). (1993). *Distributed cognitions: Psychological and educational considerations.* Cambridge, UK: Cambridge University Press.

Schön, D. A. (1983). *The reflective practitioner: How professionals think in action.* New York: Basic Books.

Snow, C. P. (1993). *The two cultures.* Cambridge, UK: Cambridge University Press.

Wenger, E. (1998). *Communities of practice: Learning, meaning, and identity.* Cambridge, UK: Cambridge University Press.

Ye, Y., & Fischer, G. (2005). Reuse-conducive development environments. *International Journal Automated Software Engineering, 12*(2), pp. 199–235.

Chapter 4
Spiders in the Net: Universities as Facilitators of Community-Based Learning

Gerhard Fischer, Markus Rohde, and Volker Wulf

Universities play an important role in the knowledge society (Brown & Duguid, 2000). Beyond their traditional role in research and education, they have the potential to exploit local knowledge in (regional) innovations and to provide opportunities for students to become lifelong learners. To realize these potentials, universities, specifically in the fields of applied sciences and engineering, will have to reinvent their conception of education by taking the importance of industrial practice and social networks into account (Tsichritzis, 1999).

Traditionally, university teaching is based on an "instructionist" understanding of learning which assumes that the instructor possesses all relevant knowledge and passes it to the learners (Noam, 1995). The learner is seen as a receptive system that stores, recalls, and transfers knowledge. Such an understanding has been criticized from theoretical and practical points of view (cf. Collins et al., 1989; Jonassen and Mandl, 1990). In a highly differentiated world full of open ended and ill-defined problems it is rather unlikely that an individual (professor) or an academic organization (faculty) alone will possess sufficient knowledge to foster learning among students and practitioners sufficiently (Arias et al., 2001).

We believe that *sociocultural theories of learning* (Bruner, 1996) and the concepts of *social capital* (Huysman & Wulf, 2004) and *social creativity* (Fischer et al., 2005) hold considerable promise as a theoretical base for the repositioning of universities in the knowledge society. Learning is understood as a collective process (Rogoff et al., 1998) that is linked to a specific context of action. In sociocultural theories of learning, communities of practice are the social aggregate in which learning and innovation take place. Knowledge emerges by discursive assignment and social identification (Lave & Wenger, 1991; Wenger, 1998). Social capital is about value derived from being a member of a social aggregate. By being a member, people have access to resources that nonmembers do not have (Bourdieu, 1985; Huysman & Wulf, 2004; Putnam, 1993). Social capital can serve as an enabler to social learning processes (Cohen & Prusak 2001; Fischer et al., 2004; Huysman & Wulf, 2004), and it represents a precondition for the emergence of communities of practice.

The *Information Systems Research Group (IS)* at the University of Siegen will be taken as an example of how universities may draw on the concepts of communities of practice and social capital to reposition themselves in societal learning

J.M. Carroll (ed.), *Learning in Communities*,

processes. Supported by research funds from public and industry sources, the IS group has grown from three to ten staff members (faculty and research associates) during recent years. Research is organized around individual, typically externally funded, projects and practice emerges within these projects or groups of them. To set up a network within the regional IT industry, the IS group got specific funding from the European Structural Fund.

In Siegen, opportunities for enculturation into specific communities of practice are considered to be a major instrument of education at the university level. This approach complements "*learning about*" with "*learning to be*" (the second objective serves as the fundamental principle underlying the *Undergraduate Research Apprenticeship Program* at the University of Colorado, Boulder; for detail see: http://13d.cs.colorado.edu/urap/). So far, experiences have been primarily gained with enculturation processes into two different types of communities of practice: those within the research group and those within regional IT companies. We have reinterpreted the following elements of the IS curriculum to offer opportunities for students to participate in our practice: seminars, project groups, and the diploma thesis. With regard to each of these elements of the curriculum, we define tasks that are relevant to actual and future research projects in our group (e.g., elaborating the state of the art of a new research area within a seminar, implementing specific software components in the framework of a project group, or designing a prototype in a Masters thesis). We also offer paid jobs for students to work within our research projects on an ongoing base. Since the relevance of these tasks is obvious to students and researchers, an important precondition for processes of enculturation is met. Enculturation processes into the research group get more likely and intense in those cases when the students follow up on more than one of these learning opportunities.

Though the research projects are typically conducted in cooperation with industry, our practice is more research oriented compared to the one our graduates will experience in industry after finishing their studies. Therefore, we offer additional types of learning opportunities to students by integrating student teams into the communities of practice of local IT companies. To host teams of two to three students, IT companies define projects close to their core business. The student teams work on these projects in close cooperation with actors from the companies. When working in industry our students are closely coached by members of the research group. The student teams are connected to each other and to their supervisors in academia by means of a community system. Rohde et al. (2005) present results of an evaluation study of an earlier implementation of this approach in entrepreneurship education.

Community-based approaches to university education provide learning opportunities for academics and companies. While enculturation into the companies' communities of practice is seen as the main mechanism for student learning, students often mediate between university and company practice. Since the students are coached by their advisers during their experience in the company, they carry ideas back and forth between the communities of practice within companies and academia. Companies get word of innovative ideas out of academia while researchers get feedback on the applicability of their concepts. This boundary spanning activity is especially intense when the students have been enculturated previously in academia.

To establish community-based approaches to university education, academic visibility and a sufficient level of social capital are required. The enculturation processes require substantial efforts from companies as well as from students. Companies are only rewarded in the end and in those cases when their proposed project turned out to be successful. Mutual trust between companies and academia is built over time through cooperation in successful projects. To get the process started, a certain reputation built through other (regional) activities is instrumental. Regional networking activities and the joint acquisition of research projects have turned out to be important means of building social capital. In the future, we will extend this community-building effort to include our network of alumni. To offer appropriate learning opportunities to their students, academics will have to building and maintain a dense web of social relations.

References

Arias, E. G., Eden, H., Fischer, G., Gorman, A., & Scharff, E. (2001). Transcending the individual human mind: Creating shared understanding through collaborative design. In J. M. Carroll (Ed.), *Human-computer interaction in the new millennium* (pp. 347–372). New York: ACM Press.

Bourdieu, P. (1985). The forms of capital. In J. G. Richardson (Ed.). *Handbook for theory and research for the sociology of education* (pp. 241–258). Westport, CT: Greenwood Press.

Brown, J. S., & Duguid, P. (2000). *The social life of information*. Boston, MA: Harvard Business School Press.

Bruner, J. (1996). *The culture of education*. Cambridge, MA: Harvard University Press.

Cohen, D., & Prusak, L. (2001). *In good company: How social capital makes organizations work*. Boston, MA: Harvard Business School Press.

Collins, A., Brown, J. S., & Newman, S. E. (1989). Cognitive apprenticeship: Teaching the crafts of reading, writing and mathematics. In L. B. Resnick (Ed.) *Knowing, learning, and instruction* (pp. 453–494). Hillsdale: Lawrence Erlbaum Associates.

Fischer, G., Scharff, E., & Ye, Y. (2004). Fostering social creativity by increasing social capital. In V. Wulf (Ed.). *Social capital and information technology* (pp. 355–399). Cambridge, MA: MIT Press.

Fischer, G., Giaccardi, E., Eden, H., Sugimoto, M., & Ye, Y. (2005). Beyond binary choices: Integrating individual and social creativity. *International Journal of Human-Computer Studies (IJHCS) Special Issue on Computer Support for Creativity* (E.A. Edmonds & L. Candy, Eds.), *63*(4–5), 482–512.

Huysman, M., & Wulf, V. (Eds.) (2004a). *Social capital and information technology*. Cambridge, MA: MIT Press.

Huysman, M., & Wulf, V. (2004b). Social capital and IT – Current debates and research. In M. Huysman & V. Wulf (Eds.). *Social capital and information technology* (pp. 1–16). Cambridge, MA: MIT Press.

Jonassen, D. H., & Mandl, H. (Eds.). (1990). *Designing hypermedia for learning*. Berlin: Springer.

Lave, J., & Wenger, E. (1991). *Situated learning: Legitimate peripheral participation*. New York: Cambridge University Press.

Noam, E. M. (1995). Electronics and the dim future of the university. *Science, 270*(5234), 247–249.

Putnam, R. (1993). The prosperious community: Social capital and public life. *American Prospect, 13*, 35–42.

Rogoff, B., Matsuov, E., & White, C. (1998). Models of teaching and learning: Participation in a community of learners. In D. R. Olsen & N. Torrance (Eds.). *The handbook of education and human development. New models of learning, teaching and schooling* (pp. 388–414). Blackwell: Oxford.

Rohde, M., Klamma, R., & Wulf, V. (2005). Establishing communities of practise among students and start-up companies. In *Proceedings of the International Conference on Collaborative Learning (CSCL 2005)*, May 30–June 4 in Taipeh (Taiwan), (pp. 514–519).

Tsichritzis, D. (1999). Reengineering the university. *Communications of the ACM, 42*(6), 93–100.

Wenger, E. (1998). *Communities of practice: Learning, meaning, and identity*. Cambridge, UK: Cambridge University Press.

Chapter 5
Designing Technology for Local Citizen Deliberation

Andrea Kavanaugh and Philip Isenhour

Citizen participation in democratic processes in the United States has been facilitated and enhanced since the mid-1990s with the diffusion and adoption of computer networking (Barber, 1984; Coleman and Gotz, 2002; Kavanaugh et al., 2005a, b; Rainie, 2005). Electronic mailing lists and Web sites pertaining to political interests grew rapidly in the late 1990s. Much of this facilitated participation consisted of increased awareness about issues and information, as well as increased capability for coordination, communication, and outreach with regard to political activities. Despite these positive outcomes, existing tools are largely used to broadcast information from a few-to-many. There is limited interaction, discussion, and deliberation online, except in specially designed centralized forums. These special Web sites are very helpful in supporting discussion and even deliberation among interested citizens (for example, in the Minnesota E-Democracy project). Yet they tend to attract and retain the most highly motivated and activist citizens. For the less motivated majority of citizens, there is a need for tools that allow easy authoring and editing and intuitive ways to comment and contribute additional content to a group discussion.

The advent of Web logs (i.e., blogs) provides an opportunity to extend the capabilities of traditional electronic mail and discussion lists toward greater social interaction, discussion, and content production. The simplicity of the tools for blogging and their free availability have lowered the bar for users interested in communicating with others in their social networks, their geographic communities, and the greater public. Community or group blogs represent a kind of self-organizing social system that allows a number of individuals to interact and learn from each other through the exchange ideas and information, and to help solve collective problems.

Components of the optimal systems that community organizations seek are in place, such as servers, network connectivity, and technical support. But gaps in software technology persist, which can be closed with applications that can be customized to meet the specific and unique needs of these organizations. For example, authoring, publishing, and archiving information; soliciting feedback from organization members and the community; holding discussions, tutorials, and forums; planning and coordinating organizational activities; and managing group resources.

J.M. Carroll (ed.), *Learning in Communities*,

The Web, in its current form, strongly favors information consumers over information producers. Emerging technologies such as Web logs and Wikis (Searls & Sifry, 2003) seek to address this deficiency. Blogs–online journals often used for commentary and content aggregation–have seen an explosive rise in popularity (Rainie, 2005). They have been adapted for diverse uses, but maintain the basic format of a column or journal entry, typically linking to external resources, and often supporting direct posting from a Web browser and discussion forums attached to each entry. Wikis (Guzdial et al., 2001) represent a more flexible and open-ended approach to direct editing. On a Wiki, any user can edit the content of any page using a shorthand language that is translated into HTML. A common element of Wiki shorthand is a simplified mechanism for linking, thereby supporting the goal of creating interconnected hypertexts.

The popularity of Web logs and Wikis, including a growing popularity of Web logs among content producers outside of technical fields, suggests that there is demand for tools that provide more direct and simplified publishing than is available with desktop Web page publishing software. Such tools seem particularly well matched to the knowledge management needs of nonprofit community organizations and small, but distributed, public sector agencies such as the public health district. These groups will often lack the resources to support full-time Web maintenance staff.

The relatively primitive nature of blogs and Wikis also suggests opportunities for technology innovation. The tools are generally focused on text publishing and often support interactivity only in the form of discussion forums. In this sense, blogs and Wikis represent something of a step backwards as end-user development tools when compared to pre-Web technologies such as MOOs and MUDs (Bruckman, 1999; Haynes & Holmevick, 1998). They also represent two extremes in their enforcement of structure, with blogs (essentially by definition) having a very specific linear structure, and Wikis having a sometimes chaotic lack of structure.

To address these issues, integrated authoring tools must support flexible representation and organization of content with format and structure based on the requirements of specific groups of users. Richer interactive tools will be required to support representation, organization, and sharing of ideas and experiences. Tools that integrate synchronous and asynchronous discussion and refinement of content objects, for example, can help capture informal and contextual knowledge that might not be captured in static Web pages.

In a series of focus group interviews conducted with adult residents of Blacksburg and Montgomery County, Virginia (Fall 2005) most citizens seemed only vaguely aware of blogs and Wikis. Nonetheless, they were clear about the affordances and functionality they wanted from emerging tools. They want to find diverse information such as news that is missing in local newspapers, and to explore different perspectives on issues of national and personal interest. Citizens reported seeking greater usability especially for novices and nontech savvy users, such as senior citizens. They observed that the local groups with which they affiliate act as important mechanisms for sharing more reliable information and sustaining discussion, since contributors are known to each other. They emphasized the need for balance between offline and online political activities, including deliberation. Peer pressure among group acquaintances helps reduce incidences of personal attacks online. Peer reviewing helps participants authenticate information, thereby fostering greater trust. The few local community groups that have set up (or converted) their Web sites to Wiki-styles benefit from simpler and easier content updating and editing, but they typically required some support and guidance to get started. The small but growing number of local blogs with at least occasional political content could be potentially more effective in educating and stimulating exchange among community members if there were mechanisms to aggregate similar content scattered across multiple blogs. Aggregators, search engines, and social bookmarking are examples of ways to facilitate the discovery of these potential connections.

References

Barber, B. (1984). *Strong democracy: Participatory politics for a new age*. Berkeley, CA: University of California Press.

Bruckman, A. (1999). The day after Net Day: Approaches to educational use of the Internet. *Convergence, 5*(1), 24–46.

Coleman, S., & Gotz, J. (2002). *Bowling together: Online public engagement in policy deliberation*. Available from: http://bowingtogether.net/

Guzdial, M., Rick, J., & Kehoe, C. (2001). Beyond adoption to invention: Teacher-created collaborative activities in higher education. *Journal of the Learning Sciences, 10*(3), 265–279.

Haynes, C., & Holmevick, J. R. (Eds.). (1998). *High wired: On the design, use, and theory of educational MOOs*. Ann Arbor: Michigan Press.

Kavanaugh, A., Reese, D. D., Carroll, J. M., & Rosson, M. B. (2005a). Weak ties in networked communities. *The Information Society, 21*(2), 119–131.

Kavanaugh, A., Carroll, J. M., Rosson, M. B., & Zin, T. T. (2005b). Participating in civil society: The case of networked communities. *Interacting with Computers, 17*, 9–33.

Rainie, L. (2005). The state of blogging. Pew Internet & American Life Project. Available from: http://www.pewinternet.org

Searls, D., & Sifry, D. (2003). Building with blogs. *Linux Journal 2003(4)*, 4. Available from: http://www.linuxjournal.com/article.php?sid=6497

Chapter 6
Supporting the Appropriation of ICT: End-User Development in Civil Societies

Volkmar Pipek, Mary Beth Rosson, Gunnar Stevens, and Volker Wulf

Introduction

Information and communication technology (ICT) has become an important factor in our personal lives as well as in our social organizations at work, at home, in our hospitals, in political institutions, and in the public media. While in work settings the dynamics of shared business goals, shared task systems, and professional delegation structures result in a relatively predictable and organized design context, the more open-ended and less-organized contexts of home or society present considerable challenges for applications of ICT. The goals and interests of the diverse actors in these more general contexts are quite unstable and unpredictable; home and society provide only weak structures of specialization and delegation regarding the use of ICTs. One approach to these challenges is to cede design power to the participating users, so that they can develop solutions that match problems and intentions for action.

There have always been motivations to involve users in the design and development of ICTs. On the one hand, the quality of products might be improved by involving end users in the early phases of design (the "User-Centred Design" tradition); on the other hand, end users have claimed the right to participate in the development of ICTs that affect their (working) environments (e.g., the Scandinavian tradition of "Participatory design"). Beyond these approaches to "change design" by changing design methodologies or other aspects of the setting of professional design work, there have also been approaches to "design for change" by offering technologies and tools that provide the flexibility to be thoroughly modified at the time of use (Henderson & Kyng, 1991). The latter approaches have been proffered under the label of "Tailoring Support" and "End-User Development" (Lieberman et al. 2005; Sutcliffe & Mehandijev, 2004), and complement earlier research on "End-User Computing" and "Adaptability/Adaptivity."

J.M. Carroll (ed.), *Learning in Communities,*

Active Support for Technology Appropriation

At some point it is no longer sufficient to provide the necessary flexibility for (re-)configuring tools and technologies while in use. It is also necessary to provide stronger support for managing this flexibility. Keeping the tool interaction simple, and providing good manuals may be one strategy, but the adaptation and appropriation of tools is often more a social activity than a problem of individual learning and use. Knowledge sharing and delegation structures often develop, although in home and other informal usage settings these structure are likely to be much more spontaneous and less organized than in professional environments. End-user development methods can address the social aspects of computing by treating users as a "(virtual) community of tool/technology users," and by providing support for different appropriation activities that users can engage in to make use of a technology. Examples of such activities (Pipek, 2005) include:

- *Basic Technological Support:* Building highly flexible systems.
- *Articulation Support:* Support for technology-related articulations (real and online).
- *Historicity Support:* Visualize appropriation as a process of emerging technologies and usages, e.g., by documenting earlier configuration decisions, providing retrievable storage of configuration and usage descriptions.
- *Decision Support:* If an agreement is required in a collaborative appropriation activity, providing voting, polling, etc.
- *Demonstration Support:* Support showing usages from one user (group) to another user (group), provide necessary communication channels.
- *Observation Support:* Support the visualization of (accumulated) information on the use of tools and functions in an organisational context.
- *Simulation Support:* Show effects of possible usage in an exemplified or actual organizational setting (only makes sense if the necessary computational basis can be established).
- *Exploration Support:* Combination of simulation with extended support for technology configurations and test bed manipulations, individual vs. collaborative exploration modes.
- *Explanation Support:* Explain reasons for application behavior, fully automated support vs. user–user or user–expert communication.
- *Delegation Support:* Support delegation patterns within configuration activities; provide remote configuration facilities.
- *(Re-) Design Support:* Feedback to designers on the appropriation processes.

These are support ideas derived from the observation of activities that users perform to make use of a technology. They have been partially addressed in earlier research, for example by providing flexibility through component-based approaches (Morch et al., 2004), or by offering sandboxes for tool exploration (Wulf & Golombek, 2001).

Supporting "Virtual Communities of Technology Practice"

Pipek (2005) also gave the example of "Use Discourse Environments" as one possibility to support the user community in some of these appropriation activities. These environments tightly integrate communication mechanisms with representations of the technologies under consideration, for instance by integrating discourse processes with the configuration facilities of tools, or by providing easy citations of technologies and configuration settings in online discussion forums. By these means, technology needs and usages become more easily describable by end users, and communication among people sharing a similar use background (typically *not* the professional tool designer) is eased. However, evaluations of these environments suggest that the problem cannot be solved by offering technological support alone; additional social or organizational measures (establishing/mediating conventions, stimulation of communication) must also be considered to guarantee long-term success.

The approach to actively support user communities in their appropriation activities promises to alleviate the lack of professional support in home/volunteering settings of ICT usage. It may stimulate the spreading of good practice among users, and it offers a platform to actively deal with conflicts that occur between different stakeholders involved in a shared activity that involves ICT use (e.g., conflicts about visibility of actions and about the configuration of access rights).

References

Henderson, A., & Kyng, M. (1991). There's no place like home: Continuing design in use. In J. Greenbaum & M. Kyng (Eds.). *Design at work: Cooperative design of computer systems* (pp. 219–240). Hillsdale, NJ: Lawrence Erlbaum.

Lieberman, H., Paternó, F., & Wulf, V. (Eds.). (2005). *End user development*. Berlin: Springer.

Morch, A., Stevens, G., Won, M., Klann, M., Dittrich, Y., & Wulf, V. (2004). Component-based technologies for end-user development. Special issue: End-user development. *Communications of the ACM, 47*(9), 59–62.

Pipek, V. (2005). From tailoring to appropriation support: Negotiating groupware usage. In *Faculty of Science, Department of Information Processing Science (ACTA UNIVERSITATIS OULUENSIS A 430) (p. 246)*. Oulu, Finland: University of Oulu.

Sutcliffe, A., & Mehandjiev, N. (2004). Introduction. Special issue: End-user development. *Communications of the ACM, 47*(9), 31–32.

Wulf, V., & Golombek, B. (2001). Exploration environments: Concept and empirical evaluation. In *Proceedings of the International ACM SIGGROUP Conference on Supporting Group Work* (pp. 107–116). Boulder, CO: ACM Press.

Chapter 7
Developmental Learning Communities

Mary Beth Rosson and John M. Carroll

Introduction

Research over the past two decades has emphasized the importance of learning communities: self-organizing groups of learners who work together on authentic tasks, describing, explaining, listening to, and interpreting one another's ideas. Learning communities often structure their learning by scaffolding embedded both in the activities and in the tools of the community (Bruner, 1960). Learners also develop by participating in the discourse of their community, where they encounter and contribute to the situated negotiation and renegotiation of meaning (Dewey, 1910). We define a *developmental* learning community as a group of learners who organize their learning activity into phases and their members into roles. The learning in such communities is developmental in the sense that members successively traverse phases and roles. An example would be a university research group including undergraduate students, graduate students, post doctoral students, and faculty.

A key feature of a developmental learning community is its members' understanding whether implicit or explicit of *phases* that they progress through as they gain community-relevant knowledge and skills. Often these communities emphasize mastery of skills (e.g., a martial arts community), where different skill levels are labeled to acknowledge members' progress (for instance, "apprentice," "practitioner," or "master"). Progress through such phases is accomplished by meeting a community standard or practice that often also includes a change in status for members, perhaps a skill test of some sort, cumulative knowledge or experiences that are judged in some fashion, a prescribed level of insight that is expressed by the member, or a critical episode that persuades the community of the member's progress.

Another characteristic of developmental communities is the relationship among members at different developmental phases. That is, we assume that members share an understanding of what is expected from them at any given phase, for example, how they should relate to less-developed members (outreach, scaffolding, other forms of mentoring); those at their same level (sharing, comparison, synthesis of experience); and those at higher levels (requesting help or mentoring, respect for suggestions).

Members of developmental learning communities also share a motivational orientation about their own and others' development. We suggest that one criterion for membership in a developmental community is a commitment to its developmental goals, that is, a willingness to spend effort in "bringing others along." One factor that may be important in creating this motivation and commitment is social ties, beyond those arising from the community's developmental activities, that cause members to care about others in the community, enough so that they work to enlist new members and encourage the growth of existing members. A developmental community may also provide rewards for members' efforts to promote co-members' learning, such as increased social capital or more explicit forms of recognition.

Examples of Learning Communities

Developmental learning communities often emerge through everyday activities and lifelong learning. Children who learn from older siblings, parents, and other relatives are a simple example (see the discussion in Dewey, 1910); another is a research group populated by members in very different phases of their professional life: senior faculty, junior faculty (e.g., pre-tenure), post-docs, advanced PhD students, junior PhD students, masters students, undergraduate research students, and wage-payroll assistants. In other cases, the community may be formed explicitly to support one another's development of some knowledge base or skill set (e.g., a gardening club).

In Table 7.1, we summarize the developmental characteristics of several community computing projects with which we have been working over the past few years.

The learning communities in Civic Nexus are nonprofit organizations; we are helping them to create sustainable informal learning processes for meeting their own IT needs (Merkel et al., 2004, 2005). Most of the nonprofits have little if any articulated knowledge about their own IT needs or trajectories, and little organizational

Table 7.1 Examples of developmental learning communities in community computing

Learning community	Learning activities	Developmental phases
Civic Nexus	Analysis of, planning for, and implementation of IT needs in a nonprofit organization	Intern, volunteer, web designer, technology committee member, technology committee chair
Teacher Bridge	Creating Web-based lessons in science and math, using a variety of interactive tools	Lurker, member, re-user, adapter, author, coach, program developer
Women in IST	Problem-based learning of the architecture and programming of Web-based collaborative systems	High school friend, college recruit, pre-major, major, alumna

infrastructure for recruiting or developing members who can meet these needs. We help them to reflect about their history and status of IT use, hoping that as the groups come to realize what they have been doing and what their needs are, they will be able to design a sustainable process for meeting and evolving their own IT requirements. These groups have a number of existing roles (intern, volunteer, etc.), but are not oriented toward recruiting and developing members through the role; if they are able to initiate a long-term process of IT learning, such an orientation may become part of their community mission.

The Teacher Bridge project (Carroll et al., 2003; Kim et al., 2003) is a group of teachers learning to build online materials. When we began the project, we deliberately recruited teachers who were already sophisticated computers users; subsequently these teachers have recruited their own peers and acquaintances and others have discovered the project and joined through word-of-mouth. The community is socially and culturally grounded through co-inhabitation of a geographical region (two contiguous counties), so many teachers join with existing place-based friendships and shared interests. These ties help to motivate peer mentoring and coaching. A typical developmental path starts with a teacher looking around at other projects for ideas; s/he may then join the group (become a member) so as to directly reuse or adapt a peer's work; after s/he has experimented in this fashion, s/he may move to more ambitious implementation projects; some teachers take on a coaching role to help others make these moves; we have even observed teachers taking a supervisory role, where one mission is to look across the whole community for opportunities to advise. In this community, the phases and activities that assist in transitions are defined only informally and anecdotally. However, one way to see this community is as a developmental community in formation.

In contrast to the other two examples, the Women in IST (Information Science & Technology) group is developmental at its core by design. Women join the community with the explicit aim to attract, mentor, and otherwise aid the development of less-expert members. It differs from similar communities (e.g., a typical chapter of the Association for Women in Computing) in that undergraduates leverage personal social ties they have maintained with their high schools, using these to contact girls with quite varied interests (e.g., sports, theater) so as to increase general awareness of computing among young women. Alumni members contact and interact with undergraduates on a similar basis. This project illustrates an effort to apply our concept of developmental community as a guiding pattern for learning community design.

Supporting Developmental Learning Communities

We are exploring two facets of developmental learning communities that might be aided by social or technical interventions: (1) recognition and acceptance of phases in community members' development, and (2) reinforcement of the social ties that motivate developmental activities within the community.

In some cases, the developmental structure may already be in place but not yet organized as a community vision. For instance, the Women in IST project is grounded on a very familiar set of phases associated with career development and as researchers our contribution has simply been to articulate these phases as a mechanism for forming a new learning community. In contrast, our work with the nonprofits has roles, but they are not associated with development of IT skills. Thus we have focused on a more bottom-up approach, carrying out extensive technology assessment activities and fieldwork aimed at understanding the IT needs and current understandings of each group. Our hope is that by taking this step the organizations can at least see some of the potential for articulating and planning a more systematic IT learning process.

With respect to social ties that might motivate members' developmental goals toward one another, one intervention is to simply highlight existing opportunities. The students and alumni at the core of Women in IST do not see "outside" friendships (e.g., from shared interests unrelated to IST) to be a key element of the learning community. But when the potential role of such relationships was outlined to them, it became obvious. The community recognition that members receive for helping (or being helped) with learning activities can also be reinforced in an online system. Making mentoring relationships is one approach; reputation tools that capture individuals' contributions to different sorts of activities could also facilitate these recognition processes.

Final Words

Our ideas about developmental communities are preliminary, inspired by our recent work with Women in IST and the perspective it has offered for thinking about our other community learning projects. Clearly, development is an inherent component of any learning community and we offer these reflections as a way of exploring the structure and dynamics of a community's developmental activities, including the implications this might have for sociotechnical design in such contexts.

At the same time we recognize the possible negative consequences of emphasizing the developmental goals of a learning community. For example Suchman (1995) discusses the tradeoffs in making "invisible" aspects of activities visible; an organization that documents employee roles and responsibilities is in a better position to track and evaluate (whether fairly or unfairly) employees' routine performance. Reifying the developmental phases within a community might convert a tacit learning process into an explicit one; perhaps it would encourage over-zealous junior members or mentors to obsess over developmental goals. Members might focus so much on skills or achievement levels that they become closed to other more interesting or unexpected learning opportunities. Coaches might compete for recognition of the "best" or the "most" successful mentoring accomplishments.

Although such downsides are real concerns for any community, we anticipate that the same social ties that prompt members to engage in developmental efforts will also prevent or at least minimize competitive and individualistic tendencies. If people contribute to one another's development not just for the good of the community, but also because they like and care about each other, then the social capital they earn through their developmental activities will be its own reward.

References

Bruner, J. S. (1960). *The process of education*. Cambridge, MA: Harvard University Press.

Carroll, J. M., Choo, C. W., Dunlap, D. R., Isenhour, P. L., Kerr, S. T., MacLean, A., & Rosson, M. B. (2003). Knowledge management support for teachers. *Educational Technology Research and Development, 51*(4), 42–64.

Dewey, J. (1910). *How we think*. New York: D. C. Heath.

Kim, K., Isenhour, P. L., Carroll, J. M., Rosson, M. B., & Dunlap, D. R. (2003). Teacher Bridge: Knowledge management in community networks. *Home and Office Information Technology: HOIT3*. April 2003, Irvine, California.

Lave, J., & Wenger, E. (1991). *Situated learning: Legitimate peripheral participation*. Cambridge, UK: Cambridge University Press.

Merkel, C., Xiao, L., Farooq, U., Ganoe, C., Lee, R., Carroll, J. M., & Rosson, M. B. 2004. Participatory design in community computing contexts: Tales from the field. *Proceedings of PDC 2004* (pp. 1–10). New York: ACM Press.

Merkel, C. B., Clitherow, M., Farooq, U., Xiao, L., Ganoe, C. H., Carroll, J. M., & Rosson, M. B. (2005). Sustaining computer use and learning in community computing contexts: Make technology part of "Who they are and what they do." *The Journal of Community Informatics, 1*(2), 134–150.

Suchman, L. (1995). Making work visible. *Communications of the ACM, 38*(9), 56–64.

Chapter 8
Social Reproduction and Its Applicability for Community Informatics

Lynette Kvasny

Introduction

For the past decade, committed researchers, politicians, policy makers, investors, and community-based organizations made concerted efforts to redress the digital divide, but the solution has remained somewhat elusive. Information and communication technologies (ICTs) have been portrayed in digital divide discourses as the great equalizer that may be leveraged by local communities to combat economic deprivation and foster social inclusion. Thus, there exists a sense of urgency in "bridging the digital divide." ICT rhetoric is generally utopian, touting innovative models for collaboration, economic activity, learning, and civic involvement.

However, as ICTs become more widely available, we cannot naively assume that historically underserved communities are reaping these highly touted benefits. The rhetoric that celebrates the "bridging of the digital divide" may in fact ring hollow in communities where questions of material existence, not ICT, prevail. People in underserved communities are often consumed with meeting basic human needs such as earning a livelihood, finding comfortable and affordable housing, and creating safe neighborhoods. In light of these persistent economic hardships and related social issues like drugs, crime, discrimination, and homelessness, our well-intended efforts for redressing the digital divide are indeed challenged.

In what follows, I present social reproduction theory as a basis for understanding how ICT may in fact serve to reproduce, rather than alleviate, inequality. When digital divide interventions are informed by Western economic and technological rationalities, they tend to rely on the financial resources and the expertise of external entities. The people experiencing economic hardships and social ills are often portrayed as passive objects, with little agency. By examining the role of ICT in perpetuating these systems of inequality, we are then able to posit transformative ways of thinking about ICT as enabling the resourcefulness of historically underserved communities in meeting their self-determined needs.

J.M. Carroll (ed.), *Learning in Communities*,

Social Reproduction Theory

Social reproduction theories are fueled by the central question of how and why relationships of inequality and domination are reproduced. This theory can be usefully appropriated by community informatics scholars interested in probing the relationship between class interests and power as exerted through the seemingly democratic practice of providing free or low-cost computer and Internet access and training.

Adopting a social reproduction standpoint, one may start from the premise that digital divide discourses tend to categorize and legitimize the power relations between those social agents with (the haves) and those without (the have nots) computing skills and access. Researchers identify and measure those who do and do not have access. Interventions based on this research seek out those without access, and provide them with opportunities to learn and acquire computing skills for little or no financial cost. Thus, one may conclude that the digital divide is a powerful discourse for socialization into a given social order (the information society).

How then does this socialization into a given social order take place? Reproduction theory provides some conceptual models for investigating this process. There is no single general reproduction theory, but reproduction processes constitute a fundamental problem that has been tackled in contemporary sociology, mostly in the study of educational institutions. In what follows, I posit three major approaches in reproduction theory.

First, Bowles and Gintis (1976) debunk the century-old ideal of public education as "the great equalizer" among disparate social classes in the United States. Bowles and Gintis instead argued that public schooling reproduces social and class-based inequities. They adopt a Marxist perspective and argue that schools are training young people for their future economic and occupational position according to their current social class position. On the one hand, students of working-class origin are trained to take orders, to be obedient, and are subject to more disciplinary interventions. On the other hand, children of professionals are trained using more progressive methods, which give them internal discipline and self-presentation skills. The schools and their curriculum structure education so as to produce workers who will fill various socially stratified occupations, thereby maintaining class-based inequities and benefiting the means of capitalist economic production and profit.

While this theory has been criticized because it assumes that futures are largely determined by the economic structure and agents place within it, it does help to raise questions about the implications around the intensity, purpose, autonomy, quality, and length of training, and access found in public access centers, libraries, universities, workplaces, and homes.

Human agency and resistance form the second explanation for social reproduction. From this perspective, dominated agents' resistance to school is a political response to oppression and limited life chances. Resistance theories privilege human agency with dominated agents being able to act, interpret, and exert some power in their lives. This agency, however, tends to keep dominated agents in the lower levels of the economic structure. In Paul Willis' (1997) study of working class male culture in the UK, he found that these males are talented enough to do school work, but they choose not to. Self-exclusion from an educational setting, which was associated with feminine qualities, was experienced as affirming a strong masculine identity. Instead of school, the youths engaged in practices such as theft, smoking, fighting, and consuming alcohol, which they perceived as masculine. The youths also engage in factory work, which became another site for expressing masculinity. While resistance was initially seen as positive, after five or so years of factory work, the young men felt locked into this working-class position and unwittingly reproduced the social structure.

This resistance-oriented approach would be useful for examining "Internet dropouts" and those who simply refuse to adopt ICT, and to understand how and why this rejection of ICT may in fact place folks at a disadvantage. The digital divide is founded on the implicit assumption that access and use provide distinct advantages, and those who fail to adopt ICT will be somehow left behind. Reproduction theory provides a lens for empirically examining this premise.

Culture represents the third explanation for social reproduction. For Bourdieu (1984), culture plays a paramount role in structuring life chances. Each class has its own cultural background, knowledge, dispositions, and tastes that are transmitted through the family. However, the culture of dominant groups forms the knowledge and skills that are most highly valued, and the basis of what is taught in schools. To possess these ways of knowing and skills, which Bourdieu calls cultural capital, means that one is considered educated or talented. To not have this cultural capital means one is considered ignorant or uneducated. Academic performance and educational credentials such as diplomas, certificates, and degrees are largely based upon the congruence between what is taught in school and the cultural capital possessed by students. Thus, those students coming from more affluent homes have greater chances of excelling in school and obtaining credentials that expand occupational opportunities because they posses larger quantities of cultural capital that are privileged in educational settings. In this way, cultural capital inculcated by families and schools plays a large role in structuring access to desirable employment and broader life chances.

Research informed by Bourdieu can provide explanations for how the dominant ideas of a society (i.e., economic development and digital divide) are related to structures of socioeconomic class, production, and power, and how these ideas are legitimated and perpetuated through ICT. This theoretical framework also provides answers to the question of how advantages fail to be passed on to dominated groups, and how we come to perceive the status quo as natural and inevitable (i.e., legitimacy through powerful institutions such as the media as well as schools).

In summary, social reproduction theories problematize taken-for-granted assumptions about the digital divide and the "people on the wrong side of the divide." These theories may inform studies of how and why social agents conceptualize, appropriate, and perhaps resist ICT, and how these practices may unwittingly lead to continued social exclusion. These theories are perhaps most useful for enabling researchers to challenge notions about the ability of ICT alone to redress uniquely human problems of social justice and equity. For instance, Bourdieu's theoretical perspective informed empirical studies of how and why the proliferation of "free" computers and Internet access regardless of mode of access (home or public) may be problematic for public life, and thus provided a rich understanding of the challenges faced by underserved groups (Kvasny, 2006; Kvasny & Keil, 2006). These empirical studies also explain the conflicts that may limit ICTs' role in contributing to broadly desirable social outcomes. These conflicts include socioeconomic class, history, race, and legitimate uses of ICT.

Breaking the Reproductive Cycle

Reproduction theories would see the digital divide as creating docile bodies and reinforcing people's place in society. Humanity is stolen from historically disadvantaged people as they come to be seen as have nots, the unemployed, and the urban poor. This loss of humanity creates a "fear of freedom" in which people acquiesce to an unfair system. Bourdieu argues that the status quo is preserved because it is essentially unquestioned and naturalized. Agents go about their business and they tend not to pose the theoretical questions of legitimacy because the social world is embodied in both their practices and in their thoughts (i.e., habitus). They reproduce it without active reflection. This does not mean that the oppressed do not reflect on their position, but their perception of themselves as oppressed is often impaired by their submersion in the reality of being oppressed (Freire, 1970).

However, education can be a "practice of freedom" with the potential to transform rather than conform (Freire, 1970). To promote transformative uses of ICT, community informatics scholars should enter into dialogue with communities to construct alternative representations of working class subjects and uses of ICT. The working class should not tacitly accept the dominant class values, but critically interrogate their class position and engage in self-actualizing activities that will enable them to integrate ICT in their everyday lives. The awakening of class-consciousness is often bound up within a process of rehabilitating and rebuilding self-esteem, and reaffirming cultural dignity (Freire, 1970; Giroux, 1983; hooks, 1994). This type of critical, participatory research is transformative in that it may help communities to critically reflect upon the structures that repress their ability to thrive. Communities can then resist these structural forces by creating innovative ways of using ICT to support the issues that are important to their social life situations.

Thus, we must respect the particular worldview as well as the social and cultural capital found in historically underserved communities. We must genuinely engage with them so as to understand the nature of their material situation, raise critical awareness of their situation, collaborate to realize alternatives, and create localized interventions for bringing about change. Engagement along the lines advocated by Freire provides a path for how community informatics researchers can promote uses of ICT that upset reproductive processes.

References

Bourdieu, P. (1984). *Distinction: A social critique of the judgement of taste*. Cambridge, MA: Harvard University Press.

Bowles, S., & Gintis, H. (1976). *Schooling in capitalist America: Educational reform and contradictions of economic life*. New York: Basic Books.

Freire, P. (1970). *Pedagogy of the oppressed,* New York: Continuum International Publishing Group.

Giroux, H. (1983). *Theory and resistance in education: A pedagogy for the opposition*. New York: Bergin and Garvey.

Hooks, B. (2000). *Feminist theory: From margin to center*. Cambridge: South End Books.

Kvasny, L. (2005). The role of the habitus in shaping discourses about the digital divide. *Journal of Computer Mediated Communication, 10*(2). Available at http://jcmc.indiana.edu/vol10/issue2/kvasny.html; last accessed April 2005.

Kvasny, L. (2006). The cultural (re)production of digital inequality. *Information, Communication and Society, 9*(2), 160–181.

Kvasny, L., & Keil, M. (2006). The challenges of redressing the digital divide: A tale of two US cities. *Information Systems Journal, 16*(1), 23–53.

Willis, P. (1997). *Learning to labor: How working-class kids get working-class jobs*. Farnborough: Saxon House.

Chapter 9
Communities, Learning, and Democracy in the Digital Age

Lynette Kvasny, Nancy Kranich, and Jorge Reina Schement

The Historical Importance of Access

Access to information networks constitutes the essential tool for enabling citizens to participate in the economic, political, and social life of their communities; and, as such, forms the basis for participatory democracy. Indeed, Jefferson, Madison, and the new Congress made concrete their commitment to an informed public as the foundation of America's nascent democracy; when, in 1789, Congress mandated the first post road. As they did 200 years ago, information networks contribute the glue that binds communities together economically, politically, and socially.

Hence, while the democratic principle for participation is inclusion, the economic principle is contribution; that is, to maximize the potential of each individual is also to maximize a community's wealth. Lack of access to a community's central networks impedes quotidian routines as well as occasional expressions of public duty; and, if persistent, enforces isolation and its derivative alienation. Accordingly, the costs and benefits of inclusivity through access may be measured in a community's progress toward maximizing the contributions of each member and of the whole.

The Challenge of Achieving Access in the Information Age

In the twenty-first century, the development of the Internet offers new hope for providing universal service in the public interest – new hope that everyone will have the opportunity to participate in our information society. Even if a household cannot afford nor chooses not to connect to the Internet from home, people can log on at their local library. Thanks to the universal service provisions of the Telecommunications Act of 1996, nearly every community is now connected, thus providing on-ramps to the information superhighway. Nevertheless, the latest research indicates that many low income, minority, disabled, rural, aging, and inner city groups remain behind in their ownership of computers and access to

J.M. Carroll (ed.), *Learning in Communities*,

telecommunications networks. No matter whose data is used to describe the "digital divide" between rich and poor, between black and white, between urban and rural, between English and Spanish-speaking, between old and young, between immigrants and Native Americans, we can be certain that there is and promises to remain differential access to the Internet and other communications tools.

The Components of Access: Context, Connectivity, Capability, and Content

Access to telecommunications services will not, by itself, guarantee success for communities. The other side of the equation requires an understanding of the resources a community must marshal to make the most of access to national and global networks. At the community level, successful access depends on four primary determinants or *4C's* of access: context, connectivity, capability, and content.

Context

For access to be achieved, a wide array of internal and external forces and trends must be considered. These include environmental (e.g., air and water pollution, waste management), economic (e.g., business incentives, tax structures), and social equity (e.g., crime, poverty, unemployment) indicators of community well-being and sustainability. And although context does not determine a community's developmental trajectory, it does suggest the pertinent needs faced by communities, what types of technology-based interventions might help to fulfill these needs, what kinds of barriers are likely to be encountered, and perhaps more importantly, what kinds of assets the community possesses. By conceptualizing the Internet as a pluralistic domain that includes the broader context in which the technical components are embedded, we explicitly connect social with technical to form the intimate interdependency of the Internet as a sociotechnical network. A sociotechnical perspective emphasizes the importance of context in determining community-level interventions and their evaluation, as well as the inherent difficulty in developing "best practices" that can be applied across diverse settings.

Connectivity

The seemingly simple fact of laying a cable to connect a household or community belies the complexity of attaining a level of connectivity sufficient to constitute a community asset. Though the Telecommunications Act of 1996 defines high-speed

Internet as connection speeds above 256 kbps, higher connection speeds are required to utilize many WWW applications in use today. Telemedicine applications call for connections of 1.5 mbps (T1.5) connections; whereas, many Internet business applications necessitate bandwidths of at least T1.5 or multiple T1.5 connections. To be sure, the level of a community's high-speed connectivity can be measured in different ways: (a) points of access: availability at public sites such as schools, libraries or community centers, in the home, in businesses or institutions, (b) the number of Internet Service Providers (ISPs) that offer high-speed Internet service in a community, and/or (c) the type and speeds of service offerings available from highspeed Internet providers: DSL, cable modem, wireless, T1.5, DS3, etc. Underserved communities may experience a "broadband digital divide" as governments, businesses and content providers increasingly develop products and services that require high-speed Internet connections.

Capability

Because the utility of any technology derives directly from the skill of the user as well as from the delivery capacity of local institutions, capability gauges the ability to deliver or acquire the service. For individuals, capability encompasses both formal and informal educational attainment and levels of technical sophistication and understanding, along with the willingness to adapt to new technologies and ways of thinking. At the institutional level, capability also relates to the amount of resources a community and its businesses commit to workforce development including teaching effective use of information technology tools and encouraging creativity, productivity, and innovations of local entrepreneurs. Capabilities are cumulative and recursive because individuals and institutions must migrate to new hardware platforms, learn new software applications, and develop new skills as new technologies are introduced and as existing technologies are upgraded. Thus, existing and emerging gaps in proficiency, knowledge, skills, and experience may lead to considerable differences in communities' abilities to leverage the Internet.

Content

Content is interdependent upon the other three C's. Once individuals and communities become connected and have the capabilities and necessary skills to use the Internet, they need a reason for use. Low-income and underserved communities face significant content barriers that include the lack of neighborhood-level information such as housing, childcare, and transportation news; limited information written at a basic literacy level; and inadequate content for culturally diverse populations, including non-English speaking Internet users. If content that is relevant to individuals and members of the community is not available, it will be difficult to encourage and sustain use. Relevant content is necessary because it provides a forum for interacting within local communities as well as a window to the outside world.

Lifelong Learning – The Persistent Challenge of Access

In contemporary communities, the 4C's converge to facilitate decentralized low- or no-cost delivery of interactive learning opportunities that enable more active, democratic participation from early childhood through adulthood. No longer confined to a classroom or educational institutions, learners are afforded greater opportunities to take advantage of emerging information and telecommunications technologies to achieve more successful outcomes. Shared spaces, both real and virtual, provide environments where people with common interests and concerns gather and benefit – the greater the participation, the more valuable the resource. These learning networks, often referred to as communities, encourage collaborative knowledge creation and sharing using all forms of media. Within these networks, learners can interact by communicating ideas and engaging in discourse and problem solving. Participants contribute new creations after they gain and benefit from access and participation. These learning spaces, or commons, may enhance both human and social capital when they incorporate democratic values, free expression and intellectual freedom prevail.

While online opportunities have the potential to serve a multitude of lifelong learning needs of all people, they are only available to those who have access to these new technologies, can afford and comprehend the content, and possess the capabilities necessary to navigate these complex systems successfully. Without equitable access within each of the 4C's, these learning opportunities pose major challenges to the democratic promise of these open anytime/anyplace educational experiences.

Chapter 10
Radical Praxis and Civic Network Design

Murali Venkatesh and Jeffrey S. Owens

Technology-powered civic networks are social constructions that develop in relation to a particular macrostructure (meaning social structure, here referring to historically-constituted relational patterns among social positions). They are proposed and are designed by incumbents of social positions (persons, groups, organizations), and the cultural practices, belief systems, and dispositions–interests, values, norms, identities–that are pervasive in that macro-structure at that historical moment should be presumed to shape network form. Macro-structural realities such as differential access to power and resources modulate how effective actors are in inscribing their preferences into the form; structurally-powerful actors tend to be more successful than structurally-powerless actors in this regard. Similar to organizational forms in general, civic networks are products of a particular intersection of the macro (macro-structure) and the micro (the developmental conditions in which human designers interact to produce design products). The network's mission, its operative strategies, and the social constituencies that are included or excluded through design choices are a function of this intersection. This sociological, institutionalist-inspired view of civic network design recommends a certain kind of reflexivity on the part of the designer, one that emphasizes her *historicity*. This, we argue, is an outlook the designer must consciously cultivate.

We view design as the locus of conflict and struggle, whereby entrenched cultural practices, beliefs, and dispositions attempt to pattern emergent artifacts in culturally compliant ways and alternative practices, beliefs, and dispositions struggle to ground themselves in concrete form. If the first wins out, the design product embodies and reaffirms prevalent macro-structure; an alternative social order finds concrete form if the latter prevails. We include among design products a broad range of artifacts including technical specifications and service contracts and project by-laws that govern the use and further development of the artifact. These products tend to be mutually-reinforcing: Contracts and by-laws, for instance, can ensure that the civic network's present technological configuration is reproduced over time and, through it, the preferred social order. As we note below, design must be conceived of in even broader terms, as design of means as well as ends: design includes specification of ICTs, contracts and by-laws, as well as the developmental (or institutional) conditions – the means – which yield these design products. Our ideal here is the reflexive designer: One who understands technology design in

J.M. Carroll (ed.), *Learning in Communities*,

these broad terms and as located in a particular historical moment and open, as such, to historical forces and structural pressures.

Our reflexive designer is aware that as a new social form, the civic network must necessarily emerge in relation to the historically-constituted relational structures in the geospatial area, and in relation as well to the practices, beliefs and dispositions prevalent there. To a greater or lesser extent, explicitly or implicitly, civic networking projects attempt to institute new relational patterns in the areas they purport to serve, whereby heretofore excluded constituencies are reinserted into the social fabric and existing relational structures are reworked in socially-progressive ways; the ideals they champion tend to center around access equity and social inclusion. The reflexive designer sees the developmental setting as an arena where the project's driving ideals encounter entrenched realities in the project area. Design activity entails social choices, which is why they are so contentious. Picking one design option over another includes some constituencies and excludes others. The contest is seldom one of equals. The embedding macro-structure and its asymmetric power distribution empower some social actors over others to effectively "limit change and create domination in the micro sphere" (Burawoy, 1991). These pressures enter the developmental setting through designers' choices to shape network form. Designers serve as conduits through which such pressures are inscribed into the form to reproduce the prevailing macro-structure. But actors can choose to channel alternative forces for "rewiring" the social order.

Individuals (as well as organizations) are host to multiple cultural logics from prior socialization. These logics – material practices and symbolic constructions (Friedland & Alford, 1991) – embed them and account for the dispositions, practices, and beliefs that define them. These logics guide situated action and encode "criteria of legitimacy by which role identities, strategic behaviors, organizational forms are constructed and sustained" (Suddaby & Greenwood, 2005). Some of these logics may be more entrenched and more institutionalized than others. Generally, more institutionalized logics tend to guide behavior more readily than do less institutionalized logics. It is conceivable that civic network designers – a category that ideally would include all potential stakeholders – enter the developmental setting with at least two sets of logics in their cultural toolkit (Swidler, 1986): One that embeds their habitual social role (for example, "community resident," "Internet service provider") and the other, the civic networking logic. The habitual, of course, is invested in and stems from the prevailing social order, while the civic networking logic may (often does) look ahead to an alternative order. The encounter between these logics in design can be more or less contentious depending on how ambitious are the civic networking project's aims to rewire the prevailing order. The more radical the aims, the greater will be the resistance from entrenched dispositions. What can our reflexive designer do to increase the likelihood that the civic networking logic will prevail in this contest, that it will, in fact, effectively counter more conservative orientations to successfully realize itself in concrete form?

Design reflects intention and yet, outcomes often are unintended. This is because design activity is usually seen in terms of products or *ends* that result from the activity. Typically, civic networking design committees (or steering committees) set out to specify a particular configuration of information and communication technologies (ICTs) that would enable the network to become operational. This would be an example of *direct design,* where the intent is to direct the product in a certain way to meet certain specifications and aims. But efforts at direct design often fail from unforeseen interactions among the interest of more and less powerful stakeholders (see Goodin, 1996). Our reflexive designer would focus not just on the *ends* of design but importantly on the *means* as well. The means of design are seldom the focus of design activity, and yet they are a crucial element in the social infrastructure of social constructions. *Indirect design* – design of the social conditions within which design activity occurs – is not only possible but a requirement, we would argue, to guard against unintended outcomes. Design of ends must start with design of the means, which, in the case of civic network design, may be seen as necessary second order public goods influencing production of the civic network – the first order public good (see Gualini, 2002). Situated actions can be guided by design of social conditions for "probabilistic activation" (Tsuokas, 1989) of preferred logics to structure design products in intended ways. How should our reflexive designer go about doing this? There are two possible targets for indirect design interventions, one internal and the other external, and they shape the design committee's social choice processes as well as the design ends that are identified and pursued. Expanding the design committee's managerial capacity (Brint & Karabel, 1991) for monitoring its own internal relations and constitutive practices is an example of the first. Instituting social controls on the committee's external relations is an example of the second.

How the committee thinks about its internal social and material relations profoundly affects the deliberative climate within which design choices are made. What formal and informal rules must be crafted to improve the likelihood that design options are openly debated by a plurality of publics in a spirit of "participatory parity" (Fraser & Honneth, 2003)? Conversation rules must guarantee individual rights while also promoting the pursuit of the common good. Assuring openness is a utopian ideal that is exceedingly difficult to accomplish in the reality of a more-or-less stratified and differentiated polity, where some constituents are more powerful than others, but we argue that this is a liberal democratic ideal worth pursuing by civic network designers. This stems from a conviction that civic networks, like the mass media, are crucial components of a community's public sphere. Conceptually, if not empirically, civic networks necessarily are sites of contestation featuring a multiplicity of publics: Targets of contestation could be the broader social agenda as well as the form of the network itself. Recognizing the civic network's obligation to be hospitable to a plurality of publics is an important amendment to a common-enough conception of such networks as *community* resources. The term *community* highlights reciprocity, mutuality, and consensus. *Publics,* on the other hand, is a broader idea connoting debate and contestation among social groups constituted around divergent interest, ideology, and identity; the term better accommodates dissensus and dissonance (Fraser, 1999). Accordingly, a civic network may be conceived of in *social process* terms rather than as an *entity*, incorporating as it grows and matures both *communities* based on consensus as well as contending *publics*. One might even argue that the desired end-state would be a normalized set of more-or-less consensual publics. A process view acknowledges that the network must stay resilient and representative, both catalyzing and reflecting broader social changes. Such a view also allows designers to think of design in incremental terms. Institutions develop through layering (Thelen, 2003), whereby changes are layered on top of more enduring "core" elements without necessarily changing them. As long as participatory parity is assured, designers can proceed on the assumption that they can respond to situational contingencies as they see fit without locking the design into an irreversible state.

Crafting a robust set of guidelines on how the committee should manage its internal relations – including rules of deliberative engagement – is an imperfect but necessary bulwark against the reality of power asymmetry in the macro-structure. Assuring *rough equality* (Fraser, 1999) in the microorder is a step toward an egalitarian macroorder; it would be hard to argue that there is no link between the means and such ends. Besides rules of engagement (everyone gets a chance to speak, for e.g.), our reflexive designer would work to include useful techniques in the committee's repertoire to augment its capacity for enlightened self-management and concerted action. For example, What cultural logics and preconceptions of civic networking do designers come into design with? Identifying these at the outset can make actors more reflexive and help "loosen themselves" from knee-jerk recourse to structural reproduction in the choices they make. Expanding capacity for deliberative action may also be helped by instituting an ethos of the long view: Actors are unlikely to focalize the near-term if they are answerable to actors with longer time horizons (Pierson, 2000). This looks ahead to social controls.

Social controls – normative or "regulative institutions that ensure individual behavior accords with group demands" (Coser, 1982) – can shape what courses of action are pursued by legitimizing some behaviors over others. Institutionalizing philanthropic (vs. self-interested) behavior by Minneapolis corporations, Galaskiewicz (1991) reports, was helped by "peer pressure and selective incentives"; philanthropic conduct was rewarded with national mass media publicity. Controls instantiate the Kantian publicity principle, which requires that design choices are "publicly defensible" (Goodin, 1996). Local mass media outlets, elected officials, urban planners, and opinion-leaders can be external controllers and sources of public oversight on the design process. The reflexive designer will incorporate such sources of control into the design process. This is easier said than done. This might require challenging well-entrenched notions of civic identity that these actors may be invested in. For example, a community that thinks of itself as driven by the logic of economic growth (and which community today is not?) may yield up few sources of social control who are prepared to go to bat for the social equity logic. Reframing civic, and individual, identity to include the latter could be especially challenging if the community lacks a history of civic activity. Successful reframing, however, would help incorporate community actors as well as other targeted social movements into the project, thus expanding the moral, rhetorical, and material resources that the reflexive designer constitutes in a *circle of solidarity*

(Jermier, 1998) to guide the committee's design choices and hold it accountable for them.

All social actors have the *capacity* for reflexivity: They are context-aware operatives who select from among logics and action repertoires when deciding how to act in a situation. This institutionalist idea is crucial to the foregoing: Indirect design can succeed only if actors are credited with this capacity. *Praxis* refers to analytic *understanding* of the sources of structural inequality and then *acting* to normatively reconstitute the prevailing social order (Benson, 1983). Our reflexive designer may be confronted with the following choices: to inscribe the design with the project's transformative aims or to compromise on those aims in light of situational contingencies. This dilemma is likely to arise in civic networking projects based on broadband ICTs. Broadband requires, as a practical necessity (Winner, 1993), significant technological, financial, and know-how resources to sustain. As such, designers may have to choose between two logics: the social equity logic and the financial sustainability logic. Affirming the former is to affirm the goal of structural change through the network; affirming the latter is to empower the prevailing macro-structural resource distribution. These logics need not be mutually-exclusive. Our reflexive designer is an enlightened pragmatist, knowing when to balance strategic structural aims against situational contingencies without, however, losing sight of the prize. She is conscious always of her capacity for social choice and works to enlighten her fellow designers of the same.

Design choices are social choices. To acknowledge one's capacity for choice is to acknowledge one's historicity. In the context of civic network design, such an outlook stems from ongoing reflection on the project's dialectical relation to broader cultural and structural forces. The challenge for civic networking cohorts everywhere is to institutionalize such an outlook to ensure that (a) designers recognize their design choices as social choices that are publicly deliberated, defended, and challenged and (b) the outlook becomes self-activating and transindividual, which means every designer – every participant in design – thinks and acts like our exemplary reflexive designer. Why should we attempt to institutionalize such an outlook? The field of urban planning offers instructive lessons. In the 1960s, Paul Davidoff argued for a new socially-progressive urban planning outlook called *advocacy planning*:

> The public interest, as he saw it, was not a matter of science but of politics. He called for many plans, rather than one master plan, and for full discussion of the values and interests represented by different plans. He brought the question of who gets what – the distributional question which the rational model had so carefully avoided – to the foreground.
>
> (Sandercock, 1998, p. 171)

Urban planning schools adapted this outlook into their curricula, as they did its successors over the years, to train planning professionals sensitized in these alternatives to the technical-rational planning model. The rational planning model and its proponents helped affirm the prevailing social order and its distribution of power and resources. This had been the taken-for-granted approach to planning practice, one that was unreflexively reproduced through urban planning research and training curricula until Davidoff's salvo. The most recent paradigm shift is represented by the radical planning approach. Radical planning praxis, Sandercock notes, is discontinuous with rational planning and is explicitly critical and progressively political in its concerns:

> Radical practices emerge from experience with and a critique of existing unequal relations and distributions of power, opportunity and resources. The goal of these practices is to work for structural transformation of these systemic inequalities and, in the process, to empower those who have been systematically disempowered (p. 176).

Bandwidth is socially-produced social space. Urban planning theorists call attention to the replication in built urban space of hegemonic power and resource distributions. Telecommunications bandwidth – broadband, in particular – is no different, wherein some interests are rendered central while others are marginalized, pushed out to the periphery. Spatialization of broadband bandwidth tends to mimic broader social distributions because of the practical necessity of resources required to sustain broadband civic networking projects; ironically, these projects often start out intending to redistribute some or all of those very same resources in socially progressive ways to effect structural change. Bandwidth, of course, can also be designed from a radical standpoint to serve as the site for distributive justice and *insurgent citizenship* (Sandercock, 1998). As an enlightened pragmatist, our reflexive designer recognizes that designs can be changed incrementally and that networks may develop through successive layering. As such, the civic network might start out serving certain publics and expand from there through concentric incorporation of new, hitherto excluded publics. The key to assuring that this occurs is to keep ongoing design discussions open and to guarantee *rough equality* (Fraser, 1999) in deliberative forums. Early adopters representing the state or market may be necessary especially in broadband networking projects: well-resourced "anchor tenants," to use shopping mall terminology, can help sustain the network financially. The trick is to view them as bandwidth *homesteaders* not *colonizers*, and to work to keep the design open to alternative developmental trajectories inspired by the promise of structural transformation.

Social learning is foundational to the means as well as ends of socially-progressive design work. Both defenders and challengers of the prevailing order may learn from the environment to press their case. Just as aggressive market logics may be (and often are) used to justify promoting financial sustainability in purportedly civic endeavors, so could reflexive designers draw on their *circle of solidarity* to mount effective cultural offensives favoring social equity. For example, framing digital inclusion as a civil right links it to broader, deeply resonant cultural tropes and may make available new resources and action repertoires to counter market logics. But establishing and sustaining such links is complex and challenging (Scully & Creed, 2005). Our plea is for higher educational institutions such as Information Schools to consider the urban planning discipline as a change model for their academic research and training programs and, through such programmatic efforts, contribute to producing an institutionalized field of socially-progressive technical practice with its own trained cadres and distinctive professional identity. Despite emerging circuits of solidarity (the Learning in Communities meeting at Pennsylvania State University in the summer of 2005 was a step in this direction) focused on civic networking, designers still tend to work in relative isolation; what they may learn from others even within the civic networking arena tends to be more or less opportunistic. Current socially-progressive civic network design practice, we would argue, is analogous to advocacy planning in urban planning, where designers advocate for social inclusion and may even empower the marginalized to fight the fight themselves. But the degree to which advocacy design – if we may call it that – is institutionalized in civic network practice is unclear. The point behind institutionalizing anything, of course, is to inform thought and action in consistent ways based on an agreed upon corpus of knowledge, and, more fundamentally, to instill a distinctive way or style of responding to challenges. We are not sure this has occurred yet. Depending on the nature and complexity of the project, civic network design choices are very much at risk of being driven disproportionately by technical–rational considerations to the detriment of properly social ones. This is regrettable and must change. As designers and educators we must continue to educate ourselves through social learning while institutionalizing cultural transmission through academic programs to train the next generation of civic network designers, so that they recognize the kinds of social and professional challenges that designers (and planners) in other fields continue to face, and, learning from them, know how to respond creatively to them through their own practice.

References

Benson, J. K. (1983). A dialectical method for the study of organizations. In G. Morgan (Ed.), *Beyond method: Strategies for social research*. Beverly Hills, CA: Sage.

Brint, S., & Karabel, J. (1991). Institutional origins and transformations: The case of American community colleges. In W. W. Powell & P. J. DiMaggio (Eds.), *The new institutionalism in organizational analysis*. Chicago, IL: University of Chicago Press.

Burawoy, M. (1991). *Ethnography unbound: Power and resistance in the modern metropolis*. Berkeley, CA: The University of California Press.

Coser, L.A. (1982). The notion of control in sociological theory. In J. P. Gibbs (Ed.), *Social control: Views from the social sciences* (pp. 13–22). Beverly Hills, CA: Sage.

Fraser, N. (1999). Rethinking the public sphere: A contribution to the critique of actually existing democracy. In C. Calhoun (Ed.), *Habermas and the public sphere*. Cambridge, MA: The MIT Press.

Fraser, N., & Honneth, A. (2003). *Recognition or redistribution? A political–philosophical exchange*. London, UK: Verso.

Friedland, R., & Alford, R. A. (1991). Bringing society back in: Symbols, practices, and institutional contradictions. In W. W. Powell & P. J. DiMaggio (Eds.), *The new institutionalism in organizational analysis*. Chicago, IL: University of Chicago Press.

Galaskiewicz, J. (1991). Making corporate actors accountable: Institution-building in Minneapolis – St. Paul. In W. W. Powell & P. J. DiMaggio (Eds.), *The new institutionalism in organizational analysis*. Chicago, IL: University of Chicago Press.

Goodin, R. E. (1996). Institutions and their design. In R. E. Goodin (Ed.), *The theory of institutional design*. Cambridge, UK: Cambridge University Press.

Gualini, E. (2002). Institution capacity building as an issue of collective action and institutionalization: Some theoretical remarks. In G. Cars, P. Healey, A. Madanipour, and C. De Megalhaes

(Eds.), *Urban governance, institutional capacity and social milieux*. Aldershot, UK: Ashgate.

Jermier, J. M. (1998). Introduction: Critical perspectives on organizational control. *Administrative Science Quarterly, 43*, 235–256.

Pierson, P. (2000). The limits of design: Explaining institutional origins and change. *Governance: An Interdisciplinary Journal of Policy and Administration, 13*(4), 475–499.

Sandercock, L. (1998). The death of modernist planning: Radical praxis for a postmodern age. In M. Douglass & J. Friedmann (Eds.), *Cities for citizens: Planning and the rise of civil society in a global age*. Chichester, UK: Wiley.

Scully, M. A., & Creed, W. E. D. (2005). Subverting our stories of subversion. In G. F. Davis, D. McAdam, W. R. Scott, and M. N. Zald (Eds.), *Social movements and organizational theory*. Cambridge, UK: Cambridge University Press.

Suddaby, R., & Greenwood, R. (2005). Rhetorical strategies of legitimacy. *Administrative Science Quarterly, 50*, 35–67.

Swidler, A. (1986). Culture in action: Symbols and strategies. *American Sociological Review, 51*, 273–286.

Thelen, K. (2003). How institutions evolve: Insights from comparative historical analysis. In J. Mahoney & D. Rueschemeyer (Eds.), *Comparative historical analysis in the social sciences*. Cambridge, UK: Cambridge University Press.

Tsoukas, H. (1989). The validity of idiographic research explanations. *Academy of Management Review, 14*(4), 551–561.

Winner, L. (1993). Social constructivism: Opening the black box and finding it empty. *Science as Culture, 3*(16), 427–452.

Part II

Chapter 11
Local Groups Online: Political Learning and Participation

Andrea Kavanaugh, ThanThan Zin, Joseph Schmitz, Mary Beth Rosson, B. Joon Kim, and John M. Carroll

Abstract Voluntary associations serve crucial roles in local communities and within our larger democratic society. They aggregate shared interests, collective will, and cultivate civic competencies that nurture democratic participation. People active in multiple local groups frequently act as opinion leaders and create "weak" social ties across groups. In Blacksburg and surrounding Montgomery County, Virginia, the Blacksburg Electronic Village (BEV) community computer network has helped to foster nearly universal Internet penetration. Set in this dense Internet context, the present study investigated whether and how personal affiliation with local groups enhanced political participation in this high information and communication technology environment. This paper presents findings from longitudinal survey data which indicate that as individuals' uses of information technology within local formal groups increase over time, so do their levels and types of involvement in the group. Furthermore, these increases most often appear among people who serve as opinion leaders and maintain weak social ties in their communities. Individuals' changes in community participation, interests and activities, and Internet use suggest ways in which group members act upon political motivations and interests across various group types.

Keywords: Social computing; Empirical methods; Survey research

Introduction

Human groups form the fundamental building blocks of society (Homans, 1950) because group affiliation permits people to coordinate action and accomplish more complex tasks than they could as lone individuals. Typically people affiliate with others who share common identities, interests, or activities (Blau, 1977; Rogers, 1995). These commonalities may be as primary as family, kin and friends; or they may reflect more general shared interests in activities (such as playing a sport, a musical instrument, or cards) or reflect shared ideas and perspectives (such as religion or politics).

J.M. Carroll (ed.), *Learning in Communities*,

The types of individual objectives participants pursue in groups may be expressive or instrumental. Individuals often join both types of groups (Parsons, 1954; Edwards & Booth, 1973) and the same group may have a mix of both types of objectives. Expressive activity goals typically are met within a group: getting together to play cards or a team sport. In contrast, instrumental activity goals typically are directed outside the group – perhaps influencing policy through advocacy.

At the group level of analysis, many groups combine instrumental and expressive goals. For example, while participants may enjoy getting together to play baseball regularly, they may also seek to influence policy by negotiating with local government for more resources, perhaps better playing fields or increased maintenance support. During these sporadic instrumental activities, groups may act as political players within their communities. Thus, average citizens typically engage in local politics in ad hoc ways, often when local law or policy change impinges on their personal circumstances (i.e., "not in my backyard") or upon the interests of a group with which they are affiliated (i.e., more ball fields). Even where goals are combined within a group, however, there generally tends to be a predominance of either expressive or instrumental type of activity objective that characterizes the group.

Expressive groups seek members who are similar in ways that construct a common group identity, e.g., common interest, social background, point of view, values or talents. In contrast, instrumental groups tend to seek and cultivate membership from high resource individuals who could help the group accomplish its goals, e.g., people with more education, expertise, greater social or material resources, or political contacts. Most groups seek combinations of these resources. Whether expressive or instrumental, all groups have structures with differing roles and crucial interdependencies (Poole & Roth, 1989).

Group affiliation is essential to a political culture of democracy and to the requisite social structures and processes that sustain it (Almond & Verba, 1963). Local clubs and other voluntary associations (e.g., church, Boy Scouts, Parent Teacher Association, and sports groups) mediate between individuals and the greater society by raising awareness of larger social issues, aggregating interests, and cultivating civic competence.

Putnam (2000) stresses that voluntary associations serve as forums for thoughtful deliberation over vital public issues just as they inculcate democratic habits and enhance political skills (p. 339). This emphasis on opportunities for participation of individuals in community power through community organizations is a pluralist – contrasted with an elite – approach to community power (Dahl, 1961; Putnam, 2000). Pluralist forms of democratic government seek broader participation and representation of the populace. Not only do voluntary associations act as communication and information dissemination forums that raise awareness among the citizenry about issues and problems, they provide training grounds to develop needed political skills. Associations also function as recruiting mechanisms that increase individuals' participation in the larger political system. Clearly, groups play essential roles in nurturing a pluralistic society.

Prior Research

Local Groups and Community Participation

In the USA, many studies have shown that typically more than half of the population is affiliated with at least one voluntary association (Almond & Verba, 1963; Edwards & Booth, 1973; Milbrath & Goel, 1982; Putnam, 2000; Stueve & Gerson, 1977; Verba & Nie, 1972; Verba et al., 1995). The most common type of affiliative group is religious (i.e., church or other congregation for worship). Both local and national studies agree about the social determinants and correlates of group affiliation. Except for religious groups, typically affiliation is most strongly related to socioeconomic status (SES). In addition to SES, common predicting factors include length of residence, gender, and stage in life cycle (Almond & Verba, 1963; Babchuk & Booth, 1973; Hyman & Wright, 1971; Stueve & Gerson, 1977; Putnam, 2000). Life cycle stage refers to whether individuals are in their school years, single, married, married with children, and whether their children are minors or adults. Life cycle stages are frequently associated with changes in social roles and groups. Parents with children are particularly involved in local communities, through their children's school and youth group activities.

People who affiliate with groups tend to participate more actively in local civic and political life (Milbrath & Goel, 1982; Putnam, 2000; Tsagarousianou et al., 1998). In this manner, participation in community groups by average citizens often leads to learning about local issues and problems that may spur greater engagement in informal and formal political discussions and foster collective responses (Kim et al., 1999). Thus, group identification and affiliation gives a greater sense of belonging and may (especially in instrumental groups) serve as a means to achieve greater political power.

Prior studies have found that people with more group affiliations are generally more politically active and involved than people who belong just to one group or to no group at all (Almond & Verba, 1963; Putnam, 2000; Verba et al., 1995). This relationship held true in our prior research as well, not only for persons with leadership positions (whom we called "leader bridges") but also for *members* of more than one group, e.g., "member bridges" (Kavanaugh et al., 2003). In that research, which was part of a larger study entitled Experiences of People, Internet and Community (or EPIC), respondents who were affiliated with multiple groups were significantly more extroverted, better educated, more informed and active than Nonbridges (i.e., people who were affiliated with one or no organization). Bridges also had a greater sense of group belonging, higher levels of trust, community attachment, and participation than did Nonbridges. Bridges were more interested in civic and political affairs. They also had greater confidence in their community's ability to collaboratively solve problems, as measured by a collective efficacy construct (Carroll & Reese, 2003). Bridges used the Internet for political purposes and civic activities significantly more than did Nonbridges. After gaining Internet access, Bridges became more involved in the local community, and in local issues of interest. (For complete statistical results about these measures, see http://epic.cs.vt.edu.)

To sum up prior research, citizens with multiple group affiliations form weak social ties (or Bridges) between diverse groups. Their higher levels of social and political engagement help to make them opinion leaders (also referred to as influentials) in their social circles and community, a topic we discuss next.

The Role of Opinion Leaders

Opinion leaders may be defined as people in social circles or groups from whom others regularly seek advice or guidance about mundane daily life, e.g., what is new, what is good, where to go for a vacation or shopping, and to hear informed political opinions (Katz & Lazarsfeld, 1955; Keller & Berry, 2003; Rogers, 1995). Opinion leaders (or influentials) exist at all strata of society, but even at the lowest strata they typically have higher education than others in their milieu. Although they represent a small minority of a population (10–15%), they not only demonstrate greater political engagement than the general public, but also display more sociability and gregariousness. Influentials are known for their keen interest in new ideas and information, greater exposure to media, and more empathy or understanding for others.

During 30 years of research about influentials, the marketing research firm Roper ASW has characterized these socially and politically active Americans as having responded positively on random sample surveys to at least 3 of 11 questions regarding government and political activities – during the past year; these are as follows: (1) served on a committee for a local organization; (2) served as an officer for a club or organization; (3) been an active member of any group that tries to influence public policy or government; (4) written or called a politician at the state, local, or national level; (5) attended a political rally, speech, or organized protest of any kind; (6) attended a public meeting on town or school affairs; (7) held or run for political office; (8) written an article for a magazine or newspaper; (9) written a letter to the editor of a newspaper or magazine or called a live radio or TV show to express an opinion; (10) signed a petition; (11) worked for a political party; or made a speech (Keller & Berry, 2003, p. 20).

Influentials often provide advice in informal contexts, often by word of mouth in conversations with friends, family, and other social groups. They tend to be active in multiple clubs and organizations in their communities. As noted earlier, people who belong to more than one group or organization create weak social ties between groups (Granovetter, 1973; Simmel, [1908] 1971; Wolff, 1950) or what Putnam (2000) refers to as "bridging" social capital. Such joint memberships form group-to-group ties that indirectly connect all persons in otherwise separate groups and strengthen bridging (across groups) when compared to bonding (within groups) forms of social capital. Evidence from earlier work (Kavanaugh et al., 2003) shows that people who act as Bridges are more involved in the local community and use the Internet to sustain, facilitate, and increase their involvement.

Group Communication and Involvement

Opinion leaders influence others in ways that differ from ad hoc interactions with others in their social circle via their participation in formal local groups (Katz & Lazarsfeld, 1955; Kim et al., 1999; Keller & Berry, 2003). Often opinion leaders serve to relay new ideas and information to other members of their social groups. In devising their two-step flow of communication model, Katz and Lazarsfeld (1955) initiated a series of subsequent studies showing that interpersonal communication, in combination with mass media, more effectively persuades people to change their attitudes or behavior than does mass media alone. Rather than making individual decisions about how to respond to new information or political ideas received from mass media, people turn to influential others in their social circles or groups to interpret and respond to new ideas (Hague & Loader, 1999; Bimber, 2003; Katz & Aspden, 1997; Scheufele & Nisbet, 2002). In this way, opinion leaders play key transmission roles by directing information and influence flows within (and across) groups with which they are affiliated. The people with whom opinion leaders share information spread that information throughout their own social circles, and the members of which also spread that information in a growing spiral of influence. By their very nature, opinion leaders share information from many sources, including mass media, the Internet, other influentials, and the groups with which they are involved.

The wide diffusion of the Internet is generally credited with expanding access to political information and with providing interested citizens with new possibilities for political learning and participation (Bimber, 2001). In one of the earliest national studies of groups and information technology use, Katz and Aspden (1997) found that long-time Internet users (3 or more years) reported belonging to more community organizations – 27% to one organization and an additional 22% to two or more (49% total) than did newer Internet users. Internet users were also affiliated with more leisure organizations than were nonusers. But they found no differences between Internet users and nonusers on measures of affiliation with religious organizations. More experienced Internet users were early adopters; as such they usually were better educated than later adopters. Higher SES was associated with more organizational involvement. Horrigan's (2001) study of Internet use (funded by the Pew Internet and American Life Project) found that a substantial majority of American Internet users accessed the Internet to explore groups. More than 80% of these users stayed in regular contact with at least one group to cultivate relationships and discuss issues of mutual interest.

This paper addresses such fundamental research questions as: Is ICT use by group members changing over time? Does level or type of involvement in the group change, and if so, how and for whom? Are there changes in community participation, interests and activities, and Internet use among group members that are similar to those of their group(s)? To what extent do opinion leaders account for any of these observed changes?

Research Method

The present paper reports on findings from two rounds conducted 1 year apart (Fall 2001 and Fall 2002) of household survey data that were part of a larger research project (EPIC) investigating community computing in Blacksburg and Montgomery County, Virginia. The EPIC project was conducted with support from the National Science Foundation (2001–2003). Our strategy to recruit households for these surveys was based upon using a representative sample that matched the population demographics of Blacksburg and Montgomery County, a total population of roughly 77,500 comprising 27,000 households (Kavanaugh et al., 2000), about half of which were in Blacksburg or the surrounding Montgomery County. Blacksburg and Montgomery County are home to the community computer network known as the Blacksburg Electronic Village (BEV).

BEV was established in 1993 with support from the land grant university, Virginia Tech, in partnership with the town of Blacksburg and Bell Atlantic, the regional telephone company now known as Verizon. Through the efforts of the BEV project, Internet adoption and use grew rapidly in the area throughout the 1990s. In 7 years more than 80% of the local population in Blacksburg and Montgomery County had Internet access (Kavanaugh & Patterson, 2001). Over 150 community groups and over 450 local businesses (>75%) maintained Web sites. Penetration has leveled off since the early years of 2000, with close to 90% (87.7%) of Blacksburg residents and close to 80% (78.9%) of (non-Blacksburg) Montgomery County residents using the Internet (Kavanaugh et al., 2005a).

While these have been among the world's highest Internet densities throughout the 1990s, in more recent years, online services throughout the USA have been growing steadily, reaching over two-thirds the total US population in 2005 and 73% by early 2006 (Madden, 2006). We can reasonably expect that the many of the secondary effects of Internet adoption and use that we have observed in Blacksburg and Montgomery County will be experienced in other rural towns throughout the United States in the near future if they are not experiencing them already. The main effect of the university presence on the rural town of Blacksburg in the early days of Internet adoption and use was to provide initial deployment of Internet infrastructure leading to a critical mass of early adopters who readily became aware of and familiar with the Internet. Such a critical mass of users is beginning to form in many rural towns and counties throughout the USA.

Sampling and Stratification

We obtained a random sample of 870 Montgomery County (including Blacksburg) residential addresses from Survey Sample, Inc. in September 2000 for a previous BEV research project and had prefiltered and eliminated 380 invalid addresses from the initial pool of 1,250. Survey Sample, Inc., generated the sample randomly by postal code, using postal and telephone directory records, and department of motor vehicles databases. Nonetheless, this approach forced us to limit our initial recruiting (one-page) survey to postal mail using the Dillman method (Dillman, 2000).

The initial recruiting survey yielded a pool of 188 respondent households (a 22% response rate). We created a 100-household sample using a stratification model with three primary stratification categories: (1) place of residence (half in the town of Blacksburg, half in the surrounding Montgomery County), (2) education level, and (3) Internet use. We asked all household members who were 16 or older to complete a 27-page "adult" survey. In order to boost response rates because the survey was long and the same individuals participated in two rounds, we compensated the respondents modestly ($25) for their participation. The following analysis reports findings from the adult respondents in the 100 representative households; since there were multiple adult members per household completing surveys, we have 156 adult respondents in Round 1 and 143 adult respondents in Round 2.

The total number of adult respondents in Round 1 (156) and Round 2 (143) changed because five households (totaling 19 respondents) dropped out of the study after the first round. We replaced the five households using households with comparable scores on the original stratification measures. Even so, we obtained only six respondents in the replacement households, yielding a net loss of 13 respondents during Round 2. This small difference in the two rounds of samples did not affect the analyses of respondents' behavior in their local groups, because we only included respondents in these analyses that were affiliated with the same types of groups in both rounds. All of the analyses presented in the results are based only on adult respondents to the surveys.

Survey Variables and Constructs

The EPIC survey used a printed questionnaire with the same questions in both rounds although Round 2 had several additional questions that are not relevant to this paper. Survey questions asked respondents about their interests and activities, attitudes and psychological attributes, affiliation with community groups, information and communication technology use, and demographic factors. This survey drew upon validated and reliable questions from prior studies, such as Robert Kraut's HomeNet study (Kraut et al., 2002), the BEV research (Kavanaugh & Patterson, 2001), and several political studies (Brady, 1999; Hyman & Wright, 1971; Robinson et al., 1999; Verba et al., 1995) that incorporated questions about known indicators of social participation.

Among the survey constructs described in this paper are measures of (1) civic, political, and social interests and activities, (2) psychological attributes, such as extroversion, collective efficacy, and trust, and (3) Internet use derived from multiple variables – most of which used Likert scales that captured respondents' agreement on frequency scales (Table 11.1). We created typologies by aggregating variables linked to common constructs. We computed variable correlations for each construct

Table 11.1 Survey constructs: Interests and activities

	Alpha		
Construct	R1	R2	Examples of survey questions in each construct
Extroversion	0.86	NA	Talkative, spend a lot of time alone (reverse-coded)
Trust	0.75	0.69	Most people can be trusted, most people help others
Activism	0.89	0.89	Work to bring change in the community, involved
Affiliation	0.70	0.54	Join many organizations, joint many groups
Belonging	0.73	0.69	Spend time with friends, help friends and neighbors in need, feel part of local community
Collective efficacy	0.86	0.88	Belief that community can achieve goals despite obstacles
Political activity	0.75	0.59	Discuss politics, call officials, attend political meetings
Civic activity	0.71	0.71	Help others, volunteer, attend local public and group meetings

Table 11.2 Survey constructs: Online interests and activities

	Alpha		
Construct	R1	R2	Examples of survey questions in construct
Online political	0.70	0.74	E-mail officials, obtain political information
Online civic	0.83	0.86	Post info, express opinions, online with local groups
Online work or education	0.7	0.66	Communicate with teachers, do work for job or school
Online social	0.79	0.8	Communicate with friends and family, meet new people
Online commerce	0.73	0.69	Buy or sell product, bank online, travel reservation
Online leisure	0.72	0.66	Play games, download music, post photos and artwork

and subjected each of these constructs to reliability tests. The reliability of each construct is indicated by an individual Cronbach alpha score shown in Tables 11.1 and 11.2. An alpha score greater than 0.7 represents good reliability for a construct. All of the constructs we used in this paper had Cronbach alpha scores of 0.7 (when rounded) or higher, with the exception of the construct Political Activity, which had an alpha of 0.59 in Round 2, and Affiliation, which had an alpha of 0.54 in Round 2. (To economize on space, Round 2 is shown as R2 in the following tables; Round 1 is shown as R1.)

Our construct Extroversion, measured by respondents' agreement on Likert scales with the statements "I am talkative" and "I spend time alone" (reverse-coded), is a proxy for measures of gregariousness (a strong attribute of opinion leaders). We did not measure this construct in the second round since the respondents were almost all the same and we did not expect their level of extroversion to change during the course of 1 year. Therefore, the Cronbach alpha is available for Round 1 only. Affiliation is measured by respondents' agreement with the statements "I belong to many groups" and "I belong to many organizations." Belonging is measured by respondents' agreement with statements about community attachment such as "I feel part of the community," and social engagement such as "I spend a lot of time with my friends," and "I spend a lot of time helping friends or neighbors in need." Collective efficacy is the belief that the community can work together to solve problems and overcome difficulties (Bandura, 2000, 2001; Carroll & Reese, 2003). The constructs for Political Activity and Civic Activity (based on frequency scales ranging from "almost never" to "several times a day") included discussing politics, attending public meetings, helping others, volunteering, and attending local group meetings.

Online Interests and Activities (Table 11.2) are based on Internet use constructs and include multiple item measures; for example Online Political Activity and Online Civic Activity included e-mailing government officials, getting information online, and expressing opinions with others online. Other Internet use constructs included Online Work or Education (working online for one's job or school, communicating with teachers or co-workers), Online Social (communicating online with friends, family, and co-workers about nonwork issues), Online Commerce (searching product or services information or purchasing products and services online), and Online Leisure (downloading music and other software, playing games, and watching video clips). (For a full description of study constructs, see http://epic.cs.vt.edu.)

To determine respondents' affiliations with local groups, we asked them to name each and all of the *local* formal groups with which they were involved. We asked respondents to check all modes of communication that each group's members used with each other (e.g., face-to-face, e-mail) and the level (or type) of involvement the respondent had in each group, specifically: was a member, contributed money, attended meetings, and/or held a leadership position. We coded these four categories as level of involvement from low to high, such that the lowest score (1) was being a member and the highest score (4) was holding a leadership position. Accordingly, each respondent was scored on their level of involvement for each of their groups.

We also coded these same categories into type of involvement: active (held a leadership position and attended meetings) and passive involvement (was a member and contributed money). Using coding schemes suggested by the US Census and other researchers (Edwards & Booth, 1973; Karsarda & Janowitz, 1974; Putnam, 2000, among others), we recoded each of the groups named by respondents into four categories of groups: (1) civic and political; (2) religious, charitable, and support; (3) educational and professional; and (4) social and recreational.

We listed seven modes of communication in the questionnaire: (1) face-to-face, (2) telephone or postal mail, (3) person-to-person e-mail, (4) e-mail discussion or listserv, (5) newsgroup, (6) chat room, and (7) online bulletin board or discussion board. We asked respondents to check all modes of communication that they used for each group or organization they had listed. We later collapsed the modes of communications into two categories: traditional communication for face-to-face and telephone, and the other five modes as electronic communication. Respondents who reported that they were involved with the same *type* of group in both rounds were selected for further analyses (the focus of this paper). Respondents who joined in or dropped out of a type of group in either round were not included in our analyses since they do not permit a longitudinal analysis. This methodological strategy helped us to control for changes that might result from different types of people entering or leaving the same type of group.

Statistical Analyses

We conducted a series of statistical analyses on the survey data. In addition to simple descriptive statistics and the creation of internally reliable composite variables (i.e., survey constructs described above), we conducted a series of paired *t*-tests that compared EPIC Round 1 (Fall 2001) and Round 2 (Fall 2002) data on selected variables and reported means, valid number of cases, and *p* values (i.e., significant differences in means) of the *t*-tests. We also used Pearson correlation coefficients to describe relationships between two variables that had been measured by ordinal or interval scales. We interpreted directions and strengths of relationships in accord with the value and sign of correlation coefficients. When both variables were nominal (no hierarchy within compared variables, as in type of group), we used SPSS cross tabs to create two-way contingency table analyses that tested relationships between the variables.

Most contingency analyses included variables with more than two categories. Hence, we reported *Cramer's V* (values ranged from 0 to1) and interpreted the direction and strength of relationship according to the value and sign of *Cramer's V*. When the *Cramer's V* was significant (a significant relation between two variables), we further examined the observed frequencies and expected frequencies in each cell. Expected frequencies are the frequencies we would expect if two variables were *not* related (independent) or if the frequency occurred by chance. Thus, cells having improbably large differences between expected and observed frequencies were identified; these variables were presumed to be related.

Results

The results show significant differences over time in modes of communication, level of involvement, and Internet use for many purposes by group members. We find evidence that much of this change stems from different intra- and intergroup dynamics for the leader and member Bridges in the present study.

Demographics and Background

Demographics for both rounds were virtually identical because the same respondents participated in both rounds with few exceptions. Descriptive statistics show that our sample respondents' were generally representative of the population of Blacksburg and Montgomery County. Respondent's education and income were relatively high, as were Internet use and experience. The average education (based on the highest in a household) was college graduation; median household income was \$35 – \$50,000. The vast majority of respondents reported using the Internet

(83% in Round 1; 84% in Round 2). This level is higher than national levels during that time: 58% of US individuals in Spring 2002, according to Lenhart (2003).

The finding of higher levels of average household income and education as well as Internet penetration is not surprising given that Blacksburg is a university town, home of the BEV, and many university affiliates live outside of town in Montgomery County. While the stratification scheme selected half Blacksburg and half County *households*, just under half the *individual* respondents lived in Blacksburg. The overwhelming majority (over 90%) of respondents were Caucasian; slightly more than half were female. About two-thirds of respondents were married. The average length of residence in the community (an indicator of local attachment) was about 18 years.

Among Internet users, about 90% had Internet access at home and more than half the respondents reported using the Internet at work. In Round 1 this corresponded to 64 households (of the study's 100 stratified households). This percentage (64%) is much higher than national (28%) and statewide (32%) households for the same period (Lenhart, 2003). Internet users in our study were more affluent and educated than were Internet users nationwide (71% of those Internet users reported some college, a college degree or a graduate degree, compared to 88% of the Internet users in the present study).

Opinion Leaders: Bridges vs. Nonbridges

Most respondents reported that they were involved with two local formal groups in both rounds. In Round 1, about a fifth of respondents did not belong to any local organization or group, and about a third belonged to only one group (Table 11.3). In Round 1, less than half (47%, $N = 75$) were Bridges; i.e., they were a leader of two or more groups (14%, $N = 23$) or they were a member of two or more groups (33%, $N = 52$). Just over half of the respondents (53%, $N = 83$) were Nonbridges in Round 1; i.e., they were affiliated with only one group (25%, $N = 44$) or they were not affiliated with any group (28% $N = 39$).

In Round 2, slightly fewer respondents were Bridges (41%, $N = 59$); leader bridges numbered roughly the same (14%, $N = 20$) and member bridges dropped slightly (27%, $N = 39$). Slightly more respondents were Nonbridges (59%, $N = 84$)

Table 11.3 Sample percentages affiliated with groups

	Round 1	Round 2
Bridge	47	41
Leader Bridge	14	14
Member Bridge	33	27
Nonbridge	53	59
One Group	25	26
No Group	28	33

Table 11.4 Group affiliation by SES, residence, and gender

	Correlations	
Variable	Round 1	Round 2
Socioeconomic status	.325**(145)[a]	.213* (134)
Length of residence	NS	.188* (143)
Gender	NS	.184* (142)

NS not significant

*$p < .05$, **$p < .01$

[a]Values in parentheses are the number of formal organizations with which the respondent affiliated

in Round 2 than in Round 1. The percentage of respondents affiliated with only one group was almost the same (26%, $N = 37$) and the nonaffiliates rose slightly (33%, $N = 47$). If a respondent was a leader in one organization and a member in another, the person was classified as a Member Bridge.

We analyzed survey data to test expected relationships between group affiliation and socioeconomic status (SES, calculated as the sum of education and income), demographics, length of residence, and life cycle stage. Significant correlations between these variables and the number of formal organizations with which the respondent affiliated are shown in Table 11.4.

In both rounds there was a modest relationship between respondents' SES and the number of formal organizations with which they were affiliated. In Round 2 data, respondents who were affiliated with more groups tended to have resided longer in the community. Women belonged to more groups than did men, and females were more likely than males to affiliate with religious–charitable–support type groups. This gender difference probably reflects not only the higher proportion of women (58%) in the study, but also the predominance of affiliation with churches or other places of worship in this region coupled with a tendency for women to join religious, charitable, and support groups more than men.

In both rounds, the majority of group affiliates (almost two-thirds) were involved with the religious–charitable–support type groups. About a third participated in civic–political types of groups, and a quarter in the educational/professional type. Affiliations remained fairly even across both rounds, with the exception of social–recreational type groups, which dropped from 42 to 34% between rounds. Religious/charitable/support type of groups also dropped slightly between rounds: from 64 to 60%. That is, among people who belonged to the same types of groups percentages sum more than 100% because some people belonged to more than one type of group (Table 11.5).

When we examine the demographics of our affiliated respondents ($N = 137$) within different types of groups, we find some clear distinctions. We cannot test for significant differences between groups because some of the same people are in different groups. However, we can see from the simple frequencies and means that there are some demographic patterns (Table 11.6). Although the data are similar

Table 11.5 Affiliation in different types of groups

Group type	Round 1 ($N = 156$)	Round 2 ($N = 143$)
Religious/charitable/support	64	60
Social/recreational	42	34
Civic/political	33	35
Educational/professional	25	25

Values are sample percentages

Table 11.6 Demographics of different groups

	Relig (79)	Social (40)	Educational (17)	Civic (26)
Age (mean years)	48	50	52	51
Gender (% female)	63	65	59	73
Education (mean)	5.0	5.4	5.7	5.8
Married (%)	59	75	77	77
Children at home (%)	43	50	29	39
Net use (mean years)	5.9	5.9	6.4	6.9
Net use (h per day)	1.6	1.7	2.0	2.2

Education ranged from 1 (*less than high school degree*) to 7 (*completed graduate degree*)

between rounds, we show here the demographics from Round 2 (the number of respondents or N is shown in parentheses under each type of group).

Average age was fairly close (ranging from 48 to 52 years) in all group types. Female affiliates were a majority in each type (even higher than the 58% of women in the total sample of respondents for Round 2.) Members of instrumental groups (civic–political and educational–professional types) had the highest mean level of education (i.e., a score of 5 means respondent completed college; 6 means respondent did some graduate degree work) and the highest measures of Internet use in years and typical hours per day. This is consistent with studies that find education to be positively correlated with civic engagement and Internet use. The religious–charitable (abbreviated *Relig*) and social–recreational type groups showed the highest percentages of respondents with children under the age of 18 at home. This finding is consistent with those of other studies that show households with children are active in social, recreational, and family- or youth-oriented activities in their communities.

Communication in Different Types of Groups

There were 137 respondents with measures for group affiliation in the same *type* of group in both Rounds 1 and 2. Over time (between Rounds 1 and 2) the use of electronic modes of communication increased significantly as did the level of group involvement (from passive to active). See Table 11.7 (t statistics are given in parentheses under the p values).

Table 11.7 Group changes: Communication and involvement (all groups)

Variable used in paired *t*-tests	Mean R1	Mean R2	*p* value	*N*
Electronic communication	0.7281	1.0304	.002[**] (−3.145)[a]	115
Level of involvement	2.3883	2.6313	.044[*] (−2.038)	115
Active involvement	1.0002	1.3705	.000[**] (−5.193)	115

[*]$p < .05$, [**]$p < .01$

[a]Values in parentheses are *t* values

When we control for Bridges vs. Nonbridges for the significant changes, we can see that in most cases, the behavior of Bridges accounts for changes over time in communication modes and levels of involvement. Bridges use more electronic communication modes (Table 11.8), and progress from relatively passive to more active levels of involvement (Table 11.9).

When we control for Bridges, we see that Bridges (and not Nonbridges) significantly increased electronic communication with other members across all types of groups. Nonbridges show nonsignificant increases. By controlling for the *type* of groups where significant changes occurred, we identified through additional paired *t*-tests that electronic modes of communication increased significantly over time for all types of groups, but that these increases still predominantly resulted from communication by Bridges. The exception is for civic–political type groups, where both Bridges (mean R1 0.8, R2 1.4; $p < .05$) and Nonbridges (R1 0.4, R2 1.4; $p < .05$) reported significant increases in electronic modes of communication.

Analysis of change in the level of group involvement over time indicates that when controlled for Bridges, again the behavior of Bridges explains increases in involvement for all group types combined (Table 11.9). By further controlling for the *type* of groups where the significant changes were observed, we identified through additional paired *t*-tests that the social–recreational type groups (R1 2.4, R2 2.9; $p < .01$) and the religious–charitable type groups (R1 2.7, R2 3.3; $p < .001$) account for these increases. In the case of social type groups, only Bridges reported significant increases (R1 2.5, R2 3.0; $p < .05$). For religious type groups, both Bridges (R1 2.7, R2 3.3; $p < .001$) and Nonbridges (R1 2.6 R2 3.3; $p < .05$) reported significant increases in their level of involvement with their group(s).

It can be argued that increases in electronic modes of communication might be expected over time in any event, as the Internet has become more pervasive and routine in our daily lives. Yet, we found significant increases to predominate only for Bridges. As for the reported changes in respondents' level and type of *involvement* in groups, these changes are not explicitly linked to the use of information technology. We can, however, investigate changes in other study variables (e.g., community participation, interests and activities, and Internet use) that might help to clarify

Table 11.8 Electronic communication modes (all groups)

	Mean			
	R1	R2	*p* value	Valid *N*
All affiliates	0.73	1.03	.002** (−3.15)[a]	115
Bridges	0.79	1.09	.006** (−2.84)	68
Nonbridges	0.63	0.94	.097 (−1.70)	47

*$p < .05$, **$p < .01$

[a]Values in parentheses are *t* values

Table 11.9 Level of involvement (all groups)

	Mean			
	R1	R2	*p* value	Valid *N*
All affiliates	2.39	2.63	.044* (−2.04)[a]	115
Bridges	2.37	2.69	.040* (−2.09)	68
Nonbridges	2.41	2.55	.481 (−0.71)	47

*$p < .05$, **$p < .01$

[a]Values in parentheses are *t* values

some of the group communication and involvement changes. These results are summarized in the next section.

Changes in Local Participation and Internet Use

To examine changes in affiliates' community participation, interests and activities, and Internet use over time, we conducted paired *t*-tests on the primary survey variables and constructs by Bridge and Nonbridge affiliates for each type of group. Although we tested all the important study variables (discussed above, as shown in Table 11.1), we report only the significant mean differences. The changes that follow show that affiliates of specific types of groups experienced some increases in various interests and activities – and/or in using the Internet for purposes that are largely political. Again, these increases in political activity are mostly attributable to opinion leaders (i.e., Bridges, meaning leaders and members of two or more groups) except in the case of civic–political type groups, where Nonbridges also reported significant increases in political activity.

Expressive Groups

Affiliates of *religious–charitable–support* type groups showed increased offline political activity for Bridges (mean R1 1.2, R2 1.3; $p < .05$). Affiliates of *social-recreational* type groups showed no significant changes in other survey variables for either Bridges or Nonbridges.

Instrumental Groups

Affiliates of *educational–professional type* groups showed increased use of the Internet for political activities by Bridges that approached significance (R1 1.3, R2 1.5; $p = .076$). Nonbridges showed increased Internet use for social purposes (R1 3.1, R2 3.7; $p < .05$) and decreased Internet use for leisure and entertainment purposes (R1 2.9, R2 2.4; $p < .01$).

Affiliates of *civic–political* type of groups showed increases among Bridges in two relevant areas: (1) online civic activities (such as using the Internet to express opinions; post factual information and answer questions; get news and information for local, national, and global events; access a community Web site; and participate in a local interest group online), and (2) community participation, a construct that comprises three subconstructs shown in Table 11.1: Activism, Belonging, and Affiliation (such as working to bring change in the local community, spending time with a group of friends, participating in community activities, and helping friends or neighbors in need). Bridges also showed increases in online leisure activities (e.g., playing games and downloading software).

Nonbridges affiliated with civic–political type groups showed significant increases in online civic activities, as well as in online leisure and commerce activities. The civic–political type of groups was the only type in which Nonbridges showed significant increases in the type of activities over time that correspond directly with the instrumental objectives of the group. Even within expressive types of groups (religious and social), Bridges showed significant increases in instrumental (political) activity.

Discussion

Voluntary associations play important roles in aggregating individual interests, shaping collective will, and cultivating civic competence. These formal and informal citizen activities remain essential to democratic participation in civil society. Voluntary associations that focus upon such activities become ever more crucial with the increasing dominance of contemporary segmented and personalized media. We have presented findings that demonstrate the interaction of information and communication technology with the roles of local voluntary associations using longitudinal survey data from two waves of a stratified random household sample in the networked community of Blacksburg and Montgomery County, Virginia. Although the sample is representative of a population in Blacksburg and Montgomery County, these findings help us to consider how information technology is presently used and how it differentially enables members in different types of local groups to participate in pluralistic community life.

Our findings show that electronic modes of communication were predominantly utilized by instrumental groups, notably, civic–political and educational–professional type groups. Religious groups were the least likely to use information technology, although this may also reflect a digital divide because church members and religious groups represent persons in all socioeconomics strata. Those with lower levels of income and education are less likely to use information technology. Therefore, such groups (as a whole) may be less likely to use electronic modes, such as e-mail, listserv, and the Internet, thinking that many of their members would not routinely access information or communication in these modes. In general, however, our thinking is that this finding does not indicate so much a digital divide, as the greater predominance of face-to-face activities among expressive groups (such as religious services, volunteer and charity work, social get-togethers, sporting events, and other similar recreational or social occasions).

For nonreligious types of groups, the results suggest that people who affiliate with multiple groups (i.e., Bridges) play an increasingly active role in communicating and disseminating information to other participants, in leading group activities and participating in face-to-face meetings within their groups. The social and political activism of people who act as Bridges indicates that they were likely to be influentials in their social circles and groups. Participation in formal local groups offers an important arena for opinion leaders to influence others apart from ad hoc interactions with friends and family. Bridges' higher levels of Internet use for both social (expressive) and political (instrumental) group purposes may help to widen their spirals of influence over time.

The increasing willingness to shoulder leadership roles in local groups is very important. The survival and strength of local groups depends on the willingness of citizens to volunteer their time and energy to support a group's activities and needs. That leaders can use information technology to communicate with fellow officers and members makes the work involved easier and less time-consuming (Kavanaugh & Schmitz, 2004). Thus, group leaders can engage in simple collaborative activities online – and even cull opinions, and obtain immediate feedback from committee members without face-to-face meetings. The distribution of information online (e.g., background documents, newsletters, and searchable archives) to a group's membership permits simpler procedures and offers cost savings for an organization or group. The vitality of a group is less likely to be sapped by mundane and routine tasks that can often lead to burn out among "all the usual" volunteers.

Our findings demonstrate increases in face-to-face interactions, including attending meetings, participating in community activities, getting together with friends, and doing volunteer work. These increases were predominant among opinion leaders.

In democratic life, voluntary associations are essential to create awareness and draw average citizens into discussions about local issues and concerns. The health of these groups and organizations directly shapes the health of democracy in the United States and in other democratic societies. Our study contributes to growing evidence that information and communication technology increases communication, interaction, and participation among members of voluntary associations, and thereby contributes to the evidence that ICT lightens the burdens of leadership, communication, and information exchange within these crucial voluntary associations.

Acknowledgments We are grateful for the support for this research from the National Science Foundation (IIS-0080864). We thank our project collaborators Albert Bandura, Robert Kraut, Philip Isenhour, Dan Dunlap, and Wendy Schafer. We greatly appreciate research assistance from Debbie Denise Reese and Steven Winters.

References

Almond, G., and Verba, S. *The Civic Culture: Political Attitudes and Democracy in Five Nations*. Princeton University Press, Princeton, NJ, 1963.

Babchuk, N., and Booth, A. Voluntary association membership: A longitudinal analysis, pp. 23–37. In J. Edwards, J. and A. Booth (Eds.), *Social Participation in Urban Society*. Schenkman, Cambridge, MA, 1973.

Bandura, A. Exercise of human agency through collective agency. *Current Directions in Psychological Science*, *9*, 3 (2000), 75–78.

Bandura, A. Social cognitive theory: An agentic perspective. *Annual Review of Psychology*, *53* (2001), 1-26.

Bimber, B. Information and political engagement in America: The search for effects of information technology at the individual level. *Political Science Quarterly*, *54*, 1 (2001), 53–67.

Blau, P. A macro theory of social structure. *American Journal of Sociology*, *83* (2001), 26–54.

Brady, H. Political participation, pp. 737–801. In J. Robinson, P. Shaver, and L. Wrightsman (Eds.), *Measures of Political Attitudes*. Academic, San Diego, 1999.

Carroll, J., and Reese, D. Community collective efficacy: Structure and consequences of perceived capacities in the Blacksburg Electronic Village. *Hawaii International Conference on System Sciences, HICSS-36*, Kona, January 6–9, 2003.

Dahl, R. *Who Governs?* Yale University Press, New Haven, CT, 1961.

Dillman, D. *Mail and Internet Surveys: The Tailored Design Method*. Wiley, New York, NY, 2000.

Edwards, J., and Booth, A. *Social Participation in Urban Society*. Schenkman, Cambridge, MA, 1973.

Granovetter, M. The strength of weak ties. *American Journal of Sociology*, *7*, 6 (1973), 1360–1380.

Hague, B., and Loader, B. *Digital Democracy: Discourse and Decision Making in the Information Age*. Routledge, London, UK, 1999.

Homans, G. *The Human Group*. Harcourt Brace, New York, NY, 1950.

Horrigan, J. *Online Communities: Networks That Nurture Long-Distance Relationships and Local Ties*. Pew Internet and American Life Project, 2001. http://www.pewinternet.org

Horrigan, J., Garrett, K., and Resnick, P. *The Internet and Democratic Debate*. Pew Internet and American Life Project, 2004. http://www.pewinternet.org

Hyman, H., and Wright, C. Trends in voluntary association memberships in American adults: Replication based on secondary analysis of national sample surveys. *American Sociological Reviews*, *36* (1971), 191–206.

Karsarda, J., and Janowitz, M. Community attachment in mass society. *American Sociological Review*, *39* (1974), 328–339.

Katz, E., and Lazarsfeld, P. *Personal Influence: The Part Played by People in the Flow of Mass Communications*. The Free Press, New York, 1955.

Katz, J., and Aspden, P. A nation of strangers? *Communications of the ACM*, *40*, 12 (1997), 81–86.

Kavanaugh, A., and Patterson, S. The impact of community computer networks on social capital and community involvement. *American Behavioral Scientist*, *45*, 3 (2001), 496–509.

Kavanaugh, A., and Schmitz, J. Talking in lists: The consequences of computer mediated communication on communities. *Internet Research Annual, 1* (2004), 250–259.

Kavanaugh, A., Kirn, K., and Willis, L. Demographic profile: Blacksburg community trends. 2000. http://www.bev.net/project/research/BEV.Demographics.00.pdf

Kavanaugh, A., Reese, D.D., Carroll, J.M., and Rosson, M.B. Weak ties in networked communities, pp. 265–286. In M. Huysman, E. Wenger, and V. Wulf (Eds.), *Communities and Technologies*. Kluwer, The Netherlands, 2003. (Reprinted in *The Information Society, 21*, 2 (2005), 119–131).

Kavanaugh, A., Carroll, J.M., Rosson, M.B., and Zin, T.T. Participating in civil society: The case of networked communities. *Interacting with Computers, 17* (2005a), 9–33.

Keller, E., and Berry, J. *The Influentials*. The Free Press, New York, NY, 2003.

Kim, J., Wyatt, R., and Katz, E. News, talk, opinion, participation: The part played by conversation in deliberative democracy. *Political Communication, 16*, 4 (1999), 361–385.

Kraut, R., Kiesler, S., Bonka, B., Cummings, J., Helgeson, V., and Crawford, A. Internet paradox revisited. *Journal of Social Issues, 58*, 1 (2002), 49–74.

Lenhart, A. *The Ever-Shifting Internet Population: A New Look at Internet Access and the Digital Divide*. Pew Internet and American Life Project, 2003. http://www.pewinternet.org

Madden, M. *Internet Penetration and Impact*. Pew Internet and American Life Project, 2006. http://www.pewinternet.org

Milbrath, L., and Goel, M. *Political Participation: How and Why Do People Get Involved in Politics* (2nd ed.). University Press of America, New York, NY, 1982.

Parsons, T. *Essays in Sociological Theory*. Free Press, Glencoe, IL, 1954.

Poole, M., and Roth, J. Decision development in small groups. IV: A typology group decision paths. *Human Communication Research, 15* (1989), 323–256.

Putnam, R. *Bowling Alone: The Collapse and Revival of American Community*. Simon and Schuster, New York, NY, 2000.

Robinson, J., Shaver, P., and Wrightsman, L. (Eds.), *Measures of Political Attitudes*. Academic Press, San Diego, CA, 1999.

Rogers, E. *Diffusion of Innovations* (5th ed.). Simon and Schuster, New York, NY, 1995.

Scheufele, D., and Nisbet, M. Being a citizen online: New opportunities and dead ends. *Press/Politics, 7*, 3 (2002), 55–75.

Simmel, G. Group expansion and the development of individuality. In D. Levine (Ed.), *Georg Simmel on Individuality and Social Forms*. University of Chicago Press, Chicago, IL, [1908] 1971.

Stueve, C., and Gerson, K. Personal relations across the life cycle. In C. Fischer (Ed.), *Networks and Places: Social Relations in the Urban Setting*. Macmillan, New York, NY, 1977.

Tsagarousianou, R., Tambini, D., and Bryan, C. (Eds.), *Cyberdemocracy, Technology, Cities and Civic Networks*. Routledge, London, 1998.

Verba, S., and Nie, N. *Participation in America: Political Democracy and Social Equality*. Harper and Row, New York, 1972.

Verba, S., Schlozman, K., and Brady, H. *Voice and Equality: Civic Voluntarism in American Politics*. Harvard University Press, Cambridge, MA, 1995.

Wolff, K. *The Sociology of Georg Simmel*. The Free Press, New York, NY, 1950.

Chapter 12
Community-Based Learning: The Core Competency of Residential, Research-Based Universities

Gerhard Fischer, Markus Rohde, and Volker Wulf

Abstract Traditionally, universities focus primarily on instructionist teaching. Such an understanding has been criticized from theoretical and practical points of view. We believe that *sociocultural theories of learning* and the concepts of *social capital* and *social creativity* hold considerable promise as a theoretical base for the repositioning of universities in the knowledge society. To illustrate our assumption, we provide case studies from the University of Colorado and the University of Siegen. These cases indicate how approaches to community-based learning can be integrated into a curriculum of applied computer science. We also discuss the role these didactical concepts can play within a practice-oriented strategy of regional innovation.

Keywords: Social capital; Social creativity; Community-based learning; Symmetry of ignorance; Distributed intelligence; Courses-as-seeds; Courses in practice; Undergraduate research apprenticeship program; Transdisciplinary education; Communities of practice; Networks of practice; Communities of interest; Regional industrial clusters

Introduction

One of the most impoverished paradigms of education is a setting in which "a single, presumably omniscient teacher tells or shows presumably unknowing learners something they presumably know nothing about" (Bruner, 1996, p. 20). Significant efforts are under way to change the nature of school discourse to make it more of a collective inquiry (Scardamalia & Bereiter, 1994) and to introduce project-based approaches to learning at university education (Cannon & Leifer, 1999; Kolmos et al., 2004). However, the traditional model of education is still widely practiced in our educational institutions, leading critics such as Illich (1971) to claim that our schools and universities are "the reproductive organ of a consumer society" (p. 107) and that people who are hooked on teaching are conditioned to be customers for everything else.

The premise of this paper is that the traditional paradigm of education is not appropriate for understanding and learning to resolve the types of open-ended and multidisciplinary problems that are most pressing to our society. These problems, which typically involve a combination of social and technological issues, require a different paradigm of education and learning skills, including self-directed learning, active collaboration, and consideration of multiple perspectives. Problems of this nature do not have "right" answers, and the knowledge to understand and resolve them is changing rapidly, thus requiring an ongoing and evolutionary approach to learning.

As an alternative to the traditional educational paradigm, we envision courses as communities of learning in which participants shift among the roles of learner, designer, and active contributor (Rogoff et al., 1998). The predominant mode of learning in this environment is peer-to-peer, with the teacher acting as a "guide on the side" rather than as a "sage on the stage." Courses are reconceptualized as seeds that are jointly evolved by all participants rather than as finished products delivered by teachers (dePaula et al., 2001). Furthermore, with close cooperation between universities and regional industries, networks of practice (NoPs) are established to enable mutual learning. University students can join companies' practices to gain industrial apprenticeship (Rohde et al., 2005, 2007).

Universities play an important role in the knowledge society (Brown & Duguid, 2000). Beyond their traditional role in research and education, they have the potential exploit local knowledge in (regional) innovations and to provide opportunities for students to become lifelong learners. To realize these potentials, universities – specifically in the fields of applied sciences and engineering – will have to reinvent their conception of education by taking the importance of industrial practice and social networks into account.

In this paper, we first describe a conceptual framework for community-based learning. We illustrate the framework by presenting our approaches to community-based learning in two settings: (1) a computer science program at the University of Colorado, Boulder, and (2) an information systems program at the University of Siegen. Empirical data evaluating the different courses indicate potentials and problem areas. Finally, we discuss lessons learned from our efforts to transform learning and to create new educational opportunities and experiences at our residential, research-based universities.

Conceptual Frameworks

We believe that *sociocultural theories of learning* (Bruner, 1996; Lave & Wenger, 1991; Vygotsky, 1986; Wenger, 1998) hold considerable promise as a theoretical base for the repositioning of universities in the knowledge society. Learning is understood as a collective process (Rogoff et al., 1998) that is linked to a specific context of action. In sociocultural theories of learning, learning and innovation take place within social aggregates that share a common practice. Knowledge emerges by discursive assignment of meaning and social identification. Therefore, *community-based learning* is used here as a concept to describe processes of collective and collaborative learning, which are based on sociocultural learning concepts and focus on the role of group membership or community participation for (collective and individual) learning.

Communities: Transcending the Individual Human Mind

The power of the unaided individual mind is highly overrated. In most traditional approaches, *human cognition* has been seen as existing solely "inside" a person's head, and studies on cognition have often disregarded the physical and social surroundings in which cognition takes place. *Distributed intelligence* (or *distributed cognition*) (Fischer, 2006; Hollan et al., 2001; Pea, 2004; Salomon, 1993) provides an effective theoretical framework for understanding what humans can achieve and how artifacts, tools, and *sociotechnical environments* (Mumford, 2000) can be designed and evaluated to empower human beings and to change tasks.

Knowledge is often portrayed as an individual possession that people carry around in their heads and transfer to each other despite the fact that work is unlikely to be carried out in isolation, let alone without the aid of external artifacts. We see *knowing* as always mediated by artifacts, situated, and often distributed in the social environment. Knowledge becomes, then, people's ability to act, *participate*, and make appropriate and informed decisions.

Owing to the complex nature of social settings in which knowledge is enacted, it is critical to understand the various aspects that contribute to the formation of the *sociotechnical conditions* for stakeholders to accomplish their work, instead of focusing solely on the knowledge-transferring problem. Our framework is based on the concepts of distributed cognition, social networks, and information ecologies, and more importantly, focuses on the role of *human agency* in enabling the work to get accomplished in the context of a *cultural practice*.

Traditionally, universities have focused on "instructionist" teaching. An instructionist understanding of teaching assumes that the instructor possesses *all* relevant knowledge and passes it to the learners (Noam, 1995). The learner is seen as a receptive system that stores, recalls, and transfers knowledge. Regional context does not play a role in these university activities. Such an understanding has been criticized from theoretical and practical points of view (Collins et al., 1989; Jonassen & Mandl, 1990). In a highly differentiated world full of open-ended and ill-defined problems, it is rather unlikely that an individual (professor) or an academic organization (faculty) will possess sufficient knowledge to foster learning among students and practitioners by itself (Arias et al., 2000).

Sociocultural theories of learning (Bruner, 1996) hold considerable promise as a theoretical base for the repositioning of universities in the knowledge society. Scholars convening at a recent National Science Foundation workshop on the future of graduate education concluded that *community* is of overarching importance for the future of graduate education (Lorden & Slimowitz, 2003). We ask, however: (a) Which categories of community provide good models for educational design and in which contexts? (b) What essential features of these categories promote desired transdisciplinary outcomes?

The following three models for knowledge creation communities can be differentiated: (1) the Knowledge-Creating Company (Nonaka & Takeuchi, 1995), (2) the Model of Expansive Learning (Engeström, 2001), and (3) Bereiter's (2002) Model of Knowledge-Building.

Even though these models are derived from different theoretical histories (activity vs. participation metaphors), are implemented in different educational contexts (work environments vs. schools), and conceptualize the outcomes of learning in different terms (tacit and explicit knowledge, new activity structures, or conceptual artifacts), they all have in common a commitment to *collective knowledge creation while developing shared objects of activity*. This common essence helps to define an important core model for transdisciplinary scholarship, although we have found it useful to further differentiate this concept into *communities of practice* (CoPs), which are homogeneous, and *communities of interest* (CoIs), which are heterogeneous (Brown & Duguid, 1991; Fischer, 2001; Wenger, 1998). Such evolving research-based concepts of community provide key discussion points for a discourse on a rethinking of education, and should become key elements of discourse within a transdisciplinary curriculum.

Communities of Practice and Communities of Interest

Communities are social structures that enable groups of people to share knowledge and resources in support of collaborative action. Different communities grow around different types of practice. Each community is unique, and in our research efforts we have identified two kinds of communities (Fischer, 2001): *communities of practice* and *communities of interest*.

Communities and Networks of Practice

CoPs (Wenger, 1998) consist of practitioners who work as a community in a certain domain, undertaking similar or at least interrelated work. Learning within a CoP takes the form of legitimate peripheral participation (Lave & Wenger, 1991), which is a type of apprenticeship model in which newcomers enter the community from the periphery and move toward the center as they become more and more knowledgeable. A CoP has many possible paths and many roles (identities) within it (e.g., leader, scribe, power-user, visionary, and so forth).

Brown and Duguid (2000) and Duguid (2003, 2005) distinguish networks of practice (NoPs) from CoPs. Within CoPs, members not only share a common practice, but work together and therefore need to coordinate their work with each other. For instance, a tailor shop in which different tailors work together and apprentices get enculturated by playing a more and more important role in the shop's practice make up a CoP. The members of a CoP have responsibility, at least implicitly, for the reproduction of their community and their practice. Within NoPs, members share a common practice but do not work together in an interdependent way by which they need to coordinate their work. For example, software engineers from different companies who do not work on the same project but who are occupied with similar problem sets, such as building e-commerce applications, form a network of practice.

Within NoPs, common practice offers a reference to members for their interaction. Common practice allows them to share information in a relatively effective and coherent way (Duguid, 2003, 2005). CoPs are typically found inside organizations, whereas NoPs often span organizational boundaries.

Sustained engagement and collaboration lead to boundaries based on shared histories of learning that create discontinuities between participants and nonparticipants. Highly developed knowledge systems (including conceptual frameworks, technical systems, and human organizations) are biased toward efficient communication within the CoP and NoP at the expense of acting as barriers to communication with outsiders. Thus, boundaries that are empowering to the insider are often barriers to outsiders and newcomers to the group.

Communities of Interest

CoIs bring together stakeholders from different CoPs or NoPs and are defined by their collective concern with the resolution of a particular problem. CoIs can be thought of as "communities of communities" (Brown & Duguid, 1991) or a community of representatives of communities. Examples of CoIs include (1) a team interested in software development comprising software designers, users, marketing specialists, psychologists, and programmers; or (2) a group of citizens and experts interested in urban planning.

Stakeholders within CoIs are considered *informed participants* (Brown et al., 1994), who are neither experts nor novices, but rather both: they are experts when they communicate their knowledge to others, and they are novices when they learn from others who are experts in areas outside their own knowledge.

As a model for working and learning in CoIs, *informed participation* (Arias et al., 1999; Brown et al., 1994) is based on the claim that for many (design) problems, the knowledge to understand, frame, and solve these problems does not already exist, but must be collaboratively constructed and evolved during the problem-solving process. Informed participation requires information, but mere access to information is not enough. The participants must go beyond the information that exists to solve their problems. For informed participation, the primary role of media is not to deliver predigested information to individuals, but to provide the opportunity and resources for social debate and discussion. In this sense, improving access to existing information (often seen as the major advance of new media) is a limiting aspiration. A more profound challenge is to allow stakeholders to incrementally acquire ownership in problems and contribute actively to their solutions (Florida, 2002).

Communication in CoIs is difficult because the stakeholders come from different CoPs and, therefore, use different languages, different conceptual knowledge systems, and perhaps even different notational systems. In his book, *The Two Cultures*, Snow (1993) describes these difficulties through an analysis of the interaction between literary intellectuals and natural scientists, who (as he observed) had almost ceased to communicate at all:

> between the two a gulf of mutual incomprehension – sometimes (particularly among the young) hostility and dislike, but most of all lack of understanding (p. 4)

and

> there seems to be no place where the cultures meet (p. 16).

The fundamental barrier facing CoIs is that knowledge distribution is based on a *symmetry of ignorance* (Rittel, 1984), in which each stakeholder possesses some, but not all, relevant knowledge, and the knowledge of one participant complements the ignorance of another. This barrier must be overcome by building a shared understanding of the task at hand, which often does not exist at the beginning, but is evolved incrementally and collaboratively and emerges in people's minds and in external artifacts. Members of CoIs must learn to communicate with and learn from others (Engeström, 2001) who have different perspectives and perhaps different vocabularies for describing their ideas. In other words, this symmetry of ignorance must be exploited.

Comparing CoPs, NoPs, and CoIs

Learning through informed participation within CoIs is more complex and multifaceted than *legitimate peripheral participation* (Lave & Wenger, 1991) in CoPs. Learning in CoPs or NoPs can be characterized as "learning within a single knowledge system," whereas learning in CoIs is often a consequence of the fact that there are multiple knowledge systems. CoIs have multiple centers of knowledge, with each member considered to be knowledgeable in a particular aspect of the problem and perhaps not so knowledgeable in others. In informed participation, the roles of "expert" or "novice" shift from person to person, depending on the current focus of attention.

Table 12.1 characterizes and differentiates CoPs, NoPs, and CoIs along a number of dimensions. The point of comparing and contrasting CoPs, NoPs, and CoIs is not to pigeonhole groups into any one category, but rather to identify patterns of practice and helpful technologies. People can participate in more than one community or network, or one community can exhibit attributes of both a CoI and a CoP. Communities do not have to be strictly either CoPs or CoIs, but they can integrate aspects of both forms of communities. The community type may shift over time, according to events outside the community, the objectives of its members, and the structure of the membership.

The different forms of social aggregates exhibit barriers and biases. CoPs and NoPs are biased toward communicating with the same people and taking advantage of a shared background. The existence of an accepted, well-established center (of expertise) and a clear path of learning toward this center allow the differentiation of a CoP's

Table 12.1 Differentiating CoPs, NoPs, and CoIs

Dimension	CoPs	NoPs	CoIs
Nature of problems	Same task in the same domain	Different tasks in the same domain	Common task across multiple domains
Knowledge development	Refinement of one knowledge system; new ideas coming from within the practice	Refinement of one knowledge system; new ideas coming from within the practice	Synthesis and mutual learning through the integration of multiple knowledge systems
Major objectives	Codified knowledge, domain coverage	Codified knowledge, domain coverage	Shared understanding, making all voices heard
Weaknesses	Group-think	Group-think	Lack of a shared understanding
Strengths	Shared ontologies	Shared ontologies	Social creativity, diversity, making all voices heard
People	Beginners and experts, apprentices and masters	Members of the network who share a common practice	Stakeholders (owners of problems) from different domains
Learning	Sustained engagement and legitimate peripheral participation	Sustained engagement	Informed participation

CoPs communities of practice, *NoPs* networks of practice, *CoIs* communities of interest

members into novices, intermediates, and experts. It makes these attributes viable concepts associated with people and provides the foundation for legitimate peripheral participation as a workable learning strategy. The barriers imposed by CoPs (and, to a lesser degree, by NoPs) are that *group-think* (Janis, 1972) can suppress exposure to, and acceptance of, outside ideas; the more someone is at home in a CoP, the more that person forgets the strange and contingent nature of its categories from the outside.

A strength of CoIs is their potential for *creativity* because different backgrounds and different perspectives can lead to new insights. CoIs have great potential to be more innovative and more transforming than a single CoP if they can exploit the *symmetry of ignorance* (Rittel, 1984) as a source of collective creativity. A fundamental barrier for CoIs might be that the participants failed to create *common ground and shared understanding* (Clark & Brennan, 1991). This barrier is particularly challenging because CoIs often are more temporary than CoPs; they come together in the context of a specific project and dissolve after the project has ended.

CoPs are the focus of approaches such as computer-supported cooperative work. They provide support for work cultures with a shared practice (Wenger, 1998). The lack of a shared practice in CoIs requires them to draw together diverse cultural perspectives. Computer-mediated knowledge communication in CoPs is different from that in CoIs. CoIs pose a number of new challenges, but the payoff is promising because they can support pluralistic societies that can cope with complexity, contradictions, epistemological pluralism, and a willingness to allow for differences in opinions.

Social Capital

Social capital (SC) is about value derived from being a member of a social aggregate. By being a member, people have access to resources that nonmembers do not have (Bourdieu, 1985; Putnam, 1993; Huysman & Wulf, 2004b; Fischer et al., 2004). SC theories provide a conceptual base to understand networks of individuals whose (economic) interactions are embedded in social relations. Through social exchanges, people build webs of trust, obligation, reputation, expectations, and norms (Coleman, 1988; Granovetter, 1973). By explaining (economic) interactions by their embeddedness in social relations, SC is a concept that can explain access to resources far beyond the domains of knowledge sharing and social creativity (Huysman & Wulf, 2004b). For this reason, SC theories can provide meaningful concepts for the strategic positioning of research universities in many different areas.

SC theories have been applied as a conceptual base to knowledge-sharing strategies (Cohen & Prusak, 2001; Huysman & Wulf, 2004b; Nahapiet & Ghoshal, 1998). Cohen and Prusak (2001) state the following, in this respect:

> Social capital consists of the stock of active connections among people: the trust, mutual understanding, and shared values and behavior that bind the members of human networks and communities and make cooperative action possible.… Its characteristic elements and indicators include high levels of trust, robust personal networks and vibrant communities, shared understandings, and a sense of equitable participation in a joint enterprise – all things that draw individuals together into a group (p. 4).

Concerning processes of gaining and fostering social capital, the approach assumes that it is accumulating SC when it is used (productively); otherwise, it is decreasing. In this sense, SC tends to be self-reinforcing and cumulative. People gain connections and trust by successful cooperation, and these achievements of networks and trust support cooperation in the future. To gain and foster SC, Cohen and Prusak (2001, p. 45 f) suggest the following (organizational) investments in trust-building processes: Social capital can be gained (1) by being trustworthy, (2) by being open and encouraging openness, and (3) by trusting others.

Duguid (2003) has pointed to some distinctions between the concepts of SC, NoPs, and CoPs. SC and practice theories all focus on the importance of social networks for the exchange of knowledge. However, practice theories focus more on the human actors' capability to share knowledge. Only those actors who engage in similar or shared practices are able to share knowledge about those practices. Thus, where SC theory points to links imposed by social networks, practice theories point to potential boundaries – boundaries shaped by practice – that divide knowledge networks from one another. These boundaries may prevent knowledge-sharing despite all the obligations of good will and SC that connect them or, indeed, all the incentives that may entice them (Duguid, 2003).

Despite the criticisms of the SC approach and the limitations of Putnam's understanding (e.g., Florida, 2002), SC seems to be useful for a pragmatic analysis of processes of community building and social networking. Since the discussion on SC focuses on the establishment of relationships of trust, we assume that SC represents a precondition for the emergence of CoPs and NoPs. Because CoIs suffer from a lack of shared practice, SC seems to be of special importance for their (well) functioning.

Social Creativity

Social creativity explores computer media and technologies to help people work together. It is relevant to community-based learning because collaboration plays an increasingly significant role in projects that require expertise in a wide range of domains. Software design projects, for example, typically involve designers, programmers, human–computer interaction specialists, marketing experts, and end-user participants (Greenbaum & Kyng, 1991). Information technologies have reached a level of sophistication, maturity, cost-effectiveness, and distribution such that they are not restricted only to enhancing productivity; they also open up new creative possibilities (National-Research-Council, 2003).

Our work is grounded in the basic belief that there is an "and," and not a "vs.," relationship between individual and social creativity (Fischer et al., 2005). Creativity occurs in the relationship between an individual and society, and between an individual and his or her technical environment. The mind, rather than driving in solitude, is clearly dependent upon the reflection, renewal, and trust inherent in sustained human relationships (John-Steiner, 2000). We need to support this distributed fabric of interactions by integrating diversity, making all voices heard, increasing the back-talk of the situation, and providing systems that are open and transparent so that learners can be aware of and access each other's work, relate it to their own work, transcend the information given, and contribute the results back to the community.

In complex projects, collaboration is crucial for success, yet it is difficult to achieve. Complexity arises from the need to synthesize different perspectives, exploit conceptual collisions between concepts and ideas coming from different disciplines, manage large amounts of information potentially relevant to a design task, and understand the design decisions that have determined the long-term evolution of a designed artifact.

Metadesign

Metadesign (Fischer & Giaccardi, 2006) is "design for designers." It extends the traditional notion of system design (including curricula, courses, learning environments, and software systems) beyond the original development of a system to include co-adaptive processes in which the learners become *co-developers*. It defines and creates social and technical infrastructures in which new forms of community-based learning can take place. Metadesign perspectives focus on the following requirements for sociotechnical environments: they must (1) be flexible and evolvable because they cannot be completely designed prior to use; (2) evolve to some extent at the hands of their users; and (3) be designed for evolution.

The goal of making courses and curricula units modifiable and evolvable by users does not imply transferring the responsibility of good design to the learner. Metadesign is a conceptual framework defining and creating social and technical infrastructures in which new forms of community-based learning can take place and new communities of learners can evolve.

Approaches to Community-Based Learning

The following discussion presents approaches to community-based learning that have been applied during the last few years to university education at the Center for LifeLong Learning and Design (L3D) (L3D, 2006), University of Colorado – Boulder, USA, and the Institute for Information Systems and New Media at the University of Siegen, Germany.

University of Colorado

Structure and Description of the Local Context

The research team at the Center for Lifelong Learning and Design has been interested and has pursued activities to understand the core competency of residential, research-based universities in the twenty-first century. A deep understanding of this issue was brought into focus by developments such as the MIT OpenCourseWare project, a free and open educational resource for educators, students, and self-learners around the world (http://ocw.mit.edu/). This project makes the course materials that are used in the teaching of almost all of MIT's undergraduate and graduate subjects available on the Web, free of charge, to any user anywhere.

Our basic assumption derived from such developments is that the core competency of residential, research-based universities is in interaction, collaboration, and constructionist activities that take place in community-based learning environments that support "learning-to-be" and "learning when the answer is not known." Interdisciplinary and transdisciplinary efforts at the University of Colorado are supported by institutes and centers such as (1) the Institute of Cognitive Science (http://ics.colorado.edu/), which brings together all disciplines contributing to Cognitive Science; (2) the ATLAS (Alliance for Technology, Learning, and Society) Institute (http://www.colorado.edu/ATLAS/), with a focus on bringing together information and communication technologies with the creative practices; and (3) the Discovery Learning Center (http://engineering.colorado.edu/DLC/), with a focus on horizontal and vertical integration. The following sections briefly describe four different activities to explore community-based learning by the Center for Lifelong Learning and Design embedded in the broader context defined by these institutes.

Our courses at the University of Colorado – Boulder are focused on creating a new understanding of design, learning, and collaboration as fundamental human activities that interact, and on how to support them with innovative computational media (for examples, see http://l3d.cs.colorado.edu/~gerhard/courses/). The goals of these courses are,

- to engage students in actively exploring technology projects of *personal interest in a self-directed way*, contributing knowledge derived from their own work;
- to support peer-to-peer learning and the emergence of a community by providing opportunities and rewards for participants to learn from each other in discussions and by working on collaborative course projects;
- to provide opportunities for transdisciplinary collaborations by supporting horizontal (e.g., students from different disciplines) and vertical (e.g., undergraduates, graduates, post-docs, professionals) integration;
- to seed the course environment with relevant information and to provide the technical possibilities and social reward structures for all participants to contribute; and
- to explore the unique possibilities that computational media can have in impacting and transforming these activities by transcending "gift-wrapping" and "technodeterminism" in order to create true innovations.

Courses-as-Seeds

Courses-as-seeds (dePaula et al., 2001) is an educational model that attempts to create a culture of collective inquiry that is situated in the context of the university courses and yet extends beyond the temporal boundaries of semester-based classes and traditional prefabricated class materials. The essential aspects of the model are that students take an active role in their own learning processes (Fischer, 2002) and that these learning processes are embedded in collaborative activities supported by innovative technologies.

The subject areas we want to investigate do not contain answers that can be found in textbooks or derived in a semester, but instead are complex, vague, and open-ended problems. Within our model, students are designers and reflective practitioners who must frame the problems they will investigate (Schön, 1983). The knowledge to understand, frame, and solve design problems does not exist a priori, but is constructed and evolved by exploiting the power of the "symmetry of ignorance" (Rittel, 1984) and "breakdowns" (Winograd & Flores, 1986). Central to the notion of design as a model of collaborative work and learning is the construction of a publicly accessible artifact (Bruner, 1996) that serves as both a reification of shared understanding and grounding for the creation of new understandings.

Collaborative technologies are providing new ways to conceptualize what such a shared artifact can be. In the past, a physical artifact was separate from the discussions and decisions that helped shape it. Modern collaborative technologies allow these discussions and decisions to be captured and considered as part of the artifact. For example, hypertext technologies enable students to create artifacts that link and extend each other's contributions to express new understandings. The result of such knowledge-building is an information space that can serve as the starting point for future students, who bring new perspectives and framings to the problem. It is this sense of ongoing, collaborative learning through design that we wish to support with the courses-as-seeds model.

Courses (examples can be found at http://l3d.cs.colorado.edu/ gerhard/courses/) taught from the courses-as-seeds perspective have the following objectives:

- to engage students in authentic, self-directed learning activities;
- to embed learning and design activities in the context of real-world activities;
- to encourage collaboration based on the interdisciplinary nature of real-world problems;
- to support peer-to-peer learning;
- to practice horizontal and vertical integration by having undergraduates, graduates, post-docs, and additional faculty members participate in the course;
- to enrich the educational experience of the students by having guest lectures;
- to encourage students to exercise judgment and self-assessment; and
- to exploit new media and new technologies in innovative ways.

Courses-as-seeds explores metadesign in the context of university courses by creating a culture of informed participation (Brown et al., 1994). It explores how to supplement community-based learning theories (Rogoff et al., 1998) with innovative collaborative technologies. Participants shift among the roles of learner, designer, and active contributor. Learning is mutual and involves all stakeholders, and the teacher acts as a guide on the side (a metadesigner) rather than as a sage on the stage. The output of each course contributes to an evolving information space that is collaboratively designed by all course participants, past and present. As in all metadesign activities, the metadesigner (i.e., the teacher) gives up some control; there is little room for micromanaged curricula and precise schedules. Because it is impossible and undesirable to precisely determine the direction and outcome of learning in the courses-as-seeds model, learning is conceptualized as an evolutionary process of "design without final goals" (Simon, 1996). From this perspective, breakdowns in understanding do not cause embarrassment to instructors and frustration to students, but rather provide opportunities for learning and new directions for inquiry. The courses-as-seeds model requires a mindset in which plans conceived at the beginning of the course do not determine the direction of learning but instead provide a resource for interpreting unanticipated situations that arise during the course (Suchman, 1987).

Learning to Be: Undergraduate Research Apprenticeship Program

The Center for LifeLong Learning and Design established an Undergraduate Research Apprenticeship Program (URAP) (URAP, 2006) in 1998 in an effort to provide a means for engaging undergraduate students in real research environments.

The underlying philosophy of the URAP is based on the fundamental objectives of complementing "learning about" with "learning to be" (Bruner, 1996). Specifically, research teams have a vertically and horizontally integrated structure: they are interdisciplinary by nature and include undergraduate apprentices, Ph.D. students, postdocs, research scientists, faculty, and industry partners from various fields. URAP emphasizes the importance of learning-by-doing: each apprentice has a personal mentor and works on ongoing projects. Our model emphasizes a long-term working relationship in which apprentices receive close guidance at first, but over time are expected to engage in more self-directed research as well as serve as mentors for newer apprentices.

Transdisciplinary Education

Our focus on transdisciplinary competencies and mindsets addresses abilities and attitudes required for successful lifelong and transdisciplinary learning that we believe are important for all students in all disciplines and that should be acquired in addition to and along with in-depth knowledge in particular specialties. We use the term *transdisciplinary* (National-Research-Council, 2003) instead of *interdisciplinary* to emphasize that interdisciplinary collaboration may create new knowledge domains outside or in between disciplines, and in the process fundamentally transform the disciplinary identities of the collaborating researchers. Interdisciplinarity requires accepting different opinions in addition to ours, but transdisciplinarity requires that we are willing to change opinions and beliefs (Snow, 1993).

The capability of crossing different knowledge spaces and nourishing a fertile middle ground between disciplines is crucial for society's problems that are far too complex for one point of view. The capability of transferring methods from one discipline to another is necessary, but mutual learning and the capability of collaborative problem framing and problem solving in a suitable sociotechnical environment are crucial. Transdisciplinary research focuses on imaging entirely new possibilities for what disciplines can do. This is achieved by transcending a distinction between designers and consumers (or providers and clients) into a relationship of peers and collaborators by exploiting the symmetry of ignorance as a source of creativity and mutual learning.

Most significant real-world problems are framed and solved by multicultural and transdisciplinary communities and organizations rather than by individuals. Human creativity emerges from activities that take place in contexts in which there is interaction among people and artifacts (e.g., tools, technologies, designs, represented ideas) that embody knowledge from various constituent communities (Bennis & Biederman, 1997; Csikszentmihalyi, 1996; Engeström, 2001). Hence goals for transdisciplinary education must include preparing citizens and professionals to live and work productively in a world in which intelligence is distributed across networks of humans and artifacts (Salomon, 1993).

Transdisciplinary education also has a critical social dimension. Theorists writing about interdisciplinary learning and collaboration have long recognized that achievement of excellence requires conceptual collisions and epistemological pluralism (Turkle & Papert, 1991) brought about by controversy and debate. Competing ideas are essential for knowledge growth, but taking advantage of them requires norms and communication practices that invite openness and lead to analysis and integration. Yet people working together often do not address communication processes openly, and they may remain unaware when communication processes are deficient (Derry & Fischer, 2005). Working and learning across time, space, people, and tools, especially when different disciplines are involved, require a community-wide social intelligence that is often not present in working groups' epistemological pluralism.

Social Networks: Lifelong Learning

The goal of our research is to explore the strengths and weaknesses of community-based learning while addressing the following question: *What and how should students learn in order to be educated citizens and to find and do interesting and important work in the twenty-first century?* Our research agenda has been grounded in the basic belief that lifelong learning is more than adult education: it forces us to rethink the core function of formal education in schools and universities. We are convinced that one of the most fundamental aspects of education at a residential, research-based university is to create a lifelong bond between the students and the university. This objective was articulated by George Norlin (1871–1942) in 1935 as president of the University of Colorado in a speech to graduating students that contained the following remarks:

> You are now certified to the world at large as alumni of the University. She is your kindly mother and you her cherished sons and daughters. This exercise denotes not your severance from her, but your union with her. Commencement does not mean, as many wrongly think, the breaking of ties and the beginning of life apart. Rather, it marks your initiation in the fullest sense into the fellowship of the University, as bearers of her torch, as centers of her influence, as promoters of her spirit.
>
> The University is not the campus, not the buildings on the campus, not the faculties, not the students of any one time – not one of these or all of them. The University consists of all who come into and go forth from her halls, who are touched by her influence and who carry on her spirit. Wherever you go, the University goes with you. Wherever you are at work, there is the University at work (Norlin, 1935).

These arguments and objectives create the following implications for community-based learning: (1) the necessity for lifelong learning, and (2) the understanding that "outreach" is more than asking alumni for money – it is a unique opportunity to integrate alumni into the fabric of community-based learning. Contrary to the times of Norlin's speech, we have now fundamental new possibilities provided by modern communication and information technologies by which alumni can stay involved and participate and be with the university not only in spirit.

University of Siegen

Structure and Description of the Local Context

The program in Information Systems (IS) at the University of Siegen is grounded in an interdisciplinary curriculum that involves the disciplines of computer sciences, business administration, and information systems. IS groups in Germany are labeled "Wirtschaftsinformatik," and are mostly parts of the departments of business administration.

The establishment of project groups of university students and company practitioners (courses in practice, or CiP groups) is part of the practice-oriented education in the IS curriculum and is one research focus of the Siegen IS group. The approach aims to strengthen regional NoPs between university and regional industry by connecting industrial CoPs with those in academia. Therefore, the academic education program is accompanied by a number of measures of networking and social capital-building activities initiated by the university.

Supported by research funds from different government sources and industries, the IS group comprises ten staff members (faculty and research associates) and a similar number of students working as research assistants. Research is organized around specific, typically externally funded projects, and practice emerges within these projects or groups of them. To initiate regional learning, the Siegen IS group tries to build SC and foster NoPs between the university and software and media industries.

Courses in Practice: Enculturation of Students into Regional Industries' CoPs

In Siegen, opportunities for enculturation into specific CoPs are considered to be a major instrument of education at the university level. This approach complements "learning about" with "learning to be." So far, experiences have been primarily gained with enculturation processes into two types of CoPs: those within the research group and those within regional information technology (IT) companies.

With regard to the latter, we offer learning opportunities to students by integrating student teams into the CoPs of local IT companies. To host teams of two to three students, IT companies define projects close to their core business. The student teams work on these projects in close cooperation with mentors from the companies. The goal of these courses is to allow the students to enter the companies' CoPs and therefore to enable processes of enculturation, mutual knowledge transfer, and the gaining of apprenticeship.

When working in industries, the students are closely coached by members of the research group. Each group is supported by an academic supervisor during the whole CiP duration. Furthermore, there are regular meetings of students, supervisors, and the professor. Coaching the CiP groups very closely is crucial for our concept. The student teams are connected to each other and to their supervisors in academia by means of a community system.

With regard to the setup of the CiP, the Siegen IS group could refer to the experiences of some of the group members with a similar CiP at the University of Aachen. On the basis of these former experiences, the initiative in Siegen aimed at establishing longer-lasting relationships between university and industry, to involve more stable companies (instead of very young start-ups), to build up "strong ties," to establish SC, and therefore, to succeed in more than short-term effects and real "regional learning."

After nearly 1 year of building up relationships with regional companies, the first CiP at the IS faculty of the University of Siegen was announced for summer term 2003. The course design is illustrated in Fig. 12.1. The figure shows the design of a CiP, in which two CoPs are established, consisting of university students and company practitioners (relation to the regional market). These CoPs are accompanied by a supervisor within the company and instructors from the university and are supported by digital media (groupware, cooperation platforms, etc.).

Since 2003, three instances of the CiP have been conducted and evaluated. Table 12.2 shows the distribution of students within six different practical projects. Two of the companies (Company A and Company C) participated in two instances of the course. The number of students assigned to the CiP project groups shows that we are working with a concept of small groups, which we expect to enculturate within the companies' practice during the project.

Fifteen IS students of the University of Siegen participated in our CiP, cooperating closely with at least an equal number of employees at the local companies. Each project group was accompanied by at least one academic supervisor and one company supervisor. During the CiP, about five presentation and discussion meetings among students and academic supervisors took place, followed by a public presen-

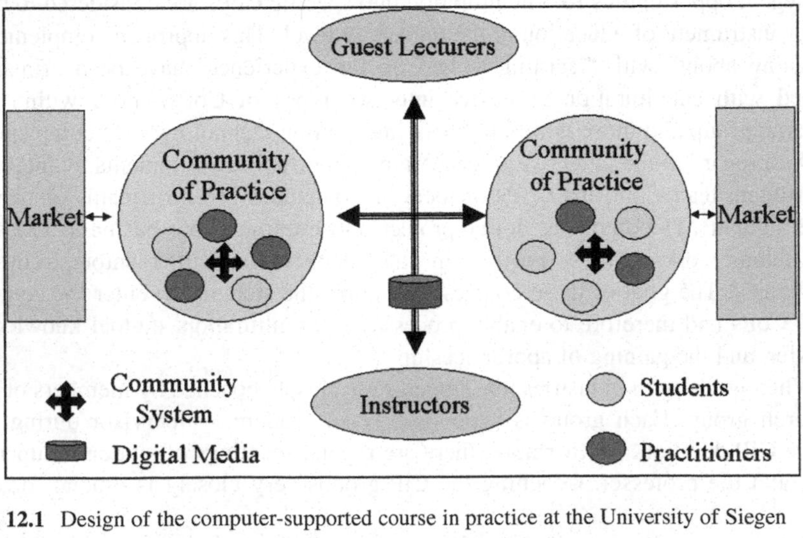

Fig. 12.1 Design of the computer-supported course in practice at the University of Siegen

Table 12.2 Project groups, tasks, and number of students

	Project Task	No. of students
Company A1	Developing a toolbar for a community-portal	3
Company A2	Developing a Web-based application to count the usage of click-per-view ads	3
Company B	Designing an offline reader for a news-paper archive	2
Company C1	Analyzing software publishing processes in a mid-size software company	2
Company C2	Developing an electronic payment tool for business software for SMEs	3
Company D	Analyzing procurement processes within a producer of caravan equipment	2

The companies' names are coded as Company A–D; the designation Company A2 means that a second project was conducted by the same Company A
SME small and medium enterprises

tation of results at the end of each course. Representatives of the local government, employees of other companies, journalists, members of other faculty departments, and others were invited to these presentations. Furthermore, an official meeting attended by the student team, the company supervisors, and the academic supervisors took place in the middle of each project.

Learning to Be: Enculturation of Students into Faculty Research CoPs

We have reinterpreted the following elements of the IS curriculum to offer opportunities for students to participate in our research practice: seminars, project groups, and diploma theses. With regard to each of these elements of the curriculum, we define tasks that were relevant to the research agenda of our group (e.g., elaborating the state of the art of a new research area by means of a seminar, implementing specific software components in the framework of a project group, or building a prototype as part of a master's thesis). We also offer research assistant positions for students to work within our externally funded projects.

Students not only assist in IS research, but also take over tasks as their own responsibilities, closely coached by research associates. Engaged students can coauthor scientific publications, and they quite often accompany the IS researchers to national and international conferences and present the research findings at the conference. Most diploma theses thereby find their way into (international) conference or journal publications.

Because these tasks are relevant to both students and researchers, an important precondition for processes of enculturation is met. Enculturation processes into the research group are becoming more likely and intense as students follow up on more than one of these learning opportunities. Some of the best students are offered employment by the IS research group after their diploma thesis – if money permits – or are recommended to other research groups. Therefore, learning as a process of diffusion from the periphery of the Siegen IS group's CoP into its center is not only possible, but seen as rather normal for the best of the IS students.

Transdisciplinary Education: Interdisciplinary Courses for Students from Different Backgrounds

Within the IS group at the University of Siegen, researchers from different scientific backgrounds – specifically, computer scientists, information systems professionals, a psychologist, a historian, a linguist, and an ethnographer – are working together. Because most research projects of the IS group in Siegen are focused on designing for different social settings, the cooperation of scientists from a range of disciplines is required.

For university courses in Siegen, there are two methods of realizing transdisciplinary teaching:

- The IS group itself provides interdisciplinary courses and lectures (computer-supported cooperative work, computer-supported cooperative learning, participatory design, etc.).
- Several courses are organized as common teaching programs for two or more departments (e.g., media sciences).

Students who attend IS courses are obviously mostly those from information systems; moreover, the courses are attended by students from other departments, such as computer science, business administration, and media sciences. Within these different types of courses, students work together and learn from each other. In this regard, Siegen, being a rather small university, can draw on a tradition of mutual acceptance of courses and transdisciplinary programs among the departments.

Social Networks: Regional Learning Between Academia and Different Firms

The building of trust and social capital is a crucial success factor to foster networks between academia and industry and among regional companies of the software and media industries. According to the approach of SC, different cooperative activities between the university and the regional industry were expected to lead to trustful relationships.

Siegen is located in a region of Germany characterized by older, down-turning, mainly iron- and steel-related industries, and is therefore challenged by the necessity of structural change. The University of Siegen tries to play a role in this process by facilitating regional development. In this context, the IS research group is trying to network the regional software and media industries, which consist of mainly small- and medium-sized enterprises, to strengthen the market position of these companies. Taking the knowledge-creating character of communities and NoPs seriously, the Siegen IS group expects to learn from the regional software and media companies as well. Innovative design concepts and methods can be evaluated, and software practice under market conditions is perceived. Market trends are closely watched. The vision behind establishing such a close cooperation with regional industries is the creation of a "learning region" in the software and media domains.

To this end, the Siegen IS group cooperates with the region's business development department. A series of networking events was set up jointly, labeled "Lyz Media Breakfast," directed toward chief executive officers (CEOs) of regional software and media companies. Following an invited talk in the early morning (8:30 a.m.), there is a joint breakfast for the participants to network with each other. Coverage by the local newspapers helped to announce the new initiative within the region.

The region's business development department was also instrumental in providing us with funding from the European Structural Fund. The funding is directed toward fostering a network of practice among six regional software and media companies. The activities of the network-building process cover joint meetings among the CEOs, meetings with the IT departments of strategic clients in the region (e.g., a brewery, a producer of switchboards), and joint public relations. These activities focus around marketing and management practice within software and media companies.

Furthermore, the IS group is in the process of establishing a joint research center in the field of interactive television. The center will focus on research and development of innovative technological features and suitable formats of interactive television. This activity is jointly pursued by a regional software company, the administrative body of the region, and the university. The software company has participated for 2 years in CiP projects and also takes part in the regional network. This initiative, therefore, was grounded in a longer history of cooperation among the different actors.

Finally, the IS research group has developed research proposals together with different member companies of the regional network. Because many university programs in Germany and Europe require participation from industry, the research proposals could be, on the one hand, grounded on an already rather established cooperation between university and industry. On the other hand, the opportunity to receive public funding via the university's activities stabilized the regional networks.

Complementary Approaches to Community-Based Learning

Although the approaches to community-based learning refer mainly to the same set of sociocultural theories on learning, the educational programs of the IS group at the University of Siegen in Germany and the LifeLong Learning and Design Center at the University of Colorado in the United States differ in some aspects. These differences in underlying community concepts, educational focus, and perspectives of networking are due to differences in the specific historical contexts in Germany and the United States and to different national regulations and

Table 12.3 Comparison of Universities of Siegen and Colorado

	University of Colorado	University of Siegen
Theoretical foundation	Sociocultural theories Social creativity	Sociocultural theories Social capital
Dominant community concept	CoI	CoP and NoP
Course concept	Courses-as-seeds: involve all stakeholders as active participants	Courses in practice: enculturation of students into regional industries' CoPs
Learning to be	Undergraduate Research Apprenticeship Program	Enculturation into faculty's research CoP
Transdisciplinary education focus	Mutual and cross-cultural peer-learning of collaborators	Interdisciplinary courses for students from different backgrounds
Social networking concept	Lifelong learning in a bond between students and university	Regional learning between academia and different regional firms
Evaluation methods	Qualitative and quantitative methods: interviews, questionnaires, personal portfolios, self-assessment	Ethnographic and qualitative methods: (participatory) observations, in-depth interviews, evaluation workshops

cultures in education and research. However, the approaches can be considered to be complementary.

According to the didactical approaches and the learning concepts mentioned above, Table 12.3 illustrates the similarities and differences between the Siegen and Colorado programs.

Empirical Findings

This section presents selected findings from evaluations of the different didactical approaches. Owing to the distributed setting, the long-term nature of our efforts, and the breadth of didactical concepts, the evaluation methods applied are heterogeneous, and the density of the empirical material varies.

University of Colorado

The University of Colorado has offered ten courses (based on two different themes) emphasizing community-based learning in the past 10 years (examples are documented at: http://l3d.cs.colorado.edu/~gerhard/courses/). Over time, we incrementally increased the embedding of these courses within the conceptual frameworks described in this paper (see the "Conceptual Frameworks" section) and improved the sociotechnical environments (see the first portion of the "Approaches to Community-Based Learning" section) supporting these courses.

Table 12.4 Selected responses from students related to our conceptual framework

Concept	Selected responses from students
Transcending the individual human mind	"The people presenting were in the same position we were all in, new to their topics and presenting everything they learned starting from nothing. They presented in a manner that we could understand and relate to."
CoPs and CoIs	"It helped us see computer science from new angles (be a part of a diverse community, not a bunch of isolated hackers)."
	"The point of this class is to 'collaborate.' By doing this, we see perspectives we wouldn't ordinarily account for, and this helps us grow in our acceptance of other ideas."
	"For some people the course was not technical enough; for some other people, the course was too technical."
Social capital	"One big difference was that we had the opportunity to present our work to the entire class, which was a great incentive since we knew our work would have a purpose (teaching others)."
Social creativity	"Have more diverse viewpoints, keep groups small so they can perform well, make sure people are satisfied with their groups and can find a way to be effective contributors."
	"We were so grateful to have an outpouring of positive feedback and suggestions from fellow classmates after our first progress report that this is an aspect of the class structure that should really be explored."
Metadesign	"I did get a chance to further explore areas I was interested in. However, I had never done serious, self-directed research before, and found that I wasn't able to explore in the directions I was really interested in, for fear of diverting too far away from the rest of the group."
Confidence	"I also would have liked to have participated more in the class discussions. I tend to be a quiet person in classes anyways, so it wasn't very unusual for me."
Horizontal integration	"This was a good idea to some extent, but was also frustrating, as the majority of non-CS people were teachers, and I wasn't particularly interested in the learning component of the course, and thus, there was a bit of a mismatch between my priorities and the priorities of most of the students of other disciplines."
Vertical integration	"As an undergrad, we have limited experience in general things that the grad students already have gained. Their insights were useful because as undergrads, we tend to be closed-minded overall because all we've been exposed to is structured curriculums."
Collaboration ("in defense of cheating")	"I am currently not comfortable with people having access to all my work before the actual termination of the assignment. I enjoy being able to let people see only the polished product. I also feel that some students could take advantage of the trusting nature of the swiki and I am not comfortable with that."
Importance of face-to-face interaction	"I learned more from group presentation because they're more interactive than posted documentation. You can ask questions and get immediate feedback."
Sociotechnical environment	"The swiki seemed to emerge largely as a submission mechanism and document repository for this class, and I felt there was little to no actual interaction among users…I like the idea [that] it will stick around, but can't immediately envision a burning need in the future for any of the information posted there. I think the biggest thing I might come back for would be participants' contact information."
	"I don't feel that people in this class used the swiki to its potential. It was more of a place to post work than to really discuss or bounce ideas."

Table 12.4 briefly summarizes responses from students related to concepts and issues discussed in the earlier sections of this paper. Data were gathered from several questionnaires over the course of a semester, including self-assessment accounts by all students.

The following two subsections discuss cultural change, risk-taking, and student reactions to the "community-of-learners" concept in more detail.

Cultural Change and Risk-Taking

Introducing a new educational model involves *cultural change* by all participants (Fischer, 1998). Regardless of how well classroom activities are designed, or how sophisticated the supporting technology, these elements will not by themselves change the culture of education (Bruner, 1996). Cultural change requires that participants critically reflect upon and possibly change their behaviors, goals, values, and attitudes toward education. Despite a growing body of research on collaborative learning, changing an instructionist classroom (in which students passively listen to a lecturer) into a community-based learning environment requires a focus not only on the role of collaborative learning in expanding students' learning experiences, but also on the cultural change needed to enable collaborative learning to take place in educational settings. Students reacted to our course with the following questions:

- Why should I learn from a peer when the faculty member knows the answer so much better?
- Why should I pay fees if the teacher is not willing to provide me with the answer?

There is overwhelming evidence in the students' self-assessments, the faculty course questionnaires, and from many of their reactions in class that a course of this kind was a "culture shock" for almost all students. The rationale for this reaction can be found in that most students' behavior is grounded in the following beliefs:

- They consider themselves as consumers of education (confirming Illich's (1971) argument that "schools and universities are the reproductive organs of a consumer society").
- They believe that problems have an answer and that the teacher has to know the answer.
- They are at best not interested, and at worst unwilling, to engage in peer-to-peer learning (which should not surprise us in a culture of education in which collaboration is mostly treated as "cheating" (Norman, 2001)).
- They are driven to learn primarily by the desire to get a good grade rather than by interest, passion, or enjoyment derived from intrinsic motivation in learning (Gardner, 1991).
- They are *not* used to being assessed by anyone other than their teachers and therefore they need to learn how to self-assess (which, like any other skill, takes time and experience to develop).

Table 12.5 Typology of teacher/student roles concerning risk-taking

Teacher	Student	Example
Authority ("sage on the stage")	Dependent, passive	Lecture without questions, drill
Motivator and facilitator	Interested	Lecture with questions, guided discussion
Delegator	Involved	Group projects, seminar
Coach/critic ("guide on the side")	Self-directed, discovery-oriented	Self-directed study group, apprenticeship, dissertation

Modified from a table in Grow (1991/1996). An expanded version is available online at http://www.famu.edu/sjmga/ggrow

Risk-Taking. Cultural change will not take place without learners and teachers taking risks as a consequence of different cultures clashing with each other. Risk-taking can be illustrated with the following example: the "mismatch problem" between teachers and learners in teacher-driven/instructionist vs. self-directed/constructionist learning environments (as summarized in Table 12.5). The major mismatches that can be derived from this table are as follows: (1) dependent, passive learners take courses with nondirective teachers; and (2) self-directed, discovery-oriented active learners take courses with directive, authoritarian teachers. The experience from our course was a mismatch of the first kind with at least half of the student population in the course.

Student Reactions to the "Community-of-Learners" Concept

A surprising result was that the students' course assessments resulted in a *bipolar distribution* that we have not experienced before. Students were either enthusiastically positive, giving faculty and the course *A*'s on the faculty course questionnaires, or totally negative, giving a substantial number of *F*'s.

This reaction is best illustrated by two comments, quoted from the students' self-evaluations:

1. A negative comment: "I will not ever take a course of this nature again in my undergraduate career, and I hope to find a more structured graduate program with an adviser that is more forthcoming. I will reinforce my strengths by continuing to study in the method that I have developed over the past 15 years, I will redirect my weaknesses by avoiding unstructured class environments. I believe that the type of self-directed learning that this class wished to promote is better done during independent studies and thesis work. (I am involved in both of the above in a very self-directed environment, I am doing well and the concept works much better there.)"
2. A positive comment: "When I signed up for this class I had no idea what it was going to be about. Once I started understanding the material, however, I was extremely thrilled and interested to be a part of one of the most progressive courses on campus. I'm not sure what specifically to say except that I rank this

class in the top three that I've taken at CU. The self-directed nature of the work ensured that I wouldn't be bored or unchallenged, and the interplay between all of us was a lot of fun. After four and a half years in college, I can honestly say that this is one of the first courses where I was treated as an adult, a fact which means more to me than I can describe."

What Can We Learn from the Student Reactions? The interesting question to ask is: What can be learned from this event for innovating and changing our university to provide an exciting, challenging, and rewarding intellectual environment for our students and our teachers in the next millennium? Here are a number of hypotheses:

- Cultural change beyond the introduction of new learning approaches and new technologies is of critical importance.
- *Risk-taking* by teachers is not necessarily rewarded by the students. With current assessments (such as faculty course questionnaires serving as primary instruments), risk-taking is not rewarded by the institution, and as a result is potentially a dangerous undertaking by young, untenured faculty members.
- Change agents are needed, but they must be aware that they take risks. These risks may "force" especially young faculty members to accommodate the existing system and conduct business as usual.

Issues to be aware of. To change a culture is risk-taking. Universities need to reward risk-taking, and using faculty course questionnaires as major instrument for assessment in most cases will punish risk-taking. New media and new technologies provide us with exciting possibilities to rethink our mission. But almost all serious educational reformers believe that new media and new technologies on their own cannot transform universities to meet the demands of the future. Technology is only one part of cultural change. This implies that goals such as (1) "supporting innovations in learning, including both undergraduate and graduate education," and (2) "using technology to improve teaching, learning, research, and management" have to be tightly integrated. Cultural change implies that all stakeholders participating in the process of change have to reflect and possibly change their behavior, their objectives, and their values. In the days where the future of universities is seen by many as occurring in the virtual world, and where education is often reduced to a commodity, we need to understand the core competencies of a residential, research-based university. Some of these core competencies should be centered around the notion that instructionist learning will be complemented with self-directed learning in learning communities, and that students of all ages will be involved in apprenticeship-like relationships that will allow them to become members of the community of scholars, researchers, proficient professionals, and educated persons.

In summary, cultural change beyond the adoption of new technologies is required in our current system in which students have been taught to take on the role of consumers of education. This change will require risk-taking by faculty members. The university needs to reward such risk-taking rather than punish it. Shaking up students' habits and mindsets is more risky, and will be met with more resistance, than dispensing knowledge.

University of Siegen

To complement the Boulder experiences, this section focuses on the evaluation of CoP- and NoP-related approaches to community-based learning at the University of Siegen.

Research Methods

To evaluate our activities, we have conducted a series of semistructured interviews and additional observational studies during a period of 3 years. The interviews and observations were conducted by researchers who were not involved in the courses. Moreover, our findings are based on experiences gained by the authors when setting up the regional networks and carrying out the community-based course program.

We conducted 25 explorative semistructured in-depth interviews with students, supervisors from academia and industry, and officers of the regional administration. Fourteen students, six company practitioners, three academics, and two officers were interviewed. During the interviews, which lasted between 60 and 180 min, students were first asked about their personal backgrounds, their educational backgrounds, and their motivation for participating in the lecture. After that, students were questioned on personal impressions and assessments of the course and its single components. Students were also asked to suggest improvements. Lecturers were asked about their personal background, and high emphasis was placed on assessments of the lecture components held by them. The regional officers were asked about their activities to encourage competition in the regional software and media industries. We were specifically interested in their experience in establishing regional networks and their evaluation of our joint activities in fostering regional NoPs between local industry and the university.

Each person was interviewed in an individual session. All interviews have been recorded with a DAT recorder and fully transcribed. In the evaluation, the answers were transformed into a table categorizing the roles of students, academic faculty, and industrial supervisors. The observational data were structured around the different events and documented in the form of written notes. Interviews and observational data have been analyzed descriptively according to our heuristic approach. The process was informed by the experiences gained when carrying out the different measures.

Courses in Practice

Since 2003, a series of three courses in practice (CiPs) has been conducted. In total, six projects had been carried out and evaluated by spring 2006 (see Table 12.6). Two of the local companies (Company A and Company C) have been engaged in two projects (in two different years with two different project tasks).

Table 12.6 Typology of projects: Structural differences and outcome

	Company A1	Company A2	Company B	Company C1	Company C2	Company D
Long-lasting activity	?	+	+	+	–	–
Collocation/ physical presence	–	+	–	+	–	+
Relevance of the project task	–	+	±	+	+	+
Fulfilment of the company-defined tasks	+	± (not finished during CiP time, but later)	+	+	± (project finished but criticized by company)	+
Enculturation	–	+	+	+	–	?

The companies' names are coded as Company A to D; the designation Company A2 means that a second project was conducted by the same Company A. A plus (+) means that the specific criterion was fulfilled, a minus (–) means that it was not fulfilled, a plus/minus (±) means that it is unclear whether the criterion was fulfilled within the project

With regard to the evaluation of the three CiPs, the interviews brought evidence of some factors that influenced the success of the project groups and the learning of lab-group members.

Long- vs. Short-Lasting Activities. Some of the project tasks were embedded in longer-lasting activities within the companies' practice, whereas others just were defined for the project and its duration. Some interviewees stated that it was important that their project task was embedded in longer-lasting activities for the degree of involvement of company practitioners, for cooperation structures, and for the success of the project. Longer-lasting activities in the companies' practice do not mean that the university was engaged in these companies for a longer term, but that the projects' tasks and results took place within longer-lasting intern processes and projects of the company itself.

Collocation and Physical Presence. Collocation of students and company practitioners had an influence on the establishment of cooperation structures between students and company practitioners. Students who were not collocated with the companies' practitioners, but worked on the project tasks at home or at the university, were less likely to build trustful relationships and SC with the companies.

Relevance of the Project Task. Some of the project tasks defined by the companies' executives had strategic relevance for the company and its product development, whereas other projects were defined more according to the company's peripheral interests. It showed that involvement, success, and enculturation are influenced by the strategic relevance the project task has had for the companies' practice.

Success of the Projects Regarding Task Fulfilment. The success of projects can be measured by the fulfilment of the project task according to the assessment of the companies' supervisors. In terms of project success, one project has been evaluated as not successful. A second was finally successful but could not be finished within the originally envisioned time frame. The other four projects have been assessed as successful by the companies according to task and goal definitions.

Enculturation in the Companies' Practice. Successful enculturation into the companies' practice is one hint for gaining apprenticeship and therefore for socio-cultural learning. These enculturation experiences were made by students who collaborated in teams within the companies and felt integrated into the companies' practice. In the three CiPs, a successful enculturation of university students into the companies' practice even means that the students continue their relationship with the companies after the CiPs end. In three cases, CiP practitioners have been employed by the companies after the project.

Table 12.6 seems to suggest that the mentioned issues of long-lasting activities, relevance, successful fulfilment of the project task, and physical presence in the company may influence the probability of successful enculturation.

Often, team building among the students had to be influenced to secure sufficient capabilities within the different teams. So the team's capabilities almost never led to problems. Almost all projects met the companies' expectations. However, the enculturation processes into the companies' CoPs varied considerably. It turned out that the students' dedication toward future work in such companies was as much a success factor as the companies' cultures and behaviors toward the students.

Table 12.6 shows a typology of projects according to the structural differences and outcomes mentioned above (University of Siegen).

Issues to be aware of: When trying to set up CiPs, the empirical findings suggest the following:

- Facilitating or engaging in regional NoPs helps to find companies that will offer their CoPs for teaching.
- Reputation and personal networks are most important to get access to companies' CoPs; alumni may play a role in the future:

> The most important point with these cooperation[s] is the personal contact. It is very important that good personal contacts emerge.... it might be due to the person of {Prof.}: He acts very open towards the companies and generates project issue. He is very supporting and demands for cooperation between university and industry. [a regional official]

- Enculturation can suffer from the relatively short duration of the CiPs, which typically take about 4 months. The short period of time can prevent the students from drifting from the periphery to the center of the companies' CoPs.
- The specific identity of students and their teams can prevent them from enculturation in case they do not see any reason to strongly engage in a company's projects:

> At the core I would look upon our three [students] group as a team. With the project running, the relationship to the {company's} members became better and closer. That made us becoming a team all together.... But the ties between us and them are not as strong as between us three students. The core is the three of us and around this core there are the members of {company}. [a student]

- A history of more than one CiP with a local company (or another form of an earlier cooperation between university and company) typically offers better opportunities for students to enculturate because companies suggest projects that are closer to their core business. The first cooperation project between the university and a local company needs to build trust, and in case of success, provides a very good basis for future cooperation.
- Mutual learning is full of conflicts because students act as boundary spanners between CoPs in academia and industries. When students are enculturated in both CoPs, conflicts come up (with regard to identity and practice). However, mutual learning (between universities and industry) and regional innovation are typically happening at these points:

  Yes, the {company's} supervisor, at the beginning I wasn't sure whether we would get problems with him, whether there would be conflicts. I didn't know because he seemed to be a strange guy, I mean, very nice but sometimes I asked myself, 'Did he mean that serious or is he joking on us? Is he thinking: There are three students from university and they try to make a show?' I wasn't able to get a right picture of him. Therefore, I kept a bit of distance at first. But [then it turned and] the {company's} supervisor is really great because he is really supporting and spends a lot of time for us. [another student]

- Social capital and mutual reliability are core to all of these processes: At the beginning of the cooperation within the projects, very often a lot of trust-building communication was necessary to enable cooperative structures and the motivation for cooperation at all:

  I have conducted one of the early interviews alone because {the other student} had to stay at university and the {company's} member with whom I was talking said to me: 'No, I don't want to talk to you.' 'Why?' Then he said: 'Because I dislike that students come to my company to sort people out' – It took me… about one hour to make clear that this was not my intention. It was rather difficult to make that clear. I noticed that there were rumors around at the beginning and that was a big problem. [another student]

- The enculturation of students into the university research CoP depends on the match between the students' anticipation of the utility of their project task with regard to their professional career expectations. Some of the students developed the topic of their diploma thesis out of their project experience. Other students who started working on projects were enculturated even for a longer period of time by being employed as research assistants or, after their graduation, as research associates.

Regional NoPs

Concerning the specific local situation in Siegen, the fostering of regional NoPs between university and local companies revealed several critical factors:

- In the Siegen region, the density of software and media companies is not very high. Therefore, NoPs focusing on specific aspects of software techniques are difficult to establish. Thus, NoPs fostered between university and companies and among different companies needed to be understood covering a broader range of practices, or a rather broad understanding of common practices.

- Because the regional market for IT services is limited as well, there is a strong competition among those software and media companies that target this market. This competition limits the chances to foster NoPs for regional learning, at least on the CEO level.
- With regard to the size (especially of small companies) and the strong competition between the local companies, cooperation in regional NoPs is rather weakly developed. The exchange of practical experiences in NoPs seems to be more likely and perform better within larger companies (e.g., local software company clusters in Silicon Valley). Within and between these NoPs of larger companies, a fluctuation of employees takes place, and people change from one local company to another one. Contrary to that, in the Siegen region, competition and the risk of "takeovers" of employees are considered the central problems.

Issues to be aware of: Our experiences and observations with establishing regional networks led to the following conclusions:

- One needs a lot of patience to successfully establish mutual relationships of trust.
- As a new player in a region, one needs a regionally well-known "door opener" to help introduce new players in the regional network structures.
- The organizational reputation of a university (in its regional context) can be enforced significantly by strategic partnerships with other well-known scientific institutions. In our case, we set up an institutional cooperation arrangement between the university and the Fraunhofer Society. In Germany, Fraunhofer has a strong reputation for transferring innovation toward industries. This alliance proved to be one of the important success factors for the fostering of regional NoPs.
- With regard to certain existing institutional and personal conflicts in a region's NoPs, one needs to be aware of them and should try to act carefully, being neutral and as fair as possible toward all actors.

Discussion

Residential, research-based universities are facing new challenges from computer-supported and Web-based offers of distance or tele-learning and tele-teaching, such as online universities and even free educational course material on the Internet (e.g., the OpenCourseWare program of MIT and similar programs at ~50 universities worldwide, planned for roll out within the next several years). The OpenCourseWare concept seems to suggest that knowledge creation is based on consumptive processes of individual learning, facilitated by filling in knowledge relevant to Web surfers, in written or multimedia formats.

On the basis of sociocultural theories of learning, the idea of instructionist teaching and consumptive learning does not represent a comprehensive model of knowledge creation in a social world. Furthermore, if concepts of "knowledge" include not only cognitive or intellectual competencies, but social, emotional, motivational, and practical competencies as well, learning (and of course university education as one core component of knowledge building) is confronted with new challenges for teachers and students.

Therefore, social and collaborative processes of learning – as well of individuals as of collectives – and the (culturally mediated) social construction of knowledge (Vygotsky, 1986) are emphasized. Specifically, the following aspects of knowledge building are focused on in a new paradigm of university education:

- Knowledge building seen as a process of *con*struction instead of *in*struction
- Knowledge building seen as a result of interaction with others instead of individual consumption
- Knowledge building seen as a function of practical experiences rather than as a function of theoretical readings
- Knowledge building seen as a challenge for lifelong learning rather than as a matter of a "once upon a lifetime" experience
- Knowledge building being influenced by the social and situational context

On the basis of these assumptions, community-based learning seems to be a quite relevant concept for learning and teaching at the university level: Lifelong learning, learning in practice, cross-cultural learning, collaborative learning, and learning in a regional context are promising concepts for residential universities to cope with the new challenges of online universities (and the emerging Web-based education programs) mentioned above.

Community-based learning has different needs for computer support than content-delivery-oriented approaches, such as the OpenCourseWare initiative. Owing to the distributed nature of the actors, we rely heavily on tools such as e-mail, community systems such as BSCW, and distributed software development environments such as CVS. These tools support cooperation, coordination, and shared knowledge building among the different actors involved, in contrast to the delivery of well-defined content from academics to students (Ackermann et al., 2003; Huysman & Wulf, 2004a). Community-based approaches to learning therefore ask for a different IT infrastructure at the university level, which needs to reach out into the relevant NoPs of the region.

Besides the question of appropriate technical support, the didactical concepts and education programs of residential, research-based universities are challenged. As far as lifelong, community-based, and practice-oriented learning is concerned, finding the right selection of CoPs and CoIs is one of the most important challenges to define a stable curriculum for students.

- A teaching curriculum could become a description of different practices a student could enculturate into (plus other forms of education).
- An appropriate mixture between traditional and community-based forms of learning needs to be found.
- A one-semester (4-month) course is often too short to create a community.

Compared to approaches that try to extract the epistemology of CoPs and bring it into the classroom (Shaffer, 2004), the Siegen experiences indicate that educational institutions should cross the boundary toward industrial practice to an even wider extent.

Supporting the enculturation of students into CoPs of companies offers occasions for mutual learning among residential universities and regional industries. So, besides students, regional industries and universities can learn while engaging in CiPs.

With regard to these suggestions, one has to concede that career patterns in academia that force professors to change university affiliations frequently are counterproductive to these (often long-term) types of learning. However, scientific competition still needs to be encouraged.

Moreover, professors need to develop new sets of skills. First, they need to be suitable facilitators to support the teambuilding and enculturation processes of the student (teams). Second, to find appropriate CoPs for their students to enculturate, they need to have networking skills to enter existing regional NoPs or even to set them up. Third, their research work needs to be, at least partly, applicable in practice. And fourth, the professors themselves, or at least the institutions with which they are involved, need to have a certain reputation to attract companies and students and bring them together.

From the point of view of necessary personal resources, it should be noted that community-based strategies of learning are labor- and qualification-intense on the part of the universities. They require coaching students intensively, particularly if these strategies are taking place in cooperation with practice (Rohde et al., 2005).

Our findings also suggest that the relationship between universities and regional industries will have to develop to a new level of intensity. Saxenian (1994) and other scholars in regional studies have already hinted at the importance of leading research universities for development in the high-tech domain (e.g., by educating a highly skilled workforce and attracting the support of high-tech companies). We stress the bidirectionality of this relationship in particular. Under a community-oriented learning paradigm, a university depends very much on its region to provide appropriate practices to nurture its different programs. In the Siegen region, however, the software and media industries lack density, thus limiting the opportunity to address specific practices.

With regard to political agendas for regional development, community-based learning offers interesting perspectives. The policy followed by the Siegen business development council points in an interesting direction. By supporting networks of practices that include the relevant actors of the university, the potentials of community-based learning are well exploited.

Implementing community-based strategies for learning requires changes on the personal as well as on the institutional level. Compared to the Colorado case, Siegen found much less resistance toward change among its IS students. This may be because Siegen's IS students selected the course by themselves from a bundle of other options.

Some students needed to understand their new role inside companies, and companies needed to develop mechanisms that allowed students to enculturate. Conflicts occurred when expectations of the university advisors and the companies did not match within this process. Our experiences indicate that the implementation of community-based educational programs requires personal and organizational development strategies on the parts of all participating actors.

Concepts such as CoPs (Lave & Wenger, 1991; Wenger, 1998) and NoPs (Duguid, 2003, 2005) as well as social capital (Bourdieu, 1985; Putnam, 1993) and social creativity (Fischer et al., 2005) guided us in developing a variety of didactical approaches for community-based learning. However, all of these concepts are analytical and do not easily provide guidelines for didactical practice in the context of residential universities.

With regard to the concept of common practice, it is especially difficult to define suitable boundaries when trying to foster NoPs or CoPs. The theories do not provide criteria of what should still be assumed as common practice and where boundaries must be expected. For instance, there was a lack of common practice among the different software and media companies with regard to their development practices. Therefore, we decided to focus our networking activities at managerial practices (e.g., process management, product innovation, and marketing). The same applies for CiPs. One needs to find sufficient common practice between university and industries to enable enculturation in a limited period of time, and to allow for the border-spanning activities of the students. When setting up practice-oriented courses, we had to rely on our "gut-feeling" rather than on well-defined criteria. So the analytic conceptualizations offer a framework of orientation but do not provide concrete guidelines for an appropriate course design, the successful establishment of CoPs, or the evaluation of networking processes.

Conclusion

New media and new technology provide us with exciting possibilities to rethink teaching, learning, and university courses – specifically, community-based learning. Almost all serious educational reformers believe that new media and new technology on their own cannot transform universities to meet the demands of the future. Technology is only one part of the necessary cultural change. Cultural change implies that all stakeholders participating in the process of change have to reflect and change their behaviors, their objectives, and their values.

We have learned from our experiences at the University of Colorado and the University of Siegen that students are strongly influenced by the values they have learned from their previous educational experiences, which are reinforced by the current university culture. Attempts to install new values cannot be conceived in isolation, but instead must take this cultural clash very seriously.

In the days where the future of universities is seen by many to lie in the virtual world, and where education is often reduced to a commodity, we need to understand the core competencies of residential, research-based universities. Community-based learning (e.g., as explored in the courses-as-seeds model) is a promising approach to evolve and enrich courses by allowing students to act as *active contributors* and not just as passive consumers. Cultural change, beyond the adoption of new technologies, is required in our current system in which students have been taught to take on the role of consumers of education. This change will require innovation and risk-taking by faculty members.

Community-based learning approaches in university education provide learning opportunities for academics and companies. While enculturation into the companies' CoPs is seen as the main mechanism for student learning, students often mediate between university and company practice. Because the students are coached by their advisors during their experience in the company, students carry ideas back and forth between the CoPs within companies and academia. Companies get glimpses of innovative ideas from academia, and researchers get feedback on the applicability of their concepts. This boundary-spanning activity is specifically intense when the students have been enculturated before in academia.

Considerable theoretical and practical problems still exist, however, when implementing community-based learning approaches at a residential research university. On a theoretical level, the different concepts discussed in Sect. 2 need to be better integrated and elaborated. By comparing practice theories with the concept of SC, Duguid (2003, 2005) offers interesting theoretical insights. On a practical level, we need to gain more experiences and develop guidelines for an appropriate course design. A still-open question is, under which circumstances CoPs/NoPs theories offer a better framework for community-based learning, compared to CoI-inspired approaches to span the boundaries between the university's and companies' practices on the one hand, and among different companies' practices on the other.

Even though these theoretical and practical problems still exist, we already can draw some conclusions from our experiences. The establishment of community-based approaches to university education is based on (academic) visibility and a sufficient level of SC. The enculturation processes require substantial efforts from companies as well as from students. Companies feel rewarded only when their proposed project turns out to be successful. Mutual trust between companies and academia needs to be built over time through cooperation in successful projects. A certain reputation built through various regional activities is instrumental in getting the process started. Regional networking activities and the joint acquisition of research projects have turned out to be an important means of building SC. In the future, we will extend this community-building effort, including our network of alumni. To offer appropriate learning opportunities to their students, therefore, academics will have to build and maintain a dense web of social relationships.

Acknowledgments We thank (1) the members of the Center for LifeLong Learning and Design at the University of Colorado, who have made major contributions to the conceptual framework described in this paper; (2) the colleagues from the University of Siegen and RWTH Aachen, with whom the courses in practice have been developed and realized; (3) Sharon Derry (University of Wisconsin), who collaborated with us to develop the concepts of transdisciplinary education; (4) Kenneth P. Morse (MIT), whose kind invitation allowed us to experience practice-based education at the Sloan School's Entrepreneurship Center; (5) the following companies: Billiton, Siegen; Buhl Data, Neunkirchen; Domestic, Siegen; and Media Dialog, Siegen, for their cooperation within the CiP education program of the University of Siegen; and (6) David Tietjen (Drexel University), who edited the final version.

The research was supported by (1) the National Science Foundation, Grant REC-0106976 "Social Creativity and Meta-Design in Lifelong Learning Communities"; (2) the Coleman Institute, Boulder, Colorado, USA; (3) the German American Fulbright Commission, which provided a scholarship for Volker Wulf; and (4) the German Federal Ministry for Education and Research (bmb+f), which funded the research projects "Wissensprojekt Informatiksysteme im Kontext – Vernetzte Lerngemeinschaften in gestaltungs- und IT-orientierten Studiengängen (Wisspro)" (Fkz.: 08 NM 052A) and "Virtuelles Software Engineering Kompetenzzentrum (VSEK)" (Fkz.: 01 IS C39E).

References

Ackermann, M., Pipek, V., & Wulf, V. (Eds.). (2003). *Sharing expertise: Beyond knowledge management*. Cambridge, MA: MIT.

Arias, E. G., Eden, H., Fischer, G., Gorman, A., & Scharff, E. (1999). Beyond access: Informed participation and empowerment. In C. Hoadley (Ed.), *Proceedings of the 1999 conference on computer support for collaborative learning. Designing new media for a new millennium: Collaborative technology for learning, education, and training* (pp. 20–32). Palo Alto, CA.

Arias, E. G., Eden, H., Fischer, G., Gorman, A., & Scharff, E. (2000). Transcending the individual human mind – Creating shared understanding through collaborative design. *ACM Transactions on Computer Human-Interaction*, *7*(1), 84–113.

Bennis, W., & Biederman, P. W. (1997). *Organizing genius: The secrets of creative collaboration*. Cambridge, MA: Perseus Books.

Bereiter, C. (2002). *Education and mind in the knowledge age*. Mahwah, NJ: Erlbaum.

Bourdieu, P. (1985). The forms of capital. In J. G. Richardson (Ed.), *Handbook of theory and research for the sociology of education* (pp. 241–258). Westport, CT: Greenwood.

Brown, J. S., & Duguid, P. (1991). Organizational learning and communities-of-practice: Toward a unified view of working, learning, and innovation. *Organization Science*, *2*(1), 40–57.

Brown, J. S., & Duguid, P. (2000). *The social life of information*. Boston, MA: Harvard Business School Press.

Brown, J. S., Duguid, P., & Haviland, S. (1994). Toward informed participation: Six scenarios in search of democracy in the Information Age. *The Aspen Institute Quarterly*, *6*(4), 49–73.

Bruner, J. (1996). *The culture of education*. Cambridge, MA: Harvard University Press.

Cannon, D. M., & Leifer, L. J. (1999). Product-based learning in an overseas study program: The ME110K course. The Second Mudd Design Workshop – Designing Design Education for the 21st Century, Harvey Mudd College, Claremont, California, May 17–19, 1999. Available at http://sll.stanford.edu/projects/me110k/HarveyMuddPaperAnnot.pdf

Clark, H. H., & Brennan, S. E. (1991). Grounding in communication. In L. B. Resnick, J. M. Levine, & S. D. Teasley (Eds.), *Perspectives on socially shared cognition* (pp. 127–149). Washington, DC: APA.

Cohen, D. & Prusak, L. (2001). *In good company: How social capital makes organizations work*. Boston, MA: Harvard Business School Press.

Coleman, J. C. (1988). Social capital in the creation of human capital. *American Journal of Sociology*, *94*, 95–120.

Collins, A., Brown, J. S., & Newman, S. E. (1989). Cognitive apprenticeship: Teaching the crafts of reading, writing and mathematics. In L. B. Resnick (Ed.), *Knowing, learning, and instruction* (pp. 453–494), Hillsdale, NJ: Erlbaum.

Csikszentmihalyi, M. (1996). *Creativity: Flow and the psychology of discovery and invention*. New York: HarperCollins.

dePaula, R., Fischer, G., & Ostwald, J. (2001). Courses as seeds: Expectations and realities. *Proceedings of the second European conference on computer-supported collaborative learning* (pp. 494–501). Maastricht, Netherlands: University of Maastricht.

Derry, S. J., & Fischer, G. (2005). Toward a model and theory for transdisciplinary graduate education. Paper presented at *the meeting of the American Educational Research Association*, Montreal, Canada. Available at http://l3d.cs.colorado.edu/~gerhard/papers/aera-montreal.pdf.

Duguid, P. (2003). Incentivising practise. Position paper for the Institute for Prospective Technological Studies of the European Commission. *Workshop on ICT and social capital in the knowledge society*, Seville, Spain, November 2–3.

Duguid, P. (2005). The art of knowing: Social and tacit dimensions of knowledge and the limits of the community. *The Information Society*, *21*, 109–118.

Engeström, Y. (2001). Expansive learning at work: Toward an activity theoretical reconceptualization. *Journal of Education and Work*, *14*(1), 133–156.

Fischer, G. (1998). *Creating the university of the 21st century: Cultural change and risk taking – Consequences of and reflections on teaching an experimental course*. Unpublished manuscript. Available at http://l3d.cs.colorado.edu/~gerhard/reports/cu-risktaking1998.pdf

Fischer, G. (2001). Communities of interest: Learning through the interaction of multiple knowledge systems. In *The 24th annual information systems research seminar in Scandinavia* (pp. 1–14), Ulvik, Norway.

Fischer, G. (2002). Beyond 'couch potatoes': From consumers to designers and active contributors. In *FirstMonday*, Issue 7. Available at http://firstmonday.org/issues/issue7_12/fischer/

Fischer, G. (2006). Distributed intelligence: Extending the power of the unaided, individual human mind. In A. Celentano (Ed.), *Proceedings of the advanced visual interfaces (AVI) conference* (pp. 7–14). New York: ACM.

Fischer, G., & Giaccardi, E. (2006). Meta-design: A framework for the future of enduser development. In H. Lieberman, F. Paternò, & V. Wulf (Eds.), *End user development: Empowering people to flexibly employ advanced information and communication technology* (pp. 421–452). Dordrecht, The Netherlands: Kluwer.

Fischer, G., Scharff, E., & Ye, Y. (2004). Fostering social creativity by increasing social capital. In M. Huysman & V. Wulf (Eds.), *Social capital and information technology* (pp. 355–399). Cambridge, MA: MIT.

Fischer, G., Giaccardi, E., Eden, H., Sugimoto, M., & Ye, Y. (2005). Beyond binary choices: Integrating individual and social creativity. *International Journal of Human-Computer Studies (IJHCS)*, *63*(4/5), 482–512. Special issue on Computer Support for Creativity.

Florida, R. (2002). *The rise of the creative class and how it's transforming work, leisure, community and everyday life*. New York: Basic Books.

Gardner, H. (1991). *The unschooled mind*. New York: Basic Books.

Granovetter, M. (1973). The strength of weak ties. *American Journal of Sociology*, *78*(6), 1360–1380.

Greenbaum, J., & Kyng, M. (Eds.). (1991). *Design at work: Cooperative design of computer systems*. Hillsdale, NJ: Erlbaum.

Grow, G. O. (1991/1996). Teaching learners to be self-directed. *Adult Education Quarterly*, 41(3), 125–149.

Hollan, J., Hutchins, E., & Kirsch, D. (2001). Distributed cognition: Toward a new foundation for human–computer interaction research. In J. M. Carroll (Ed.), *Human–computer interaction in the new millennium* (pp. 75–94). New York: ACM.

Huysman, M., & Wulf, V. (Eds.). (2004a). *Social capital and information technology*. Cambridge, MA: MIT.

Huysman, M., & Wulf, V. (2004b) Social capital and IT – Current debates and research. In M. Huysman & V. Wulf (Eds.), *Social capital and information technology* (pp. 1–16). Cambridge, MA: MIT.

Illich, I. (1971). *Deschooling society*. New York: Harper and Row.

Janis, I. (1972). *Victims of groupthink*. Boston: Houghton Mifflin.

John-Steiner, V. (2000). *Creative collaboration*. Oxford, UK: Oxford University Press.

Jonassen, D. H., & Mandl, H. (Eds.). (1990). *Designing hypermedia for learning*. Berlin: Springer.

Kolmos, A., Fink, F. K., & Krogh, L. (Eds.). (2004). *The Aalborg PBL Model – Progress, diversity and challenges*. Aalborg: Aalborg University Press.

L3D. (2006). *Center for lifelong learning and design homepage*. Boulder, CO: University of Colorado. Available at http://l3d.cs.colorado.edu/.

Lave, J., & Wenger, E. (1991). *Situated learning: Legitimate peripheral participation*. New York: Cambridge University Press.

Lorden, J., & Slimowitz, J. (2003). NSF workshop examines the future of graduate education. *CGS Communicator*, *36*(5), 3–5.

Mumford, E. (1987). Sociotechnical systems design: Evolving theory and practice. In G. Bjerknes, P. Ehn, & M. Kyng (Eds.), *Computers and democracy* (pp. 59–76). Aldershot, UK: Avebury.

Mumford, E. (2000). Socio-technical design: An unfulfilled promise or a future opportunity. In A. Sloane & F. van Rijn (Eds.), *Proceedings of the IFIP TC9 WG9.3 international conference on home oriented informatics and telematics, "IF at home: Virtual influences on everyday life": Information, technology and society* (pp. 45–60). Devender, The Netherlands: Kluwer.

Nahapiet, J., & Ghoshal, S. (1998). Social capital, intellectual capital, and organizational advantage. *Academy of Management Review*, *23*(2), 242–266.

National-Research-Council (2003). *Beyond productivity: Information technology, innovation, and creativity*. Washington, DC: National Academy Press.

Noam, E. M. (1995). Electronics and the dim future of the university. *Science*, *270*(5234), 247–249.

Nonaka, I., & Takeuchi, H. (1995). *The knowledge-creating company: How Japanese companies create the dynamics of innovation*. New York: Oxford University Press.

Norlin, G. (1935). Norlin's speech on charge to the graduates. Available at http://ucblibraries.colorado.edu/about/norlin.htm

Norman, D. (2001). In defense of cheating. Available at http://jnd.org/dn.mss/InDefenseOfCheating.html

Pea, R. D. (2004). The social and technological dimensions of scaffolding and related theoretical concepts for learning, education, and human activity. *The Journal of the Learning Sciences*, *13*(3), 423–451.

Putnam, R. (1993). The prosperous community: Social capital and public life. *American Prospect*, *13*, 35–42.

Rittel, H. (1984). Second-generation design methods. In N. Cross (Ed.), *Developments in design methodology* (pp. 317–327). New York: Wiley.

Rogoff, B., Matsuov, E., & White, C. (1998). Models of teaching and learning: Participation in a community of learners. In D. R. Olsen & N. Torrance (Eds.), *The handbook of education and human development – New models of learning, teaching and schooling* (pp. 388–414). Oxford, UK: Blackwell.

Rohde, M., Klamma, R., & Wulf, V. (2005). Establishing communities of practice among students and start-up companies. In T. Koschmann, D. D. Suthers, & T. W. Chan (Eds.), *Proceedings of CSCL 2005. Computer support for collaborative learning: The next 10 years!* (pp. 514–519). Mahwah, NJ: Erlbaum.

Rohde, M., Klamma, R., Jarke, M., & Wulf, V. (2007). Reality is our laboratory: Communities of practice in applied computer science. *Behavior and Information Technology (BIT)*, 26(1), 81–94.

Salomon, G. (1993). *Distributed cognitions: Psychological and educational considerations*. Cambridge, UK: Cambridge University Press.

Saxenian, A. (1994). *Regional advantage: Culture and competition in Silicon Valley and Route 128*. Boston, MA: Harvard University Press.

Scardamalia, M., & Bereiter, C. (1994). Computer support for knowledge-building communities. *The Journal of the Learning Sciences*, *3*(3), 265–283.

Schön, D. A. (1983). *The reflective practitioner: How professionals think in action*. New York: Basic Books.

Shaffer, D. W. (2004). Pedagogical praxis: The professions as models for post-industrial education. *Teachers College Record*, *106*(7), 1401–1421.

Simon, H. A. (1996). *The sciences of the artificial*, 3rd ed. Cambridge, MA: MIT.

Snow, C. P. (1993). *The two cultures*. Cambridge, UK: Cambridge University Press.

Suchman, L. A. (1987). *Plans and situated actions*. Cambridge, UK: Cambridge University Press.

Turkle, S., & Papert, S. (1991). Epistemological pluralism and the revaluation of the concrete. In I. Harel & S. Papert (Eds.), *Constructionism* (pp. 161–191). Norwood, NJ: Ablex.

URAP. (2006). Undergraduate research apprenticeship program. Available at http://l3d.cs.colorado.edu/urap/

Vygotsky, L. (1986). *Thought and language*. Cambridge, MA: MIT.

Wenger, E. (1998). *Communities of practice – Learning, meaning, and identity*. Cambridge, UK: Cambridge University Press.

Winograd, T., & Flores, F. (1986). *Understanding computers and cognition: A new foundation for design*. Norwood, NJ: Ablex.

Chapter 13
Sustaining a Community Computing Infrastructure for Online Teacher Professional Development: A Case Study of Designing Tapped In

Umer Farooq, Patricia Schank, Alexandra Harris, Judith Fusco, and Mark Schlager

Abstract Community computing has recently grown to become a major research area in human–computer interaction. One of the objectives of community computing is to support computer-supported cooperative work among distributed collaborators working toward shared professional goals in online communities of practice. A core issue in designing and developing community computing infrastructures – the underlying sociotechnical layer that supports communitarian activities – is sustainability. Many community computing initiatives fail because the underlying infrastructure does not meet end user requirements; the community is unable to maintain a critical mass of users consistently over time; it generates insufficient social capital to support significant contributions by members of the community; or, as typically happens with funded initiatives, financial and human capital resource become unavailable to further maintain the infrastructure. On the basis of more than 9 years of design experience with Tapped In – an online community of practice for education professionals – we present a case study that discusses four design interventions that have sustained the Tapped In infrastructure and its community to date. These interventions represent broader design strategies for developing online environments for professional communities of practice.

Keywords: Sustainability; Community of practice; Participatory design; Social capital; Human–computer interaction

Introduction

Community computing refers to sociotechnical interventions and infrastructures that support community interactions and civic activities among people sharing common resources (Carroll, 2001). For example, the Blacksburg Electronic Village community computing infrastructure supports a Web-based network that hosts local, online community information and activity (Carroll, 2005). Community computing, in general, supports human–computer interaction and computer-supported cooperative work (CSCW) among community members, both local and distributed, working toward shared goals.

J.M. Carroll (ed.), *Learning in Communities*,

A core issue in developing and maintaining community computing infrastructures is sustainability. Many community computing projects fail because the underlying infrastructure does not meet end user requirements; the community is unable to maintain a critical mass of users consistently over time; there is insufficient social capital to support significant contributions by community members; or, as it typically happens with funded community computing initiatives, financial and human resources become constrained or even unavailable to adequately maintain the infrastructure. When community activities and practices are supplied hierarchically, such as by formal institutions, instead of developing organically and being maintained by the community, they are often construed as belonging to others and are typically underutilized (Rheingold, 1993; Schuler, 1996). As a result, the community fades away and its infrastructure fails.

In this paper, we present a case study of successfully and iteratively designing and sustaining a community computing infrastructure. Our case study is an online environment called Tapped In® (http://tappedin.org/) that supports activities of a large and diverse community of distributed education professionals. Drawing on more than 9 years of participatory design experience with Tapped In users, we present design interventions that were introduced in the Tapped In community to sustain its computing infrastructure. Our participatory design interactions with the Tapped In community have enabled end users to articulate problems and propose high-value improvements to the infrastructure. These recommendations, in turn, have enabled Tapped In designers to continually improve the infrastructure over time.

Our contribution in this paper is a case study analysis of developing Tapped In. Specifically, we present four design interventions that have helped sustain the Tapped In community computing infrastructure. These interventions represent broader design strategies for developing online environments to support professional communities of practice. These design interventions and strategies would be of interest to software designers and community computing developers.

In the following section, we present our conceptual framework with respect to prior literature. We explain our participatory design methodology and research methods in the section "Methodological Approach and Research Methods." The section "Background of Tapped In" provides background of Tapped In that sets a historical context for our case study. In the section "Case Description and Analysis," we present four design interventions that have been successful in sustaining the Tapped In infrastructure and its community of users. Under the section "Discussion" three broader strategies for technology design to support online communities of practice are discussed.

Related Work

Over the past several years, we have been developing and refining the Tapped In infrastructure, which is intended to support the online activities of a large and diverse community of education professionals. The community of practice framework (Lave & Wenger, 1991; Brown & Duguid, 1991; Wenger, 1998; Orr, 1996; Cothrel

& Williams, 1999) has guided us over the years to develop online teacher support activities and the community computing infrastructure to support such activities. Communities of practice are described as emergent, self-reproducing, and evolving entities that are distinct from, and frequently extend beyond, formal organizational structures, with their own organizing structures, norms of behavior, communication channels, and histories. Members often come from larger professional networks spanning multiple organizations, drawn to one another for both social and professional reasons.

The community of practice framework suggests that a teaching professional's community of practice can have a direct (positive or negative) impact on professional growth through various forms of informal collegial interactions (Barab & Duffy, 2000; Brown & Duguid, 2000). The recognition that communities of practice can play an important role in professional learning has spurred a great deal of interest in how to harness the power of such communities in the context of systemic school reform and professional development projects. Researchers (Garet et al., 2001; Smylie et al., 2001; Loucks-Horsley et al., 1998; Little, 1990; Stein et al., 1998), practitioners (Wilson & Berne, 1999; Rényi, 1996), and policymakers (President's Committee of Advisors on Science and Technology, 1997; National Commission on Mathematics and Science Teaching for the 21st Century, 2000) are converging on a shared vision of effective teacher professional development as more than a series of training workshops, institutes, meetings, and in-service days. It is a process of learning how to put knowledge into practice through engagement within a community of practitioners.

A major part of the challenge in designing and developing community computing infrastructures is *sustaining* the infrastructure and its critical mass of users over time. The theme of sustainability has long been addressed from different perspectives in the community informatics literature. Merkel and colleagues (2005) provide an overview of what sustainability means in community computing settings. Broadly, sustainability is centered on how people in community computing settings can best achieve their goals consistently over time. According to Merkel and colleagues (2005), this question has been asked in different ways, with researchers and practitioners focusing on (a) the feasibility of various models and the physical, social, and technical requirements that must be in place to ensure technology access to citizens (Clement & Shade, 2000; Benassi et al., 2004); (b) the role of the government in addressing issues that affect the public good, such as providing access to government information through Web portals and to the Internet itself, especially for marginalized members of society who may lack the resources or training necessary to access such services (Doody, 2004; Musgrave, 2004; Malina & Ball, 2004; Rideout & Reddick, 2004; Schauder et al., 2004); (c) outcome-based approaches that study factors needed to encourage long-term changes in the lives of users (Gordon & Gordon, 2004); and (d) sociotechnical investigations of information technology adoption and features of one's social network (e.g., social capital) that tend to support or inhibit technology adoption (Day & Cupidi, 2004; Prell et al., 2004).

For Tapped In, our concern with sustainability is related to developing design interventions to keep up with the changing needs of our community of users. Our mantra has been that design interventions that enhance end user participation and interaction with the designers of the community infrastructure can lead to sustainability. When end users have a greater stake in the community computing infrastructure, they feel empowered as they have the ability to guide design, and they are actively engaged in discussions with peers and designers, motivating subsequent community interaction and contribution.

Previous literature outside the domain of teacher professional development has looked at factors that motivate participation (Lampe & Johnston, 2005; Lakhani & Hippel, 2003; Ling et al., 2005) and enhance sociotechnical capital (Resnick, 2002) in online communities. Our interest lies in enhancing participation and social capital between end users and designers of the community in order to foster collective initiatives to improve the underlying community computing infrastructure.

The work most closely related to our investigation is the practitioner-oriented set of design lessons by Amy Jo Kim (2000). Kim proposes specific design principles that characterize successful, sustainable online communities. We reiterate five of Kim's design principles that we have used directly to design the four interventions for Tapped In that we present in this paper.

- *Build flexible, extensible gathering places:* Online gathering places provide a flexible medium for end users and designers to work together to evolve and continually define and articulate the purpose of the community.
- *Design for a range of roles:* As the community grows, it will become increasingly important to provide guidance to newcomers while offering leadership and ownership opportunities to more experienced members.
- *Develop a strong leadership program:* Develop a leadership program because community leaders are the fuel in the community – they greet visitors, encourage newbies, teach classes, and answer questions.
- *Facilitate member-run subgroups:* To grow a large-scale community, provide technologies to help community members create and run subgroups to drive member loyalty.
- *Create and maintain feedback loops:* Successful community building is a constant balancing act between the efforts of management (designers) to plan, organize, and run the space and the ideas, suggestions, and needs of community members.

Our integrated conceptual framework draws inspiration from the various pieces of literature mentioned earlier, especially Kim's design principles. Our framework has been developed over several years to support professional collaboration and peer support among teachers (Schlager & Schank, 1997; Fusco et al., 2000; Schlager et al., 1998, 2002; Tatar et al., 2002; Derry et al., 2000). The major conceptual components of our framework that we directly leverage in this paper are as follows:

- *Multiple interaction formats and technologies*. Our framework calls for a range of tools and workspaces that (a) support work practices of large numbers of different groups; (b) enable users to know with whom they are interacting and what is going on around them; (c) allow users to create, store, and share discourse objects (e.g., notes, overhead slides); (d) communicate in real time or asynchronously, as the need arises; and (e) engage in group activities hosted by designers as well as their own circle of colleagues.

- *Identity and trust.* User profiles and induction activities are aimed at building trust in the system and developing a strong sense of community and group identity.
- *Ownership and empowerment.* The framework facilitates a sense of ownership and empowerment in the community by encouraging members to contribute to community activities and resources, assist other members, and use the online environment to support their own collaboration with others.
- *Heterogeneity.* A key indicator of community health is the participation of a population with diverse interests and a range of expertise. The framework encourages the participation of teachers at all levels and from all disciplines, as well as district staff, researchers, university faculty and students, staff developers, and administrators.
- *Community management, leadership, and sustainability.* No professional community can be sustained without management and committed community leadership. Recognizing and rewarding informal leadership and centralizing community management can help coordinate activities across projects, increase efficiency, and create economies of scale.

One facet of our research deals with understanding the kinds of online activities and content that teacher professional development organizations can develop to achieve their goals and support teachers more effectively (Schlager et al., 1999). A second facet of our research, which is thc focus of this paper, addresses the issue of sustainability with respect to the long-term and evolving design interventions that allow the online teacher professional development community to engage in participatory design with the designers of the infrastructure.

Methodological Approach and Research Methods

Our methodological approach most closely resembles participatory design. Participatory design is a practice among design professionals that explores conditions for user participation in the design of technology (for detailed discussions, see Clement & van den Besselaar, 1993; Greenbaum & Kyng, 1991; Kensing & Blomberg, 1998; Schuler & Namioka, 1993). Participatory design, as it is referred to in human–computer interaction and CSCW, has its roots in sociotechnical systems theory (Mumford, 1983). Historically, Emery and Trist (Emery & Trist, 1960; Emery, 1993) were pioneering thinkers in understanding the importance of including the membership of a community in the design process.

Our approach to participatory design brings end users and designers together in mutual commitment, where users learn about what computer technology can do for them and designers learn about the application domain in order to build a flexible and efficient system to fit the users' needs (Bjerknes, 1993). Most of our participatory design interactions occur online in an asynchronous manner.

Our participatory design approach also has a flavor of action research. We assume that the end users who are scrutinized in our research and are potentially affected by our research can be, or can be qualified to become, co-researchers. Overall, our methodological approach can be described as a design experiment, in which our investigation includes research to design professional activities and technical capabilities that we conjecture will help establish and sustain online teacher professional development communities.

Since the Tapped In project started in 1996, it has spawned many different smaller projects (e.g., theses and dissertations). It is difficult to briefly describe how data were collected, analyzed, and evaluated over such a long period of investigation. For the purposes of this paper, we refer to snapshots of our efforts with data collection, analysis, and evaluation that have occurred during multiple instances in the 9 years of our research with Tapped In. These snapshots establish that we followed a rigorous and systematic research investigation.

Data Collection

Field research began in 1997 when Tapped In went online. We have used a multitude of quantitative and qualitative instruments in collecting data. Because our methodological approach was guided by participatory design mostly through online interactions, the primary methods of data collection were online observations recorded through field notes, surveys, activity logs, and interviews. Secondary sources of data included documentation (e.g., newsletters), archival records (e.g., e-mails), and physical artifacts (e.g., design mockups and scenarios).

As reported in Schlager et al. (1999), we have collected data for online member activities (e.g., objects they access, rooms they visit, when they log in and out). All Tapped In members are informed of such research data collection efforts when they apply for membership. Strict confidentiality is maintained, and the content of conversations is never recorded without additional explicit permission from the participants. The only exception is our After School Online (ASO) sessions, which are recorded and posted in Tapped In's transcript archive for Tapped In members and guests to access in the future. Participants are informed that by participating in an ASO session, they agree to the publication of their transcript.

Our membership and list of partners have grown steadily over time. As of January 1999, we had more than 2,500 members and an average of more than 60 logins a day. In July 2006, we had about 20,000 members and ~1,200–1,500 member logins a day. As membership has grown, the monthly login rate has remained steady at ~10–20% of the membership. For example, in July 1998, 378 different members (of 1,700+) logged in. In July 2006, 2,100 different members (of about 20,000) logged in. Members log in every day of the week and almost around the clock. Logins are relatively equally distributed from Monday through Friday and shrink by about two-thirds on weekends. Currently, about 40% of our members describe themselves as K-12 teachers and 25% are composed of researchers, university faculty and graduate students, staff developers, school support and administration staff, and preservice teachers. The remaining 35% describe themselves as "other."

Over the years, we have also held summer institutes, workshops, training sessions, and online seminars to expand our data collection efforts. One of our largest efforts started in summer 1997, when we were part of two 2-week summer institutes in July and August. We followed seven teams of two to four high school and/or community college teachers who attended each institute to gain hands-on experience with software and techniques used in earth and space science. Periodic follow-up online meetings with the 14 teams also occurred over the course of the school year. At least one representative from each of the 14 teams was asked to log in and report on their progress, obstacles, and lessons that they wanted to share with other teams. Transcripts of all the meetings were collected via Tapped In's automated transcript logging mechanism. We analyzed these meetings and learned a great deal in this research about how people learned to communicate, share information, and collaborate online. In the course of three meetings, we observed people being able to work and accomplish things online (Schlager et al., 2002).

We have also administered surveys with Tapped In users. For example, one such survey was developed to help us learn who our members are and how their experiences in Tapped In have affected their professional lives. We collected data on standard demographics and professional development activities, technology use, and Tapped In use, affordances, and barriers (Fusco et al., 2000).

Data Analysis

The data collected were analyzed by using the general analytic strategy of developing case descriptions (Yin, 2003). A descriptive approach was followed to help identify the complex stages of designing and sustaining a community computing infrastructure for Tapped In. Our perspective on participatory design guided our analysis of the data, reflecting important sociotechnical elements of designing the Tapped In infrastructure. However, the data were also used to inform the participatory design approach itself, in that the design emerged as an iterative process taking place throughout the data collection and analysis phases. For example, the designers and researchers of Tapped In addressed many features and bugs in the order end users prioritized them.

We have used discourse analysis on meeting transcripts to interpret our data (Schlager et al., 2002). As an example, one of our transcript analyses shows that even with a group that uses technology minimally over a period of several months, the structure of their meetings shifts from a focus on technology and group norms to a predominantly task-oriented focus, similar to dialogue captured in face-to-face meetings (Olson et al., 1992).

We have also coded our data to address specific research questions (Schlager et al., 2002). For example, with the data we collected from the summer institutes, a coding scheme was developed to quantify the structure and flow of the online meetings, based in part on studies of face-to-face dialogue in collaborative design group meetings (Olson et al., 1992). We coded each utterance and nonverbal action as an instance of one of several categories of discourse. As an example, the four most common categories of discourse that emerged were business focused, meeting management, technology related, and social.

Data Evaluation

To achieve rigor in our data analysis and interpretation, we triangulated the multiple sources of data collection. To ensure reliability and plausibility of our results, the Tapped In research group attended biweekly meetings to discuss their field observations. The research group included developers and designers with considerable experience in online communication technology. All members of the group reflected on the collected data to generate collaborative interpretations. Discussions related to design and improvements of the Tapped In infrastructure were the primary focus of these meetings. This process of collectively reflecting on data interpretations helped to remove individual researchers' subjective biases, thus increasing the reliability of data analysis. During our coding efforts, the transcripts were read by two researchers, who coded independently and then came together to calibrate their findings. Differences between the two coders' ratings were resolved by a third reviewer.

Because many of our research group members were geographically dispersed, we often used Tapped In ourselves as a communication and collaboration mechanism for our research meetings. We analyzed our meeting transcripts as well. These analyses revealed many episodes of knowledge building, mentoring, argumentation, and resolution, all key characteristics of productive group work. A research issue that we encountered in our multidisciplinary research group was learning each other's jargon and interpersonal styles (Schlager et al., 2002). We also had to develop our own norms for interacting as a dispersed group. We were all used to the social constructs of face-to-face meetings – rapid-fire dialogue, long monologues, whispered side comments, topic shifts – and the skills needed to break into the dialogue at just the right moment or guide a meeting through the items on an agenda. Online collaboration requires adjustments to these constructs and skills.

The data we present in the forthcoming sections have been anonymized. For screenshots, we have blocked out the last names of the participants. In some cases, staff members have given permission to leave their names unaltered.

Background of Tapped In

From 1996 to 2002, we developed and hosted the Tapped In Testbed, a MOO-based platform (Curtis, 1992) in which we cultivated a diverse education community of more than 20,000 members with the aim of understanding the nature and affordances of online communities of practice in the service of teacher professional development. Two critical pillars of the infrastructure were the establishment of a live Help Desk and a discussion series called ASO. We felt that greeting new members was an important first step in welcoming them into the Tapped In community. We established the Help Desk in the reception room for this purpose. Although the Help Desk was originally staffed by members of the research group, community members acknowledged its importance by adopting it to such a degree that it was eventually staffed primarily by volunteers. ASO was originally conceived of as a venue for our partner organizations and community leaders to reach out to teachers, but it grew over time into a way for members to meet others with similar interests, to gain comfort with the technology, and to develop online discourse and leadership skills in a low-pressure, motivating context.

To further support the key activities of an online community of practice and move forward with our research, we decided to abandon the MOO platform for a more modern, flexible, and extensible architecture. The MOO used an unsupported language, was single-threaded and hence scaled poorly, and was a text-based system at odds with the increasing use of multimedia to support online learning and collaboration.

Starting in mid-2001, we began working with our partners and community to incorporate new features and capabilities, including groups, discussion boards, and search, among others. We used a scenario-based, participatory design approach (Rosson & Carroll, 2001), bringing together a design team representing researchers, teacher educators, technology developers, regional education support providers, national teacher professional development organizations, and our core constituency, the Tapped In members. After a rigorous needs assessment process and multiple design iterations, mockups, and user tests, the resulting feature set and interface design were reified in a Web-based demonstration and a set of functional specification documents, including feature prioritization.

The development team chose open-source, scalable, Java-based solutions in which to implement a redesigned system that would be robust, versatile, and scalable. By building on open-source foundations, we benefited from and contributed back to existing development communities. We released a basic system for alpha testing ahead of schedule in September 2002. As a result of a second formal round of user testing, we made a major conceptual design change to the "place" metaphor employed in the user interface (Schank et al., 2002). We continue to develop features in the system based on suggestions by community members. Screenshots of the current system are shown in Fig. 13.1.

Case Description and Analysis

We presented a brief history of Tapped In's evolution. Many design interventions have been introduced in Tapped In's infrastructure to facilitate the participatory design process. In this section, we discuss four such design interventions that we

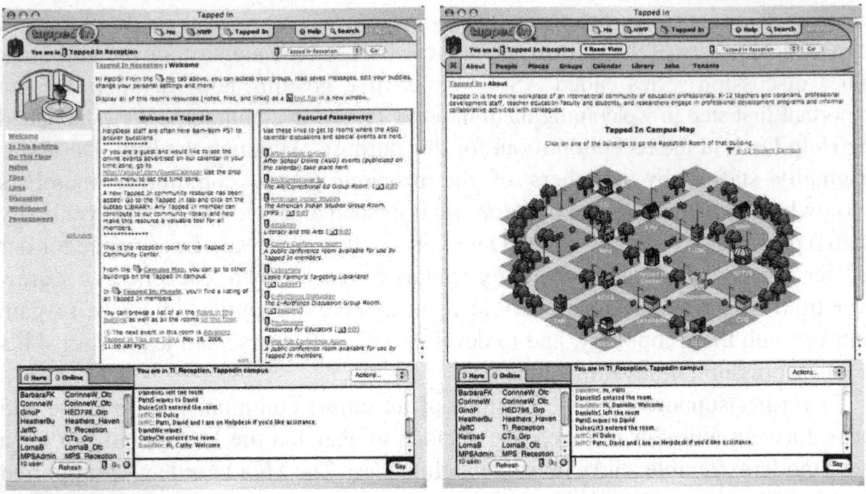

Fig. 13.1 Redesigned Tapped In user interface, with the addition of many new tools and services. Information tabs and navigation support are at the *top*; content and room tools are in the *center*; and awareness, chat, and instant messaging tools are at the *bottom*. Clicking a tab at the top overlays the tab content over the room until you close the tab overlay. The screenshot on the *left* shows the reception room and a variety of tools available in the room (notes, files, links, etc.). The screenshot on the *right* shows the campus map overlaying the reception room view

believe have been instrumental in successfully enhancing and sustaining the Tapped In community and its infrastructure. We believe these design interventions represent useful strategies for designers of online communities of practice.

Table 13.1 summarizes our contribution in this paper in terms of the four design interventions. We chose these specific interventions because they are significantly distinct from each other on at least four dimensions: goal of the design intervention, primary mode of communication, core participants (primary users of the design intervention), and implications for use. These interventions have allowed Tapped In community members to weigh in on and influence the design in the spirit of our participatory design methodology.

Contact and Bug Forms

An early design intervention through which Tapped In community members and guests (who did not create a Tapped In user name and password but could still log in) contributed to the design process was a submission form available on Tapped In's Web site. One part of the submission form, known as the contact form, was dedicated to contacting the staff for technical help, suggestions, and general comments. The second part of the submission form, known as the bug form, was specifically

Table 13.1 Design interventions summary

Design intervention	Goal	Primary mode of communication	Core participants	Implications for use
Contact and bug forms	To provide a feedback mechanism external to Tapped In	E-mail	Tapped In staff and peripheral participants (nonmembers and new members) who sent the communication	External feedback mechanism encourages participant buy-in and exploration of Tapped In features
Needed Features group	To provide an interactive discussion forum for Tapped In features	Group discussion board	Visiting groups (with read-only access; e.g., K-12 students), Needed Features group members (e.g., proactive educators), and any Tapped In member	Emphasizes an open line of communication between the Tapped In design team and community members (who own the group discussion)
Task list	To organize and prioritize enhancements to Tapped In features	Published document (PDF file) in the Needed Features group	Tapped In staff and core participants in Needed Features group	Feature development process becomes more transparent for Tapped In community members
Help Desk	To provide orientation and assistance to Tapped In members	Chat	Experienced Tapped In volunteers engaged in communication	Volunteers act as conduits between Tapped In community members and design team

used for reporting bugs. End user input from these two form submissions was e-mailed to a mailing list that several Tapped In team members monitored daily. Using contact and bug forms, Tapped In community members could establish direct communication with the designers and developers. Although users sometimes reported suggestions for new features or enhancements of existing ones that spawned e-mail discussions, the vast majority of submissions related to technical difficulties with lost passwords, chat configuration, and firewalls. However, community members did often engage the Tapped In design team in clarifying various features of the infrastructure. For example, the following was a request by one Tapped In community member:

> Date: July 3
> Subject: Saving info in my Music History Room
> Comment: I'd like to save ALL the information from my Music History Room, including discussions, postings, and mail to me. If I can't do this directly, how can I access this information in the future? I may have students come back at a later date for grade information …

The first responder to this request was Kari from the Tapped In design team. She did not know the exact answer to the query, and so she engaged the rest of the team within a couple of days. She sent the following message to the Tapped In team mailing list:

> Date: July 5
> Would archiving save this info for him? Or should he just keep renewing the group?

One of the other members of the Tapped In team, Patti, was also unsure how to answer the original query. To achieve consensus, she drafted a reply and asked for confirmation:

> Date: July 5
> Archiving will record the discussion messages and notes, I believe (right Zaz)? He'll lose any files that were attached, though. When he says "mail to me" that's totally separate from the group (I assume he means Saved Messages?)

In this message, Patti tries to engage another team member, Zaz, a programmer who developed the group archiving feature. Zaz has the final response to this internal discussion thread:

> Date: July 5
> That's right, everything is recorded (except perhaps folders? not sure about that) but binary files are deleted. So he'd have any metadata (title, description) but not the file itself.
>
> Saved messages have no relation to groups, and we don't keep records of any messages sent to the group (from About Us, e.g.) not via the discussion board.

The first respondent, Kari, finally replies to the Tapped In community member:

> Date: July 6
> You could either just keep renewing your group so that it does not expire or you could archive the group. Archiving will record the discussion messages and notes, but you'll lose any files that were attached.
>
> Let me know if this helps or if you have any further questions.

Such a discussion thread is a frequent occurrence within the Tapped In team. All design team members are active in promptly replying to end user queries. Such prompt action reinforces that Tapped In community members are important and that their queries are being addressed.

One of the most important ways to sustain a community infrastructure is to retain and increase critical mass by constantly engaging users to contribute to the infrastructure. Because the contact and bug forms are external to the Tapped In infrastructure – they are simply Web forms on the Tapped In Web site – the Tapped In design team also encourages end users to share their contribution and learning experiences with the larger Tapped In community. For example, in the following e-mail, an end user contacted the Tapped In design team to share educational Web resources:

> Thought your users/members would appreciate this information on our social studies curriculum involving the use of popular song lyrics to engage students and raise their aware-

> ness of important environmental, historic, social, and political issues as a prelude to action and activism.
>
> Our Web resource for teachers and students has recently moved to… http://www.learningfromlyrics.org/
>
> Be sure to check out numerous examples of student works including photos of the 2006 Student Memorial Projects in the Gallery Section… http://www.learningfromlyrics.org/gallery.htm
>
> and here's a recent Web posting about the student Memorial Projects… http://www.eltonjohnworld.com/coranto/news/2006/April/SittinginTheClassroom.html

The lead Help Desk member (part of the Tapped In design team) urged this end user to be a guest speaker in one of the Tapped In community sessions:

> What a wonderful resource! Why don't you present this information yourself as a guest speaker during one of the Tapped In After School Online discussions? I didn't see your name in the member directory, so that would be my first recommendation…
>
> I lead a monthly Arts and Literacy discussion (one is scheduled for July 3 at 7pm EDT/4pm PDT) and a monthly ArtsSites discussion that covers a variety of arts topics (your resources would fit nicely in either discussion). Please get back to me if you're interested in more information or would like to schedule a date and time to be a guest speaker.

The contact and bug forms have been instrumental over the years to serve as a medium for the Tapped In design team to interact with end user community members and achieve participant buy-in. Many characteristics of these forms have led to the sustainability of the Tapped In infrastructure. Prompt replies by the design team have reinforced the importance of the presence of community members. These replies have not just been one-way dialogue. They have led to constructive discussion threads and have engaged end users in exploring further features of Tapped In, a mechanism that encourages the community to keep coming back. Involving end users in community-wide sessions has also helped to ensure that, ultimately, Tapped In is co-directed by the larger end user community and the design team.

Needed Features Group

As Tapped In has evolved, community members and guests have also taken advantage of the infrastructure's new features to create additional avenues by which to inform the designers of their suggestions, frustrations, and experiences interacting with the online environment and its denizens. For example, a prominent Tapped In community member used groups and discussion boards to foster a lively subcommunity expressly to provide a place for other community members to contribute their thoughts on the design of Tapped In. This group, "TI2 Needed Features," evolved into a valuable resource for the Tapped In team (TI2 refers to Tapped In, version 2.0). An important characteristic of this group is that it was not created by the Tapped In design team but rather by one of Tapped In's community members.

Kathleen, who created this group in 2002, was motivated to incorporate features from Tapped In's predecessor MOO-based system.

Because the Needed Features group is public and open, any member in the community can join and post to the group's discussion. These discussions include musings on the differences between the old and new systems, bug notifications, wish lists for new features, and feedback to the staff on recently introduced features. The simple "me too" recurrence of the same request or the enthusiasm expressed by users helps the Tapped In team decide how to prioritize the implementation of new features and assess which features from the old system are most sorely missed. The group also provides a means for staff to announce when new features are made available, allowing for an informal beta test before the feature is mentioned in the monthly newsletter or advertised by Help Desk volunteers. This open line of communication also engenders a positive feedback cycle in which users feel that the Tapped In team is attuned to their needs and informs them as progress is made and features are prioritized. The Tapped In team has directly experienced the gratitude of community members when they post their thanks after the introduction of a new feature.

The following are two typical examples of discussion threads in the Needed Features group that document the interplay between the community and the design team. The first example (see Fig. 13.2) shows an unsolicited feature request from a user for foldering and hyperlinks within note text and the responses from a member of the design team letting the group know the priority of the features requested and when they were completed.

The second example (see Fig. 13.3) comes from several prominent Tapped In community members, emphasizing the need for being able to create K-12 student groups. This example demonstrates the open lines of communication between users and the design team and illustrates that the urgency of the needs of these users is taken into account when prioritizing and implementing features and enhancements to the system.

In 2003, we created a technological mechanism to allow K-12 teachers to bring their students online. Many teachers had asked whether they could bring their students online, and then a discussion about the wish for this feature came up (in the TI2 Needed Features room). Tapped In staff wanted to create a way that would make it safe for the students and also keep them from entering and disrupting the Tapped In community. (We imagined that some teachers might view Tapped In as a sanctuary from students.)

While we were creating the technology that would give K-12 students their own special accounts and a place of their own to interact in the system, we also created a group room for the teachers who would be bringing their students online so that they could easily find others who were doing so. We imagined that they would want to discuss how the technology could be used in new, interesting, and effective ways. This was a deliberate effort to increase the social capital among a subset of members and the first time we had invited people to join a group because of an action (getting a K-12 student group room) they took in the system. The invitation to join was automatic during the K-12 group creation process.

TI Needed Features : Discussion : View Thread

Discussion > Resolved (This folder is for requests and suggestions that have been addressed)

Show Message Subjects Only

Hyperlinks and files folders
posted by Susan *on Aug 21, 2003, 1:53 PM PDT* reply

It would be great if we could put a hot hyperlink on a note. This way we could leave specific links for different people or groups.

Also, I really need a way to sort my files my topic. I know that would mean another layer of folders, but it would help me.

You guys are great--it's an awesome place.

There are 3 replies to this message.

Re: Hyperlinks and files folders
posted by Zaz Harris (ZazH) *on Aug 21, 2003, 2:12 PM PDT* reply

Hi Susan,

I'm sure you'll be pleased to know that both of these items are on our to-do list (and both are medium high priority)

Zaz

Re: Hyperlinks and files folders
posted by Zaz Harris (ZazH) *on Mar 28, 2004, 2:01 AM PST* reply

We don't have file folders yet, but url's work in notes and discussion posts (since January). Let me know if there are any other text areas that you think we missed...

zaz

Re: Re: Hyperlinks and files folders
posted by Zaz Harris (ZazH) *on Aug 13, 2004, 4:17 PM PDT* reply

Folders are live! (For files, links, discussion threads, and notes)

Fig. 13.2 A discussion thread in the TI Needed Features group room, showing a request for foldering and hyperlinks

Student Center
posted by Kathleen *on Sep 16, 2003, 9:50 AM PDT* reply

The urgency for the Student Center to be completed continues to grow for me. Is there anyone else that is in the same need? I have groups of teachers I have trained in Global Learning that would greatly benefit from being able to do their projects with students in an isolated area for students. Any news?

There are 6 replies to this message.

Re: Student Center
posted by Zaz Harris (ZazH) *on Sep 16, 2003, 11:07 AM PDT* reply

That's all I'm working on right now, all day every day.

Re: Re: Student Center
posted by Kathleen *on Sep 16, 2003, 11:32 AM PDT* reply

Bless you Zaz - keep us posted when that ribbon is ready to be cut and I'll bring the refreshments and a big gold metal for you

Re: Re: Student Center
posted by Jim *on Oct 26, 2003, 8:06 PM PST* reply

Thank you...I have wanted to try online Science forums for awhile now. Its great to see it up and running. Hope to do a training with a small group of students by Nov. 11 or 12

Re: Student Center
posted by Zaz Harris (ZazH) *on Oct 2, 2003, 5:15 PM PDT* reply

I've finished the bulk of this and we're closing in on a first pass. I think we'll definitely have something live in the next week or two. You may have already noticed the student campus!

Re: Student Center
posted by Zaz Harris (ZazH) *on Oct 21, 2003, 1:20 PM PDT* reply

K-12 Student groups are LIVE! We don't have any documentation yet, but I'll try to stay online when I can to answer questions. To create a student group, go to the Groups tab and click "Create a K-12 Student Group".

Re: Student Center
posted by Zaz Harris (ZazH) *on Oct 30, 2003, 6:31 PM PST* reply

Wednesday, November 5
* Special! Student Center Grand Opening
4:00-5:00pm PST/7:00-8:00pm EST
http://ti2data.sri.com/ti2web/calendar/ti2nov03.html#ti2

I'll be there to answer questions and take suggestions...

Fig. 13.3 A discussion thread in the TI Needed Features group room, showing a request for K-12 student groups

Currently, there are 310 K-12 group rooms in Tapped In and 446 members in the group to support teachers interested in bringing their students online. In early 2004, a member learned that it was possible to bring K-12 students online, and that there was a group to support teachers doing this, and asked whether she could work with and support the teachers in the group room. We were delighted to have a member take charge in this way. The member was a doctoral student and an education consultant. Previously, she was a middle school teacher, a curriculum developer, a professional development facilitator, and an education researcher.

Task List

As development of the redesigned Tapped In began to ramp up in 2001, the number of features to implement and bugs to fix rapidly became too high to manage without some formal process. The Tapped In design team created a list of these items, the initial purpose of which was simply to record the features and bugs. However, the list soon also came to function as a mechanism for designating a priority category (ranging from 1 (high) to 4 (low)) to each item, assigning items to individual developers, establishing the status of each item (e.g., in progress), and organizing items into types (e.g., enhancement vs. bug). As development continued, this priority list was continuously updated and added to as new features were dreamed up, bugs were reported, and the design of the new system was refined. Eventually, the list was also used to estimate development time and record how long items took to be completed. With the small Tapped In design team and the varied nature of the items (e.g., features vs. bugs), a simple Excel document with a single individual as the primary gatekeeper was easier to maintain than a more sophisticated bug-tracking system such as Bugzilla (http://www.bugzilla.org/).

Table 13.2 shows a part of the task list. Darker colored rows indicate high-priority items. The tasks in the list are also organized according to three categories (not shown in the table): ongoing tasks, possible vendor bugs, and completed tasks/unverifiable bugs.

The task list is shared among the Tapped In design team. One person maintains the list for synchronization purposes. The team members typically e-mail about new tasks and/or talk about them face-to-face to clarify the scope and identify the best person to do the task. The developers estimate the time, and management sets the priority. During periods of intense development, the Tapped In team meets at least weekly to discuss the task list and prioritize tasks. In times of sparse development (such as when funding is low), the team focuses on tasks requiring the least time and cost.

The following is an exchange of e-mails within the Tapped In team to discuss addition of new features. The original e-mail thread started off with the following:

> Here are some top features Zaz and I came up with for TI2 … any you want to add? Do the estimates look right?

For private messages, make it easy to delete multiple messages, e.g., add select all and delete selected buttons (1 day?)

Buddies Tab working (5 days?)

Login Aliases (2 days?)
Calendar Search (2 days?)

Implementing Resources jsp for TI2 (3 days?)

Implementing Newsletter jsps for TI2 (3 days?)

Preference for timestamps (hide/show) in transcripts (1 day?)

User Reaper (3 days?)

Allow custom header/footer for login and registration pages (2 days?)

Integrate search indexing into results for discussion, other (5 days?)

Make "new" marker smart (new to you) (5 days?)

The following reply from one of the developers reassessed one of the features and estimated times for all the tasks:

I would double all those estimates :-)

Is "transcript access via Web" worthy of this list?

Once Tapped In users began to migrate from the MOO-based system to the new one and as they became a source of input – particularly via the Needed Features group – the developers found themselves frequently referring to the task list when communi-

Table 13.2 Sample rows from the task list

No.	Task	Category	Type	Status	Pri.	User req.	Who	Est. time (Days)
563	Tenant default room image	Edit room	2 – Feature	4 – Implement	1	1	Zaz	0.5
15	Tenant Tab Libraries (Files, etc., tabs in Directory)	Room items	2 – Feature	2 – Specify	1	–	Zaz	4
494	Indexing rest of search	Search	4 – Optimization	5 – In progress	1	0	Larry	3
305	Transfer identity (discussion posts, saved messages)	Admin	2 – Feature	4 – Implement	2	0	Zaz	0.5
524	Make notifications either e-mail or saved message, not both	Async. comm.	5 – Enhancement	4 – Implement	2	–	Zaz	0.5
554	Check jobs are working properly	Back-end	1 – Bug	4 – Implement	2	NA	Zaz	0.5

cating with the community. As more active community members became aware of the existence of the priority list, it became obvious that the next logical step was to periodically publish the list to the community in the interest of strengthening and making more transparent the feature development process. In the following example, one of the Tapped In community members encourages the developer team to consider his improvements:

> Spent 2 plus hours on Tuesday participating and observing two of the sessions in the TI2 Launch Festival. Exciting to see the level of interest and to see the activity. The two sessions I participated in were well attended – 40 plus and 50 plus people in attendance.
>
> I hope you don't mind, but I noted some issues that I ran into while using the system and, where appropriate, took the liberty of offering my ideas for addressing them. I know that given resource constraints, you are very limited in terms of what you can afford to do, but I wanted to capture my observations so that you have a record. Please accept as food for thought as you move ahead with the system.
>
> …[suggestions]
>
> Fred

The Tapped In team was prompt in replying to this e-mail and explicitly referred to the task list. For instance, in reference to the private message window icon in Tapped In, one of the developers replied with the following:

> each time the private message icon is clicked whether previously opened or not, it should be given focus and moved to the foreground. [Fred's suggestion]
>
> Hmm, this may be on our list, I'll check. [Developer's response]

For one of the other features (a help button in Tapped In), the developers realized that it should be put on their list:

> Explore the possibility of creating a separate help button outside of the "Actions" menu that spawns a small window in which the help can be viewed statically and concurrently with the Chat window. [Fred's suggestion]
>
> Good idea; we can put that on our list. [Developer's response]

The list is an Excel file, so publishing it as an uneditable PDF file in the Needed Features group room is a straightforward task. To enhance the usefulness of the task list, we recently began recording for each item the number of times it is mentioned or requested by Tapped In users. Keeping in tune with the needs of the community and prioritizing the items on the list are particularly critical, given the small development team and the minimal funding for Tapped In. As such, sometimes larger, more complicated items that may not be as frequently used drift down the list in favor of more pressing needs, which often are "low-hanging fruit" – that is, smaller features or fixes that make a large difference to users.

Overall, we consider the use of the task list a success for systematically monitoring feature updates to the infrastructure. The task list is also helpful as a tangible resource when communicating with the Tapped In community. Most important, we feel that the task list facilitates the management of tacit knowledge within the Tapped In developer and design team. Although documentation plays an important role in managing knowledge within an organization, it is often considered a "side task." The Tapped In team's view on the task list – a lightweight version of formal documentation – is that it promotes sustainability because it helps to legitimize less formal mechanisms of documentation.

Help Desk Volunteers and Long-Standing Members

Originally, in 1996–1999, Tapped In staff members were the leaders and managers of the community and were online continuously. However, as the community grew, the leadership and governance transferred (as is necessary for a successful community) to the community members. Tapped In staff members still take part in the community and know many community members well, especially the most dedicated and long-standing members. The community volunteers and leaders are highly dedicated and provide assistance and a warm welcome to new members for as many as 12 hours a day, sometimes more.

While they are online, these members help guests and new members get oriented, lead tours, provide technical assistance, and grease the wheels of the community in many other subtle ways. They are often present as members or guests arrive in Tapped In Reception for the first time, try out new features, or exclaim as they discover a useful aspect of the system. By helping scores of new members and guests every day, Help Desk volunteers become aware of misconceptions or problems users may have, perhaps indicating design choices of the system that require clarification or modification.

Problems and successes are communicated to the Tapped In design team through various means. There is no single formal process for Help Desk volunteers to report experiences and impressions, but the Tapped In team and the volunteer community are close-knit, and so they see each other regularly online and make themselves available to each other. Positive feedback and ideas for improvements are often communicated informally online or through e-mail. There is also a group room, Helpdesk Central, where some of the more formal communication occurs. Figure 13.4 illustrates information flow from a Tapped In staff member (Mark) to a core Help Desk volunteer (BJ), who in turn posts it to the Help Desk Central group room discussion board, where it is disseminated to the 54 volunteers who are members of the group.

In addition, there is a link between the Help Desk and the Needed Features group, since most of the Help Desk volunteers are members of the Needed Features group and add requests and suggestions there. In this way, Help Desk volunteers act as conduits between newer community members and the design team. Because the Help Desk volunteers have a great deal of experience with using the system, their comments are often given more weight as they can usually better articulate the feature request or frame an idea for a new feature and suggest how it might be integrated into the current design. Perhaps more important, the experienced volunteers can usually provide a concrete design rationale for a new feature and express why it supports the overarching goal of

Helpdesk Central : Discussion : View Thread

Show Message Subjects Only

Kudos to the Help desk!
posted by* BJ Berquist (CIC : BjB) *on May 2, 2006, 3:42 PM PDT

Hi, Everyone!

This email was forwarded to me by Mark Schlager, the director of Tapped In. If you ever doubt that you are providing an important service by being a helpdesk volunteer, read this message from Helen. For anyone thinking about spending some time at helpdesk, DO IT! We need you. The Tapped In membership is now over 19,500 with lots of newbies. Just one hour a week gives all the other regular helpdesk volunteers a much needed break.

Hugs, BJ
bjb@tappedin.org
=====================
From: Helen
Date: April 24, 2006

Dear all,

I joined the Tapped In community last night and I just wanted to write and say how impressed I am.

I am reaching the end of my training to be an ESOL teacher to adults in London, and want to exploit elearning as much as possible.

I love this site and the ability to tap in to 'resources' from around the world. The navigation is wonderful particularly the doors!!! - no rushing round school corridors from one 'class' to another, I also love the fact that I get an email with a transcript...... was there a special program used to set this up? I'm asking as I'd like to set up an ESOL learning site in the college where I teach, and would love to make it so my students can 'individualise' in the same way.

The people (BjB and DavidWE) manning your helpdesk yesterday were very friendly, welcoming and helpful and I had a wonderful tour of the site with MaryFT.

Although it will take a while for me to find exactly what I need, I can already see the potential is enormous.

Thank you for setting up this site and I look forward to many years of happy use.

Best

Helen.

Fig. 13.4 An example of positive feedback flowing through the close-knit Tapped In team and volunteer Help Desk community

the Tapped In community. All of these "extras" that an experienced member provides help the Tapped In design team to make better decisions about where to invest their limited resources.

The Help Desk volunteers are so much a part of the design cycle and so in tune with the community that they recently (October 2005) noticed a slight decrease in ASO session attendance and alerted Tapped In staff. Tapped In staff called a meeting of all interested members and held a brainstorming session about what could be done. Some members hypothesized that new technologies (e.g., audio or video capabilities, blogging tools, or a new look and feel) might make Tapped In more useful and interesting to members. Others thought that Tapped In was just fine as it was, but that more outreach had to be done by staff and volunteers. The solution will most likely require social infrastructure improvement, but new technologies also might help. The important thing is that through the mechanisms we have set up, developed, and allowed to grow organically, the community brings these issues to the attention of the Tapped In staff as they arise.

Summary

We have presented four design interventions (contact and bug forms, Needed Features group, task list, and Help Desk) that have contributed to the sustainability of the Tapped In infrastructure. We perceive these interventions as a measure of our success in iteratively designing the Tapped In infrastructure and keeping the community members interested in using the infrastructure for their online teacher professional development and social networking. Although the four interventions we presented may be considered as standard design practice, the value lies in their integrated use as participatory design mechanisms to enhance end user participation and interaction with designers.

The community design processes we established to collect feedback and suggestions from users have led to many improvements to the community infrastructure that supports Tapped In. These processes grew organically from minimal structures we had in place initially – such as simple contact and bug report forms – into a more complete feedback system of task lists, discussion boards, and interactions with Help Desk staff and long-standing members. These processes also help members feel ownership in the community: members feel that they are recognized, helpful, and contributing to a larger cause.

The design interventions introduced through the process of participatory design were instrumental in empowering the Tapped In community members. Data in the preceding sections indicated that end users had a stake in the design process and on many occasions drove this process. We think achieving such buy-in through participatory design is essential for maintaining and increasing the critical mass of users and improving the community computing infrastructure.

Discussion

Although the social sciences provide a rich body of theoretical and empirical literature about human behavior from a sociopsychological perspective, CSCW has rarely taken advantage of such research (Kraut, 2003). This is partially because CSCW is primarily a design-oriented domain (Farooq et al., 2006). Although our contribution in this paper is targeted to advancing the design science of developing sustainable community computing infrastructures, the design interventions we presented are interwoven with theoretical and empirical foundations acknowledged in prior literature.

In our previous work (Schlager & Fusco, 2004), we proposed several guideposts for technology design to support online communities of practice for teacher professional development. Here, we expand on these guideposts by reflecting on *three design strategies* that tie back to theoretical and empirical literature in community computing. These higher-level design strategies, as defined by Dourish (2001), comment upon the general characteristics of design interventions articulated in the previous section.

First, *investing in bonding social capital* is critical for maintaining feedback loops between community end users and designers. Putnam (1993) uses the phrase *bonding social capital* to refer to the relationships that are developed within a homogeneous community. For online communities of practice, such as Tapped In, one important aspect of bonding social capital between the end users and developers of the community computing infrastructure is the feedback that end users provide. This type of social capital grounded in participatory design (between end users and designers) is not typically discussed when people think about designing an online community and its potential social support or resources. However, we would argue that it is necessary to keep the community moving forward, improving its offerings and growing at the same time. Through our design interventions, we have facilitated the creation of social capital in the Tapped In community, evidenced by the steady growth of Tapped In users and their contributions in the online community. The Needed Features group is a good example of bonding social capital with the goal of getting feedback by the community; the group is led by Tapped In community members and serves as a primary channel for requesting new infrastructure features from the designers.

A second design strategy is to *provide multiple online gathering places* for engagement with a range of community end users. The need for communities in general to have a gathering place of some sort is well acknowledged. For face-to-face geographical communities, these gathering places might take the shape of coffee shops, bars, and bookstores. Oldenburg (1989) refers to these as *third places*, the first being home and the second being work. For distributed online communities, providing effective gathering places is a design challenge. On the Internet, a gathering place can be a mailing list, a chat room, a virtual world, a blog, or some combination of these spaces (Kim, 2000). Online gathering places, just like their geographical counterparts, nourish relationships, develop a sense of community, and promote social interactions (Kim, 2000). For online communities of practice, where participants can range from being legitimate peripheral participants to core members (Wenger, 1998), an important aspect is to design multiple gathering places for the different types of community end users. Tapped In provides such multiple gathering places. The contact and bug forms provide an asynchronous gathering place that caters to peripheral participants who may not have transitioned into core participants of Tapped In but still want to explore Tapped In features and weigh in on design. The Needed Features group and the Help Desk provide interactive gathering places for more committed and experienced Tapped In community members.

A third design strategy is to *reinforce leadership roles organically* from within the community. Community leaders perform organizing, governance, networking, brokering, and other social support services for the community (Lieberman, 1996; Spillane et al., 1999). They empower and sustain the community and maintain order and etiquette (Kim, 2000). Community leaders are instrumental in developing, managing, and participating in multiple overlapping social networks within and across community of practice boundaries (Wenger, 1998; Cothrel & Williams, 1999). A major difference from other online communities is that Tapped In facilitates organic growth of leadership rather than well-defined and highly structured leadership roles that are put in place by designers or administrators. Indeed, it is plausible that leadership by community members, who are intrinsically motivated to give back to the community, entails longer-term sustainable consequences than designing contrived and possibly constraining leadership roles. In Tapped In, for example, the Help Desk continues to be a viable option for developing organic leadership; it leverages experienced volunteers, who are self-motivated, as conduits between other community members and the design team.

Although community computing research in general has been discussed in CSCW, design work on community computing infrastructures has been less well documented. In this spirit, we have presented a rich history of a successful community computing infrastructure, Tapped In, to support an online community of practice for education professionals. We used a case study analysis to reflect on four design interventions that were instrumental in sustaining the Tapped In infrastructure on a community-wide scale for more than 9 years. The case study was not just technical in presentation but was based on our integrated conceptual framework, which emanated from broad and interdisciplinary, theoretical and empirical literature. The follow-up discussion points abstracted from our case study analysis represent broader design strategies that serve as a source for constructive debate and future investigation in the CSCW design community.

We are currently exploring the viability and application of our design interventions and strategies for other community computing infrastructures. On the basis of Tapped In technology, we started CLTNet (pronounced as C-L-T-Net; http://cltnet.org/) in 2003 as an online network to support the US NSF-funded (National Science Foundation) Centers for Learning and Teaching (CLTs). This network helps the CLTs share knowledge and resources, disseminate findings and expertise to the education community at large, and provide information on training, professional development, and job opportunities to teacher education researchers and practitioners. In contrast to the Tapped In community, the CLTNet community is quite small (~800 members) because of the limited number of people participating in CLTs. The meeting space is used infrequently and was intended primarily to support scheduled online events. Because CLTNet members rarely use the meeting space facilities (such as chat), there are fewer opportunities for informal interactions between CLTNet members and staff, less need for Help Desk staff (mainly to answer questions sent by e-mail), and far fewer feature requests received from the community. As such, we have noted that CLTNet has not grown into a community of practice to the same extent as Tapped In has.

It is important to acknowledge that not all online communities become communities of practice. CLTNet has similar technology support as Tapped In. Many members certainly make use of CLTNet resources for various activities, such as organizing courses, working groups, and events, but no community of practice has specifically moved into CLTNet to do its work. Why? It may be that the main users of CLTNet (university faculty and graduate students participating in a Center for Learning and Teaching) have existing communities of practice that are not fully defined or are not catered to by CLTNet. For example, many university professors in education belong to communities of practice through the networks of professionals that they or their universities have developed. Given the technologies available to them, they may not see a need to move their existing communities of practice to a specific online environment such as CLTNet. It also may be that their visions for their communities of practice are still being defined; certainly, a vision for a community of practice is key to success. We are continuing to leverage our Tapped In experience to investigate the successes and failures of our design interventions and strategies in other case studies such as CLTNet.

It was our intent in this paper to serve a broad audience of scholars interested in sociotechnical interventions that lead to the design of successful community computing infrastructures. We believe that our contribution is of value to researchers and practitioners interested in designing online communities and using information technology to build community capacity, enhance social capital, and achieve sustainability. In general, scholars in community computing can reuse our design interventions and strategies in their own research investigations to engage their communities of users and apply our design knowledge in their own contexts. We also recognize that, as architect Ludwig Mies van der Rohe is quoted as saying, "God is in the details." We conclude this paper with a few pragmatic details of our four interventions that, although perhaps not standard design practices, may benefit community computing practitioners in particular.

The first pragmatic detail is our practice of always closing the communication loop in order to establish and gain trust and confidence of end users in our leadership. We achieve this by respectfully responding to users who submit a bug, complaint, or suggestion, and as appropriate, informing the community concerning what is being done. If we cannot address the problem (e.g., solution is too costly) or choose not to address the issue at that particular time, we explain why. Explaining our rationale and theoretical underpinnings simply and succinctly typically quelled any anger or frustration on part of the end users. In some cases, the self-reflection we engaged in as a result of eliciting our rationale and theoretical underpinnings helped reinforce existing, or establish new, community policies.

Regarding our Help Desk, an important pragmatic detail is that although we envisioned it as helping users learn to use the system, in practice, it quickly became a set of services more aptly described as those of a doorman and concierge. The Tapped In team members shed the researcher and developer persona to put a friendly face on the community from the first moment a new member logged in (note that a vast majority of our users had never experienced a "chat room"). We tried to help with all questions people asked, regardless of whether the question or problem was professional, academic, or personal. This stance built tremendous good will and set the tone for all interactions among Tapped In members (we like to say that new members "imprinted" on the Help Desk staff). We believe that this is the chief reason Tapped In has had so few problems with inappropriate behavior.

Regarding prioritization of our task list, design teams must recognize that there is an inherent tension (especially with limited funding) between what the users want and what we ultimately prioritize on the list. It is easy to implicitly discount the priorities expressed by the community (after all, we are the experts!). We were able to recognize and overcome this bias by having a user ambassador on the core team who sincerely and consistently represented the will of the community in all design and development discussions.

Finally, we cannot emphasize enough the value of applying the adage "eat your own dog food" to every member of the design team. We were most effectual in identifying and fixing problems when we got frustrated trying to participate in an online group or activity. Moreover, we learned to understand what was truly important to the community by interacting with the members on their terms and on their virtual turf.

Acknowledgments We thank Melissa Koch and Larry Hamel for their contributions to our work and thoughtful comments on earlier drafts of this paper, Aaron Becker for helping us create an attractive and usable interface, and BJ Berquist, Kari Holsinger, and countless other volunteers for their ongoing help in making Tapped In a success. Critical revisions to the original manuscript would not have been possible without the valuable insights of several anonymous reviewers. This material is based on work supported by the United States National Science Foundation (NSF) under grants REC-0106926, REC-9725528, and ESI-0314484. Any opinions, findings, and conclusions or recommendations expressed in this material are those of the authors and do not necessarily reflect the views of the National Science Foundation.

References

Barab, S.A., and Duffy, T.M. (2000). From practice fields to communities of practice. In D. Jonassen and S. Land (Eds.), *Theoretical foundations of learning environments*. Mahwah, NJ: Erlbaum.

Benassi, M., De Cindio, F., and Ripamonti, L. (2004). Online communities: A costs vs. benefits analysis. Paper presented at CIRN 2004: Sustainability and community technology, Monash University, Prato, Tuscany, Italy.

Bjerknes, G. (1993). Some PD advice. *Communications of the ACM*, *36*(6), 39.

Boehm, B.W. (1981). *Software engineering economics*. Englewood Cliffs, NJ: Prentice-Hall.

Brown, J.S., and Duguid, P. (1991). Organizational learning and communities-of-practice: Toward a unified view of working, learning and innovation. *Organization Science*, *2*, 40–57.

Brown, J.S., and Duguid, P. (2000). *The social life of information*. Cambridge, MA: Harvard Business School Press.

Carroll, J.M. (2001). Community computing as human–computer interaction. *Behaviour and Information Technology*, *20*(5), 307–314.

Carroll, J.M. (2005). The Blacksburg Electronic Village: A study in community computing. In P. van den Besselaar and S. Koizumi (Eds.), *Digital cities 2003*. Lecture notes in computer science, Vol. 3081 (pp. 43–65). Berlin: Springer-Verlag.

Clement, A., and Shade, L.R. (2000). The access rainbow: Conceptualizing universal access to the information/communication infrastructure. In M. Gurstein (Ed.), *Community informatics: Enabling communities with information and communication technologies* (pp. 32–51). Hershey, PA: Idea Group.

Clement, A., and van den Besselaar, P. (1993). A retrospective look at PD projects. *Communications of the ACM*, *36*(6), 29–37.

Cothrel, J., and Williams, R. (1999). Online communities: Helping them form and grow. *Journal of Knowledge Management*, *3*(1), 54–60.

Curtis, P. (1992). Mudding: Social phenomena in text-based virtual realities. *Proceedings of the 1992 conference on the directions and implications of advanced computing*, Berkeley, CA. Available at http://citeseer.ist.psu.edu/curtis92mudding.html/

Day, P., and Cupidi, R. (2004). Building and sustaining healthy communities: The symbiosis between community technology and community research. Paper presented at CIRN 2004: Sustainability and community technology, Monash University, Prato, Tuscany, Italy.

Derry, S.J., Gance, S., Gance, L.L., and Schlager, M.S. (2000). Toward assessment of knowledge building practices in technology-mediated work group interactions. In S. Lajoie (Ed.), *Computers as cognitive tools II* (pp. 29–68). Mahwah, NJ: Erlbaum.

Doody, M. (2004). Social capital and community networking: Ethno-cultural use of community networking initiatives in Canada (phase I). Paper presented at CIRN 2004: Sustainability and community technology, Monash University, Prato, Tuscany, Italy.

Dourish, P. (2001). *Where the action is: The foundations of embodied interaction*. London: MIT Press.

Emery, F.E., and Trist, E.L. (1960). Sociotechnical systems. In C.W. Churchman and M. Verhurst (Eds.), *Management science, models, and techniques* (Vol. 2, pp. 83–97). London: Pergamon.

Emery, M. (1993). *Participative design for participative democracy*. Canberra: Australian National University, Center for Continuing Education.

Farooq, U., Fairweather, P.G., and Singley, M.K. (2006). Grounding CSCW in social psychology. In C. Ghaoui (Ed.), *Encyclopedia of human computer interaction* (pp. 257–260). Hershey, Pennsylvania: Idea Group.

Fusco, J., Gehlbach, H., and Schlager, M. (2000). Assessing the impact of a large-scale online teacher professional development community. In J. Willis (Ed.), *Proceedings of the 11th international conference of the Society for Information Technology and Teacher Education* (pp. 2178–2183). Charlottesville, VA: Association for the Advancement of Computing in Education.

Garet, M.S., Porter, A.C., Desimone, L., Birman, B.F., and Yoon, K.S. (2001). What makes professional development effective? Results from a national sample of teachers. *American Educational Research Journal*, *38*(4), 915–945.

Gordon, A., and Gordon, M. (2004). Sustainability and community technology: The role of public libraries and Gates Library Initiative. Paper presented at CIRN 2004: Sustainability and community technology, Monash University, Prato, Tuscany, Italy.

Greenbaum, J., and Kyng, M. (Eds.). (1991). *Design at work: Cooperative design of computer systems*. Hillsdale, NJ: Erlbaum.

Kensing, F., and Blomberg, J. (1998). Participatory design: Issues and concerns. *Computer Supported Cooperative Work (CSCW): The Journal of Collaborative Computing*, *7*(3/4), 167–185.

Kim, A.J. (2000). *Community building on the Web: Secret strategies for successful online communities*. Berkeley, CA: Peachpit.

Kraut, R.E. (2003). Applying social psychological theory to the problems of group work. In J.M. Carroll (Ed.), *HCI models, theories, and frameworks: Toward a multidisciplinary science* (pp. 325–356). San Francisco: Morgan Kaufmann.

Lakhani, K.R., and Hippel, E.V. (2003). How open source software works: "Free" user to user assistance. *Research Policy*, *32*, 923–943.

Lampe, C., and Johnston, C. (2005). Follow the (slash) dot: Effects of feedback on new members in an online community. *Proceedings of the international SIGGROUP conference on supporting group work*, Sanibel Island, Florida, November 6–9, 2005 (pp. 11–20), New York: ACM Press.

Lave, J., and Wenger, E. (1991). *Situated learning: Legitimate peripheral participation*. Cambridge, UK: Cambridge University Press.

Lieberman, A. (1996). Creating intentional learning communities. *Educational Leadership*, *54*(3), 51–55.

Ling, K., Beenen, G., Ludford, P., Wang, X., Chang, K., Li, X., Cosley, D., Frankowski, D., Terveen, L., Rashid, A.M., Resnick, P., and Kraut, R.E. (2005). Using social psychology to motivate contributions to online communities. *Journal of Computer-Mediated Communication*, *10*(4), Article 10. Available at http://jcmc.indiana.edu/vol10/issue4/ling.html

Little, J.W. (1990). The persistence of privacy: Autonomy and initiative in teachers' professional relations. *Teachers College Record*, *91*(4), 509–536.

Loucks-Horsley, S., Hewson, P.W., Love, N., and Stiles, K.E. (1998). *Designing professional development for teachers of science and mathematics*. Thousand Oaks, CA: Corwin.

Malina, A., and Ball, I. (2004). ICTs and community and suggestions for further research: Lessons learned from Scotland. Paper presented at CIRN 2004: Sustainability and community technology, Monash University, Prato, Tuscany, Italy.

Merkel, C., Clitherow, M., Farooq, U., Xiao, L., Carroll, J.M., and Rosson, M.B. (2005). Sustaining computer use and learning in community computing contexts: Making technology part of 'who they are and what they do'. *The Journal of Community Informatics* (online), *1*(2), 158–174.

Mumford, E. (1983). *Designing human systems*. Manchester: Manchester Business School.

Musgrave, S. (2004). Telematics in the context of community portals. Paper presented at CIRN 2004: Sustainability and community technology, Monash University, Prato, Tuscany, Italy.

National Commission on Mathematics and Science Teaching for the 21st Century. (2000). *Before it's too late*. Washington, DC: U.S. Department of Education. Available at http://www.ed.gov/americacounts/glenn/

Oldenburg, R. (1989). *The great good place*. New York: Marlowe.

Olson, G.M., Olson, J.S., Carter, M.R., and Storrosten, M. (1992). Small group design meetings: An analysis of collaboration. *Human–Computer Interaction*, *7*, 347–374.

Orr, J. (1996). *Talking about machines: An ethnography of a modern job*. Ithaca, NY: IRL Press.

Prell, C., Harrison, T., Zappen, J., and Hubacek, K. (2004). Sustaining community/building social capital: The case of connected kids. Paper presented at CIRN 2004: Sustainability and community technology, Monash University, Prato, Tuscany, Italy.

President's Committee of Advisors on Science and Technology (PCAST), Panel on Educational Technology. (1997). Report to the President on the use of technology to strengthen K-12 education in the United States. Available at http://www.ostp.gov/PCAST/k-12ed.html/

Putnam, R. (1993). The prosperous community: Social capital and public life. *The American Prospect*, *4*(13), 35–42.

Rényi, J. (1996). *Teachers take charge of their learning: Transforming professional development for student success*. NEA Foundation for the Improvement of Education. Available at http://nfie.org/publications/takecharge.htm/

Resnick, P. (2002). Beyond bowling together: Sociotechnical capital. In J.M. Carroll (Ed.), *HCI in the new millennium* (pp. 247–272). Reading, MA: Addison-Wesley.

Rheingold, H. (1993): *The virtual community: Homesteading on the electronic frontier*. Reading, MA: Addison-Wesley.

Rideout, V., and Reddick, A. (2004). Community digital divide sustainability: Who should pay and why! Paper presented at CIRN 2004: Sustainability and community technology, Monash University, Prato, Tuscany, Italy.

Rosson, M.B., and Carroll, J.M. (2001). *Usability engineering: Scenario-based development of human computer interaction*. Redwood City, CA: Morgan Kaufmann.

Schank, P., Harris, Z., and Schlager, M. (2002). Painting a landscape onto Tapped In 2. Paper presented at the CSCW 2002 workshop on the role of place in virtual community, New Orleans, LA. Available at http://tappedin.org/tappedin/web/papers/2002/TI2PlaceCSCW.pdf

Schauder, D., Stillman, L., and Johanson, G. (2004). Sustaining and transforming a community network. The Information Continuum Model and the Case of VICNET. Paper presented at CIRN 2004: Sustainability and community technology, Monash University, Prato, Tuscany, Italy.

Schlager, M., and Fusco, J. (2004). Teacher professional development, technology, and communities of practice: Are we putting the cart before the horse? In S. Barab, R. Kling, and J. Gray (Eds.), *Designing for virtual communities in the service of learning* (pp. 120–153). Cambridge: Cambridge University Press.

Schlager, M., and Schank, P. (1997). Tapped In: A new on-line teacher community concept for the next generation of Internet technology. In R. Hall, N. Miyake, and N. Enyedy (Eds.), *Proceedings of the second international conference on computer support for collaborative learning* (pp. 231–240). Hillsdale, NJ: Erlbaum. Available at http://tappedin.org/tappedin/web/papers/1997/NextGenCSCL.pdf

Schlager, M., Fusco, J., and Schank, P. (1998). Cornerstones for an on-line community of education professionals. *IEEE Technology and Society Magazine*, *17*(4), 15–21, 40. Special issue: Wired Classrooms: The Internet in K-12. Available at http://tappedin.org/tappedin/web/papers/1998/CornerstonesIEEE.pdf

Schlager, M., Schank, P., and Fusco, J. (1999). Online communities [Position Paper]. Presented at the CHI 1999 "Online communities" workshop, Pittsburgh, PA.

Schlager, M., Fusco, J., and Schank, P. (2002). Evolution of an on-line education community of practice. In K.A. Renninger and W. Shumar (Eds.), *Building virtual communities: Learning*

and change in cyberspace (pp. 129–158). New York: Cambridge University Press. Available at http://tappedin.org/tappedin/web/papers/2002/TIEvolution.pdf
Schuler, D. (1996). *New community networks: Wired for change*. Reading, MA: Addison-Wesley.
Schuler, D., and Namioka, A. (Eds.). (1993). *Participatory design: Principles and practice*. Hillsdale, NJ: Erlbaum.
Smylie, M.A., Allensworth, E., Greenberg, R.C., Harris, R., and Luppescu, S. (2001). *Teacher professional development in Chicago: Supporting effective practice*. Chicago, IL: Consortium on Chicago School Research.
Spillane, J.P., Halverson, R., and Diamond, J.B. (1999). *Toward a theory of leadership practice: A distributed perspective*. Evanston, IL: Northwestern University.
Stein, M.K., Silver, E.A., and Smith, M.S. (1998). Mathematics reform and teacher development: A community of practice perspective. In J.G. Greeno and S.V. Goldman (Eds.), *Thinking practices in mathematics and science learning* (pp. 17–52). Mahwah, NJ: Erlbaum.
Tatar, D.G., Gray, J., and Fusco, J. (2002). Rich social interaction in a synchronous online community for learning. In G. Stahl (Ed.), *Proceedings of the conference on computer support for collaborative learning*, Hillsdale, NJ: Erlbaum.
Wenger, E. (1998). *Communities of practice: Learning, meaning, and identity*. New York: Cambridge University Press.
Wilson, S.M., and Berne, J. (1999). Teacher learning and the acquisition of professional knowledge: An examination of research on contemporary professional development. In A. Iran-Nejad and P.D. Pearson (Eds.), *Review of research in education* (Vol. 24, pp. 173–209). Washington, DC: AERA.
Yin, R.K. (2003). *Case study research: Design and methods*. Thousand Oaks, CA: Sage.

Chapter 14
Expert Recommender: Designing for a Network Organization

Tim Reichling, Michael Veith, and Volker Wulf

Abstract Recent knowledge management initiatives focus on expertise sharing within formal organizational units and informal communities of practice. Expert recommender systems seem to be a promising tool in support of these initiatives. This paper presents experiences in designing an expert recommender system for a knowledge-intensive organization, namely the National Industry Association (NIA). Field study results provide a set of specific design requirements. Based on these requirements, we have designed an expert recommender system which is integrated into the specific software infrastructure of the organizational setting. The organizational setting is, as we will show, specific for historical, political, and economic reasons. These particularities influence the employees' organizational and (inter-)personal needs within this setting. The paper connects empirical findings of a long-term case study with design experiences of an expertise recommender system.

Keywords: Expertise recommender systems; Expertise sharing; Knowledge management; Yellow pages

Introduction

Approaches to knowledge management (KM) have attracted both practitioners and scholars in the field of organizations and IT. The basic assumption underlying this trend is that knowledge creation and distribution will become core processes in a complex, fast-changing world. However, the focus of research in knowledge management has shifted. Ackerman et al. (2003a,b) have proposed the concept of "expertise sharing" as a step beyond traditional KM approaches which mainly focus on the externalization of codified knowledge. To label these developmental stages, Huysman & de Wit (2004) recognize two distinct waves of knowledge management. The "first wave" of knowledge management concentrated on the analysis, modeling, storing, and retrieval of codified knowledge. These initiatives focused either on the knowledge of individuals or on knowledge management from a managerial perspective. IT tools were mainly designed to support acquisition and retrieval of codified knowledge to improve knowledge bases, i.e., also the externalization

J.M. Carroll (ed.), *Learning in Communities*,

of knowledge itself. By contrast, the "second wave" of knowledge management focuses on the tacit and emergent aspects of knowledge (on those forms which cannot be easily externalized), and on knowledge sharing within communities.

In a sociotechnical understanding of KM, the importance of IT tools is contested (e.g., Cohen & Prusak, 2001). The primary function of these tools is not to represent codified knowledge but to support processes of informal interaction within communities (e.g., communication tools, such as email or instant messaging, and tools that help to find partners for communication). Compared to first-generation knowledge management tools, little research on expertise sharing and expert recommendation has been conducted so far. Only few case studies distill technical requirements from real world settings (e.g., McDonald, 2000) or evaluate the impact of these technologies on organizational performance. Given our understanding of codified knowledge as just one relevant dimension of knowledge, it still needs to be investigated how knowledge sharing as a part of mundane work practices can be supported by appropriately designed technologies.

There are several challenges in investigating the fit of KM technologies designed for such purpose (Ackerman et al., 2003a,b; Huysman & Wulf, 2004; Lindgren et al., 2004). Employees often have different skills, goals, or cultural backgrounds which can lead to failures of IT systems (Pipek & Wulf, 2003; Normark & Randall, 2005). Even the successful application of new technologies can have unexpected individual or organizational outcomes that are contrary to the initial goals as Orlikowski (1996) and Pipek & Wulf (1999) describe.

Research in this area needs to explore specific organizational settings, identify requirements, introduce dedicated KM systems, and observe actors appropriating the system. The connection between a specific field of application and its design outcomes is another point of interest. The research area of KM is not yet mature enough to come up with general concepts. Instead, KM can be seen as a kind of mosaic that still needs to be further completed before one may hope to be able to identify "general patterns" in applying KM strategies.

In this paper, we present yet another mosaic stone – experiences when designing an expertise recommender system for the specific needs of a major European national industry association (NIA[1]). The design is based on a long-term field study. We outline basic requirements for KM derived from the field study and present a system which deals with the particularities of the identified problems. We conclude by discussing our design experiences.

Technical Support for Second-Generation Knowledge Management

There are several computer applications that have the potential to play a role within initiatives of second-generation knowledge management. Most of these applications are designed to overcome spatial or temporal boundaries by making

[1] "NIA" is actually not the real name but a pseudonym.

users aware of each other or of artifacts others have created. Among the systems that bridge spatial and temporal boundaries, topic- and member-centered communication spaces are common examples. While member-centered communication spaces, such as the Babble or Loops system presented by Ackerman & Halverson (2004), foster social ties in existing communities, topic-centered communication spaces, such as news groups, allow members (or guests) to exchange ideas and find solutions to given problems.[2] An important motivational factor to participate in topic-centered communication spaces seems to be the gain of personal reputation. Beyond pure communication, applications may foster knowledge exchange by offering virtual spaces which allow creating, developing, and storing of topic-centered materials. These repositories of materials are typically augmented with communication and annotation functionality (cf. Buckingham Shum, 1997; Stahl & Herrmann, 1999; Pipek & Won, 2000). Editing tools support the development of materials and may have additional functionality to distill content out of communication spaces (Ackerman et al., 2003a,b). The Answer Garden (cf. Ackerman & Malone, 1990; Ackerman, 1998) is one of the most influential approaches in integrating shared repositories within communication spaces. It was mainly built to encourage learning within organizations. While the general functionality of these systems may be similar, their concrete implementation is specific with regard to the topic under discussion and the application domain (e.g., Chapman, 2004). The systems discussed so far offer places in virtual space where human actors can direct themselves to and exchange knowledge through intended but informal communication.

By contrast, awareness features capture selected activities of individual actors and make them visible to their cooperation partners. Won & Pipek (2003) suggest the application of specific awareness services to make knowledge creation perceivable for others within an organization. Furthermore, they propose to collect users' data on these computer-supported activities, which are regarded as indications for their personal expertise. After different steps of aggregation, their Expertise Awareness mechanism supports finding human participants who possess a required skill profile which is dynamically updated.

We will now have a closer look at a case study of another class of applications in the field of second-generation knowledge management: *expert recommendation systems*. In this class of applications, the system suggests knowledgeable actors. Contrary to first-generation KM tools, these applications do not focus on externalizing and representing knowledge but on calculating the participants' level of expertise. These applications therefore require personal data of all users and domain-specific algorithms that can match actors appropriately.

Considering the latest approaches of KM applications, five *sources of personal data* have been applied to generate user profiles:

[2] Member-centered communication spaces may include some topic-centred functionality. However, their design assumes a rather stable group of users basically known to each other.

1. *Content of textual documents*: Documents that were written, read, or reviewed by a user appear to be an indicative source of data for users' expertise. Documents can include work reports, www-pages as well as emails or newsgroups postings. Systems such as *Who Knows* (Streeter & Lochbaum, 1988), *Yenta* (Foner, 1997), *Lotus Discovery Server* (Pohs et al., 2001), *MII Expert Finder* and *XperNet* (Maybury et al., 2003), *HALe* (McArthur & Bruza, 2003), or the *ExpertFinding Framework* (Reichling et al., 2005) automatically extract personal data about human interests or knowledge from text-based documents.
2. *Yellow pages (YP)/Directories:* Documents created with the specific intent to portray a human actor's interests and expertise can be a highly relevant source. In an E-learning platform, Becks et al. (2004) ground their matching algorithm partly upon a self-classification of the learners concerning their educational and professional background.
3. *Inscriptions into software artifacts:* Software – like many other artifacts – can contain inscriptions that allow referring to the expertise of its creator. Concepts of a programming language applied when realizing an application can indicate a programmer's skill level (Vivacque & Lieberman, 2000). Comments within the documentation of the source code can indicate who was responsible for the specific module (McDonald, 2000).
4. *Data on interaction history:* Structured data about a user's history in interacting with specific applications can be an indicator for his interests or expertise. Vignollet et al. (2005) proposes to make use of similarities in browsing histories for expert recommendation. In a similar way, Becks et al. (2004) presented an approach that is integrated into an E-learning platform. Interacting with certain learning modules out of a well-structured hierarchy of learning materials is interpreted as an indication of interest in that domain.
5. *Social network analysis:* Analyzing the user's social environment is another method of user assessment. The basic idea is that users who have collaborated in the past are likely to successfully collaborate in the future. Referral Web tries to support scientific communities based on an analysis of coauthorship in publications (Kautz et al., 1997a,b). McArthur & Bruza (2003) as well as Tyler et al. (2003) analyze email traffic to learn about social networks within organizations. The latter approach focuses on discovering Communities of Practice (CoPs) that coexist with the formal organizational structure. McDonald (2003) suggests integrating data of organizational structure and social networks into the algorithms for ranking potential experts.

Interestingly, almost all approaches on expert recommender systems are technology-driven – which means that the authors do not refer to any empirical study that grounds their design to real world practice. The major exception is McDonald's (2000) work. He analyzed in depth the related needs of a smaller sized medical software company. His tool's functionality is therefore very specific for this software company. However, he also abstracts some of his experiences into a software architecture for expert recommender systems (ER Arch). Groth & Bowers (2001) have challenged some assumptions underlying this architecture by means of a second case study conducted within a Swedish consultancy. Consultants showed patterns of behavior when searching expertise, which were not considered in ER Arch, e.g., choosing accessibility and availability for prioritizing which expert to contact. ER Arch suggests prioritizing experts solely according to data concerning expertise and personal/organizational relations between the information seeker and potential experts.

Due to the lack of empirical grounding, the discourse on expert recommender systems has not yet developed a sufficient understanding on the requirements in real world settings. It is also unclear which type of user profiles and matching algorithms will lead to acceptable matching results. Most of the expert recommenders stand alone in the sense that they collect the required user data from just one application. A more practice-oriented perspective could investigate how to integrate expert recommender systems into a given software infrastructure on specific fields of application.

In the following sections, we will present NIA as a case to explore the potentials of expert recommendation systems. Our research with NIA is still ongoing. We discuss findings from the first two stages of our longitudinal study. Up to this point, we have completed the design of the system based on a comprehensive field study and have implemented a first version of an expertise recommender system. Hence, the software design is based on results of an empirical study which put light on the requirements of different subjects within the underlying heterogeneous organization.

Setting

With almost 3,000 member companies from a large variety of different branches, NIA is one of the biggest confederations of industries in Europe. The association is divided horizontally into 37 sections, each dedicated to companies from a certain industry sector[3] (e.g., "agricultural technology," "lifts and escalators," or "pumps and systems," but all related to machine and plant construction) and vertically into general departments (e.g., "business administration," "law," or "taxes"). In addition, NIA consists of several spin-offs and other specific organizational units such as forums, projects, and regional offices. At the NIA headquarters, about 450 employees work in one of the organizations' sections or departments. Member companies pay for their membership according to their size. These fees are received directly by the corresponding sections. The sections pay a certain percentage of their fees for organizational overhead to finance the vertical departments (among other parts of the organization). The payments of member companies are the main source of income for NIA.

[3]In the following we will use the term "sector" in the sense of branch of industry, whereas "section" will refer to NIA's sectoral departments.

Member companies in turn are welcome to request NIA's services, when needed. NIA defines its core competencies as:

- *Networking* (introducing member companies to each other for business transactions)
- *Technical* or *professional support*
- *Representation* (lobbying at governmental (or other important) institutions – this kind of service is offered by NIA exclusively[4])

Knowledge management initiatives are regarded as a means to deal with a slight decline in membership registrations. While membership in an industrial association was given to companies in technical sectors during the past decades, companies today are expected to justify their expenses by claiming a "return on investment." This can be difficult to calculate for the membership in an organization "dealing" with *support*, *network*, and *representation.* So one of the projects goals is to better define and present its services to the members and to make NIA and its members "move closer to each other." This should be done by improving the mutual awareness of one another, i.e., the awareness of NIA's services on the members' side and the awareness of the members' needs on NIA's side.

An illustrative example should sharpen the project's vision. In short, when developing a new agricultural tractor, one member company got into trouble as they realized (after the design phase was over) that their machine did not conform to certain regulations related to its physical dimensions. This was a very costly error that could have been avoided by turning to NIA where this information was available. In turn, NIA was not aware of the company's intention of developing this kind of agricultural machine and thus was unable to inform the company. KM strategies are now expected to connect both NIA and its members more efficiently to each other in order to avoid situations like the one described. It is especially the communicative level of knowledge sharing between member companies and NIA that needs to be improved or at least supported.

However, there are also serious intraorganizational challenges in communication. As mentioned above, NIA consists of 37 sections which serve 37 sectors of national machine and plant construction industries. Earlier, many of these sections were autonomous associations and in the 1990s these former rivals were merging into a single organization. There is still a considerable level of rivalry remaining since many member companies are hardly associable with just one section of NIA.[5] Still, quite a number of sections consider members which they had enlisted long before the creation of NIA as their exclusive customers.

[4] Since about 10 years there are additional organizations which offer networking and knowledge services to – mainly small and medium sized – companies. NIA, however, is the only officially recognized industry representation in these branches. Thus, it can provide exclusive links to political committees and policy-makers.

[5] As an example, some agricultural companies need support from the "agricultural technology" and from the "pumps and system" section since many agricultural machines and tractors are additionally equipped with systems and machines that are developed by member companies of other sections.

The members' obvious advantage of being served by just a single section becomes a problem when deficits in communication within NIA lead to suboptimal services. So, in our field of application, it seems that two distinguishable challenges in knowledge management and especially in communication behavior exist. On the one hand, NIA has considerable problems in providing qualitative and quick help for their member companies. On the other hand, there are also KM problems among NIA sections which seem to be the main reason for the communication problem between the member companies and NIA.

Research Methods

The methodological approach taken in the field follows the theoretical framework of *Integrated Organization and Technology Development* (OTD). Wulf & Rohde (1995) and Rohde (2006) describe OTD as an evolutionary concept which tries to take technological, organizational, and human factors into consideration. As commonly known, the introduction and establishment of novel technology influences not only work processes but also organizational structures and human habits. Keeping that in mind, human and organizational needs have to be taken into account when new software solutions are supposed to support work practices. One particular characteristic of the NIA project is to implement technical opportunities for additional collaborative work processes. NIA's existing work processes often seemed to fail when employees looked for expertise beyond their own section, e.g., when answering a request of a member company. With regard to this general problem statement, our empirical study tried to deal with three specific questions. First, what are the relevant work processes within NIA? Second, why do they often seem to fail? And third, which alternatives could be envisioned and which type of technical support would be required? Through our field study we tried to understand the formal organization, the employees' *interpretation* of it, and the informal patterns employees apply in order to deal with these types of problems.

With regard to the empirical case study, we applied the OTD framework by employing the ethnomethodological concept of "Studies of Work" to focus on personal and interpersonal issues (cf. Flick, 2002: 39 ff; Bergmann, 2003: 129 ff; Harper et al., 2000). Beyond workplace observations, investigations into the technical infrastructure, and workshops on specific topics, our research included three cycles of 16 semistructured interviews conducted with 14 different employees and two managers of NIA. The majority of the employees worked in the agricultural section; the others worked in several vertical units such as the staff-, IT departments, or standardization committees. The two managers headed the agricultural section and the IT department, respectively.

In addition to the interviews, we conducted continuous field observations which we documented in written form. Central to our observations were KM-related work practices and the use of corresponding software applications. We also looked at the employees' (electronic) documents when conducting interviews and observations.

We observed mainly employees who took part in the interviews. Most of the "formal" observations took place in conjunction with the interviews or were carried out after the interviews were conducted. Since a researcher was present in the field at least twice a month for almost three years, observations happened additionally in an informal way. These sources provided further empirical material for analysis.

For each interview cycle, we created a particular interview guideline. This allowed us to modify the guidelines evolutionarily as we assimilated the experiences gained before. The guidelines included issues such as "everyday's life on the job," "working history within NIA" (both were main topics in cycle 1 which included six interviews), "communication and cooperation with others," and "knowledge management and expertise sharing" (treated already in cycle 1 but became the main focus in cycle 2 which included seven additional interviews). In cycle 3, technical and sociotechnical issues, such as problem solving and dealing with IT, were brought up in three more interviews.

The interviews lasted between 60 and 120 min. We set up the interviews in a relatively open and talkative manner, since guided questions were accompanied by narrative elements. By doing so, we had the opportunity to reflect upon the interviews with regard to the organizational and cultural environment. We recognize and situate our findings in an interpersonal, organizational context (cf. Randall & Bentley, 1994). Therefore, we tried to steer the interviews as little as possible, i.e., we followed an open-ended protocol. In order to guarantee solid and valid results, we used a tape recorder to avoid note taking during the interviews which would have influenced the fluency of the conversations negatively.

To facilitate data reduction and to spend time efficiently, we decided to split the analysis phase into five specific steps (cf. Schmidt, 2003):

1. Based on the written materials, we constructed "ex-post" categories for analysis. This categorization was mainly in line with the three aspects of OTD: technology, organization, and human factors; however, the specific subcategories resulted mainly from the interviews.
2. We put together the analytical categories to create a coding guideline which helped us to cluster the data in terms of meaningful units. Each unit focused on a specific problem.
3. We coded the material in order to make critical data anonymous and to generalize the data into meaningful patterns.
4. We constructed nodes of correlating units which provided a quantitative overview of the material. This also gave us a clue which questions and problems might be most prominent and urgent, and had to be reconsidered in later steps of the project.
5. Finally, we thought about possible hypotheses which had been derived from the previous steps of analysis. Based on those, we modified the guideline for the next interview cycle.

We employed the five steps mentioned above for each interview cycle. By doing so, we believe to have satisfied two important requirements: (1) participation of NIA's employees and (2) consideration for processes and practices.

Following the OTD approach, we also looked at the empirical findings from a design perspective. A part of the interviews was dedicated to "brainstorming and discussing KM solutions." In the beginning, we had only a very coarse vision of which KM strategy could be applied within NIA. In later interview sessions, we focussed on KM concepts which potentially offered a solution to problems already been identified. As a result of the empirical analysis, we came up with a set of specific design requirements for NIA. To evaluate their validity, we created mock-ups and early prototypes and discussed them with employees of NIA.[6]

Empirical Findings

After analyzing the interviews, certain issues appeared to be central in terms of KM. These issues can be roughly assigned to the domains of work processes, organizational transparency, and knowledge management. Here, we will focus mainly on those issues which have technical implications for the design of the expert recommender system. More detailed insights of the study are provided by Reichling & Veith (2005). In the following section, we will have a closer look at the results which form a starting point for deriving design requirements.

Working for Member Companies

The work of NIAs' employees (especially those of the agricultural sector) is dominated by a high and varying workload as targeted events (e.g., internal work groups, standards committee meetings, exhibitions, trade fairs) structure their work activities seasonally. The services directly delivered to member companies, such as technical support and representation, strongly depend on the members' requests and can hardly be anticipated in advance.

Handling customers' requests for help is an important task in the agricultural section. Responses in the interviews indicate that handling inquiries can often be reduced to "finding the right expert." In a first instance, employees try to find experts within their section. In particular cases, even contacts to member companies or ministries are utilized to answer certain questions. A few requests demand further inquiries or are delegated to other work units within the association. A common way to deal with costumer requests – as indicated in the interviews – is to sort them according to their "importance" for NIA.[7]

Especially newcomers find it hard to deal with this dynamic organization of knowledge work. Moreover, new employees are often overwhelmed by NIA's institutional complexity. In this domain, experienced employees have an advantage

[6] About 20 users participated in evaluating the expertise recommender. We conducted another 21 more interviews and workplace observations with users (some of them twice at different stages) during the evaluation period. These participants overlapped partly with those of the early empirical study.

[7] This importance is defined by two major criteria: first, the actual size of a member company, as the membership subscription is based on size, and second, by micropolitical considerations regarding the engagement of a member company within NIA's policies.v

over novices because they are already experienced in dealing with this structural labyrinth. Some of the interviewees claimed that the internal complexity is a result of NIA being created out of the merger of several independent associations.

Particularly in situations of urgent requests from member companies, knowledge about who has expertise in a certain field is crucially important. Participants described their expectations this way:

> "If we had a rough idea of what everyone is doing [within NIA] – which of course is unmanageable for 450 people – then for us this would be a giant step forward."

> "The goal is to create transparency. Responsibilities must be clearly defined and assigned unambiguously."

Due to the complex organizational structure and the missing transparency, it is not surprising that requests from member companies were redirected without being answered appropriately. Situations occur, as interviewees reported, where requests were handed over from one colleague to the next without being finally answered. It was considered to be difficult to identify actors possessing specific competencies, responsibilities, or skills within the organization.

Building and maintaining social networks is a task of central importance for NIA's employees. It was reported to take years to have established appropriate networks externally within the industrial sector and toward ministries as well as internally within the different sections of NIA. Moreover, once established, social networks cannot be simply transferred among NIA's employees.

Tools for Expertise Sharing

For internal networking purposes, NIA provides two tools that allow employees to seek for experts and maintain social networks: First, a printed catalogue lists internal experts for specific topics. In response to the question whether this booklet eases the search for experts within NIA[8] appropriately, some interviewees stated that it is often pure chance to find an expert within the booklet. The information was often outdated or imprecise.

Similar problems were identified when discussing the second tool, the central *Address Information Management System* (AIM). The AIM system suffered from being designed in order to meet diverse requirements defined by different organizational units. For instance, as one participant stated, she would like AIM to be capable for seeking persons within the organization carrying certain competencies or responsibilities. However, AIM's functionality did not allow this type of inquiries.

To compensate for the problems of AIM and the paper catalogue, we found an interesting approach. One employee described his way to manage external requests

[8] These experts may work in certain horizontal sections (e.g., the agricultural section) or in vertical sections (e.g., the IT or standardization department).

by means of a personal archive of contacts. He had built up this archive continuously over time by adding contacts and skills sets every time a human actor proved to be "useful." His archive allows seeking for skills and experts, but it was not commonly shared since the employee considers it to be his private property.

When discussing technical functionalities to overcome the given problems, the most illustrative suggestion was described as "Google for NIA," an extended *yellow pages system* (YP) that supports finding people based on an extended set of personal attributes, such as *activities*, *interests*, *experiences*, or *responsibilities*. One of the participants explained his vision in the following way:

> "It would be heaven, just to enter a keyword and then to get back exactly those ten experts [that I am seeking for]."

Yet another interviewee had a vision:

> "... that it becomes transparent, who's responsible for what, would be surely helpful. And this might be some kind of compliment for certain people; they can see themselves in a leading position within the organization (...). This can even be motivating."

In the latter quotation, another issue is addressed, namely, the interviewee gives a subtle reason for employees to take part in the system: People might feel some kind of "glory" when being assigned as an expert for a certain topic area. Such a feeling, as some interviewees stated, may improve the employees' motivation to keep their profiles up to date and to share their knowledge with others. As we see in the following subsection, the willingness to share expertise must not be assumed to be naturally given at NIA.

A controversial question with regard to YP systems in general is how to create and update the user profiles (cf. Ehrlich, 2003; Pipek et al., 2003). Since most of the interviewees typically worked under time pressure and high work load, it seems to be unlikely that they would update their profiles periodically. On the other hand, it became clear from the interviews that a YP system would not be used in case the stored user profiles appeared to be outdated or simply erroneous.

An alternative suggestion was made by one of the interviewees outlining the idea of a "virtual notice board." In her assessment, NIA was too complex to be effectively covered by a YP system. Her idea was to simply change from a "pull" to a "push" concept. By having such a virtual notice board, the system would no longer be required to seek people – but have the users themselves responding to the requests they feel qualified for. Even though the "virtual notice board" approach has obvious advantages over the Google idea, it is expected to lead to problems when urgent requests were to be handled. As another participant stated, it was impossible for him to wait for "someone who is willing to accept a request."

Obstacles to Expertise Sharing

When discussing KM strategies during the interview sessions, we primarily focussed on the management of human resources rather than of content. The concepts of a YP system ("Google for NIA") require the employees to actively take part in, i.e., share their knowledge/expertise which they must be willing and ready to do. Several interviewees found it perfectly natural to share their expertise with others and expected others to follow suit. Others, however, expressed good reasons not to do so. Additionally, some participants stated that the "potential of knowledge sharing" was highly overestimated.

As one participant assumed, KM was primarily required by the younger employees with limited experiences. These are the ones who could benefit most from "sharing" expertise. In contrast, some of the more experienced employees seemed to be more short-spoken with regard to expertise sharing. An interviewee stated that expertise sharing would endanger his status by "making his unique knowledge accessible for others." So he suggested that it could be a good idea to create incentives for sharing knowledge in the sense of monetary rewards. According to his assessment:

> "[…] everything inside my head is mine. And I must keep it to myself […] to increase or to keep up my market value."

Besides this obvious reason not to share his knowledge, other impeding factors of organizational or cultural nature were brought up by the same participant. As he stated, it was a typical behavior of some of his colleagues to "strut in borrowed plumes." They would solve certain problems with the help of colleagues within NIA, and thereafter declare it to be their own work. Therefore, colleagues with lower qualification appeared as "experts" who would be requested exclusively in future. Such behavior would reduce the colleagues' willingness to share their knowledge. In his eyes, the only way to make colleagues share their knowledge would be to pay them money (see above). Asked whether standardizations or guidelines (mandating colleagues to share expertise as part of their work) were capable of increasing the colleagues' willingness to share knowledge, he spontaneously responded that "guidelines are to be avoided."

Assuming that a YP system such as "Google for NIA" would be introduced, employees are expected to spend time on helping each other. Taking the workers' heavy workload into account, cooperation among colleagues could be fostered by creating a balance sheet to bill internal services. Some of the interviewees argued that such a balance sheet would make it easier for them to legitimate the amount of time spent on helping or cooperating with colleagues. Otherwise these efforts had to be labelled as "lost time."

Requirements for Technical Support

Based on the findings from the analysis phase, we discuss requirements for a KM tool. We will first summarize the requirements and then link them to appropriate system features. The subsequent section will describe the actual implementation of the expert recommender system for NIA which was designed to meet these requirements.

Basic Requirements

The empirical findings can be summarized as follows: NIA is a large organization with a decentralized internal structure consisting of 37 sections and several general departments. The boundaries among the sections are strongly developed. This is an effect of the organization's history since the sections were formerly independent associations. The mode of dividing the member fees within the organization further strengthens the independence of the different sections. Especially the section heads act in a highly self-determined manner.

The decentralized organizational structure fosters the dedication of NIA toward the individual branches. However, the strict borders between the sections lead to losses in potential synergies. Due to 37 sections and several other departments, the formal organizational structure within NIA is very heterogeneous and the relevant social networks – formal as well as informal – are very complex. Several interviewees stated that increasing mutual awareness about skills, expertise, experiences, and knowledge among the employees would be a "giant step forward."[9] Based on such an awareness, occasional sharing of expertise may happen which many (but not all) of the interviewees assumed to be highly promising. Our study shows that this awareness information is not yet available within the existing organizational and IT infrastructures. It is neither provided by the AIM database nor by the employees' catalogue. Employees requested an efficient and reliable search function (that is what the Google metaphor was used for) for appropriate experts in a given domain. However, we cannot assume that a sufficient amount of employees are willing to continuously or periodically update their profile data which "traditional" Yellow Pages systems would require. Hence, information about the employees' expertise needs to be extracted from well-chosen, indicative sources of existing data.

Indicators for Expertise

When considering expert recommender technology, we had to find appropriate indicators for human actors' expertise. With regard to the indicators found in the literature, our field of application offered the following opportunities:

1. *Content of textual documents:* Textual documents were a major means to report inside the sections and toward member companies. So, most of the employees created considerable amounts of textual documents as part of their daily work practice. For instance, project documentation, protocols, correspondence, or articles for the organization's Website could be widely found. Almost all textual

[9] It becomes obvious from the empirical findings that not only high level expert knowledge is requested. Even lower degrees and different aspects of "expertise" (namely interests, experiences, activities, or abilities) belong to the requested properties (cf. Hinds & Pfeffer, 2003 or Ackerman et al., 2003a,b).

documents were given in PDF or MS Office file formats such as Word, PowerPoint, or Excel. The textual documents were typically organized in a directory system hosted on the department's file server. Documents stored on local hard drives, though a rare phenomenon, do still exist.

Email was an important means of communication inside as well as outside NIA. Lotus Notes was commonly used as an email client and time scheduler.

2. *Yellow pages:* Except for the limited information AIM provided, NIA did not run any personal profile system. Personal profiles were updated, e.g., in case an employee moved to another office. However, employees found it hard to use AIM efficiently for matching people. AIM is – as its name indicates – a database to administrate address information; Neither did it function as a YP-system nor as an expertise recommender system.
3. *Social network analysis:* The organizational structure given by the sections plays a major role for expertise sharing inside NIA. However, the sections seem to be small enough that expert recommendation is not needed inside. Social network analysis might play an important role in sharing knowledge beyond the individual sections. For privacy reasons, we did not access email information (see below). Beyond email, there was not any other comprehensive base for social network analysis available.

Taking the given sources for data on the human actors' expertise into account, we decided to base a first version of the expert recommender system on textual documents. We assumed that a collection of textual documents would be a rather good indication of an employee's interests and expertise. Based on a choice of the employees' text documents, a keyword vector was derived using methods of automatic text analysis (see below). We also assumed that the given folder structure would make it easy for the employees to quickly and reliably select relevant and indicative documents from their working environment.

Since NIA did not have its own Yellow Page system, we decided to integrate a YP component into the expert recommender application. Employees could use it to create a personal expertise profile based on their self-assessments. We extracted the personal data as another indicator of an employee's expertise. Moreover, we presented this information when visualizing the list of experts found by the system. Beyond "ordinary" contact information, the YP component allows users to enter information describing their educational background, professional experiences, interests, and organizational involvement – properties which are relevant for expertise matching, as well.

Hence the users' expertise profile consists of two components: A YP component containing self-assessments that can be directly edited by the users and the keyword vector which is created automatically from a personal selection of the employees' text documents. Both profile components are distinct with respect to their content and the level of accessibility by the (other) users. So, these two components are likely to complement each other. The keyword vector which is supposed to contain several thousands of keywords adds to the self-assessments provided by the YP component. Its creation requires much less effort, since the employees just need to specify the folders from which the textual documents should be extracted.

Privacy Issues

Further requirements emerged from the legal situation in the German context. According to German law, the storage and exploitation of personal data, which can be used to monitor employees' behavior and performance, is a matter of workers' co-determination. Therefore, we designed a system architecture that allows the users to determine which of their documents or document folders should be taken as an indicator of their expertise (instead of an automatic selection of an employee's entire hard disk or the "My Documents" folder).[10] When documents or folders were selected to be an indicator of expertise, the system's client just extracts the keyword vector but does not upload the whole documents to the server. The system also provides a function to let the user manually delete specific items from the keyword vector in case of a misleading or privacy-threatening extraction. Hence, none of the user's documents is uploaded to the server or could be inspected by other members anyway. As a result, our system – unlike the original Google – does not actually support detecting documents, which makes the usage of the Google metaphor appear somewhat misleading at this point (an example of the systems output is given in the subsequent section). Finally, the keyword profile is uploaded at the explicit request of a user (when s/he has pressed the upload button).

For privacy reasons, we decided not to include email folders or time schedulers as indicators for expertise. While emails and scheduling information may be highly promising indicators for a person's interests and expertise, we assumed that their integration would be perceived as a violation of the actors' privacy. The question of how to preserve privacy without violating legal constraints or employees' attitudes needs to be further investigated within NIA after the systems roll out.

With regard to the YP component, similar methods of privacy protection are included: For each item that can be entered, its visibility can be set up to be: "not visible for others," "internally visible," or "externally visible." The last option is relevant in case member companies are connected to the system. This feature is described in more detail in the subsequent section.

Feedback Component

In order to guarantee reliable and trustworthy recommendations, the tool should provide some kind of "social control" to prevent negative or opportunistic behavior. For instance, users may handle other users' requests for help carelessly or let themselves inappropriately appear as experts in certain domains – as reported by employees during the analysis phase. The latter might be done by entering wrong or misleading personal information to the system or release misleading text documents.

[10] We believed that such a design approach would also improve the quality of the keyword vector since we included only relevant documents for matching.

In order to achieve some kind of social control, we include a feedback mechanism that allows users to evaluate the support they received from an expert.

Different "methods" of providing feedback can be implemented: Scores (i.e., from 1 to 5), tendencies (i.e., "+," "–," or "neutral"), or comments (i.e., free-style text of defined maximum length) are popular elements of user feedback in groupware systems. Another design issue concerning feedback mechanisms is the "degrees of freedom": Will users be able to provide negative feedback as well as positive? Or will negative feedback be indicated by lacking feedback or the lowest number of positive scores? And will other users have access to the feedback details (i.e., the comments)? In case they have, will they be provided with the overall number of feedback statements, such as the feedback ratio (positive feedback divided by the overall amount of feedback)?

Another problem may come up by different "feedback cultures." While some people are used to give honest and straightforward responses, others may use a euphemism to describe poor cooperation. Others in turn may intentionally return undeserved bad feedback in order to keep up their own "market value" compared to others (see section above).

In order to avoid this kind of behavior and eventual resulting conflicts, our feedback system does not permit negative scores. In detail, after a request is answered, the requestor is given the opportunity to score by assigning between one to five points (where one means "thanks for trying" and five means "great assistance") to each actor who was involved in answering. Assigning scores, however, is not mandatory. When feedback information is presented, the members' overall number of received feedback statements (and thus, the feedback ratio) is also displayed. We believe that only the combination of both values provides an impression of the actors' actual performance.

Bringing It All Together

Table 14.1 gives an overview of the central requirements mainly taken from our empirically derived scenario and describes the resulting recommender functionalities. The application can be described as a *text-based recommender system for expertise* inside NIA (and its member companies). Each user can provide personal information about himself, including typical yellow page information, such as contact information, a photo, and work-related information. We assume that most of the basic functionalities, i.e., text-based indication of expertise, would be relevant for the second application scenario, as well. However, the privacy-related functionality and the feedback mechanisms will probably need design adaptations with regard to the interorganizational setting.

The architecture of the system is designed in an extendible manner to allow more sophisticated recommendation strategies which include additional indicators of expertise. It allows integrating modules which connect a variety of different applications to access further types of personal data. For instance, in future system versions email content, interaction histories, Internet bookmarks or newsgroup postings may provide additional insights into the employees' expertise or interest.

Table 14.1 Requirements and potential according KM technology

Issues and requirements	Technical functionalities
Creating organizational transparency and gathering expertise-related information	Search for experts based on textual documents and YP data
Identifying competencies, abilities, and responsibilities	
Reflecting the potentially rapid developments in expertise, skills, and interests	Semiautomatic generation of user profiles
Preventing users from time-consuming profile updates	
Encouraging users' motivation and reliability	Feedback mechanisms
Handling sensible, expertise-indicating data in a trustworthy manner	Local creation and editing of expertise profiles; upload on users' explicit request
Ease of use and learning	Pure expertise recommender engine, no undesired extra functionality
Extendibility in terms of expertise indicators and matching functionality	Server *and* client rely on an open, modular architecture, allowing for extensions and adjustments
Interoperability with the existing IT infrastructure	*Web Service* interface for connecting other systems and databases

Appropriate modules capable of accessing these data sources can extend the system's ability to create indicative user profiles.

In order to enable interoperability with and integration into NIA's IT infrastructure, we included a *Web Service* interface into the system, allowing clients' access to the system via standardized interaction technologies and protocols like HTTP, XML, SOAP, and WSDL (Alonso et al., 2003). This technology allows for embedding expert recommender functionality into other applications such as AIM or NIA's Intranet Website. When analysing the KM needs within NIA, many interviewees pointed to the fact that they did not want to get yet another additional application. They felt already overwhelmed by the number of applications they were using. Web Service technology thus enables (limited) access to the system without installing the ExpertFinding's client application.[11]

Expert Recommender for NIA

We will now have a closer look at the implementation of the expert recommender system for NIA. It is a specific instance of a more widely applicable software framework which we call the *expert finding framework* (EFF) (cf. Becks et al.,

[11] The Web Service interface allows only for expertise recommendations. Since local creation of the users' keyword profiles is a central part of our approach and a Web Service would require uploading entire files, the client system still needs to be installed locally in order to generate and eventually edit keyword profiles before uploading them.

2004; Reichling et al., 2005). We will first outline the system's basic attributes. Afterward we will describe the most important and distinctive features in more detail. Finally, the application on the client side is presented.

Expert Finding Framework

EFF is implemented in Java using the Java 1.5 language specification. We rely on a client-server architecture (rather than on peer-to-peer architecture) since user profiles need to be stored on a central server instance in order to guarantee for continuous and quick access to expertise profiles even when clients are offline. Hence, the server-side application manages storage, update, and eventual deletion or renaming of user profiles. Furthermore, requests for expertise are handled by the server. In turn, the client-side application offers a user interface for editing the personal data, generating a keyword profile from text documents, generating requests for expertise, accordingly displaying the results (which may be seen as the realization of the Google metaphor), and managing emerging requests for help which are facilitated by the system. Both, server and client side applications allow for extensions ("plug-ins") in order to enrich the system's functionalities. This way, further data sources serving as indicators for expertise may be included.

The creation of keyword profiles from text documents is done by using statistical methods of keyword analysis (Heyer et al., 2002). Since the text documents generally are present in some proprietary file format, plain text needs to be extracted from the files in a first step. Namely, we are able to extract plain text from MS Word documents, MS PowerPoint presentations, PDF, and HTML files. For this purpose, we rely on open source projects capable of reading these file formats (Apache POI, 2005; PDFBox, 2005). So, we cover the most common text file formats used also as standard formats within NIA.[12]

The steps to extract keywords and create keyword profiles are explained in more detail in Reichling et al. (2005). In short, plain text is extracted from documents of diverse file formats. Afterward, stop words (terms such as "the," "a," "me," or "with") are filtered using stop word listings. The remaining terms are regarded as meaningful terms – i.e., keywords. Together with their frequency within all the recognized documents, these keywords are stored within a large keyword vector – the "keyword profile." It has to be pointed out that the documents that users release for their keyword profile are not shared with other users. Only the keyword vector is used to match human actors.

The use of personal data is highly restricted by the users' privacy concerns. Careless handling with these data would threaten the users' acceptance of the system. In order to avoid this, none of the users' personal data is released without the users'

[12] MS Excel files are widely used as well at NIA. However, Excel files are not yet supported since we assumed these files to include numbers rather than meaningful keywords. Our latest investigations show that this is actually not true for NIA since some Excel sheets appeared to include meaningful keywords. Hence, support for Excel files will be included in the next version of the system.

explicit agreement. By default, personal data (after uploading to the server) still remains invisible to other users unless they are explicitly released by the owner of these data. None of the text documents used for automatically generating the user's keyword profile is uploaded to the server or can be inspected by other users. Instead, the keyword profile is generated locally and then sent to the server on the users' demand.

Software Architecture

Figure 14.1 presents the software architecture of the expert recommender. It shows nine system components, realized as plug-ins. Furthermore interactions among modules are depicted as dotted lines. Such interaction occurs when matching components access corresponding storage components for user data or when the feedback collection component "feeds" the feedback storage component. As described above, a Web Service interface acts as a standardized interface for interaction with the "world outside."

The users are represented by three types of profiles. They are stored in different modules (storage modules). We will refer to single components of the user profile as "profile components," whereas the collection of each user's profile components is referred to as the "user profile." The first profile component consists of the yellow page information that users provide about themselves. This component is strongly motivated by our empirical findings (see above). It includes contact information (name, telephone number, email, etc.), information about their role within the

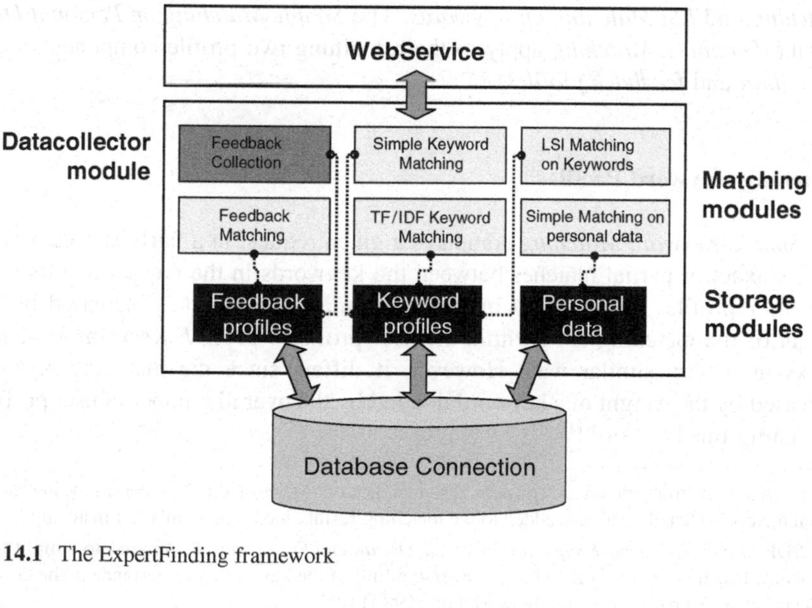

Fig. 14.1 The ExpertFinding framework

organization (position, tasks, job description) and information about skills, experiences, and expertises (apprenticeship, study, publications, presentations, etc.). We assume this information to be rather static since it's only infrequently changed.

The second profile component is given by the keywords derived from the users' text documents which are created, manipulated, or read in the context of the actors' actual work. The extraction is carried out semiautomatically as described above. The third profile component is created from feedback events that occur during continued usage of the system (see above). For each user, the overall score is stored in the *feedback* component. The average value of scores gained by others is likely to reflect properties like the participants' *willingness to help* or their *engagement in users' requests*. This component is not a part of the first rolled out version of the implementation of the EFF. It is a plug-in which will be further developed in a second cycle.

In order to match the user profiles against requests and in order to give recommendations, we draw from a set of five matching algorithms ("matching modules"), rather than from just one. We do so in order to deal with possible failures of single matching modules (that may occur as a result of missing, obsolete, or insufficient profile data). We further believe that over time certain matching components will prove to be useful while others may emerge as rather useless. So, eventual adjustments of the systems configuration over time (e.g., removal of useless components) are part of our concept.

The overall matching result is given by the average value of theses five modules (we will later see that users can adjust the weight of each module according to their individual needs). In Fig. 14.1, these five different matching modules are depicted as light gray boxes, each implementing one single matching strategy. Five strategies might be a surprising number since only three different types of profile data sets are stored. However, by no means is it given that only one matching strategy can be applied to a specific profile component. In this case, three different matching strategies can apply to the *keyword profile*: *Simple Keyword Matching*, *TF/IDF Keyword Matching* and *LSI Matching on Keywords*. The *Simple Matching on Personal Data* and the *Feedback Matching* apply to the remaining two profile components (*personal data* and *feedback profiles*).

Matching Keyword Profiles

The *Simple Keyword Matching* compares a given request in a fairly simple way: It detects exact or partial matches between the keywords in the request and those in each user profile. For all exact matches, the matching result is increased by the weight of the matching term within the user profile.[13] *TF/IDF Keyword Matching* works in a very similar way: However, it differs since the matching result is increased by the weight of a keyword divided by the overall number of user profiles containing this keyword.[14]

[13] Partial matches (truncations) are considered as matches of "lower quality". Accordingly, in cases of partial matches a smaller value is added to the matching result, due to the number of matching letters.

[14] TF/IDF stands for *Term Frequency Inversed Document Frequency*. Compared to simple term frequency, this method provides a better understanding of the keyword's importance in the context of the other user profiles (cf. Salton & McGill, 1983).

A more sophisticated method of comparing user profiles is implemented in the LSI algorithm (Berry et al. 1995). LSI (Latent Semantic Indexing) applies to a set of documents that reveal hidden ("latent") similarities between documents.[15] In the case of a "proper" set of documents (some of the keywords should occur in more than one document), similarities are discovered even if there are not any exact matches of terms to be detected (Deerwester et al. 1990). Again, in our case, it is the user's profile rather than the documents that is being considered.

Matching Personal Data and User Feedback

Another matching strategy fairly similar to the *Simple Keyword Matching* is the *Simple Matching on personal data.* Again, exact or partial matches between a given request and the user profile are detected. In case of the Matching on Personal Data, the users' personal data are used instead of keyword profiles. The matching result is computed in the same way as with the *Simple Keyword Matching* method.

Finally, *Feedback Matching* is applied to the *Feedback Profiles*. The matching result is computed independently to the actual request since no matching needs to be performed. It computes an average value describing the users' engagement in answering requests (see above) based on all received feedback items. For privacy reasons, no detailed information about these data is presented. The feedback is included as part of the result list that is displayed on demand. The results are colour-coded: green indicates a positive feedback whereas white indicates negative or missing feedback.

Since feedback needs to be gathered, a *Feedback Collection* module is part of the software architecture and depicted in the upper left part of Fig. 14.1. This component gathers user feedback after a cooperation among users was initiated and communication took place. Collected feedback is stored in a profile (*Feedback Profile*).

User Interface

Now we describe the client-side component ("user client") of the system. The design rationale was to provide a gentle slope of increased complexity to allow users to manage the system and its inherent flexibility (cf. McLean et al., 1991). On the lowest level of complexity, the client provides "preconfigured parameters" for

[15] Presenting this method in detail would exceed the scope of this paper. Therefore, we refer to Berry et al. (1995) for a detailed description.

nonexperienced users to apply the five different matching strategies. However, users can adjust these parameters to fit their individual needs. Some users may want a configuration of the matching modules, which takes the personal profiles to be the most important data to base the matching on. Others might be interested in the users' willingness to help rather than their pure qualification. The flexibility in the weighting mechanism is an attempt to deal with partly controversial empirical findings in which participants' motivated technical strategies strongly grounded in their actual work contexts. These contexts again, partly differ tremendously due to NIA's organizational structure.

Searching for Experts

Figure 14.2 shows the system's search interface. In Fig. 14.2a, users can select which type of search is required. The options for search include *keyword-based search, document-driven* search, and the *search for similar users*. To set parameters for individual search strategies, a fourth button needs to be pressed.

The keyword-based inquiry can be seen as "straight forward" search functionality. It approximates most closely to the aspired *Google for NIA* idea, which is motivated by the empirical findings. However, the two other search functions need further explanation: First, the document-driven search allows users to select one or more text files from their file system. When starting the search, a vector of weighted keywords is derived from these documents in the same way as it is done when creating keyword profiles. In this case, the inquiry is conducted by matching the resulting keyword vector with the user profiles stored in the system. The inquiry for similar users compares the requestor's own profile with those of other users. The goal of this type of search is to find user profiles that are similar to the requestor's profile. Since the user profiles consist of keywords (in cases of the keyword profile and the personal data), similarities between user profiles are detected in the same way as it is done with keyword-based requests. These search methods are meant to offer additional access to the expertise indicators. While they were not explicitly required by the NIA interviewees, we assumed that specifically employees in member companies would benefit from these additional search options.

In Fig. 14.2b, a list of experts for an exemplary search inquiry for the terms "market," "agriculture," and "china" is shown. From this list, users can directly create requests to experts or add the contact data to their personal address book. The result list shows the expert's name and a photo as long as the data are released to be displayed. By doing so, we dealt with legal concerns as well as with NIA-specific privacy issues (see above). The overall matching result (defined as the average of the results returned by all the involved matching modules) is indicated by the vertical bar chart (Fig. 14.2b). Finally, the right part of each row shows details of the matching results in natural language, explaining *why* the results are as they are and which are the actual matching terms. Since three matching modules (the *Simple Keyword Matching*, the *LSI Matching*, and the *Simple Matching on Personal Data*) were involved in answering this search inquiry, three comments are

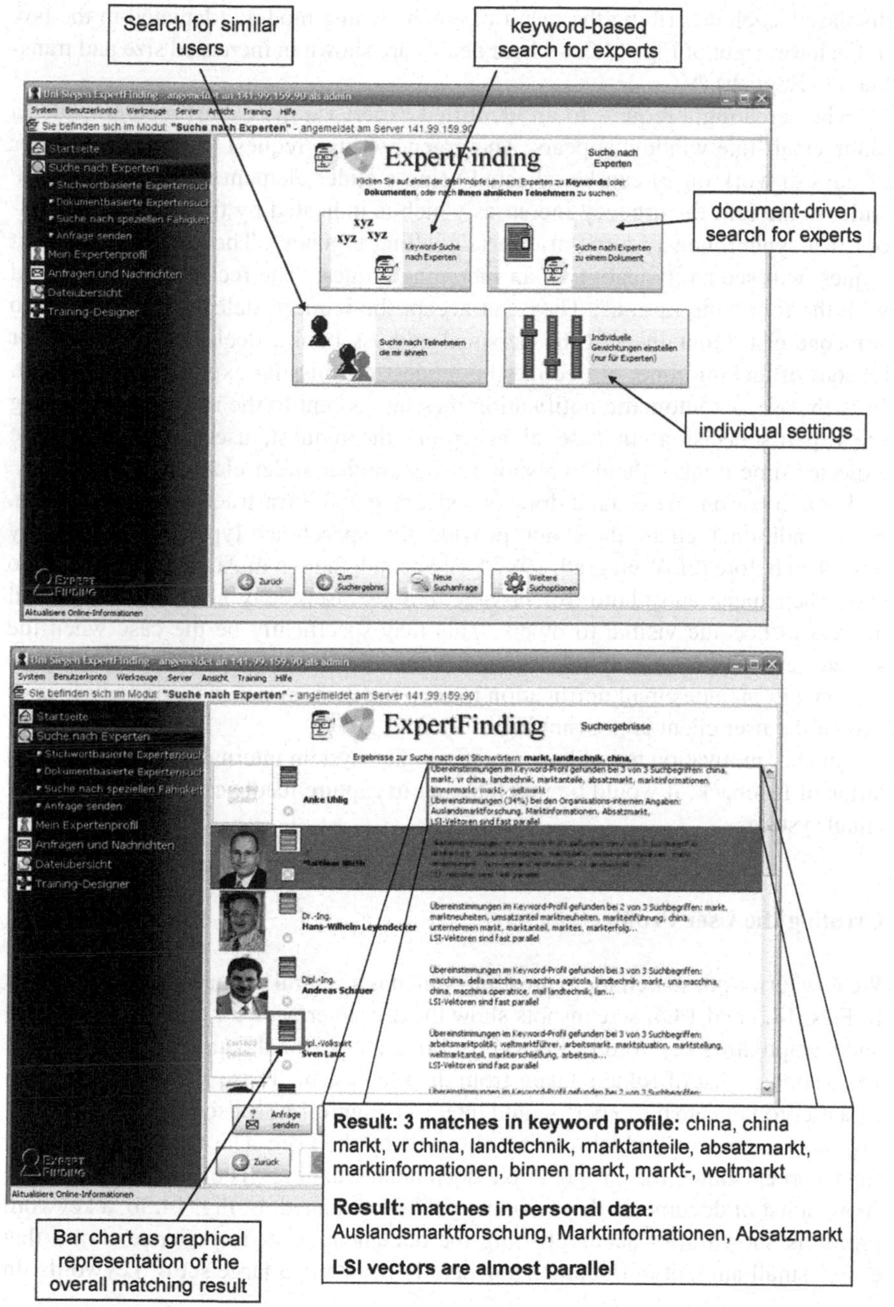

Fig. 14.2 (**a**) Interface to select the preferred type of search (**b**) Interface presenting the list of experts

displayed, each describing the result of one matching module (depicted in the box in the lower right of Fig. 14.2b, where details are shown in increased size and translated to English).[16]

When creating a request to an identified expert via the expert recommender a blank email-like window appears. The urgency of the request (maximum number of days to work on it) can be adjusted using a slider element. When moving the slider to the left, the urgency increases which is indicated by the background colour that synchronously turns orange (signalling urgency). The receiver(s) of that request will see an indication of an incoming request. The receivers are provided with the following options: They can accept the request, delegate the request to someone else (contained in the personal address book), decline the request for reasons of lacking time, or decline the request for missing expertise to handle it. In each case, an automatic notification message is sent to the requestor providing the expert's decision. In case of accepting the request, users can specify the expected time it takes them to respond using another slider element.

For two reasons we did not draw on existing email infrastructure for messaging. First, traditional email does not provide the speech-act type of functionality described before (cf. Winograd, 1987/88). Second, though most users are willing to show their name and photo, for privacy reasons, users may not wish their email address to become visible to others. This may specifically be the case when the system reaches out into member organizations. However, the next version of the system will include email notification to keep the users aware of incoming requests even if the user client is not running.

Another motivation to implement a messaging system internally is the documentation of feedback. It would be much harder to capture feedback from a traditional email system.

Creating the User Profile

We now turn from searching to profiling which is a central element in our approach. In Figs. 14.3 and 14.4, screenshots show the user interfaces for creating, checking, and manipulating keyword profiles (Fig. 14.3) and personal data (Fig. 14.4). Figure 14.3a shows a list of folders taken from the file system. These folders are selected by a user to indicate his expertise and interests. Figure 14.3a also indicates an ongoing "document scan" which can be observed by the user: The frame in the upper right corner shows the progress on document scanning. The lower right frame shows a list of documents that have not yet been scanned. In Fig. 14.3b, a keyword profile is shown after accomplishing the document scan. Experience shows that even a small amount of documents generally results in a large set of keywords. In

---

[16] The current implementation offers information on the quality of the automatically generated recommendations. However, in case member companies deploy the system to a large extend, we may need to reconsider the display of too many details at this point. For example, NIA may not like to let its member companies know that the best match with regard to a 'hot topic' has a score of only 26%.

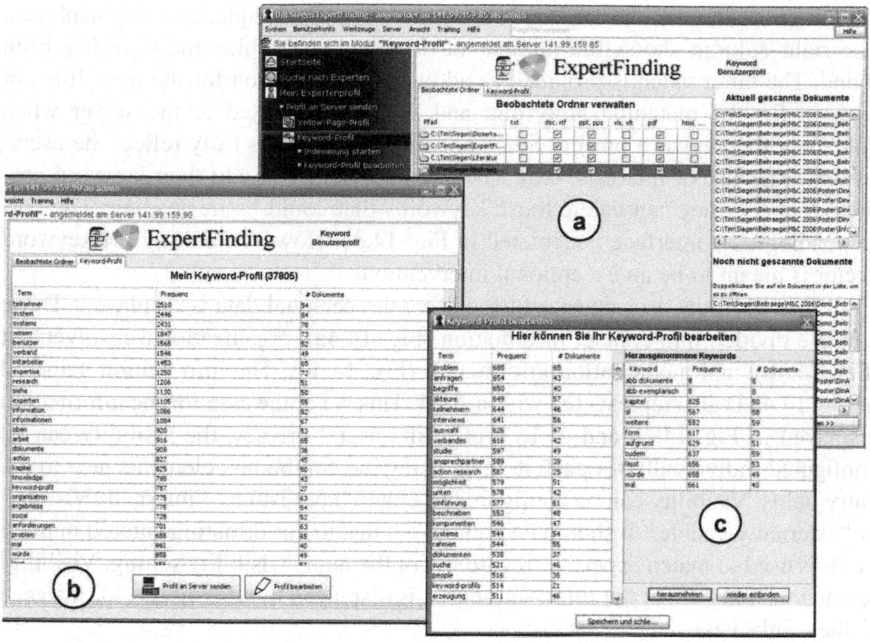

Fig. 14.3 Screenshots of (a) the selected folders, (b) the generated keyword profile, and (c) the interface for editing the keyword profile

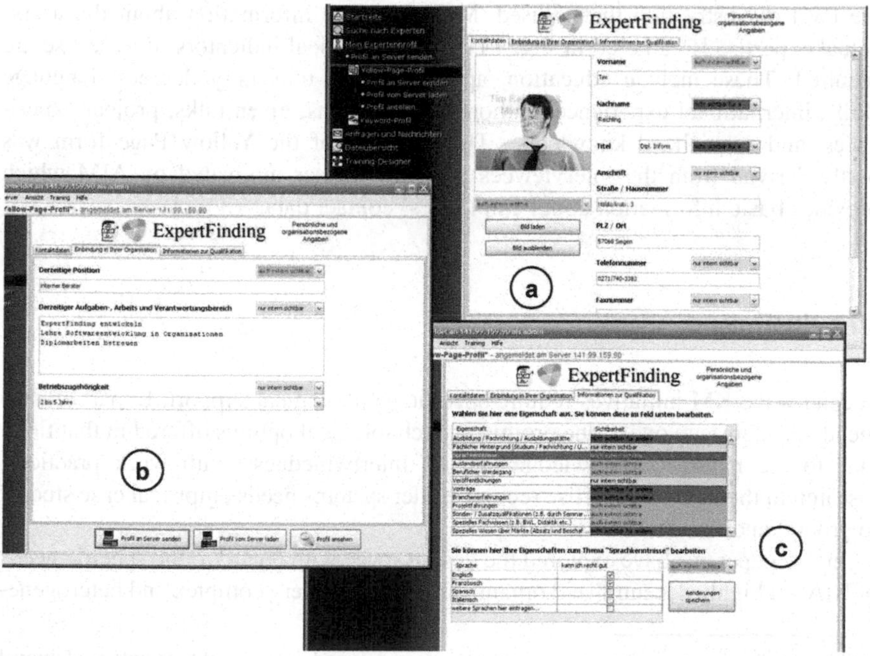

Fig. 14.4 User interface for editing the personal profile: (a) contact information, (b) organizational involvement, and (c) qualification information

the left two columns, the keywords and corresponding frequencies are displayed. The right column shows the number of documents in which the term has been found. The latter value is provided as additional information for the user. It is not relevant for the matching algorithm and is not transmitted to the server when uploading the keyword profile. Since not all of these terms truly reflect the users' current expertise or interests, they have the opportunity to edit their keyword profiles. Namely, they can delete those keywords that could be misleading. The corresponding user interface is depicted in Fig. 14.3c. However, editing the keyword vector is meant to be an exceptional intervention.

In Fig. 14.4, the user interface for editing the personal data is displayed. Those data are divided into contact information (Fig. 14.4a), organizational involvement (Fig. 14.4b), and qualification information (Fig. 14.4c). The information gathered in Fig. 14.4a is also represented within AIM. This is not the case for the information displayed in Fig. 14.4b and c. To protect the users' privacy, the visibility can be configured individually for each item by using the combo box elements next to the entry fields. Visibility can be configured to either "not visible," "internally visible," or "externally visible." It should be pointed out that the information entered in these fields is used to match expertise, regardless of the item's visibility setting. Visibility restrictions only affect the information that is displayed to other users (for instance in the result lists).

The information about organizational involvement (Fig. 14.4b) includes information about the recent position, a description of the actual tasks, and the number of years spent in the organization. The value of these data may vary according to the level of abstraction that is used. More concrete information about the users' actual expertise is gathered in Fig. 14.4c, where typical indicators of expertise are inquired. These include education, apprenticeship, university degrees, language skills, international experience, authored publications, given talks, project experiences, and specialized knowledge. The structure of the Yellow Page form was partly derived from the interviewees and was further motivated by AIM which provides basic information about employees' contact data.[17]

Conclusion

Second wave KM initiatives require specific technological support. Expert recommender systems are one of the promising technological options offered in that field. Due to the nature of knowledge and its intertwinedness with work practices, research in the field of expertise recommender systems needs empirical case studies to ground and evaluate the design space.

In this paper, we have explored the design space with regard to the specific needs of NIA – a highly decentralized organization which is very complex and heterogene-

[17] NIA's employees are used to work with these sets of data and do not want to maintain additional information.

ous in its structure. We have conducted an investigation into the knowledge-related work practices of NIA. Contrary to earlier field studies (e.g., Pipek & Wulf, 2003), NIA had considerable problems in locating appropriate human experts beyond the boundaries of specific sections. Work activities and the related division of labour remained hidden within the individual sections. This pattern seems to result from the organization's history and its internal reward system. These structural patterns seemed to have shaped a culture of competition among the different sections. The size of the organization and its regional distribution only add to the problems.

However, at least on the operative level, the inefficiency of the current mode of expertise sharing is strongly felt. During the empirical case study, it became clear that the services provided to member companies and employees' job satisfaction would benefit from better means of expertise sharing. New employees and actors from member companies can be expected to benefit the most from better organizational transparency within NIA. However, we also experienced considerable reservations from the side of other users. Some of the experienced employees and section heads felt threatened by the potentials of a wider culture of expertise sharing. Such a multiperspective study allows us to better understand potentials and obstacles to the appropriation of expert recommender systems. Moreover, it helps us to conceptualize an appropriate strategy for the rollout of expert recommender systems.

Based on the results of the empirical study, we designed an expert recommender system. Compared to most other implementations of expert recommendation systems (e.g., Maybury et al., 2003; Streeter & Lochbaum, 1988; Foner, 1997), we have implemented an application which is specific for an organizational setting. While we were able to draw on a software framework that provided modules for different matching strategies and their parameterization (cf. Becks et al., 2004; Reichling et al., 2005), many design decisions were grounded in the specific requirements of NIA.

Expert recommenders often rely on structured data such as source code or histories of interaction (Vivacque & Lieberman, 2000, McDonald, 2000, Becks et al., 2004). Structured data typically allow extracting and interpreting expertise-related information in a more straight forward way than plain text. However, this kind of data was not easily available inside NIA and its member companies or problematic for privacy reasons. Since dealing with textual documents was an important aspect of the work practices, we took these documents as an indicator of expertise and complemented them with Yellow Page information. Our approach is conceptually close to the "Who Knows" application (Streeter & Lochbaum, 1988), since it builds on a similar strategy to generate expertise profiles from textual documents. However, our system architecture allows dealing with different sources of expertise indicators in a specific manner. Moreover, our architecture and implementation consider privacy issues explicitly.

The Lotus Discovery Server (LDS) collects a wide variety of textual documents automatically, analyzes, and clusters them. Human actors are associated with certain document clusters. Search queries display documents as well as related human actors. Users can decide whether to be associated with a certain document cluster (Pohs et al., 2001; Schirmer, 2003). While LDS combines search for documents and experts, our approach focuses solely on finding expertise. Therefore, indicative documents are selected manually by the users and text analysis happens in a decentralized manner. Such an approach is more selective with regard to indicative documents and sensitive toward privacy concerns. Enterprise Content Management systems (ECM) contain typically some sort of expert recommender functionality, as well. However, this functionality is not designed for the particularities of a specific organizational setting and does not offer sufficient flexibility. So, matching results are probably suboptimal and privacy concerns are not dealt with in accordance to the legal and cultural particularities.

Alternatively, one could think of applying (commercial or noncommercial) pull technologies to locate and engage experts. For instance, Usenet technology or Virtual Notice Boards meet some of the requirements. Once a participant engages in answering a request, it is a clear indicator of his readiness to share expertise in this domain. However, the empirical prestudy made clear that actors often cannot wait for "someone who is willing to accept a request." We assume that (specifically in noncooperative environments) a "push" mechanism of directly asking a potential expert would have a positive impact on the way requests are received: Dedicated requests which are exclusively directed toward a potential expert may be – due to their stronger social and communicative character – much harder to decline than requests launched in a pull-medium.

We are not aware of any existing technology covering the functionality that NIA (and its member companies) require. While our approach is mainly based on textual documents, the quality of recommendation could be improved by taking parts of an employee's communication, such as email messages or phone calls, additionally into account. Further indicators, such as U1senet postings, Internet bookmarks, or browser histories, could be considered, as well. For three reasons we decided to base our matching algorithms mainly on textual documents. First, there are still considerable technical and algorithmic problems with regard to voice recognition, which prevent the integration of spoken language. Textual documents are easily accessible and there exists an elaborated set of matching algorithms. Second, privacy issues kept us from utilizing email messages or browser histories. The integration of employees' content of communication or detailed activity protocols seemed to be more delicate than dedicated textual documents. Third, we could not rely on a significant number of users applying other text-based communication channels which could become additional indicators of expertise. For instance, Usenet or similar technologies are not widely used at NIA.

Another important issue when designing expert recommender systems is to find a balance between the control a user needs to have over his profile and the effort which is involved in keeping it updated. We believe that the solution developed for NIA, which draws on textual documents stored in the users' file system, is a promising approach to deal with this design issue. Therefore, changes in a user's document base can be tracked and used to update his profile. This approach can be applied to other document collections which are organized by means of a container structure, as well.

From a privacy perspective, a high level of control on a user's profiles is essential for any expertise recommender system. The German legal setting, with its high demands on privacy, has a great influence on our design considerations. However, the importance of controllability has also been emphasised outside the German setting, as well (e.g., Belotti & Sellen, 1993). Indeed at this point, design requirements for appropriate expert matching and the requirements for the protection of the users' privacy seem to point in the same direction.

A third lesson we learned involves integrating expert recommender systems into the given IT infrastructure. McDonald (2000) and Becks et al. (2004) already pointed out the fact that important aspects of the users' profile data need to be taken out of existing IT systems. Our study confirms this finding. However, in our case, the data source was less obvious and the quality of data probably less precise for matching than in the case of McDonald's (2000) work. Our case study shows that "fitting into the given infrastructure" can have a broader meaning. On the one hand, NIA employees requested an integration of the expert finder functionality into the user interface of already given applications, e.g., their Intranet portal. Since the use of expert recommender systems will be deeply embedded in a range of different work practices, this fact has to be reflected by the interface design. The software architecture of expert recommenders should allow the integration into a range of different applications with little efforts. Finally, the extent of the functionality of an expert recommender system needs to be designed in relation to the already existing software functionality. In NIA, a Yellow Page system was missing. To gain additional profile data and to offer potentially relevant functionality to the organization, we decided to integrate a Yellow Page component into our application. So our design case indicates that fit with an existing IT infrastructure is a more complex construct than just allowing importing external data.

There are also lessons to be learnt with regard to the design of the software architecture of an expert recommender system. To integrate expert recommender technologies into given IT infrastructures, a flexible software architecture and standardized software interfaces are essential. Flexibility allows to access additional sources of expertise indicators and to extend the functionality, e.g., by adding feedback mechanisms or a Yellow Page component. Standardized software interfaces allow for integration of the application into the user interfaces of another application. While the need for flexibility with regard to expertise indicators has already been discussed in the literature (McDonald, 2000; Becks et al., 2004), our study provides a broader set of architectural requirements. Some of them are also the result of privacy concerns which have not yet been widely explored with regard to expertise recommender systems.

Groth & Bowers (2001) challenge expert recommender systems which base their algorithms mainly on indicators of expertise or interest. They found situational factors such as accessibility and availability of human actors more relevant when employees asked for help. To add to this discussion, our empirical study revealed the importance of social and organizational factors when employees select potential experts. These factors include the level of competition across sectors, the level of competition among NIA peers, and the importance of a member company. Groth & Bowers (2001) concluded that the situatedness of human strategies in finding expertise prevented algorithms for expertise location from being effective in case they were solely based on indicators of expertise or interest. Based on our material, one could argue that matching algorithms which do not take social and organizational factors into account would hardly be effective.

However, our interpretation of the empirical findings is rather different. NIA (and the network of its member companies) is an organizational setting in which potential experts are often unknown to the internal and external actors in need of support. So the current version of the recommender system offers information which has not yet been made available to the human actors. The system architecture allows taking further types of data into account when recommendations are computing, e.g., data dealing with situational, social, or organizational factors. However, our design experience indicates that these data may be hardly available and highly sensitive. Data such as the actual workload of an expert is currently not available within NIA's software infrastructure. Other types of data may even be too sensitive that employees would not state them openly or make them available to a computer system. This refers in our case to data such as the level of competition between sections or peers.

However, the lacking availability of these types of data may not be a too serious threat to the usefulness of expert recommender systems. These applications need to be seen as tools supplementing rather than replacing human activities in expert finding (see Pipek & Wulf, 2003). When selecting an actor out of the list of potential experts, the users can "manually" bring into play all those factors which have not been considered within the algorithms. The results of matching algorithms which take too many different factors into account may be difficult to interpret by users. Therefore, a design approach grounding its recommendations in data sources which are semantically homogeneous, i.e., indicators of expertise and interests, has its merits. Further information helpful to choose among potential experts could be displayed as additional items in the output window which listed the matching results (see Fig. 14.2b). Our study indicates that it is still a challenge to find homogeneous data sources and to configurate the matching algorithms appropriately for specific organizational settings.

While the design of the expert recommender is grounded in the empirical case, further studies on the system's appropriation by NIA's employees are needed. NIA's organizational structures and culture does not guarantee the experts' willingness to cooperate or to use the system at all (see section "Obstacles to Expert(ise) Finding"). So the question is whether the recommender is doomed to fail if certain high-level experts will not take part. It is not clear whether those actors will become users of the system as long as they are not intrinsically motivated to contribute to expert sharing in the organizational network.

Obviously, the introduction of the expert recommender system should be best accompanied by measures of organizational and personal development (e.g., Wulf & Rohde, 1995). For instance, a modification of NIA's internal reward system, which would take efforts spent on expertise sharing more into account, would be very beneficial for the appropriation of the expert recommender system and, most likely, for NIA's overall organizational performance. Such a reward system could be partly based on data derived from the feedback component of the expert recommender system.

However, NIA's decentralized nature seems to make changes in the overall organizational structure more difficult than the introduction of a technical system. Orlikowski (1996) as well as Pipek & Wulf (1999) show empirically that the appropriation of groupware may change organizational practices and processes even beyond the originally intended level. So, it will be an interesting issue to investigate to which extent the introduction of the expert recommender system will have an impact on the pattern of expertise sharing.

While expert recommender technologies have been discussed for quite some time, the focus was so far rather on conceptual and algorithmic issues (Maybury et al., 2003; Streeter & Lochbaum, 1988; Foner, 1997). We presented a case where we evaluated its fit into a complex organizational setting. Based on this finding, we designed and implemented a specific functionality and came up with new requirements for the software architecture of expert recommender systems. We believe that further studies of this type are needed to better understand the design space for expert recommender systems and make this promising technology useful in real world settings.

Acknowledgments The research has been funded by the German Federal Ministry for Economics and Technology. During the time of writing, Volker Wulf was supported by a Fulbright Scholarship. We would like to thank April Bowen, Andrea Bernards, and Aditya Johri for proof reading the manuscript.

References

Ackerman, M.S. (1998) Augmenting organizational memory: a field study of answer garden. ACM Transactions on Information Systems (TOIS), 16(3), 203–224.

Ackerman, M.S. and Halverson, Ch. (2004) Sharing expertise: the next step for knowledge management. In: Huysman, M.H. and Wulf, V. (eds.), Social Capital and Information Technology. MIT Press, Cambridge, MA, pp. 273–299.

Ackerman, M.S. and Malone, T.W. (1990) Answer Garden: a tool for growing organizational memory. In: Proceedings of the ACM Conference on Office Information Systems. ACM Press, New York, pp. 31–39.

Ackerman, M.S., Pipek, V., and Wulf, V. (eds.) (2003a) Beyond Knowledge Management: Sharing Expertise. MIT Press, Cambridge, MA.

Ackerman, M.S., Swenson, A., Cotterill, S., and DeMaagd, C. (2003b) I-DIAG: from community discussion to knowledge distillation. In: Huysman, M., Wenger, E., and Wulf, V. (eds.), Communities and Technologies. Kluwer, Dordrecht, pp. 307–326.

Alonso, G., Casati, F., Kuno, H., and Machiraju, V. (2003) Web Services – Concepts, Architectures and Applications. Springer, Berlin.

Apache POI (2005) http://jakarta.apache.org/poi/, seen November 2005.

Becks, A., Reichling, T., and Wulf, V. (2004) Expertise finding: approaches to foster social capital. In: M. Huysman and V. Wulf (eds.), Social Capital and Information Technology. MIT Press, Cambridge, MA, pp. 333–354.

Belotti, V. and Sellen, A. (1993) Design for privacy in ubiquitous computing environments. In: de Michelis, G., Simone, C., and Schmidt, K. (eds.), Proceedings of the Third Conference on Computer-Supported Cooperative Work – ECSCW'93. Kluwer, Dordrecht, 77–92.

Bergmann, J.R. (2003) Ethnomethodologie. In: Flick, U., von Kardorff, E., and Steinke, I. (eds.), Qualitative Forschung: Ein Handbuch. Rowohlt Taschenbuch Verlag, Hamburg, pp. 118–135.

Berry, M.W., Dumais, S.T., and O'Brien, G.W. (1995) Using linear algebra for intelligent information retrieval. SIAM Review, 37(4), 573–595.

Buckingham Shum, S. (1997) Negotiating the construction and reconstruction of organisational memories. Journal of Universal Computer Science (Special Issue on IT for Knowledge Management), 3(8), 899–928.

Chapman, R. (2004) Pearls of wisdom: social capital building in informal learning environments. In: Huysman, M.H. and Wulf, V. (eds.), Social Capital and Information Technology. MIT Press, Cambridge, MA, pp. 310–333.

Cohen, D. and Prusak, L. (2001) In Good Company: How Social Capital Makes Organizations Work. Harvard Business School Press, Boston.

Deerwester, S., Dumais, S., Furnas, G., Landauer, T., and Harshman, R. (1990) Indexing by latent semantic analysis. Journal of the American Society of Information Science, 41(6), 391–407.

Ehrlich, K. (2003) Locating expertise: design issues for an expertise locator system. In: Ackerman, M., Pipek, V., and Wulf, V. (eds.), Sharing Expertise – Beyond Knowledge Management. MIT Press, Cambridge, MA, pp. 137–158.

Flick, U. (2002) Qualitative Sozialforschung: Eine Einführung. Rowohlt Taschenbuch Verlag, Hamburg.

Foner, L.N. (1997) Yenta: a multi-agent, referral-based matchmaking system. In: Proceedings of the First International Conference on Autonomous Agents. ACM Press, New York, pp. 301–307.

Groth, K. and Bowers, J. (2001) On finding things out: situated organizational knowledge in CSCW. In: Proceedings of the 7th ECSCW. Kluwer, Dordrecht, pp. 279–298.

Harper, R., Randall, D., and Rouncefield, M. (2000) Organizational Change and Retail Finance: An Ethnographic Approach. Routledge, London.

Heyer, G., Quasthoff, U., and Wolff, Ch. (2002) Möglichkeiten und Verfahren zur automatischen Gewinnung von Fachbegriffen aus Texten. http://wortschatz.informatik.uni-leipzig.de/asv/publikationen/HeyFachbegriffe100902.pdf, seen: 20 November 2004.

Huysman, M. and de Wit, D. (2004) Practise of managing knowledge sharing: towards a second wave of knowledge management. Knowledge and Process Management, 11(2), 81–92.

Huysman, M. and Wulf, V. (2004) Social Capital and Information Technology. MIT Press, Cambridge, MA.

Kautz, H.A., Selman, B., and Shak, M. (1997a) Referral web: combining social networks and collaborative filtering. Communications of the ACM, 40(3), 63–65.

Kautz, H.A., Selman, B., and Shak, M. (1997b) The hidden web. AI Magazine, 18(2), 27–36.

Lindgren, R., Henfriedsson, O., and Schultze, U. (2004) Design principles for competence management systems: a synthesis of an action research study. MIS Quarterly, 28, 435–427.

Maybury, M., D'Amore, R., and House, D. (2003) Automated discovery and mapping of expertise. In: Ackerman, M., Pipek, V., and Wulf, V. (eds.), Expertise Sharing: Beyond Knowledge Management. MIT Press, Cambridge, MA, pp. 359–382.

McArthur, R. and Bruza, P. (2003) Discovery of implicit and explicit connections between people using email utterance. In: ECSCW 2003 – Proceedings of the Eighth Conference on Computer Supported Cooperative Work, Helsinki, Finland, pp. 21–40.

McDonald, D.W. (2000) Supporting Nuance in Groupware Design: Moving from Naturalistic Expertise Location to Expertise Recommendation. Ph.D. Thesis. University of California, Irvine.

McDonald, D.W. (2003) Recommending collaboration with social networks: a comparative evaluation. In: Proceedings of the 2003 ACM Conference on Human Factors in Computer Systems, Ft. Lauderdale, pp. 593–600.

Normark, M. and Randall, D. (2005) Local expertise at an emergency call centre. In: Proceedings of the Ninth European Conference on Computer Supported Cooperative Work. Springer, Dordrecht, pp. 347–366.

Orlikowski, W.J. (1996) Evolving with notes: organizational change around groupware technology. In: Ciborra, C. (ed.), Groupware & Teamwork. Wiley, Chichester, pp. 23–60.

PDFBox (2005) http://www.pdfbox.org/, seen December 2005.

Pipek, V. and Won, M. (2000) Wissenslandschaften und Kommunikation, Position Paper for the Workshop on 'Communication and Cooperation in Knowledge Communities' German Conference on Computer-Supported Cooperative Work (DCSCW), München, 2000.

Pipek, V. and Wulf, V. (1999) A groupware's life. In: Proceedings of the Sixth European Conference on Computer Supported Cooperative Work, ECSCW'99. Kluwer, Dordrecht, pp. 199–218.

Pipek, V. and Wulf, V. (2003) Pruning the answer garden: knowledge sharing in maintenance engineering. In: Proceedings of the Eighth European Conference on Computer Supported Cooperative Work (ECSCW 2003), Helsinki, Finland, 14–18 September. Kluwer, Dordrecht, pp. 1–20.

Pipek, V., Hinrichs, J., and Wulf, V. (2003) Sharing expertise: challenges for technical support. In: Ackerman, M., Pipek, V., and Wulf, V. (eds.), Sharing Expertise – Beyond Knowledge Management. MIT Press, Cambridge, MA, pp. 111–136.

Pohs, W., Pinder, G., Dougherty, C., and White, M. (2001) The lotus knowledge discovery system: tools and experiences. IBM Systems Journal, 40(4), 956–966.

Randall, D. and Bentley, R. (1994) Tutorial on 'Ethnography and collaborative systems development II: practical application in a commercial context'. CSCW'94, Chapel Hill, North Carolina, September 1994.

Reichling, T. and Veith, M. (2005) Expertise sharing in a heterogeneous organizational environment. In: Proceedings of the Ninth European Conference on Computer Supported Cooperative Work. Springer, Dordrecht, pp. 325–345.

Reichling, T., Schubert, K., and Wulf, V. (2005) Matching human actors based on their texts: design and evaluation of an instance of the expert finding framework. In: Proceedings of GROUP 2005. ACM Press, New York.

Rohde, M. (2006) Integrated organization and technology development (OTD) – a process model for action research. Ph.D. Thesis. Department of Communication, Journalism and Computer Science, Roskilde University, Roskilde.

Salton, G. and McGill, M.J. (1983) Introduction to Modern Information Retrieval. McGraw-Hill, New York.

Schirmer, A.L. (2003) Privacy and knowledge management: challenges in the design of the lotus discovery server. IBM Systems Journal, 42(3), 519–531.

Schmidt, C. (2003) Analyse von Leitfadeninterviews. In: Flick, U., von Kardorff, E., and Steinke, I. (eds.), Qualitative Forschung: Ein Handbuch. Rowohlt Taschenbuch Verlag, Hamburg, pp. 447–456.

Stahl, G. and Herrmann, T. (1999) Intertwining perspectives and negotiation. In: International Conference on Supporting Group Work (GROUP'99). ACM Press, New York, pp. 316–325.

Streeter, L.A. and Lochbaum, K.E. (1988) Who knows: a system based on automatic representation of semantic structure. In: RIAO'88, Cambridge, MA, pp. 380–388.

Tyler, J.R., Wilkinson, D.M., and Huberman, B.A. (2003) Email as spectroscopy: automated discovery of community structure within organizations. In: Huysman, M., Wenger, E., and Wulf, V. (eds.), Communities and Technologies 2003. Kluwer, Dordrecht, pp. 81–96.

Vignollet, L., Plu, M., Marty, J.C., and Agosto, L. (2005) Regulation mechanisms in an open social media using a contact recommender system. In: Proceedings of Communities and Technologies (C&T 2005). Springer, Dordrecht, pp. 419–436.

Vivacque, A. and Lieberman, H. (2000) Agents to assist in finding help. In: Proceedings in the Conference on Human Computer Interaction (CHI 2000). ACM Press, New York, pp. 65–72.

Winograd, T. (1987–88) A language/action perspective on the design of cooperative work. Human-Computer Interaction, 3(1), 3–30.

Won, M. and Pipek, V. (2003) Sharing knowledge on knowledge – the eXact peripheral expertise awareness system. Journal of Universal Computer Science, 9(12), 1388–1397.

Wulf, V. and Rohde, M. (1995) Towards an integrated organization and technology development. In: Proceedings of the Conference on Designing Interactive Systems: Processes, Practices, Methods, & Techniques. ACM Press, New York, pp. 55–64.

Chapter 15
Patterns as a Paradigm for Theory in Community-Based Learning

John M. Carroll and Umer Farooq

Abstract Learning about information technology is typically not a first-order goal for community-based volunteer organizations. Nonetheless, information technology is vital to such groups for member recruiting and management, communication and visibility to the community, and for primary group activities. During the past 12 years, we have worked with community groups in Centre County, Pennsylvania, and Montgomery County, Virginia. We have built partnerships with these groups to better understand and address their learning challenges with respect to information technology. In this paper, we suggest that *patterns*, standard solution schemata for recurring problems (as used in architecture and software engineering, among other design domains), can be a paradigm for codifying and developing an understanding of learning in and by community organizations. Patterns are middle-level abstractions; they capture regularities of practices in ways that are potentially intelligible, verifiable, and perhaps useful to the practitioners themselves. We present two example patterns and discuss issues and directions for developing patterns as a theoretical foundation for community-based learning.

Keywords: Community informatics; Community-based learning; Design; Informal learning; Information technology; Organizational informatics; Patterns

Introduction

Most adult learning occurs in *informal* contexts, that is, contexts outside educational programs. People learn through recreational, civic, and work activities from and/or with their peers. During the past 12 years, we have been studying informal learning about information technology (IT)v as it occurs in communities and community groups (e.g., Carroll & Rosson, 1996, 2003). Informal learning about IT is a pervasive challenge in modern society. Many recreational, learning, and work activities require at least some IT skill, and this is becoming more pervasive. While some business and governmental organizations make use of formal IT training programs, much of this learning occurs informally.

J.M. Carroll (ed.), *Learning in Communities,*

Community groups provide an interesting arena for informal IT learning. Such groups have very distinctive resources and constraints. On the one hand, they are social linchpins of our communities and our society. Community-based groups are everywhere, in every community; the majority of people belong to at least one such organization (Kavanaugh, Reese, Carroll, & Rosson, 2005). Churches, service organizations, arts and cultural groups, clubs and recreational groups are bastions against the "decline of community," as described by Bellah, Madsen, Sullivan, Swindler, and Tipton (1986) and by Putnam (2000), among others. They are in fact a fast-growing and increasingly important category of organization. In the state of Pennsylvania, USA, where our current research site is located, there are 700,000 nonprofit organizations, compared to only 12,500 in 1940. Nonprofit organizations, which are largely community based and rely heavily on volunteer labor, now account for about 10% of total employment in the state (Grobman, 2002).

On the other hand, community groups are underfunded and understaffed to cope with the complexity and the rate of change in information technology. Maintaining PCs, networks, and software, perhaps servers, and obtaining or otherwise organizing personnel support – including support for training and learning – is expensive, both financially and with respect to organizational capacity. Community groups lack material resources of all sorts (money, skills, telecommunication infrastructure), as well as organizational structures, protocols, and continuity to effectively cope with technology. Relying on volunteers to organize, manage, and carry out most vital organizational activities, including learning about technology, entrains knowledge-management risks. Volunteers come and go, often taking with them organizationally vital knowledge and skill (Farooq et al., 2007).

In this paper, we reflect on a set of participatory action research partnerships we built with various community-based groups to better understand and address their learning challenges with respect to information technology. In other papers, we have described various aspects of these partnerships, and the organizational learning we facilitated and observed (Carroll et al., 2000; Merkel et al., 2004, 2005; Farooq et al., 2005). Our specific concern in this paper is to develop a model for *codifying and reusing* problems and solutions across varied contexts. This is the practical sense in which we invoke the sometimes-problematic term "theory" in the title of this paper.

We suggest that *patterns*, standard solution schemata for recurring problems – used in architecture and software engineering, among other design domains – can be a paradigm for developing a theory of community-based IT learning. Patterns, in this sense, consist of a *problem*, a description of the problem's *context*, an analysis of relevant *forces* (that is, resources and trends that enable or constrain possible solutions to the problem), a statement of a *solution* to the problem, a discussion of how the *resulting context* was changed by the solution, and *examples* of the solution (pointers to instantiations of the pattern in our on-going work).

Patterns are a good example of what C. Wright Mills (1959) famously called "middle-level abstractions." They capture regularities of practices in ways that are potentially intelligible, verifiable, and perhaps useful to the practitioners themselves. For example, among Alexander's (Alexander et al., 1977) patterns is the Street Café pattern. The *problem* this pattern addresses is the need to enhance feelings of openness and access to people and activity in city spaces. The *context* is tightly packed, tall buildings and narrow streets, with many people anonymously hurrying along. The *forces* are construction and operation costs, the hassles of getting municipal approvals to open a café onto the sidewalk, the personal approach avoidances of making eye contact and meeting others in public, and so forth. Documenting and analyzing the pattern provides a resource to designers and other design stakeholders for sharing and improving solutions.

In the balance of this paper, we discuss two key patterns of community-based learning: *informal developmental learning* and *scaffolded documentation*. Informal development learning is a solution to the problem of paralyzing lack of control over IT. Scaffolded documentation is a solution to the problem of knowledge loss through turnover in volunteers. Both of these are truly common problems for contemporary community-based groups. The solutions are authentic – we have observed them – but they cannot be claimed to be typical. In that sense, we are proactively tailoring the concept of pattern for participatory action research, extending its somewhat anthropological conception: "standard solution to a recurring problem," to that of a program for social intervention: "potentially effective solution to a crippling problem." The notion of pattern we are exploring here is similar to what has been called "emerging pattern" (Chung et al., 2004) or "prepattern" (Saponas et al., 2006).

This more activist interpretation of patterns is highly consistent with the developing methodological vision of pattern languages in computer-supported cooperative work (CSCW), computer-supported collaborative learning (CSCL), and community informatics (Erickson, 2000; Schuler, 2002; Avgeriou et al., 2003; Goodyear et al., 2004). Indeed, the intelligibility of patterns to the people whose practice is described by the patterns, and the use of patterns as self-regulatory social mechanisms, is an important direction in this work that we return to in the discussion.

Informal Developmental Learning

Many community groups are paralyzed in a sense with respect to information technology. They are dissatisfied with some or perhaps all of their IT applications – their Web pages, databases, newsletter publishing, and so forth. But they cannot articulate a plan to address these problems.

Problem: Lack of Control Over IT

Not so many years ago, it was a radical proposition to assert that community organizations could maintain information and manage activities through the Internet. Through the 1980s, community groups used the Internet to facilitate information dissemination, discussion, and joint activity pertaining to municipal government, public schools, civic groups, local events, community issues and concerns, and regional economic development and social services. Some of these projects have become touchstones of Internet activism – jobs, housing, and veterans' issues in the Berkeley Community Memory (Farrington & Pine, 1997), community health in the Cleveland Free Net (Beamish, 1995), problems of the homeless in the Santa Monica Public Electronic Network (Rogers et al., 1994), and public education and Native American culture in the Big Sky Telegraph (Uncapher, 1999).

In their decade, these projects were the leading edge of community networking. But in fact they were implemented on relatively simple networking software platforms – the file transfer protocol (ftp). People were inspired to be able to use this new medium to exchange civic information and perspectives with fellow citizens. But of course the broader context was that most civic and community-based organizations, and indeed most commercial and governmental organizations as well, were still operating in a world of typewriters and telephones.

Today, baseline expectations throughout western society about communication are different. One expects to be able to identify and access an organization's URL (universal resource locator). One expects to be able to send or receive an email announcing a meeting. The pervasive adoption of email and the WWW present opportunities and challenges to community-based volunteer organizations. The opportunities are obvious: Organizations can get their message out for "free," Web communication may result in more time-efficient management of work, and so on.

The challenges are less obvious. The Web is easy and accessible to all, if accessibility means browsing. But when a community organization wants to post and serve current information about activities and new programs, it faces a host of issues – Who will design and create the Website, the various pages, and the content in the pages? Who will maintain the site and contents, run the Web server, and update software? It is likely that no one in the organization has these skills. If so, it is unlikely that anyone wants to invest much time and effort into acquiring these skills.

The problem we are addressing is that community-based volunteer organizations experience a lack of control over their own IT. What makes the problem worse is that these organizations can have so little in-house expertise that they are not even able to recognize the extent to which they lack control, or to diagnose how they might begin to remedy the situation. An example from our own fieldwork was an environmental group who felt they were participating in IT activities over which they had control, because they had hired a commercial vendor to produce their Website. Indeed, when they wished to change the Website design, they discovered that this outsourcing had deprived them of control. The vendor had all the knowledge, all the content, and all the code (Farooq et al., 2005). Hence, part of the problematic lack of control over IT is not realizing that this problem exists in the first place.

Context: American Society and the Internet

A key context for the challenges that community-based organizations face with respect to control of their own IT is the rapid and pervasive growth of computing and the Internet during the past two decades. The WWW began as a way for elite military and academic groups to exchange information, but it has evolved rapidly into a powerful information source for ordinary citizens.

Our empirical work takes place in North America, chiefly in Pennsylvania and Virginia in the United States. Sixty-three percent of American adults now use the Internet. Since 2000, the distribution of Internet users across gender, income, and race is surprisingly regular. Use of the Internet has become normal in daily life. On a typical day in 2004, 70 million adult Americans logged on to the Internet (about 35%), up from about 50 million in 2000. Fifty-eight million used email; 35 million got news; 24 million did job-related research; 24 million looked for political information. Ninety-four million Americans have used the Internet to find or to share health-related information; 97 million Americans have used government Websites. Sixty-five percent of American Internet users believe that the Internet has helped their relationships with friends; 56% believe it has helped their relationships with their own family members. Sixty million American homes now have broadband Internet access, compared to 6 million in 2000. (All data are from Rainie and Horrigan, 2005.)

These facts and trends contrast interestingly with trends relating to the ability and interests of Americans in preparing for more active roles with respect to IT. For example, undergraduate enrollments in computer science fell about 25% between 2000 and 2003 (Computer Research Association, 2003).

Moreover, as the Web has evolved, browsing, searching, and carrying out purchases has become easier and more accessible, while creating dynamic, interactive Web content has become increasingly more difficult, requiring server-based mechanisms (e.g., servers that support Web-based discussion forums), embedded components written in other programming languages (e.g., Java applets, ActiveX controls, Flash, or JavaScript), or plug-ins that augment the user's browser and allow it to receive data in closed, proprietary formats. These advances create richer experiences for the passive information consumer on the Web, but they add technical obstacles for users interested in constructing novel, interactive functionality to their own creations.

Forces: Lack of Resources and Rich Social Capital

Two key forces shaping the solution to the problem in this pattern are the lack of resources among volunteer community-based groups and the important role such groups play in social capital formation.

Community volunteer organizations generally lack financial resources, telecommunications infrastructure (high-bandwidth connectivity), equipment, skills, and access to training. They lack almost every relevant resource to support an IT strategy. In our studies, we have found that it is typical for community organizations to have no budget line item for technology. In one case, a community organization we worked with only had Internet access via the home connections of its members; the organization as such had no connectivity other than its own phone line. Lack of resources is a force – it affects how community volunteer organizations will address the problem of having less control of their IT.

Lack of relevant resources is exacerbated by the fact that IT is generally *not* a core concern of these organizations. Not surprisingly, a local historical society is chiefly concerned with preservation of sites and artifacts, informal education programs, and interactions with school and community groups. Even though an outside consultant might conclude that IT is a key to addressing their primary concerns in an efficient and effective manner, they do not necessarily see it that way.

Social capital is the generalized trust, social interaction, and mutual reciprocity throughout a group, a community, or a society (Coleman, 1990). Because community volunteer organizations depend upon intrinsic motivation and personal commitment, rather than material rewards, social capital formation and preservation is especially critical to their survival and growth (King, 2004). And the social capital produced through participation in these organizations is critical to the whole society (Putnam, 2000).

Indeed, many studies of contemporary American society have concluded that traditional mechanisms of social capital formation in American communities are in decline (e.g., Bellah et al., 1986; Putnam, 2000). For example, between the 1960s and the 1990s, participation rates in a variety of civic activities declined: Red Cross volunteering declined by 60%; participation in parent–teacher organizations declined by nearly half, membership in the League of Women Voters and in the Jaycees both declined by 40%; the number of people reporting that they attended a public meeting on town or school affairs in the past year has declined by more than a third; volunteering of Boy Scout troop leaders declined by a quarter; voter turnout in national elections declined by nearly a quarter; churchgoing and church-related activities declined by a sixth; the proportion of Americans who socialize with neighbors more than once a year declined by nearly a sixth.

In this societal context, the formation and preservation of social capital through participation in community groups has become of greater importance to the larger society.

Solution: Informal Developmental Learning

An important alternative to formal pedagogy is learning *informally*. Informal learning refers to learning that occurs outside of classrooms, schools, and other formal instructional environments and activities, and it includes incidental, self-directed, and lifelong learning. People with existing and active commitments to their communities may find it more meaningful to learn about Web programming, for example, by helping to create a Web application for a community service organization than by attending an intensive programming class. What we know about adult learners suggests that this would indeed be the case (e.g., Knowles, 1973).

In fact, informal learning represents an important part of the common culture of the Internet and its democratic and community roots (Rheingold, 1993). Informal learning of Web technologies often involves "learning by doing," for example, learning in the course of downloading and exploring new software, posting on newsgroups, getting product technical support, or copying and editing useful or appealing Web pages. Such activities are often situated in "authentic" tasks, providing solutions to real, concrete problems that the learner faces either as an individual or as part of a group or community.

One solution to the problem of lack of control over IT is a self-sustained process of informal learning, in which organizations identify and analyze their technology needs, and then learn about IT through continuing engagement in solving their own problems. We describe this solution as comprising three facets: *reflection*, *analysis*, and *enactment* (see Fig.15.1). Reflection is a self-assessment on part of the community organization of its relationship to its own IT. It is more effective to come to the realization that there is a lack of control on one's own than to be told there is a problem by another. Technology self-assessments and discussions of critical incidents within the organization are good approaches for this reflection. In the example we discussed above, when the environmental group wanted to change their Website and found that this would be a long and difficult process, they realized that they were not in control to the extent they wanted and needed to be.

Organizational competition with peer groups may also prompt reflection, such as multiple environmental organizations in a proximate community competing for project or operations funding from one government source.

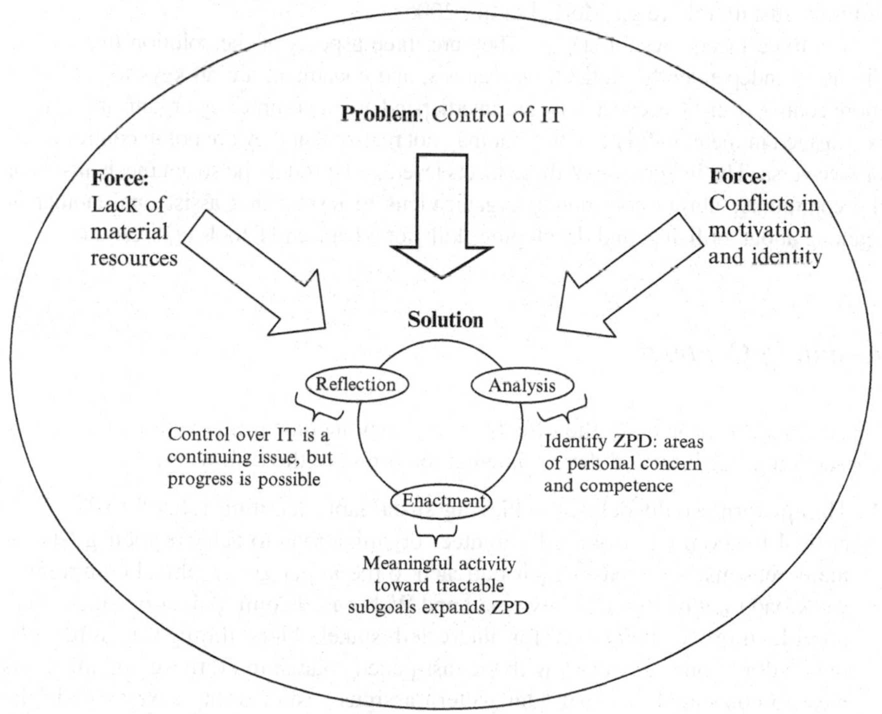

Fig. 15.1 Schema for informal developmental learning pattern

The second facet is identification and analysis of organizational practices, needs, and issues related to IT. Community-based volunteer organizations are unique in that their work activities may be loosely coupled and minimally coordinated (Carroll, 2001). They depend primarily on volunteerism; they face a lack of financial and temporal resources, and so forth, which makes them unique. Technology needs and issues must be identified and analyzed in context of these unique structural features of community-based volunteer organizations. While technology provides many opportunities for these organizations to achieve their civic-oriented goals, community-based volunteer organizations still face formidable challenges in sustaining the use of technology (Merkel et al., 2005). Part of the reason is that the adoption and use of technology is not aligned with their unique structure. Hence, these organizations must identify and analyze their organizational practices to see how IT can become a part of their organizational day-to-day activities. One way to achieve this is to develop technology plans by assessing the current status of work practices and technology-related activities in the organization (e.g., Techsoup, 2005).

The third facet of our pattern solution is enactment. The solution must be assimilated into everyday practices of the organization. In other words, learning about IT is an on-going facet of everyday activity, in the sense that Dewey (1916) described traditional models for situated learning as integrated into community activities, and in the sense that Lave and Wenger (1991) describe learning as the process of becoming a full participant in a socio-cultural practice. Enactment makes the solution sustainable (e.g., Merkel et al., 2005).

The three facets are not stages. They are three aspects of the solution that can be discussed independently. Reflection, analysis, and enactment are all keys to achieving more control over IT because they are interdependent. A community organization could be engaged in meaningful activities but may not realize that they are not in control of IT, or vice versa. The integration of these facets leveraged through the social mechanisms of the community allows community organizations to inspire and assist one another in learning about, utilizing, and developing skills for advanced IT tools and resources.

Resulting Context

It is difficult to project all the effects of any sociotechnical innovation. Two likely consequences of informal developmental learning are the following:

1. This pattern would help in achieving sustainable learning related to IT. IT is critical for community-based volunteer organizations to achieve their goals for many reasons: it increases their outreach to the larger geographical community, workload may be lightened by email and Web-based communication, and it may provide more convenience for interested stakeholders through features like online donations. However, with the fast-paced change in IT, these organizations have to continuously learn. Our pattern assigns sustainability a key role in the solution by emphasizing the need for *continuous* engagement in meaningful activities *over time*.

2. This pattern would help to recast organizational practices related to IT. In our pattern solution, community-based volunteer organizations are cognizant of the fact that sustainable use of technology is key to their long-term success. Decision makers in such organizations make decisions by following a reflexive and proactive process of thinking about how particular technology-related decisions will affect the organizational goals and use of that technology in the near and far future. Part of this process involves perceiving how technology learning will be managed in their organization over time (e.g., Who will update the site when you are on vacation? Who will maintain the site if you, your technology person, or a volunteer leaves the organization?) and how will a long-term technology plan be incorporated as organizational practice (e.g., What will happen to the site when the grant runs out? Who is going to add content to these more dynamic features of the site?).

These consequences are some of the major ones that result from following our pattern solution. They all converge toward greater control over IT for community-based volunteer organizations. We now discuss our pattern solution with two examples that also illustrate some of the resulting context.

Example: Spring Creek Watershed Community

The informal developmental learning pattern can be illustrated in many community-oriented participatory action research (PAR) projects. Spring Creek Watershed Community (Spring Creek, http://www.springcreekwatershed.org) is a sustainable development, volunteer organization committed to regional environmental and economic planning, specifically planning by watershed area rather than by individual municipalities. The organization works to explain this vision to the larger community and to show how watersheds have an impact on quality of life and the local economy. We worked with this organization for approximately 14 months (Merkel et al., 2004).

A major technology issue that Spring Creek faced was to redesign their Website. Before our involvement with the organization, Spring Creek hired a commercial vendor to develop and maintain their Website. Spring Creek was dissatisfied with the Website because it did not reflect their mission, overall goals, or the fact that they were a local organization concerned with environmental and economic planning. For example, whereas the goal of Spring Creek was local economic planning, influencing decision makers, and encouraging quality of life through watersheds, the Website depicted them as a generic tree-hugger group. Moreover, the vendor resisted any major restructuring of the Website and often times used his/her sole control over the community organization's technology to avoid changes. Critical incidents such as this forced Spring Creek to realize the problem. By delegating their Website design and maintenance to a commercial vendor, Spring Creek lacked control of IT because they were not active participants in Website-related activities.

To address this problem, key stakeholders in Spring Creek first analyzed the situation. This was achieved by holding a kickoff meeting, initiated by the Spring Creek lead coordinator, in which many volunteers from Spring Creek's social network were involved. The result of this meeting was that Spring Creek would itself redesign their

Website so that they retained control over its management. The volunteers who attended this first meeting formed, by default, an informal technology committee that would deliberate over subsequent meetings to see Spring Creek's vision through.

During the Website redesign process, committee members had different perspectives on "design" that created tension between technical requirements and the need to organize information on the Website effectively. One of the more technical volunteers wanted to follow a rapid prototype approach by proposing several new designs for the Website, whereas another volunteer who had been working previously with Spring Creek suggested that content design should be done first. The latter proposal meant that layout design would be done afterward – this would allow Spring Creek to focus on the organizational message they want to convey through their Website. Key stakeholders in Spring Creek agreed to the latter idea by being active participants in this negotiation process, trying to tease out the pros and cons of the different proposals put forward. This resulted in the creation of an expert–novice zone of proximal development that concretely led to achieving common ground and understanding through hierarchical modes of learning (Farooq et al., 2005).

One way that key stakeholders from Spring Creek became active participants in the social context of the Website-redesign process was through the use of scenarios as conceptual tools (Farooq et al., 2005). The lead coordinator used scenarios to convey her input into the design process. Active engagement through scenarios had a direct effect in eliciting design, communicating design rationale, and resolving design conflicts. It also had an indirect effect by resulting in increased learning on part of the key stakeholders as they were now transitioning from legitimate peripheral participants to more core actors in the redesign process (Lave and Wenger, 1991).

The solutions adopted by Spring Creek had both short- and long-term implications. In the short-term, the current stakeholders in Spring Creek's Website have become more technology literate. For example, earlier, one of the key stakeholders did not even know what HTML denoted, and now, after having engaged meaningfully in technology-related activities, is heavily involved in technical discussion forums and basic HTML coding. In the long term, this solution will result in more autonomy over time, where learning is being captured and transformed into organizational expertise. Some evidence of this is currently being seen. For example, Spring Creek has incorporated technology-related knowledge management practices within the organization and has thus reduced the dependence on outside technical experts. Spring Creek now keeps a documented record of all their Website management activities, so that newer volunteers can come in and learn how Website maintenance and update is done. Another example of this pattern is described in Carroll and Farooq (2005).

Scaffolded Documentation

Community nonprofits typically rely on volunteer members – even for organizationally critical roles. A positive consequence of this personnel paradigm is that much organizational problem solving and learning is intrinsically motivated.

A negative consequence is that it is common for volunteers to drop out, often suddenly, in response to exigencies in their lives. As a result, community nonprofits are relatively more vulnerable to organizational knowledge losses through turnover than are other organizations.

Problem: Managing Tacit Knowledge Held by Nonorganizational Stakeholders

Financial support and technical expertise are critical factors for organizations in order to effectively integrate information technologies into their daily work process. The problem of technology adoption and integration in community organizations goes beyond getting newer versions of software, better hardware, or obtaining general advice on technology issues like installing new software or creating community Web pages. The community organizations need advice and assistance that fit their context, which cannot be provided by a general agency. Also, with limited funding resources, it is often not an option for nonprofit organizations to hire technical consultants for long-term support on technology projects. Community organizations are often forced to grow their own expertise to take on technology projects and manage technical issues in their organizations.

Growing expertise means coming up with sets of strategies to manage the limited resources for technology adoption and integration. One set of strategies tackles the problem of the scarcity of the human resource. Several other studies have discussed the importance of recruiting a stable network of technical expertise into nonprofit organizations (Corder, 2001; Eisinger, 2002). The use of volunteers is part of this broader strategy to develop expertise in the organization and to develop a network of support. Growing expertise in small, nonprofit community organizations implies developing longer-term knowledge management strategies.

The use of volunteers can be a problematic strategy. Volunteers may either not have the required skill set or be more interested in working on the social mission of the organization. In a similar vein, a volunteer may design a system that matches his or her own skill set and experience. Berlinger and Te'eni (1999) noted some of the same tensions when incorporating volunteers into an organization. They found that sometimes volunteers design systems that are idiosyncratic based on his/her knowledge of a particular technology (not necessarily the best solution). They also found that sometimes the advice can be short-sighted, especially if a volunteer is new to the organization or is not familiar with its work practices.

The problem we are addressing is the management of tacit knowledge held by nonorganizational stakeholders (volunteers, part-time staff members, etc.). This is a major issue for nonprofit organizations because when they lose a volunteer, they may also lose the only person that held the tacit knowledge required to complete technology work (e.g., the password needed to upload files, the location of files critical to the organization). An example from our fieldwork was a food bank that relied on a volunteer to develop and maintain their Website. After the volunteer left, the organization was unable to retain any knowledge of their Website, including trivial information such as the user name and password to access their Website domain.

Context: Technology Sustainability Through Participatory Design

A concern with sustainability is prevalent in the participatory design literature (Bodker et al., 2000; Clement & Van den Besselaar, 1993; Kensing, F. & Blomberg, J. (1998); McPhail et al., 1998). In the Civic Nexus project, our view of sustainability is tied to approaches that explicitly connect design to learning. Sachs (1995), for example, argued that "technology design should enhance the human capacity of finding problems and solving them" (p. 40). Similarly, Trigg and Bodker (1994) argued that "system development should be organized as a learning process where the participants, collectively and as individuals, improve their ability to understand and manage processes of technological and organizational change" (p. 46). Design should involve finding ways to help users maintain the new competencies that they have gained through the participatory design process (Bodker et al., 2000).

In our fieldwork, sustainability involves finding ways of working with community organizations in ways that give them greater control over the use of technology in their organization. We think of sustainability as a dynamic multifaceted process in which users learn to apply technology to address challenges and opportunities in their work, taking into account local contingencies. We define technology broadly to include technical innovations (e.g., software, hardware, Websites) and shifts in routines, procedures, practices, etc. Users within an organization and the organization itself are involved in a learning trajectory. They are learning to identify ways that technology can enhance their work, marshal resources within their social network to get work done, solve problems that inevitably occur along the way, and attend to the shifts in roles, practices, and process that result from technology adoption.

Force: Volunteer-Driven Workforce

Part of the value system for community organizations is their consideration for volunteerism. For example, the Johns Hopkins Nonprofit Sector project reported that the number of people working in civil society organizations in the 35 countries they studied exceeds 190 million, which represents over 30% of the adult population in these countries (Salamon et al., 2003). Valuing participation by community organizations is relevant to adoption and design of technology because it is likely that volunteers will participate in and manage technology-related activities.

Because technology is typically not part of the core mission for community organizations, the use of a community-based workforce creates tensions as the organizations work to harness a diverse set of skills. Volunteers and staff members possess a diverse set of technology skills, which makes it difficult to prescribe a skill set while still being participative (McPhail et al., 1998). In addition, managing such diverse constituents requires additional articulation work. This is because it involves increased coordination of the cooperative work processes and operationalization of subtasks (Gerson & Star, 1986; Gross, 1999).

Solution: Lightweight Knowledge Management

Our solution can be decomposed into three facets, although more fine-grained constructs can be substituted or augmented. These three facets of our solution – lightweight knowledge management – are *technology assessment*, *contingency planning*, and *lightweight documentation* (see Fig. 15.2).

Technology assessment deals with evaluating needs of community organizations. Community organizations often have ideas about what they would like to do with technology, but they often need a way to make their plans more concrete. A community technology assessment includes, but is not limited to, descriptions of the organization's: (a) mission, decision-making structure, stakeholders, and values; (b) current technology infrastructure (e.g., the number and types of computers they have, do they have an organizational Website, do they have Internet access); (c) use of technology (e.g., office tasks, information dissemination, commercial or noncommercial pursuits) in decision-making and to achieve their communitarian goals; (d) human and technical resources that can be leveraged (and that have been used in the past) to work on a technology project; and (e) vision for how they would like to use technology if obstacles were removed and a list of potential projects. Our intent in using the technique is to encourage the group to reflect on their current technology needs, prioritize potential technology projects, and assess their resources to get projects done.

The second facet is contingency planning. Part of the work that community groups need to do is to manage the trade-offs involved in managing volunteer labor. A major site of breakdowns for nonprofit organizations is the loss of a volunteer or a staff member who was primarily responsible for some aspect of a technology project. This problem is exacerbated because nonprofits do not have the money to hire a new person to take over these responsibilities. If there is a great deal of turnover, the nonprofit is put in the position of continuously starting over, delaying temporarily and sometimes permanently the achievement of their technology goals. We have addressed the need for long-term planning in our participatory design process by prodding our community partners with questions related to contingency planning. Asking contingency question evokes learning because it helps the organizations make planning more a part of their practice. The organizations learn to ask the kinds of questions that are relevant when initiating and managing technology projects in their organization. They then start asking these questions about other technology projects that they initiate.

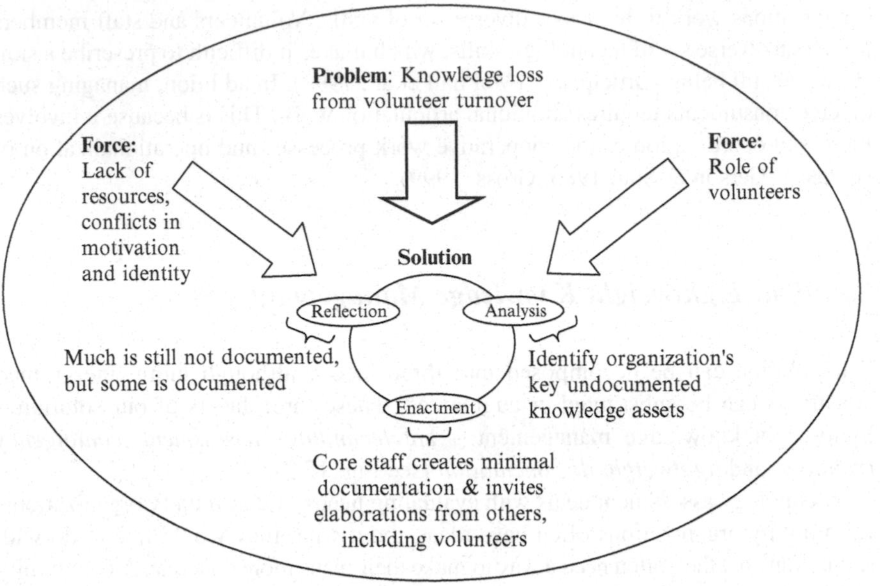

Fig. 15.2 Schema for scaffolded documentation pattern

The third facet is lightweight documentation. This involves finding a balance between processes that need to be documented and those that do not. Most people do not enjoy the process of documentation even though it plays an important role in managing tacit knowledge within the organization. Documentation evokes sustainability because it is a technique that nonprofits can use to manage knowledge in their organization. Our emphasis on documentation helps to legitimize less formal methods of documentation that people might not recognize as such (e.g., note-taking and "cheat sheets"). These are resources that can be shared with others in the organization and future volunteers. This puts nonprofits more in control of technology in their organization in the sense that they are not continuously starting over every time they lose a staff member or a new volunteer.

Resulting Context

Again, with the disclaimer that one can never fully project the effects of any sociotechnical innovation, two likely consequences of the scaffolded documentation pattern are:

1. This pattern would encourage informal learning. The community technology assessment promotes learning because the organizations start to prioritize their current technology needs and the resources that they have available to carry out

their technology goals. Asking contingency questions evokes learning because it helps the groups make planning more a part of their practice. The groups learn to ask the kinds of questions that are relevant when initiating and managing technology projects in their organization.

2. This pattern would enhance organizational preservation of technical expertise. For community-based volunteer organizations, technical experts, just like other volunteers, are temporally volatile. They come, do an IT-related project(s), and go. Since these organizations cannot afford a continual supply of technical experts around the clock, it is natural for these organizations to consider preservation of technical *expertise* rather than *experts*. Our pattern solution, in effect, allows community organizations to develop IT-related knowledge management within the organization. Since community organizations would breed their own technical expertise, and would continuously learn and develop their IT skills over time, a culture of eliciting and packaging organizational memory emerges.

Example

An example of this pattern can be illustrated through our yearlong fieldwork with the State College Food Bank (Food Bank). Food Bank is a nonprofit organization that provides emergency food and clothing to those in need. The Food Bank also provides support to a network of other food pantries in the region. The organization has two paid staff members and a steady base of volunteers that serve the organization. They have a Board of Directors that is active in providing oversight for the organization.

One major concern that the Food Bank had when we began to work with them was shortcomings in their technology infrastructure. The staff members wanted to be able to access the Internet at the office and they wanted more control over their organizational Website. However, the organization did not yet have Internet access, so when staff members needed to email or access the Web, they were forced to do so at home. The management of Web resources, including the organization's Website, was another major concern. Food Bank relied on a volunteer to update their Website. This strategy worked well until the volunteer left the organization. As a result, they decided to do this work in-house. This formed the basis of our participatory design work with Food Bank. We helped to train a staff member to take over responsibility for updating and maintaining the Website.

As a first step, Food Bank wanted to carry out a technology assessment of their organization in relation to what kinds of resources they needed to get access to high-speed Internet and to maintain their Website in-house. Food Bank relies on volunteer effort in the form of their Board of Directors to address technology infrastructure issues. They used this expertise, for example, to conduct a technology assessment for their organization. A member of the board recommended that they utilize the services of a technology consultant who was a personal acquaintance to evaluate the organization's current technology capacity and to make recommendations for technology upgrades. The assessment that was done served as a roadmap that Food Bank followed to enhance the technical infrastructure of their organization and to make software purchases for the organization. This assessment report also had social implications because it provided evidence that they could use with members of their board to justify technology expenditures.

When the volunteer who was maintaining Food Bank's Website left, they decided to assign responsibility for updating the Website to a staff member. We worked with this staff member to teach him how to update and refine Food Bank's Website. Our goal was to work with him in such a way that he was able to transfer his knowledge to others in the organization. This was important because the staff member hoped that eventually he would be able to pass this task on to volunteers who would update the Website from within Food Bank. We consistently encouraged the staff member at Food Bank to document tasks related to the design and update of the Website. The staff member was somewhat resistant to this process. He was a hands-on person preferring to learn by doing the same task two or three times. He once commented "Our intelligence is in our hands," referring to the value of hands-on experience in learning new skills. However, we did realize that after we fade from the setting as researchers, he might forget the knowledge he gained from us. Even worse, if he left the organization, Food Bank would lose this tacit knowledge again. The staff member we worked with was convinced that for operational tasks (e.g., how to add a link to a Web page), he was more than capable of retaining such knowledge. However, for higher level and complex tasks, we prompted him to take notes. For example, it was critical to understand the hierarchical structure of the Website in order to add a new Web page. He wrote down how the Website was organized, what each of the directories meant, and the associated content of each subdirectory folder. This documentation would be useful as he continued to work on the Website, but it will also be useful in the future if someone else takes over this role.

One of our roles in our interaction with Food Bank was to keep this staff member on track with the theme of sustainability when the maintenance of the Website is deferred to volunteers. We asked the staff member questions to prod his thinking about the long-term use of volunteers. For example, how long does a particular volunteer plan on working for the organization? What will you do if he/she leaves? How can the work done by one volunteer be transferred to another?

Discussion and Program

We described and illustrated two patterns from the domain of community-based learning. *Informal developmental learning* is a specific solution to the recurring problem of lack of control over IT in community volunteer organizations. *Scaffolded documentation* is a solution to the loss of organizational knowledge due to reliance on a volunteering workforce. These patterns closely, and thereby usefully, couple codification and application of design knowledge. This is a highly desirable property in practical design domains like CSCW and CSCL, where many kinds of scientific knowledge necessarily converge and interact (see Carroll and Rosson, 2003, for general discussion).

The dominant paradigm in community computing is *case study research* (Yin, 2003). This approach is renowned, of course, for bringing to light important nuances of human behavior and experience, and producing revelatory interpretations. It is regarded as particularly indispensable in the analysis of real-world social systems. However, case study research presents classic challenges with respect to abstraction and generalization. For example, Yin (2003) emphasizes that a theoretical framework for case study research must state conditions under which a particular phenomenon is likely to occur as well as conditions under which it is likely not to occur. The context and forces fields in a pattern schema achieve this. Moreover, case study descriptions, no matter how rich and revelatory, do not provide prescriptive advice. Accordingly, from the standpoint of action research and design, case studies improve our understanding of instances, but do not explicitly guide the creation of new solutions.

Patterns do not replace case studies; they do not provide the vivid narrative view into complex social data. But patterns can complement case studies and provide a theoretical framework for abstracting and generalizing case study descriptions. The two patterns we discussed illustrate this, and the pattern schema we employed to present them indicates how this approach might be extended. Of course, patterns themselves raise many further questions about theory in design and comprise a research program more than a finished solution (Dearden & Finlay, 2006). One of the advantages of considering patterns as a paradigm for theory is that design knowledge is codified in self-contained chunks that include descriptions of the domain contexts and recurring problems in those contexts. But in such a program, what guarantees the coherence and commensurability of the chunks? As an example, suppose we were to go through the effort of creating a more complete pattern language (Alexander, 1979) for community-based learning, what would we have? Is a set of patterns a theory? In the balance of this discussion, we consider the notion of *frameworks* from software engineering as a direction for further work.

In software engineering, a framework is a reusable design of all or part of a system that is the skeleton of an application customizable by a software developer (Gamma et al., 1994). Frameworks are expressed in a programming language – they are code. A single framework usually contains several to many patterns, and in this sense patterns are narrower than frameworks (Johnson, 1997). Patterns are embodied in and illustrated through their roles in frameworks. Patterns are more abstract, and can be viewed as microarchitectural elements of frameworks. A well-known example in software engineering is the role of the observer, composite, and strategy patterns in the model-view-controller framework (Gamma et al., 1994).

Our concern is how frameworks can be adapted to help guide the instantiation and use of patterns in design and analysis in community-based learning. We believe that frameworks are an important area for further development of patterns as a paradigm for theory in community-based learning.

In the CSCW and CSCL domains of community computing, frameworks are the various types of community networks, community portals, and community organization Websites. For example, the Spring Creek Website (discussed earlier) instantiates a design framework: it consists of a shallow information hierarchy navigated by a permanently displayed dynamic menu that foregrounds a statement of the organization's mission, a rationale, and a newsletter archive. The primary graphical content is a set of images depicting typical landmarks throughout the Spring Creek Watershed. This Website is literally code, but more specifically it is a code base over which the Spring Creek organization now exerts substantial control. It exemplifies an application skeleton that could be immediately repurposed with a few cut-and-paste operations.

The *informal developmental learning* and *scaffolded documentation* design patterns are architectural elements of the Spring Creek Website framework; that is, articulating the patterns provides language constructs for design and analysis of Websites instantiating this framework. As described earlier, Spring Creek stakeholders became active participants in the Website redesign process (informal developmental learning) and later maintained organizational documents that logged their Website management activities (scaffolded documentation).

Frameworks are a design nexus for patterns. Spring Creek's Website framework embodies and integrates the two patterns described in this paper. But this framework also describes how the knowledge codified in the two patterns interacts in design implementation with further patterns. For example, another recurring problem for community organizations is that of *preparing and disseminating newsletters* (Merkel et al., 2004). This pattern is also evident in the Website framework; the current newsletter and the newsletter archive are one click away from the homepage display of the organization's mission and strategic goals. The preparing and disseminating newsletters pattern (which we have not yet analyzed in the same detail as *informal developmental learning* or *scaffolded documentation*) highlights the need to organize members to contribute content and editorial assistance, and to streamline the formatting of newsletter content into email, Web pages, and other formats (e.g., *pdf* files). It suggests, for example, solution approaches like a wiki-based interface through which organizational stakeholders can add newsletter content without worrying about the details of formatting tags, and possibly pressing a button to generate the newsletter as a *pdf* file styled according to a predefined template.

Yet another community-based learning design pattern might address the problem of *managing diverse volunteers* who have a variety of technical skills and vested interests. Within the Website framework, this pattern implies the problem of who does what on the Website while keeping organizational goals in mind. In our fieldwork, we have observed that community organizations want to micromanage volunteers in relation to specific Website tasks. In our work with Spring Creek (Farooq et al., 2007), it was noted that they did not want all volunteers to be able to update the entire Website because it may be detrimental to the organization (volunteers' interest may not match organizational mission, volunteers may inadvertently delete vital content, etc.). One possible solution that was discussed was to grant access rights to specific volunteers so they could change Website content only for the sections to which they had privileges.

Frameworks, in the sense described above, help to develop a pattern-oriented program for research and theory development in community-based learning in two complementary ways. On the one hand, they help to ground patterns more richly in experience. Frameworks make patterns easier to use by illustrating how a given pattern was applied in a particular kind of problem situation, and in the context of other patterns. Even though patterns themselves are rich and contextualized, they focus attention of analysts and designers on the context and dynamics of a single solution schema. However, solution patterns ultimately succeed or fail in a larger context of related problems and their forces, solutions, and contexts. In other words, patterns – ultimately – must be synthesized into implementations, and those implementations are both more comprehensive and more deeply contextualized.

On the other hand, frameworks also provide rubrics for organizing and refining patterns as descriptions and as tools. Although patterns are often induced bottom-up from data, they can also be deduced by factoring a framework that instantiates several known patterns. As in our example of the Spring Creek Website framework, two known patterns in this framework were factored out, helping us to identify two further patterns. Indeed, we think it is significant that Schuler's (2002) collection of community informatics patterns, and Alexander's (1979) original collection of urban design patterns are considered unwieldy by many practitioners; these two pattern languages are essentially long lists of patterns, albeit with some cross-referencing and examples, but without frameworks to integrate and operationalize them.

The key idea in Alexander's (1979) pattern language program is to identify consequential invariants in existing design solutions, to ground them in the domain context and problems from which they arise, and to articulate their specific consequences for people and for human activity. This core idea is simple and powerful, and it has had extraordinary resonance through a wide variety of design communities. It is not a finished system; the idea of frameworks, for example, which itself is under development, seems essential to make pattern languages more than mere lists of knowledge nuggets. The pattern language program seems particularly appropriate for design domains like community computing in which users and user organizations must participate in every aspect of design.

Acknowledgments A predecessor of this paper, discussing only the informal developmental learning pattern, under the more general name "community-based learning," appeared in the proceedings of the European Conference on Computer-Supported Cooperative Work (Carroll and Farooq, 2005). We are grateful to the US National Science Foundation (grant numbers 0106552, 0342547, 0353101, 0429274) for supporting this research. We thank our colleagues and collaborators Mary Beth Rosson, Cecelia Merkel, Lu Xiao, and Craig Ganoe for helping us refine our ideas on patterns for community learning. Our research would not have been possible without the wonderful support of the various community groups we worked with as part of the Civic Nexus project.

References

Alexander, C. (1979). *The Timeless Way of Building*. Oxford, UK: Oxford University Press.

Alexander, C., Ishikawa, S., Silverstein, M., Jacobson, M., Fiksdahl-King, I., & Angel, S. (1977). *A Pattern Language: Towns, Buildings, Construction*. New York: Oxford University Press.

Avgeriou, P., Papasalouros, A., Retalis, S., & Skordalakis, E. (2003). Towards a pattern language for learning management systems. *Educational Technology & Society, 6*(2), 11–24.

Beamish, A. (1995). *Communities On-Line: Community-Based Computer Networks*. Masters Thesis, Department of Urban Studies and Planning, MIT.

Bellah, R., Madsen, R., Sullivan, W., Swindler, A., & Tipton, S. (1986). *Habits of the Heart: Individualism and Commitment in American Life*. Berkeley, CA: University of California Press.

Berlinger, L. & Te'eni, D. (1999). Leader's attitudes and computer use in religious congregations. *Non-profit Management and Leadership, 9*(4), 399–411.

Bødker, S., Ehn, P., Sjögren, D., & Sundblad, Y. (2000). Cooperative design – perspectives on 20 years with "the scandinavian IT design model". In *Proceedings of the Nordic Conference on Human-Computer Interaction (NordiCHI 2000)* (pp. 1–9). Stockholm, Sweden, October 22–24.

Carroll, J.M. (2001). Community computing as human-computer interaction. *Behaviour and Information Technology, 20*(5), 307–314.

Carroll, J.M. & Farooq, U. (2005). Community-based learning: design patterns and frameworks. In H. Gullersen, K. Schmidt, M. Beaudouin-Lafon, & W. Mackay (Eds.), *Proceedings of the 9th European Conference on Computer-Supported Cooperative Work* (pp. 307–324). Dordrecht, the Netherlands: Springer.

Carroll, J.M. & Rosson, M.B. (2003). Design rationale as theory. In J.M. Carroll (Ed.), *HCI Models, Theories and Frameworks: Toward a Multidisciplinary Science* (pp. 431–461). San Francisco, CA: Morgan-Kaufmann.

Carroll, J.M., Chin, G., Rosson, M.B., & Neale, D.C. (2000). The development of cooperation: Five years of participatory design in the virtual school. In *Proceedings of ACM Symposium on Designing Interactive Systems: DIS'2000* (pp. 239–251). New York: ACM Press.

Chung, E.S., Hong, J.I., Lin, J., Prabaker, M.K., Landay, J.A., & Liu, A.L. (2004). Development and evaluation of emerging design patterns for ubiquitous computing. *Proceedings of the ACM Conference on Designing Interactive Systems: DIS 2004* (pp. 233–242). New York: ACM Press.

Clement, A. & Van den Besselaar, P. (1993). A retrospective look at PD projects. *Communications of the ACM, 36*(6), 29–37.

Coleman, J.S. (1990). *The Foundations of Social Theory*. Cambridge, MA: Harvard University Press.

Computer Research Association. (2003). Taulbee Survey. Last accessed March 1, 2005. Available at http://www.cra.org/.

Corder, K. (2001). Acquiring new technology: Comparing nonprofit and public sector agencies. *Administration & Society, 33*(2), 194–219.

Dearden, A. & Finlay, J. (2006). Pattern languages in HCI: a critical review. *Human Computer Interaction, 21*(1), 49–102.

Dewey, J. (1916). *Democracy in Education*. New York: Macmillan.

Eisinger, P. (2002). Organizational capacity and organizational effectiveness among street-level food assistance programs. *Nonprofit and Voluntary Sector Quarterly, 31*, 115–130.

Erickson, T. (2000). Lingua francas for design: sacred places and pattern languages. *Proceedings of ACM Symposium on Designing Interactive Systems: DIS'2000* (pp. 357–368). New York: ACM Press.

Farooq, U., Merkel, C., Nash, H., Rosson, M.B., Carroll, J.M., & Xiao, M. (2005). Participatory design as apprenticeship: sustainable watershed management as a community computing application. *Proceedings of the 38th Hawaii International Conference on System Sciences: HICSS-38*. Washington, DC: IEEE Computer Society.

Farooq, U., Ganoe, C.H., Xiao, L., Merkel, C.B., Rosson, M.B., & Carroll, J.M. (2007). Supporting community-based learning: case study of a geographical community organization designing their web site. *Behaviour and Information Technology, 26*(1), 5–21.

Farrington, C. & Pine, E. (1997). Community memory: a case study in community communication. In P. Agre & D. Schuler (Eds.), *Reinventing Technology, Rediscovering Community: Critical Explorations of Computing as a Social Practice* (pp. 219–228). Greenwich, CT: Albex.

Gamma, E., Helm, R., Johnson, R., & Vlissides, J. (1994). *Design Patterns: Elements of Reusable Object-Oriented Software*. Reading, MA: Addison-Wesley.

Gerson, E.M. & Star, S.L. (1986). Analyzing due process in the workplace. *ACM Transactions on Office Information Systems, 4*(3), 257–270.

Goodyear, P., Avgeriou, P., Baggetun, R., Bartoluzzi, S., Retalis, S., Ronteltap, F., & Rusman, E. (2004). Towards a pattern language for networked learning, In S. Banks, P. Goodyear, V. Hodgson, C. Jones, V. Lally, D. McConnell, & C. Steeples (Eds.), *Networked Learning 2004* (pp. 449–455), Lancaster: Lancaster University.

Grobman, G.M. (2002). *Pennsylvania Nonprofit Handbook: Everything You Need to Know to Start and Run Your NonProfit Organization.* Harrisburg, PA: White Hat Communications.

Gross, T. (1999). Computer-supported community work: old wine in new bottles? *Workshop on Broadening Our Understanding: Community Networks and Other Forms of Computer-Supported Cooperative Work, Proceedings of the European Conference on Computer Supported Cooperative Work.* Dordrecht, the Netherlands: Kluwer.

Johnson, R.E. (1997). Frameworks = (Components and Patterns). *Communications of the ACM, 40*(10), 39–42.

Kavanaugh, A., Reese, D.D., Carroll, J.M., & Rosson, M.B. (2005). Weak ties in networked communities. *The Information Society, 21*(2), 119–131.

Kensing, F. & Blomberg, J. (1998). Participatory design: issues and concerns. *Computer Supported Cooperative Work: The Journal of Collaborative Computing, 7*(3–4), 167–185.

King, N.K. (2004). Social capital and nonprofit leaders. *Nonprofit Management & Leadership, 14*(4), 471–486.

Knowles, M.S. (1973). *The Adult Learner: A Neglected Species.* Houston, TX: Gulf Publishing Company, American Society for Training and Development.

Lave, J. & Wenger, E. (1991). *Situated Learning: Legitimate Peripheral Participation.* New York: Cambridge University Press.

McPhail, B., Costantino, T., Bruckmann, D., Barclay, R., & Clement, A. (1998). CAVEAT exemplar: participatory design in a non-profit volunteer organisation. *Computer Supported Cooperative Work (CSCW): The Journal of Collaborative Computing, 7*(3–4), 223–243.

Merkel, C.B., Xiao, L., Farooq, U., Ganoe, C.H., Lee, R., Carroll, J.M., & Rosson, M.B. (2004). Participatory design in community computing contexts: tales from the field. *Proceedings of the 8th Conference on Participatory Design: Artful Integration: Interweaving Media, Materials and Practices* (pp. 1–10). New York: ACM Press.

Merkel, C.B., Clitherow, M., Farooq, U., Xiao, L., Ganoe, G.H., Carroll, J.M., & Rosson, M.B. (2005). Sustaining computer use and learning in community computing contexts: making technology part of "who they are and what they do". *The Journal of Community Informatics* [Online], *1*(2), 134–150. Available at: http://ci-journal.net/viewarticle.php?id=53&layout=html

Putnam, R. (2000). *Bowling Alone: The Collapse and Revival of American Community.* New York: Simon & Schuster.

Rainie, L. & Horrigan, J. (2005). A decade of adoption: how the Internet has woven itself into American life. *Trends 2005,* Pew Research Center. Last accessed March 1, 2005; Available at: http://pewresearch.org

Rheingold, H. (1993). *The Virtual Community: Homesteading on the Electronic Frontier.* Reading, MA: Addison-Wesley.

Rogers, E.M., Collins-Jarvis, L., & Schmitz, J. (1994). The PEN Project in Santa Monica: interactive communication, equality, and political action. *Journal of the American Society for Information Science, 45*(6), 401–410.

Sachs, P. (1995). Transforming work: collaboration, learning, and design. *Communications of the ACM, 38*(9), 36–44.

Salamon, L.M., Sokolowski, S.W., & List, R. (2003). *Johns Hopkins Comparative Nonprofit Sector Project: Global Civil Society At-a-glance: Major Findings of the John Hopkins Comparative Nonprofit Sector Project.* Baltimore, MD: John Hopkins Press.

Saponas, T.S., Prabaker, M.K., Abowd, G.D., & Landay, J.A. (2006). The impact of pre-patterns on the design of digital home applications. *Proceedings of the ACM Conference on Designing Interactive Systems: DIS 2006* (pp. 189–198). New York: ACM Press.

Schuler, D. (2002). A pattern language for living communication. *Proceedings of the 6th Conference on Participatory Design* (pp. 434–436). Palo Alto, CA: CPSR.

Techsoup. (2005). *Technology Planning*. Accessed March 2, 2005; Available at: http://www.techsoup.com/howto/articles.cfm?topicid=11&topic=Technology%20Planning

Trigg, R.H. & Bødker, S. (1994). From implementation to design: tailoring and the emergence of systematization in CSCW. *Proceedings of the Conference on Computer Supported Cooperative Work* (pp. 45–54). New York: ACM Press.

Uncapher, W. (1999). Electronic homesteading on the rural frontier: Big Sky Telegraph and its community. In M. Smith & P. Kollock (Eds.), *Communities in Cyberspace* (pp. 264–289). Oxford, UK: Routledge.

Yin, R.K. (2003). *Case Study Research: Design and Methods*. Thousand Oaks, CA: Sage.

Chapter 16
Architecture, Infrastructure, and Broadband Civic Network Design: An Institutional View[1]

Murali Venkatesh and Mawaki Chango

Abstract Cultural values frame architectures, and architectures motivate infrastructures – by which we mean the foundational telecommunications and Internet access services that software applications depend on. Design is the social process that realizes architectural elements in an infrastructure. This process is often a conflicted one where transformative visions confront the realities of entrenched power, where innovation confronts pressure from institutionalized interests and practices working to resist change and reproduce the status quo in the design outcome. We use this viewpoint to discuss design aspects of the Urban-net, a broadband civic networking case. Civic networks are embodiments of distinctive technological configurations and forms of social order. In choosing some technological configurations over others, designers are favoring some social structural configurations over alternatives. To the extent that a civic network sets out to reconfigure the prevailing social order (as was the case in the Urban-net project considered here), the design process becomes the arena where challengers of the prevailing order encounter its defenders. In this case, the defenders prevailed and the design that emerged was conservative and reproduced the status quo. What steps can stakeholders take so that the project's future development is in line with the original aim of structural change? We outline two strategies. We argue the importance of articulating cultural desiderata in an architecture that stakeholders can use to open up the infrastructure to new constituents and incremental change. Next, we argue the importance of designing the conditions of design. The climate in which social interactions occur can powerfully shape design outcomes, but this does not usually figure in stakeholders' design concerns.

Keywords: Network architecture; Network infrastructure; Network design, Institutional conditions

---

[1] Early versions of parts of this paper were presented at seminars, conferences, and workshops at Syracuse University, Pennsylvania State University, Carnegie Mellon University and the Massachusetts Institute of Technology. The authors wish to thank the Editor and reviewers for valuable comments that have greatly improved the paper.

J.M. Carroll (ed.), *Learning in Communities*,

Introduction

The design of a civic network infrastructure serves as the context for the present paper. Design entails specification: stakeholders specify network *functions* (what it will do) and a configuration of information and communications technology (ICT) *components* that would enable the functions to be used. Each of these steps entails tradeoffs and choices among alternatives, occasioning conflict and negotiation. Our account below pertains to the Urban-net (pseudonym), a broadband network located in and purporting to serve an urban area in New York State. We are not concerned with virtual online networks.

Social constructivism has emerged as a vigorous alternative to the determinist view on the development of artifacts generally, including ICT artifacts. Determinists believe that artifacts arise from forces inherent in technology, outside the purview of social processes. Such a view tends to motivate a concern with impacts that the artifact is assumed directly to have produced without the benefit of social mediation. Constructivists, such as Bijker (1995), for example, refute the case for autonomy, modeling artifacts and their effects as socially constructed products of social processes. We subscribe to the constructivist view.

We hold that it is important to understand how an artifact acquired its characteristics – its functions and distinctive configuration of enabling components – before we can account for its impacts. Analyses of an artifact's impacts are necessary. A robust literature exists – and continues to evolve – on the impacts of ICT artifacts on individuals, organizations, groups, entire populations. The civic networking literature is certainly well served in this regard (e.g., Kavanaugh et al., 2005). However, constructivists, as a matter of principle would direct attention to what has been termed the *prior* question: "What has shaped the technology that is having effects? What has caused the […] changes whose impact we are experiencing?" (Mackenzie & Wajcman, 1985, p. 2). In this paper we draw on sociological institutional ideas to complement constructivist ideas in conceptualizing artifact design.

We start with the assumption that ICT-based civic networks, as a class of systems – and as public artifacts – share a commitment to promoting open access to resources available through them. To the extent that civic networks purport to be so, their constitution (their specification and material embodiment) raises the *prior* question with particular urgency. The constructivist analyst would study the social process and historical context in which the design was produced. What (or whose) interpretations of the artifact won, and whose lost out? What (or whose) values, norms, interests and ideologies prevailed in the process and why? The investigation would be incomplete, we believe, without a consideration of the structural realities embedding the social process of design. A key question here would be: How was power distributed in that milieu? What groups and cultural *logics* (Friedland & Alford, 1991) – standing for preferred meanings, practices, and dispositions, including interests – influenced the design, and what groups could not? How were cultural conflicts resolved? Did the process promote or frustrate the open access ideal?

Emphasizing the lens of culture – as in cultural logics – in explaining the emergence and stabilization of and change in organizational forms gives sociological institutional theory its "theoretical distinctiveness" (Tolbert & Zucker, 1983). ICT artifacts are instantiations of organizational form. They embody distinctive configurations that are simultaneously technological and social. Typically, when designers select a set of enabling components, they do so based on some understanding of the artifact's functions and its target users. If, for instance, they see a civic network primarily as a vehicle for delivering public services to needy people, their technological choices would incorporate databases and transaction trackers. If they see it primarily as a platform for open dialog among citizens and elected officials, one would expect them to include interactive capabilities like electronic mail. These *technological* choices obviously have *social* consequences, selecting some groups in, selecting others out. In the first instance, the network is a service delivery mechanism intended for users of public services; in the second, it is a platform intended for use more generally by the public. By designing the network for delivering services to underserved populations, for example, designers are attempting to change a social structure which, as it exists, may provide few viable avenues to the needy to conveniently satisfy their needs. Intended or not, the design becomes a social intervention which, if successful, changes relations between this social group (the needy) and others in that social structure.

Our institutionalist approach to artifact design uses what Rao (1998) labels the cultural frame analysis of organizational form. Cultural frames are cognitive schema that actors rely on in making technological choices. More generally, frames allow actors to make sense of the world. Actors acquire these sense-making resources from their professional background, training, and organizational socialization. Actors are assumed to bring their schema with them into social situations. As a result, a design setting involving multiple actors can feature multiple, possibly incongruent and conflicting schema. For example, technical professionals may see a civic network in technical terms and their task narrowly as specification of a technically elegant design. Schema differences with nontechnical actors can trigger conflict, and how these conflicts are resolved affects the artifact's form and the technological choices leading up to it. In the present case, certain schema helped shape collective cultural preferences (answering the question *What are meaningful uses of the Urban-net?*) and social choices (*What social groups should the Urban-net serve?*) more than others. These were, of course, technological design decisions, and the network infrastructure that resulted from these decisions diverged substantially from the project's original aim of structural change.

After Porpora (1989), we understand social structure as patterned relations among social entities (groups, individuals, organizations) in a given social order. In any structure, some entities tend to be more powerful than others from superior access to scarce resources. A large organization, for example, may have greater clout over local decisions relative to a smaller organization due to its status as a large employer in the community. Individuals representing this larger organization may command more attention in collective decision processes. Nevertheless, assuming that these processes are democratic, even structurally powerful actors must mobilize support for their preferences from other actors before they can realize them. Behavior is said to be political (or *micropolitical*, when individuals are involved) when actors use others "as resources in competitive situations" (Burns, 1961). Cultural framing is political (or micropolitical) activity in this sense of the term, wherein actors attempt to garner support by persuading other actors to back their design.

From this perspective, we view design as the site of micropolitical conflict and struggle pitting *challengers* against *defenders* of the social structural status quo (Fligstein, 1999), wherein interacting designers with a vested interest in the prevailing structure attempt to configure the artifact in culturally meaningful ways while challengers of the status quo push to obtain structural definition for preferred alternative cultural logics by grounding them in the emergent form. Design negotiations play out between old and new cultural logics, between institutionalized and emergent structures (Hargadon & Douglas, 2001). The social process of design is the arena for these conflicted encounters, and the design outcome bears their imprint.

In course of time, the artifact is said to stabilize – when a degree of consensus emerges on its meaning(s) among stakeholders. When this happens, social relations embodied in the artifact are on their way to institutionalization – when the form is reproduced, perpetuated – through the everyday practices of actors implicated in these relations (Jepperson, 1991). The artifact's distinctive configuration – both technological and social – becomes taken-for-granted when this happens and is rarely open for further negotiation thereafter. Here, *artifact* refers to the Urban-net's technological (ICT) infrastructure.

Infrastructures tend to stabilize and become institutionalized for a variety of cultural and structural reasons. An institutionalist view of the micropolitics of design is sensitive to the very real possibility of cultural inheritances and structural allegiances acting on the designers to more or less effectively constrain design decisions along conservative lines.

Artifacts in general and ICT infrastructures in particular are usually not constituted anew; they tend to be extensions of existing systems. Taken together then, designers' cultural inheritances (the schema they bring with them into the design process) and pressure for backward compatibility exerted by existing systems set up path dependencies – wherein past commitments intrude on present and future developmental trajectories. Accordingly, an institutionalist response to the *prior* question would examine human design behavior in relation to such cultural and structural constraints, documenting the nature of influence attempts (e.g., designers pushing design in a conservative direction) and their relative success as formative forces on the design as it emerges and stabilizes. As public projects, civic networks necessarily develop in relation to entrenched cultural logics and structures prevailing in a given social order. As such, their design and ongoing development tend to invite activist intervention from challengers as well as defenders of the status quo.

Civic network projects often are socially progressive structural interventions, challenging the status quo and promising to (literally) *rewire* structure by enabling relations between hitherto unconnected individuals, groups, and organizations and by bringing marginalized or excluded interests into the public sphere by affording them a public platform. The task for designers is to materialize this aim in the network's constitution so that it is routinely enacted – thus institutionalized – in the new social practices made possible by the design.

For example, every time a K-12 school uses the network to link to a medical hospital for primary healthcare, the new network-enabled practice helps solidify the relation between these organizations. In course of time, both entities come to see the once-new practice as routine, taken-for-granted, legitimate. Delivering and receiving healthcare services over the civic network become institutionalized practice at the sites, inviting financial budgets and staff resources to sustain the practice. If this phenomenon recurs at a number of other sites, a new social structure characterized by new relational patterns will have been set up and stabilized in the area served by the network. However, those with a vested interest in the status quo should be expected to resist the structural intervention – because they stand to lose most from any change – and co-opt the network instead to serve their conservative purposes. If they win, the network will reaffirm prevailing cultural logics and structures: no new practices will be legitimized; no new relational patterns will be activated.

Broadband refers to a class of ICTs capable of data transfer speeds significantly greater than the 56k dial-up rates of telephone modem technology.[2] For instance, cable modem and digital subscriber line (DSL) services – widely available broadband solutions used in the US for Internet access – are capable of transfer speeds in the megabit (millions of bits per second) range compared to the kilobit range (thousands of bits a second) common in telephone modems. Broadband speeds stem from greater technological complexity, and this often means users must upgrade their ICT devices and technical skills in order to use broadband, or to use it well. Monthly service charges tend to be considerably higher than dial-up, so there is an increased financial burden on the user as well.

Broadband telecommunication directs attention to important social structural realities. By demanding, as a matter of *practical necessity* (Winner, 1993), significant additional resources – financial, technological, know-how – of users, broadband penetration in the US tends to reflect the income distribution, with the higher income populations far more likely to have access to it. This has produced a new type of divide – between broadband haves and have-nots.[3] Financial transactions, public information databases, and services are increasingly migrating online but are not available to those on the wrong side of this new Digital Divide. These citizens must expend time and effort to avail of amenities that the digitally privileged citizens take-for-granted and can access with a mere mouse-click from the workplace or home. Broadband access can go significantly farther than dial-up access in promoting a

---

[2] Broadband, according to the US Federal Communications Commission's use of the term "advanced telecommunications capabilities," refers to "services and facilities with an upstream (customer-to-provider) and downstream (provider-to-customer) transmission speed exceeding 200 kbps" (McGarty & Bhagavan, 2002, p. 4).

[3] Moyers (2006), for example, notes disparities in broadband access inside the US and comparatively between the US and other nations in the "New Digital Divide."

higher quality of life: their higher data transfer speed – their higher *bandwidth* – allows the provision of enriched or *high-touch* services, such as video-based telemedicine, where the physician provides mental health counseling remotely to needy populations, for example. Those without broadband must forgo such conveniences.

Broadband civic networks afford one way to mitigate inequitable access and narrow the divide. If the community health center in a poor neighborhood is on such a network along with the local hospital, a needy patient without broadband access at home could go to the first location to receive care. Sick children can get care from the hospital nurse over the network if schools were connected. Broadband's expressive capacity (i.e., its speed) can enrich social *production* (not just consumption) by providing marginalized groups a point of entry into an expanded public sphere. An inner city youth group, for example, can broadcast street theater productions over the network, bypassing local mass media outlets and their biases. Civic networks based on broadband can multiply possibilities for human flourishing both on the consumption and production fronts, but they can also confront stakeholders with tough design challenges.

Broadband's higher technological complexity coupled with its financial and know-how demands can bias civic network design toward individuals, groups, and organizations that are well resourced in these terms. The network can serve no one if it cannot sustain itself financially, and such a concern, which is legitimate and well founded, may bias design in favor of entities that can help sustain it. Given that distribution of resources tends to be asymmetric in any social structure (in that some entities are better resourced than others), designers are faced with a fundamental tension sooner or later: that between designing for (access) *equity* and (financial) *viability*. Should the civic network be designed to serve all or only the well resourced? We have stated this tension in stark, black-and-white terms for rhetorical reasons. The choice need not be, cannot be, equity *or* viability: arguably, it has to be both. How then should designers negotiate this tension? We offer pointers from a case study.

The Urban-net project sought to rewire social structure in the project area. The project steering committee set out to materialize this aspiration in the design of the Urban-net's technological infrastructure. But the specifications that emerged fell short of this aim and reaffirmed instead the existing social structure, with large, resource-rich organizations as network users. The network was priced out of reach of community-based organizations (smaller nonprofits) who lacked the necessary resources for broadband. The tension between viability and equity logics was resolved in favor of the first in the infrastructure design that emerged, as was that between the prevailing social structure and the promise of structural change. The cultural–political struggles in the committee that produced this design outcome are analyzed elsewhere (Venkatesh & Shin, 2005) and are not revisited here. Instead, we consider a crucial *developmental* issue: What can the committee do now so that the Urban-net's future does not merely reproduce its present form but continues to progress toward the project's original goal? The question is meaningful considering the path dependency pressure that infrastructures often generate, pressure that would tend to constrain the Urban-net's future development along present lines. Users currently rely on Urban-net for "mission critical" applications and are likely to resist any proposed change that threatens existing arrangements. Is it possible then to steer its future development in new directions? Is it possible to keep the design open to change when the stabilized state generates pressure against change?

The following section provides the background to the Urban-net project. We then discuss two relevant and connected ideas: architecture and infrastructure. Architectural desiderata – values, norms, interests that designers seek to promote in and through the architecture – may be viewed as framing design activity in cultural terms. An infrastructure, for its part, materializes these desiderata (wholly or selectively) in ICT components. Once stabilized, infrastructures are known to resist change. We propose two strategies to assure openness. First, it is important to articulate desiderata in a layered architecture to help stakeholders better manage open access to the infrastructure. Second, we use the ideas of *architecture* and *infrastructure* to think about the conditions within which individuals interact to make collective design choices. We hold that these microsocial conditions should be designed. For instance, norms and rules covering interaction and deliberation, and management of social relations inside and outside the design setting should themselves be design objects.

Such elements may be manipulated to increase the probability of collectives materializing intended outcomes in the design. When stakeholders agree to design the social conditions under which they will conduct design work, they agree that the proper starting point is the social dynamic of the design process itself. To the extent that civic network projects wish to rewire the macrostructure (the broader social order), designers would do well to start with the microstructure, the microsocial order. If relations *among* designers cannot be characterized in terms of the aspirations envisaged for the larger order, such as equity, what are the chances they will be realized in the design? The social conditions of design may be seen as second-order resources that can powerfully shape the first-order resource – the civic network (see Gualini, 2002), but the design of such resources frequently does not figure among designers' concerns.

Background to the Research

The Urban-net project was funded by a New York state program. Per a 1995 regulatory settlement, Telco (pseudonymous telecommunications provider) committed $50 million to develop/deploy advanced telecommunications infrastructure/services in economically poor, technologically underserved zip code areas.[4] A state-level program committee was established to solicit proposals from consortia of

[4]"Economically disadvantaged areas means zip codes within Standard Metropolitan Statistical Areas (SMSA's) and cities, towns and villages outside SMSA's that are within the operating territory for (the Telco) in New York State…Median household incomes for the listed zip codes, cities, towns and villages are below 75% of the statewide median household income" (NY State Advanced Telecommunications Program, First Round RFP, 1996). Underserved zip codes were defined as those "where the percentage of households without telephone service is at least 50% above the statewide average…" (NY State Advanced Telecommunications Program, First Round RFP, 1996).

public organizations (local government agencies, K-12 and higher educational institutions, public hospitals), community-based organizations or CBOs (small public and private nonprofits), and small business units via a competitive request for proposals (RFP) process. Only organizations located in or serving approved zip code areas were eligible to subscribe to program-funded networks. State and federal government agencies were ineligible, neither were individuals, families, and households. Two rounds of grants were given out before the grant program closed in 2000. Twenty-two projects received funding overall under the program.

Network subscribers (users) paid subsidized telecommunications service charges and were eligible for additional funds for user training or ICT resources; only subscribers were eligible for these additional resources. Subscribers were required to connect to the network's shared backbone (explained below) to avail of these benefits. Eighty percent of every grant returned to Telco to fund development/deployment of infrastructure and services; the remainder went to subscriber sites for ICT resources or training. Grant funds could not be used to hire technical staff or consultants or to fund software development. When implemented, the Urban-net would serve as a hardwired intranet locally to enable high-speed multimedia exchange among subscribers; it would also connect subscriber organizations to the Internet at broadband speeds.

The program sought proposals connecting large and small organizational entities across *functional sectors* (for example, K-12 education qualified as a distinct sector; hospitals, clinics, and nursing homes belonged in a different sector – healthcare). Proposals with a single-sector focus were discouraged. Explaining the decision to use a competitive RFP process in awarding grants, a member of the program proposal selection committee said: "We were not interested in putting technology in place. (Proposers) had to make a strong case that the investment would make a difference… in economic and social terms." Selectors further hoped that the grant opportunity would motivate local organizations to come together and propose cooperative uses of advanced technology to meet local needs and resolve local problems. They saw program-funded networks serving as *community networks* – as civic resources helping forge "coalitions and partnerships" and "common ground" among diverse organizations to facilitate access to social services and public information in poor neighborhoods. These ideas, shaped by civic networking models of communitarian uses of ICTs, influenced the Urban-net steering committee right from the project's outset. At the steering committee's behest, a member assembled and distributed information on operational civic networks in North America, including dial-up Free-Nets, to guide thinking on the design of the Urban-net. A selector encouraged the committee to envision and realize a "true" community network – an interactive civic amenity flexible in design to accommodate changing community needs and affordable by "pockets of all sizes and depths" – by both large and small organizational subscribers.

Consequently, the steering committee envisaged the Urban-net as a technology-enabled social innovation promoting broadband access and social equity by incorporating small and large organizational subscribers and enabling new relational patterns across sectors and organizations – thus literally rewiring social structure in the project area – to serve needy residents. Public organizations were providers of a broad range of critical social services used by significant segments of the project area's economically poor residents – services such as Medicaid, which provides financial support to those whose income and resources fall below what they need for medical care. CBOs were smaller in size relative to public organizations, but they were a significant presence in poor neighborhoods and were heavily used locations where residents accessed the services provided by the public organizations. Neighborhood service providers (adult and children's day care centers, for instance), public assistance law agencies, neighborhood media arts initiatives – these are some examples of CBOs. Comparing CBOs to public organizations, one selector noted: "They (CBOs) may be more creative…more aware of what communities need." Linking public organizations and CBOs over the Urban-net would instantiate the *common ground* idea of organizations working together to meet local needs through network applications.

In 1996, area residents formed a voluntary association to submit a grant proposal in the program's second round solicitation. Most represented eligible public organizations and CBOs and were prospective subscribers of Urban-net; others were private citizens with an interest in public interest projects (small business participation was negligible and is left out of this analysis). The group was self-selected in response to the grant opportunity, which was publicized by Telco in the area. By the time the proposal was submitted a year later, the group had formalized into a steering committee. A technology (sub) committee was also formed. The proposal won a $3.8 million grant. The committee considered the grant as the first in a series and committed itself to ongoing grant-seeking to continually grow the Urban-net and advance the project's original plan.

The committee's goal for the infrastructure design process was to secure subscription commitments from CBOs and public organizations. The project's cross-organizational, cross-sectoral connectivity objective could only be realized if diverse agencies signed on. There was broad agreement in the committee on other desired architectural elements that members wished to see incorporated in the infrastructure, including centrality of Internet Protocol (IP), availability of more and less expensive broadband access network services to enable subscription by public organizations and CBOs, and support for diverse service providers (elaborated below). The design process brought together the steering committee and Telco professionals (with the committee as client) to specify the infrastructure. Once the design was completed, Telco would deploy the infrastructure and make the Urban-net operational.

The infrastructure comprised two parts: network backbone and access network. *Backbone* refers to the ICT equipment at Telco switching centers and the telecommunications lines that linked them together. For the Telco designers assigned to the project, the design task was specification of backbone capacity – number of subscribers it would support and the data transfer speeds at which it would support them. *Access network* refers to the wired links between a Telco switching center and a subscriber site. Users are linked to other users and the Internet over the backbone.

The design task here entailed specification of access network service demand and end-points: what sites would connect to the backbone over what services?

For a host of reasons (discussed in Venkatesh & Shin, 2005) internal and external to the steering committee, the design product failed to realize the project's aim. Today, public organizations are the only users, and they use the backbone to tie together their physically distributed systems and local area networks, and for Internet access. Instead of bridging organizations and sectors, the backbone extends intraorganizational networks. This was not the only change from original intentions. Preceding design, the first author completed a comprehensive planning effort to elicit user needs, which revealed broad-based interest in software applications. Applications would enable area residents to access services and information. But during the design process, public organizations grew more interested in intraorganizational connectivity for moving data across their distributed campuses and worksites. Applications meant additional costs because they would have to be developed first. Public organizations wished instead to cut their telecommunications costs using the subsidized connections available through the project.

Urban-net's present form is attributable in part to broadband resource requirements; as was noted, broadband demands a certain level of resources of users. Public organizations had these resources; CBOs did not. This asymmetry, objectively real in the project area, had nonetheless to be persuasively framed before it could sway collective design choices. This occurred when the design process stalled and pressure from the program mounted on the steering committee to show evidence of progress in signing up users or risk losing the money. Whereupon, some committee members alluded to the resource asymmetry when arguing in favor of promoting project viability over equity: public organizations, by being willing and able *right now* to sign on as subscribers, could save the grant. CBOs could be brought in subsequently to realize the equity aim. This framing was influential and helped sway the committee's collective design choices favoring public organizations. Ironically, it was this very same structural resource asymmetry that motivated program authorities to target poor neighborhoods for broadband deployment.

Architecture and Infrastructure

Architecture embodies a worldview (McGarty, 1992), an ideological stance on who the target users will be and what needs will be met; this worldview motivates the design of the technological infrastructure. More specifically, an architecture organizes a structured set of *functions* that work concertedly to ensure reliable information exchange between two or more end systems (e.g., personal computers). A classic insight from the early work on ARPAnet called for breaking down this communications challenge into subproblems and equipping each *layer* in an architecture to handle them (Whitt, 2004). A layer defines a set of closely related functions; a layer is *modular* to the extent it satisfies this criterion. Functions involved in transferring information between two end systems over a local area network (LAN), for example, would include the following: the sender (PC) must address the data to ensure delivery to the destination PC (receiver) and not any other on the LAN and encode the data for transmission over the network. The intended receiver would have to check the data for transmission error and request retransmission if necessary. This set of functions is part of the data link layer in LAN and wide area networking. Note that this layer contributes one of set of capabilities for reliable data transfer. Other modular layers in the architecture contribute other necessary functions to collectively solve the challenge of reliable data transfer between sender and receiver.

Whitt (2004) traces the concept of layers to the work of the network working group in 1969 on what became the ARPAnet, precursor to the Internet: "the general view was that any protocol was a potential building block and so the best approach was to define simple protocols, each limited in scope, with the expectation that any of them might someday be joined or modified in…unanticipated ways. The protocol design philosophy adopted by the NWG…broke new ground for what came to be… accepted as the layered approach to protocols" (p. 360). The layered approach underpins the Internet and its dynamism today.

Protocols implement layer functions in hardware and software, rendering them usable. Protocols, in this context, refer to conventions and rules governing reliable data transfer. A network interface card, for example, implements data link layer functions in hardware and software. One is buying and installing these functions when one buys and installs an Ethernet card (or adapter) in their PC. Later, if the user decides to replace this card with a better card, or replaces it with one that works wirelessly, modularity helps localize effects of the change to the data link layer; the other layers are not affected. Modularity promotes flexibility, allowing "products and services to evolve by accommodating changes made at appropriate layer rather than having to rework the entire set of protocols" (Whitt, 2004).

The user benefits from flexibility since he is not locked into a particular configuration of system capabilities. If he can find a better or cheaper card than the one he uses at present, he can change into it without the effects of the change ramifying wildly across the entire architecture. Flexibility helps designers and vendors too, as is the enterprise of innovation itself. Innovators can design an improved card and market it widely, reassuring users that disruption would be minimal. A modular set allows them to provide this reassurance.

Modularity requires vertical (hierarchical) integration of layers. As a modular layer only supports a small, closely related set of functions, it depends on other layers below in the architecture for other necessary functions. More formally, layer n provides functions to layer $n + 1$ and depends on functions provided by layer $n - 1$. Interlayer dependencies are enabled via standardized interfaces; it is through these interfaces that layers request functions from other layers in the architecture. Standardized interlayer interfaces ensure minimal disruption when a user, for example, switches to wireless Ethernet as long as the layer above *(n + 1)* can request functions in the standard way. Similarly, the layer below *(n − 1)* is not disturbed as long as standardized interfaces are used. Actual implementation of layer functions in, for instance, the Ethernet card is of no concern to other layers; their only concern is with the interface. In this sense, each modular layer may be thought of as a black box: the "effect of black-boxing is that only the interface (the outside) of the box matters" (Hanseth et al., 1996).

The layered approach has been influential in data communications but is also useful in characterizing ICT artifacts like the PC. A PC is usually not a monolithic device but an integrated system of layered, interconnected parts. PCs rely on two classes of software: the operating system and utility programs that work directly with hardware, and software applications (e.g., a word processing program) that depend on the operating system and utilities to request and receive hardware services. These components are "hierarchically segmented" (Williams, 1997); they perform specialized tasks, are more or less modular. They are also, for that reason, necessarily interdependent. The hierarchy's base is system hardware, which includes components like the microprocessor (or CPU) and others that determine a PC's capabilities. The operating system and other utilities form the next layer up the hierarchy, with applications on the third and topmost layer (from the human user's standpoint). The bottom layers (system hardware, operating system/utilities) may be said to constitute the PC's technological infrastructure. Applications run *on top of* and rely on this infrastructure to be useful. An exploded, architectural view permits a configurational (versus monolithic) portrait of the PC as an ensemble of more or less standardized pieces. System capabilities are constrained within material and design considerations by vendors' interest in product differentiation, standardization, and efficiency at infrastructural layers, but some customization usually is possible to accommodate user tastes/needs. Modularity of the PC architecture helps localize the effects of changes occurring in, for example, the LAN to the PC's Ethernet card without disrupting the PC itself; similarly, changes to the PC are kept from affecting the network.

Infrastructure

McGarty (1992) characterizes an ICT infrastructure as "a shareable, common, enabling, enduring resource that has scale in its design, is sustainable by an existing market, and is the physical embodiment of an underlying architecture" (p. 235). Elaborating this view of infrastructure – networks in particular – yields the following portrait:

Physical embodiment of architecture: Infrastructure is the embodiment of stakeholders' worldviews (including values, norms, interests), their ideologies. As products of human design, both architecture and infrastructure include as well as exclude, recognizing some users and needs as more in line with valued goals than others. Design choices in both instances are also, therefore, social choices. However, well-designed products typically permit a degree of flexibility to accommodate needs as they evolve and change.

Shareable: Infrastructure is usable by and available to disparate users and applications to access a broad variety of shared resources. It is a *global* enabler defined with reference to a community of users which supports their disparate needs by allowing a degree of *local* customization and flexibility (Star & Ruhleder, 1996).

Common: Infrastructure's shareability is premised on its presentation of a "common and consistent interface to all users, accessible by standard means" (McGarty, 1992). While particular applications may be customized to the user's needs, those applications typically access the infrastructure and the resources connected to it using standard means.

Economically sustainable: Given the capital-intensive nature of infrastructure projects, they must be economically viable, attracting a sufficient number of providers and serving a sufficient number of paying users to stay viable. The more advanced the technological constituents of an infrastructure, the more expensive it is to build out and sustain, and the more urgent its economics become. As we remarked previously relative to the practical necessity demands (Winner, 1993) of broadband generally and the Urban-net project in particular, the financial viability imperative can clash with the logic of equity that tends to drive civic networking projects, producing tensions between architectural desiderata and their implemented reality and confronting stakeholders with difficult social choice dilemmas.

Enduring: Building out an infrastructure is a time-consuming and capital-intensive effort, and, as such, the product is intended for the long term. But to the extent that target users, needs, and architectural desiderata change over time, the infrastructure must be capable of change too. An infrastructure must be stable without precluding its ability to change, and it must change in a way that is transparent to its users (McGarty, 1992). The scope of the infrastructure will determine the scope of change that is feasible. With infrastructures that are ultralarge, like the Internet, change of limited scope is far more feasible than a global overhaul – when foundational building blocks change across the board – due to the scale of anticipated disruption. With infrastructures of smaller scope, as in civic networks, even global change may be feasible under appropriate conditions.

Infrastructures tend to endure for many reasons. As enablers of applications and social practices that, over time, come to depend on them, their reliability and availability on a continuous basis are foundational to modern organizations. Service contracts, vendor relations, and organizational budget allocations are institutionalized to ensure the disruption-free operation of the infrastructure. Technical staff are recruited, trained, and managed in light of the same ends. These support personnel are critical to organizational computing, which would be impossible to sustain without them. In time, sunk investment in the infrastructure – which is both financial and cognitive (e.g., skills training) – begins to pay off as its operations stabilize. Later technology choices are powerfully constrained by their assessed backward fit with the technology and support infrastructure, and "these path dependencies can result in lock in to established solutions and standards" (Williams, 1997). These are structural reasons. Infrastructures endure for cultural reasons as well. As critical elements embedded deep in the fabric of organizations and in work processes they directly or indirectly enable, infrastructures are central constituents of a social reality that users and technical staff come to take for granted, as "always there." Infrastructures cease to be socially visible the more they are taken for granted, and thinking of them as such, as "always there," or rather, not thinking of them (taken for granted things are, by definition, rarely objects of conscious thought processes) only confirms and deepens the invisibility. As enablers of "how we have always done things around here," not only are they seen as legitimate but they also often define the notion of legitimacy itself. As such, changing them is unthinkable. Infrastructures can constrain change and thinking about change. We expand on some of these ideas below using institutionalist insights.

Infrastructure: An Institutional View

At project outset, stakeholders were starting with a "blank sheet of paper" more or less and were free to conceptualize the Urban-net within the parameters of the program and civic networking models. But during design, the "interpretive flexibility" (Bijker, 1995) of the Urban-net was effectively circumscribed by the institutionalized technological and technical support infrastructure at Telco and public organizations. This infrastructure was well entrenched at these locations and could not be readily changed to accommodate the Urban-net. Rather, as the *younger* artifact Urban-net was forced to fit with the *older* base (see Hughes, 1996). Institutionalized infrastructures tend to *infect* elements connected to them for structural and cultural reasons, institutionalizing them in turn over time (Zucker, 1977).

A hallmark of institutionalization is the institutionalized entity's progressive invisibility.

Invisibility – as occurs, for instance, when "any propensity to question (it) has halted due to elimination of alternative institutions or principles" (Jepperson, 1991, p. 152) – results from, and further reinforces it's taken for granted status. As an entity deeply embedded in public organizations' institutionalized structures and practices, the Urban-net is at risk of dropping from public view as an object of questioning. The less visible an entity is in the social sense, the higher the degree of institutionalization and the higher the assurance of continuing institutionalization along prevailing lines. It would present "a near insuperable threshold" (Jepperson, 1991) for change interventions if it is an institutionalized aspect of organizational reality and cannot, as a consequence, be "seen."

Institutionalized infrastructures can constrain an artifact's initial as well as future form due to path dependency pressures. Tying Urban-net's infrastructure to that of the public organizations helped to stabilize the design and get the network off the ground at a time when the committee was under pressure from the program. In line with the "contagion" phenomenon, the institutionalized base at public organizations can be expected to infect the newer artifact so that the Urban-net's present form will likely continue at least for the span of Telco service contracts (multiple years). Under the circumstances, it is legitimate to ask if Urban-net can be changed at all consistent with the project's original ideals. But before this question can be answered, it is useful to recall the notion of layering and ask:

> What "*aspects* of a(n)…institutional configuration are (or are not) negotiable and *under what conditions*" (Thelen, 2003)?

Writing on the forces and pressures that shape developmental trajectories of institutions in general, Thelen (2003) urges researchers to examine what aspects or layers of a given social organization, for example, are changing (or are changeable) and what are "staying the same," locked in because of path dependency. Some aspects may indeed be locked in for this reason, but it may still be possible for change proponents to add on new elements "without dismantling the old." US political institutions (like the Congress, for instance) have in fact evolved in this way, wherein "institutional innovators accommodated and in many ways adapted to the logic of the preexisting system" while successfully pursuing change; importantly, their success, Thelen observes, "did not push developments further along the same track" as path dependency might suggest.

With technological artifacts, as previously noted, pressures for back compatibility exerted by preexisting systems and from social relations and practices implicated in and enabled by this institutionalized base tend to set up conditions for path-dependent developmental trajectories. While some actors stand to benefit from the continuation of such trajectories, those who are excluded could be a source of pressure favoring change. Excluded interests could bring political pressure for change by increasing the artifact's social visibility via mass media and the World Wide Web. In the case of civic networking projects, excluded constituencies and their advocates could partner with social movement organizers in the area (or with organizations of broader scope) to tap into new cultural framing strategies. "Digital inclusion is a Civil Right" is an example.[5] By connecting their grievances to a broadly resonant frame like Civil Rights, advocates may be able to mobilize new support constituencies to effect change.

The scope of the change sought would depend on the success of the mobilization effort, and radical redesign of the infrastructure is certainly possible. Alternatively (taking the Urban-net as an example), proponents could start by targeting (software) applications so as to not disrupt the network's present source of financial stability, which stems from its linkage to subscribers' infrastructures. Mass media outlets and the Web could be used to publicize unmet needs and to demand that applications be developed to meet these needs and made accessible over the Urban-net. If such strategies are successful, the Urban-net's social visibility would rise, lowering the threshold for further change interventions. Path-dependent, lock-in effects could continue at the infrastructural layers while new uses are layered on incrementally and transparently at the application layer. Layering on of such uses could occur together with, or as catalyst or consequence of incremental redesign of the steering committee's mission, structure, and composition, and of service contracts and project by-laws motivated by the digital inclusion criterion.

A layered understanding of ICT artifacts blunts the determinism of path-dependent, lock-in models of stabilization and accommodates the possibility of "incremental or

---

[5] Apropos, access to certain services by populations with special needs is presently covered under the provisions of the US Civil Rights Act of 1964, as noted, for example, by a New York State Department of Health press release from 2005: "Currently, federal Title VI of the Civil Rights Act and state regulations require hospitals to provide interpretation services to patients with difficulty speaking English or who have disabilities affecting their communication." (NY State Department of Health Press Release, September 16, 2005).

bounded change" (Thelen, 2003): even stable artifacts may be modified via "partial renegotiation" of some layers without necessarily touching the others. While assuring public visibility is crucial to creating the conditions for network change, it is not by itself enough actively to aid and abet new uses of the infrastructure. In order for this to occur, stakeholders would need to articulate desiderata in a modular architecture so that vendors and providers of a range of services can do their work at the appropriate layer or layers independently of the other layers. This is the promise, after all, of a modular design. Architectural desiderata may never get so articulated. As occurred in the Urban-net case, stakeholders may simply agree on a few broad principles that they may then refer to shape infrastructure design. They may never flesh out and organize these principles in a system of layered functions. We believe it is vital that they are so articulated, as we show with the Systems Reference Architecture (SRA).

The first author as chair of the Urban-net technology committee began work on the SRA in the course of a program of application demonstrations/trials initiated during the design process. With the SRA, we initiated the process of identifying and describing the Urban-net's functional specifications spanning both the upper and lower layers, building on the infrastructural specifications provided by participating Internet Service Providers (ISPs) and Telco. By starting to document protocols across the whole architecture, we wished to facilitate participation by diverse service providers by publicizing actionable information.

With the SRA, we started defining multiple entry points for service providers interested in doing business with users.[6] The SRA was not authorized or commissioned by the Urban-net steering committee, nor was it used by the committee in deliberations. The first author used it to organize discussions in and outside the committee on the Urban-net's ongoing development consistent with the original aims of the project. The SRA contributed to the development of a local market for high-technology services (which is still in its fledgling stage). The SRA embodies an attempt to articulate a coherent conceptual system linking the project's aims, present and prospective future service providers and network users. It outlines one path for realizing network change.

The Services Reference Architecture (SRA)

The SRA was sketched out as an open, modular six-layer architecture (Fig. 16.1). The bottom three layers describe the basic functions of signal propagation

[6] The SRA presents a sketch of Urban-net specifications. It could be further developed by adding more detail. It could, for example, list current applications by name, as well as client/server hardware and wiring specifications. In addition to technical specifications at each layer, projected future changes could also be documented, as in "Market changes may move supported file/printer server platform away from X to the Linux operating system" and provide a timeframe for the anticipated migration, as in "eventually Protocol X will be phased out as the Internet Protocol under platforms Y and Z becomes more prevalent across the enterprise. We project that Protocol X will be dropped in the next two to three years (confidence 0.80)."

Network Management
Application Implementation
Value-added IP
Basic Internet Protocol
Layer 2
Physical

Fig. 16.1 The Services Reference Architecture (SRA)
(Copyright *Community and Information Technology Institute* (CITI), 1999)

(Physical), data link (layer 2), and network (basic Internet Protocol functions). Urban-net's broadband infrastructure today implements these functions using fiberoptic physical links on the access network and backbone (physical layer) and gigabit Ethernet and Asynchronous Transfer Mode/Cell Relay Service (ATM/CRS) services at three different (broadband) data transfer speeds at layer 2. Subscribers use the network to get on the Internet using third-party ISPs. Technical specifications at these layers were made available to users and the steering committee by Telco and the ISPs.

The upper layers – Value-added Internet Protocol (covering functions beyond basic IP), Application Implementation, and Network Management[7] – reference prospective uses (applications) of the infrastructure. Desired applications were identified and prioritized via a comprehensive planning process prior to the start of design. Video-conferencing for telemedicine and distance learning, integrated databases, high-speed Internet access, and "one-stop shops" for public network access emerged as top needs. There was community-wide interest in using the Urban-net for cross-organizational, cross-sectoral connectivity. While the application needs were known, technical specifications at the upper layers were far less clear in 1998, when the design process commenced. Products compliant with the new H.323 video standard[8] (which supports desktop video-conferencing over LANs and the Internet), for example, had started to appear in the market. Relative to the older H.320 ISDN video-conferencing standard and implementations based on the broadband multichannel video system specifications (called MVS) that were fairly common in New York State's K-12 schools, the H.323-compliant products promised to sharply lower the cost of desktop Internet video-conferencing while adding useful capabilities not offered by older systems, such as applications sharing. Given its lower costs and the steering committee's interest to assure the Internet Protocol's centrality in the infrastructure, it made sense to envisage Urban-net video applications using the H.323 video specifications.

[7]Referred to as "Application" in a previous version of the SRA. Changed to "Network Management" to avoid confusion with end-user applications such as word processing software.

[8]"H.323 is an umbrella recommendation from the International Telecommunications Union Telecommunication Standardization Section (ITU-T) that defines the protocols to provide audio-visual communication across any packet network" (Wikipedia, accessed October 25, 2006).

The nature of the technical services required to sustain such applications only acquired definition during the course of the demo/trial program (elaborated below) initiated under the aegis of the infrastructure design effort. For example, appropriate technical services at the value-added IP layer, it became clear, would include *back-end* services like switching for video-conferencing sessions linking multiple (over two) user sites. The Applications Implementation layer services would include *front-end* services – such as developing and implementing customized video-conferencing applications for administrative and clinical uses, each set seamlessly integrated, for example, with its particular desktop applications, image and data stores by means of customized software hooks. Both back-end and front-end services could be provided by service providers or by users themselves. The Services Reference Architecture started to document service requirements at upper layers in order to spell out the relevant technical specifications and help (a) service providers interested in providing targeted back-end/front-end services and (b) better manage points at which service hand-offs occurred between users and service providers. Network management layer's concerns were network monitoring, management of service hand-offs and help-desk trouble-shooting for the network overall.

Recall that for all funded projects, Telco was the designated service provider charged under the program with building out and deploying the infrastructure. During the design process, some committee members argued that other smaller service providers (some of whom were locally owned businesses) who had emerged in the increasingly competitive local telecommunications market be allowed to compete with Telco to provide services to subscribers at the bottom three layers. This argument, which had been made by no other project in the state, found favor in the committee, resulting in formal requests for quotes going out to Telco rivals. Although providers did respond to the RFQ and the committee went as far as contract negotiations with one of them, at the end of the day, for a number of reasons, Telco emerged as the only provider. However, the RFQ interlude prompted the committee to mull development of a neutral meet point – referring to a physical point of access to the Urban-net backbone that would be neutral in that it would be controlled by the committee or committee-designated entity and not be any provider. Furthermore, the meet point would not be located on any provider's premise but in a neutral location.

The committee was focused on the bottom three layers because of influential members representing public organizations. As previously noted, these individuals saw networked applications as avoidable expenses. A neutral meet point was later set up to allow service providers to offer infrastructural services to Urban-net users. It exists today, but its role is largely symbolic, representing the *possibility* of open access by a diverse cadre of service providers. In reality, a very small number of them use it to provide largely infrastructural services.

The demo/trial program, which was focused on applications, helped extend the scope of the project's open access aims beyond the bottom layers while adding operational detail to the meet point function. There were at least two motivations for this scope expansion. By starting to articulate specifications across the board in the SRA, we hoped to promote participation in the Urban-net by not just the larger providers of infrastructural services but also by smaller start-ups interested in providing services at other layers. For example, a provider interested in offering services at the application implementation layer could do so independently of providers lower down in the architecture if specifications were well enough documented. By adding detail to upper layer specifications based on the known set of desired applications (as determined through the planning process) and protocols, we hoped to define multiple points of entry into the Urban-net for a wide range of service providers. But the SRA would only be a sketch. We recognized the strategic importance of publicizing the SRA and inviting input from all concerned parties in developing it. We saw the SRA as an open project to be grown collaboratively. The architecture would have to be visible if it was to promote this intent and succeed in opening up broad-based access to the meet point.

Second, a critical set of issues relevant to committee control over the meet point centered on overall network management. Being telecommunications/Internet service providers, neither Telco nor its rivals in the local market wished to assure service levels on any but the bottom three layers, and they would only be concerned with their specific service or services at these layers. The meet point itself, as a whole, would have to be managed by an entity other than these service providers. The need to coordinate management control across service providers and layers became clear when technical problems arose during the demos and trials. These problems stressed the importance of centralized processing of trouble reports as part of a coherent overall network management strategy that this entity would be responsible for. When a user called in a problem, for example, a trouble ticket would have to be issued identifying the problem before it was routed to the appropriate provider (at one or more layers) for further action. The entity responsible for managing the meet point would have to develop the skills and procedures necessary to carry out this initial triage function while also assigning financial resources for supporting 24/7 access (24 h access 7 days a week) over the phone and the Internet. Details such as this, on what the meet point management responsibility would actually involve day to day on the ground, only emerged during the demos and trials.

The Demonstration/Trial Program

The Urban-net planning process revealed the lopsided distribution of ICT resources and technical know-how in the project area, with public organizations qualifying as resource-rich and CBOs, as the resource-poor. Broadband telecommunications was an unfamiliar subject area for CBOs, some of whom were relatively new even to the standard business technologies such as LANs. Public organizations were long-time users of PCs, LANs, and older broadband technologies like T carrier services (e.g., T1 leased line) and knew them all well, but they were far less familiar with the broadband services – ATM/CRS, gigabit Ethernet – available through the Urban-net. Newer specifications like the H.323 protocol was unfamiliar territory as well. Under the circumstances, the steering committee charged the technology committee with a dual responsibility to ensure that the design process and outcome served the interests of all prospective users. First, technology committee would represent agencies' needs (in particular the CBOs') to Telco and translate the broadband technical jargon at meetings to facilitate broad participation in design discussions. Next, technology committee would develop applications prototypes and organize public trials and demonstrations of these prototypes to showcase broadband capabilities and also to help prospective subscribers make informed adoption decisions. The demos/trials were intended to educate prospective adopters through what we called *show-how* – practical illustrative applications of broadband capabilities intended to foster learning-by-using – to augment the technical information or *know-how* provided by Telco and other vendors and service providers. We reasoned that show-how, along with know-how, would equip prospective users to be smarter consumers of broadband.

The first author's research and development group at the Community and Information Technology Institute (or CITI, which is located in the School of Information Studies at Syracuse University) designed, tested, and installed the demos and trials. Telco and local ISPs donated DSL and Internet access services free. Applications selected for prototype development came out of the Urban-net planning effort and focused on Internet video-conferencing for administrative and clinical tele-medicine. We selected the H.323 video standard for use with the demos and trials. A technical manager at a large hospital which participated as a trial site observed of H.323: "Internet video-conferencing…is new to us. We are quite familiar with ISDN-based video-conferencing. With ISDN, it is like dial-up, it is not on the office network, so it was easy. We didn't have to worry about bandwidth issues. But now, with the IP video stream shared on the office network and needing at least 400 kbps or so per stream, we have to look into bandwidth sharing. So far it has not been a problem. But if you are running several (video) sessions at the same time on top of all the office traffic, bandwidth availability may become an issue. The whole world has changed." This quote captures the kinds of questions participants needed information on; by participating in the trial, they hoped to find the answers through learning-by-using.

CITI staff organized two well-attended live public demos. The demos were designed to illustrate technology capabilities through generic, sample applications. The demos used ADSL (asymmetric digital subscriber line) and Internet video-conferencing; groupwork and office applications-sharing (widely used Microsoft desktop programs like the Office suite) by three dispersed groups was the sample application on both occasions. The focus of the demos was on technology capabilities. The demos provided proof of concept that DSL bandwidth was adequate for high-quality video and audio and that connecting three points over the Internet at peak usage times (mid-morning) did not appreciably degrade signal quality. CITI staff evaluated the demos on technical criteria.

The trials occurred after the demos. Trials were installed at the participant site free of charge and left there for a few months to permit extended use directly by the user with their ICTs and organizational work processes. The trials were evaluated on technical and organizational criteria. Three applications were trialed; two of these were in clinical tele-medicine: tele-radiology (networked access to radiological image databases) and pediatric cardiology diagnostics using sonogram imaging. The third was administrative: eligibility screening for Medicaid/Chronic Care benefits certification. All three trials were designed, installed, and tested by CITI staff, who also evaluated the Medicaid application trial (trial participants evaluated the other two and shared reports with the first author). Participants were public organizations like hospitals (as well as affiliated physicians' offices), nursing homes, primary health centers, etc. – all prospective Urban-net subscribers. CBOs could only afford DSL from the eligible services, and this was a consideration in designing the trials around DSL as the access network service. CBOs did not take part as trial sites for many reasons, lack of appropriate ICT resources being one of them, but we wished to illustrate technologies that were relevant to them.

Actionable information on cost and performance of Internet video-conferencing was not readily available because the technologies involved were new. For example, hospitals had well-defined needs suitable for video-conferencing applications, such as remote radiology (tele-radiology) and sonogram-based diagnostics, and were interested in assembling useful information and hoped to offer such applications over the Urban-net at some point in the future. The technical manager quoted above signed on as a participant because she lacked this information. Would H.323 applications cut into bandwidth availability on her LANs and Internet connection so much so that she would be forced to upgrade her networks? If costs prohibited upgrading, could users live with a lower level of network performance? Because user demand for video applications was as yet unknown, service providers were reluctant to develop and offer support services. The trials helped both prospective users and service providers by furnishing a basis for starting to define demand – and a market – for such applications in the project area.

The Medicaid/Chronic Care eligibility certification trial linked the county Department of Social Services, a hospital, and a nursing home over DSL for video-interviewing. County Medicaid staff now conducted the eligibility interview (mandatory under Medicaid) with the applicant using H.323 video-conferencing over the link. The conventional eligibility interview occurred face-to-face and required the applicant to go to the County Medicaid office, and this was inconvenient given that the typical applicant was old and often frail.

With video-interviewing, the applicant could be interviewed right at the nursing home or hospital they happened to be at that time. This trial is noteworthy for a few reasons. First, it linked organizations across sectors (social services and healthcare) with an *application* to serve *needy residents* – satisfying key elements of the project's original aims. Second, the county decided in 2004 to regularize video-interviewing as a standard option (with the face-to-face interview being the other) available to applicants. Many large nursing homes are linked into the video network and offer both options; more expect to enroll. Urban-net services some of these intersite connections. The software used by the sites and back-end services (in SRA's Value-added IP services layer) are provided by a local start-up service provider, exactly as hoped for by the SRA and the demo/trial program.[9]

[9] At this writing, the Urban-net's governing body is exploring the possibility of new infrastructural service providers connecting to the meet point to serve users with layer 2 and Internet access services.

The benefits of open, layered architectures have been explored in relation to wide area networks like the Internet[10] (Cooper, 2004; McGarty, 1992). Barring a few exceptions (e.g., Clement and Shade, 2000), the benefits of the layered approach to civic networking have not received the same level of attention from analysts. Clement and Shade advance a sociotechnical access model to the ICI (the information/communication infrastructure) and use it to organize a wide-ranging sociotechnical and policy design discussion around important questions, questions that lie at the very heart of public interest projects: access for what purposes, access for whom, access to what? The scope of the Services Reference Architecture is local and focused on the Urban-net project area but our aim in articulating the architecture is consistent with Clement and Shade's and stemmed from a commitment to open access. We recognized that, given the SRA's layered and modular format and our commitment to documenting and disseminating its contents widely in the area, and under the appropriate set of conditions, the category *Urban-net user* and *service provider* could expand well beyond the project's geographical boundaries. Given the Internet Protocol's centrality in the Urban-net infrastructure, what is to stop a user anywhere from accessing the network's services over the Internet? Or a service provider anywhere from offering these services? If this were to occur, it would mean a significant expansion of the notions of *user, service provider*, and *service area* as originally envisaged by steering committee: recall that the project's service scope was defined with reference to program-designated zip code areas and limited to users and providers connected directly to the infrastructure. The steering committee did not intend to restrict access to the Urban-net, but neither did it develop mechanisms like the SRA and appropriate policies to actively facilitate open access. The SRA represents a step toward such a development.

Clement and Shade (2000) touch on the basic tension between the open access ideal and "market-led forces and industry initiatives" tasked with developing the information and communication infrastructure. As we noted in relation to the financial viability pressures that surfaced during Urban-net design, such tensions are very real and can, and very often do (as in this case) deflect purportedly public interest initiatives from their original aims. As one CBO representative remarked in frustration during design, alluding to broadband resource demands: "ATM/CRS and underserved don't belong in the same sentence." To counteract market pressures and reassert public interest in the ICI "specific protections or promotion via collective public initiatives may be required" (Clement & Shade, 2000). We wholeheartedly agree on the need for special provisions. Using Urban-net design process as point of reference, we outline the basis for a microsocial architecture: an architecture that articulates desiderata generally for

[10] Cooper (2004) lists principles of openness identified with reference to the Open Data Network (ODN) as follows: open to users, open to providers ("provides an open and accessible environment for competing commercial and intellectual interests"), open to network providers ("It makes it possible for any network provider to meet the necessary requirements to attach and become a part of the aggregate of interconnected networks"), and open to change ("It permits the introduction of new applications and services overtime" … and "It also permits new transmission, switching and control technologies to become available over time"). See the Stockholm Declaration on Open networks (INEC, 2006) for a more recent take on this idea.

open, democratic deliberation and choice-making in civic network design situations. A resource like this – embodying a set of *protections* inspired by norms underpinning discussions around civic networking and communitarian ICT uses generally – was unavailable to the Urban-net steering committee during design; the design outcomes might have been quite different had such a resource been available.

Microsocial Architecture

The Urban-net project was a *political* project as it sought to rewire social structure using technology. But the steering committee's understanding of its project role – which was to materialize this aspiration in design and help institutionalize it through social practices – was technology centered and apolitical, indeed ahistorical. The committee's expectation was that the structural rewiring would be accomplished by appropriately designing the technological infrastructure: the first would flow straightforwardly from the second, with technology serving as the formative force behind social change. If beliefs about "what is morally or materially desirable underlie decisions about ends", factual premises "about how the world operates empirically" influence decisions about means (Scott & Backman, 1990). The committee failed to anticipate resistance to structural rewiring from defenders of the prevailing structure and failed to account for the reality of power relations wherein structurally powerful actors (those with access to scarce resources) typically prevail over relatively poor actors in shaping collective choices. Structurally powerful entities tend to be status quo defenders because they have more to lose from change. The committee, in retrospect, had a naïve appreciation of how the world worked empirically and thus failed to anticipate the need for and equip itself with the appropriate *means* to pursue its *ends* by negotiating the power asymmetries obtaining in the social structure it wished to change.

Civic network design tends to be focused on ends, seldom the means. This case outlines a few of the challenges that can confront designers when the means are neglected.

Design reflects intention and yet, outcomes often are unintended (as in the present case). According to institutional design theorists, attempts at direct design – when stakeholders attempt to direct outcomes – are often unsuccessful because, typically, "there is no single design or designer. There are just lots of localized attempts at partial design cutting across one another…" (Goodin, 1996, p. 28). Conflict resulting from "interactions among intentions" as actors jockey for dominance impact the design in unpredictable ways. The microsocial conditions under which actors interact to make design choices can influence what intentions prevail and how *interactions* among intentions are collectively resolved, but they are usually not objects of design. We would argue that design interventions are better off targeting these conditions (Goodin, 1996), i.e., the *means*. This is the province of indirect design.

Indirect design is not merely a matter of pragmatics (Goodin, 1996) but proceeds within a framework of ends and the values that inform them. Articulation of what we have termed the *microsocial architecture* might start with the thinking that a civic network committed to equity, for example, would be designed in a setting committed to ensuring that design options and decisions are debated openly and actively by a plurality of publics in a spirit of *participatory parity* (Fraser & Honneth, 2003). Such a commitment linking means and ends could be part of a larger set of architectural desiderata – value-based first principles that are intended to serve as a basis for evaluating stakeholder actions by their conformity to overarching norms. The architecture might inform development of pragmatic, dialogic rules – the means – for regulating the mechanics of social interaction, like "everyone gets a chance to speak." Such rules, simple as they may be, rise from a pragmatic appreciation of how the world works empirically and embody efforts to sustain first principles through the hurly-burly of design activity as it unfolds on the ground by serving as infrastructural resources for regulating microsocial intercourse. An *architectural* commitment to open deliberation of design alternatives could be tied to *infrastructural* resources like devil's advocacy, for example. Such resources can facilitate civic dialogue on choices pertinent to the public interest or even to substantive definitions of the public interest. They can be the means for grounding and enacting microsocial architectural desiderata in the design encounter. For their part, the architectural desiderata give actors a reason for voluntarily permitting such resources to regulate situated behavior. It must be emphasized that these resources provide no guarantees that a collective will realize intended outcomes; they can however increase the likelihood thereof (Goodin, 1996).

The Urban-net steering committee failed to anticipate the need for such resources. Public organizational representatives' interest in using the Urban-net backbone to link together their internal systems and networks, for instance, was not adequately debated committee-wide. If this had occurred, the committee might have identified creative ways to leverage this interest to advance the project's original equity aims. Public organizations' interest was a manifestation of the institutionalized cultural inheritances – cultural legacies – and prior occupational socialization that their representatives brought into the design setting. ICTs, these actors believed, could (should) help their organizations to contain operating costs. They operated in an organizational environment of doing-more-with-less and cost containment, hence it is not surprising that they framed the project narrowly using cost-to-user criterion. Given their organizational role, professional background, training, and affiliations (all of which were technical), such a criterion was institutionally sanctioned and therefore legitimate. We argue that microsocial infrastructural resources might have helped to moderate the influence of such legacies by prompting self-introspection. Stated in the form of a rule, all actors could be required, for example, to surface their legacies so that incongruities pertinent to the project may be located and addressed both individually and collectively. Such rules make actors more self-aware and deliberate in their response to the situation and can prompt self-questioning: *Are my actions conducive to furthering the project's aim? When I act, am I doing so wearing my organizational hat or the hat of the steering committee member?* Additionally, the collective may appoint a "conscience-keeper" to periodically subject choice alternatives to collective introspection and debate in light of project aims, for example.

Expanding collective capacity for introspection may also be promoted by instituting the ethic of the *long view*: actors may less readily displace collective aims to the extent that they are accountable to actors with long "time horizons" (Pierson, 2000). This looks ahead to social controls.

Social controls – described as normative or "regulative institutions that ensure individual behavior accords with group demands" (Coser, 1982) – can shape what courses of action are pursued by legitimizing some behaviors and delegitimizing others. In one example, mass media notice helped institutionalize philanthropic (over self-interested) behavior by Minneapolis corporations (Galaskiewicz, 1991). Social controls instantiate the publicity principle attributed to the philosopher Kant, which, as applied here, requires that actions pertinent to the public interest are "publicly defensible" (Goodin, 1996). The Urban-net lacked any such controls. Local mass media outlets, elected officials, urban planners, and opinion leaders – who constitute the so-called *third groups*, i.e., individuals and bodies other than designers and intended users (Shin, 2004) – who might have served as civic-minded external controllers and conscience keepers tended to interpret the project as a technology (rather than social) initiative and ignored it. Consequently, there was little public pressure on the steering committee during the design to stay focused on the project's original aim, nor the means effectively to incentivize and legitimize preferred courses of action or the ethic of the perspective view. Had such controls been available, representatives of public organizations might have been challenged more when they chose to promote their private legacies and interests over the project's aim.

The committee's collective capacity for pursuing valued ends would have benefited from enhanced self-consciousness in regard to its constitutive processes, practices, and internal and external relations. The committee failed to anticipate the importance of designing the appropriate means conducive to working through the empirical obstacles it faced. A more introspective group would have understood design activity appropriately as a contentious cultural–political endeavor considering the project's aspiration: to rewire social structure. The design process should have commenced by equipping steering committee members to enact, in their cognitions, social relations and practices, the new order that the project wished to materialize in the area.

Conclusion

The constructivist assertion that there is nothing *inevitable* about the form assumed by an artifact – that it could have developed along different lines had the circumstances been different – challenges determinism and opens out usefully to the possibility of activism in shaping it (see Williams & Edge, 1996). Our focus is activist in this sense. We ask: What should stakeholders do to increase the likelihood that purportedly civic ICT artifacts do in fact develop as intended? By way of an answer, we discussed two strategies: articulation of a layered functional architecture and, second, articulation of architectural desiderata and derivative infrastructural resources for regulating social behavior in design settings.

We see these strategies as complementary.

Historically, the development of the Services Reference Architecture occurred within the context of the demonstration/trial program. While the impetus for the SRA was primarily forward-looking, we recognized that the claims of the past – in the form of pressure from institutionalized infrastructures (technological, social) at subscriber and service provider sites – could not be discounted and could very well pattern the Urban-net's stabilization and development in path-dependent ways. But the SRA's scope and layered format allow for constructive activism to shape (or reshape) the form over time. ICT artifacts are not monolithic and seldom institutionalize all at once. Rather, they tend to institutionalize in layers, with some layers (usually infrastructure) stabilizing more readily due to pressure for *historical continuities* from infrastructures they are linked to. An institutionalist view analyzes artifact stabilization in relation to other ongoing processes of institutionalization in organizations, permitting a historical understanding of these complex phenomena. The Urban-net's present form and likely future developmental trajectory cannot be understood without reference to the contagion pressures exerted by already-institutionalized elements connected to it. But optimism and possibility are also possible. To see the ICT artifact as a monolith is to assert a politics of fixity and path dependency. To see it as comprised of layers, as described by the SRA, allows a politics of accommodation, where the new can coexist with the old (and upper layer uses, for example, can work without necessitating changes in the layers lower down in the architecture) and negotiated new developmental trajectories are possible going forward.

The microsocial architecture outlines foundational provisions to assure social inclusion and openness in collective deliberations within the civic network's governing body (e.g., the steering committee in the present case). However, the principled linking of means and ends that motivates the architecture – as in, for example, the thinking that a civic network committed to promoting equity would be designed in a setting promoting open access and participatory parity, inquiry, and debate – is readily extensible to cover social interactions generally around the network's proper role in the community. A geographical *community* is usefully seen as comprised of a plurality of publics defined more-or-less tightly around shared identity, interest, and ideology, with some publics commanding greater centrality and power for cultural and structural reasons. If the term *community*, as an ideal type in the social sense, highlights reciprocity, mutuality, and consensus, *publics,* in the plural, recognizes the empirical reality of divergent interests, conflict, and dissensus (see Fraser, 1999). In light of this, a civic network has the obligation, we believe, to (a) serve as an open forum on issues pertinent to a diverse set of publics both central and marginal, (b) catalyze formation of new publics around new needs and aspirations, and (c) facilitate the progressive expansion and diversification of the civic discourse space in the community in order to continue to fulfill its catalytic civic role as the community changes. A civic network that assumes this set of obligations facilitates the community's dialogue with itself by facilitating broad-based discursive membership in the social order through the space it creates, sustains, and continually reaffirms. But whether the network is able to take on, sustain, and continually reaffirm this role is a design choice, one that can affect not just the network's form but also the character of the broader community it helps to produce. The microsocial architecture we have outlined may be seen as a generalized normative resource for regulating discursive encounters – in the network's governing body, between this body and the community's publics, between dominant and marginal publics (Fraser, 1999) – that shape such choices.

Substantively, the term *public interest* incorporates a "collective moral imperative that transcends particular or private interests" (Alexander, 2002). Highlighting the dialogical sense of the term, stakeholders may voluntarily adopt democratic discursive resources for use among themselves and with other publics in defining public interest in the substantive sense of the term (Alexander, 2002). Microsocial conditions under which such norms are debated can powerfully inform the degree of inclusiveness of the definitions that emerge. In light of this, civic network stakeholders must work to ensure that the network's design stays open and responsive to demographic changes over time as new publics emerge and new, expanded interpretations of the public interest struggle to register themselves on the collective agenda. As evidenced by the present case, the economics of advanced ICTs can impede attempts to specify a socially inclusive design. But even if stakeholders had been successful in specifying such a design, the challenge would be to keep it that way, to keep it open and inclusive. Both the two strategies we outlined share this commitment.

Sociological institutional theory affords a cultural–political view of civic network design. The design of civic artifacts unfolds, as it must, in relation to social structures and logics (or cultural logics) already prevailing in the social order, and these antecedents impinge more or less effectively on design choices at the microlevel through designers' mindsets and behavior. Differential power from superior resource access and cultural legitimacy is often a political factor explaining how design products emerge and stabilize and whether they materialize dominant or marginal interests, the entrenched order, or an alternative to it. But structurally powerful or not, actors must successfully mobilize social support if their preferences are to influence collective decisions. Recent work in institutional theory (Davis et al., 2005, for example) provides new insights for extending constructivist activism by stressing the role played by culture in strategic collective action and ultimately, in understanding how an artifact got its distinctive form and the structural choices embodied in it. Power – at least one form of power – is relational and flows from advocates' effectiveness in garnering support for their preferences. Advocates often rely on resources like frames to do this. Cultural framing provides a useful analytic lens to understand and explain micropolitical behavior in the social construction of an artifact, directing attention to the discursive strategies framers employ to forge coalitions. These strategies, as previously noted, may reference entrenched logics and structures or favor alternatives to these. We used insights from the institutional design literature to outline activist interventions of the *indirect* variety: the intent here is to design the conditions of design rather than the artifact directly so that stakeholders, singly and collectively, invoke shared frames and voluntarily "deactivate" self-serving cultural legacies (Tsoukas, 1989) to give the former a reasonable chance of material expression in the design outcome.[11]

The Urban-net project started out with a commitment to a utopian vision of rewiring the project area's social structure. Critical social theorists (such as Horkheimer, 1972) will recognize the attempt by the steering committee (and the program authorities) to correct systemic structural inequalities by improving access to advanced technology and online resources through the project. However, the economics of broadband moved center stage during design and diluted the commitment, and assuring Urban-net's viability became an overriding concern and source of influence on the design that emerged. A civic network built on broadband technology cannot easily avoid questions of viability, for if it cannot sustain itself, it can serve no one. To recognize this moderates the critical theoretic stance: the socially responsive designer recognizes the need to be resilient and resourceful as he searches for the appropriate balance. The Urban-net steering committee has continued to struggle with the tension resulting from a need to assure project's viability and a desire to support equity. Facilitating open access to the network can bring a plurality of voices into the community's discourse space. It is customary to see this space as separate and distinct from state and market-sponsored spaces. Realistically, however, as shown by the present case, these demarcations may not be quite as clean as one might prefer when broadband technology enters the equation. Resource pressures may well push stakeholders to court state and market participation in the network in order to sustain it and to develop a base of funding to underwrite development of network uses targeting hitherto excluded groups and unaddressed needs. We outlined two complementary strategies to assist stakeholders in the struggle to secure network sustainability but without compromising on the ideals of equity and open access.

References

Alexander, E. R. (2002). The public interest in planning: from legitimation to substantive plan evaluation. *Planning Theory*, 1(3), 226–249.

Bijker, W. E. (1995). *Of Bicycles, Bakelites, and Bulbs: Toward a Theory of Sociotechnical Change*. Cambridge, MA: The MIT Press.

Burns, T. (1961). Micropolitics: mechanisms of institutional change. *Administrative Science Quarterly*, 6(3), 257–281.

Clement, A. & Shade, L. (2000). The Access Rainbow: a social/technical architecture for community networking. In M. Gurstein (Ed.), *Community Informatics: Enabling Communities with Information and Communications Technologies*. Hershey, PA: Idea Group Publishing, 32–51.

[11] We recognize that an institutonalist theory of artifact design must consider the design of what we term instruments of institutionalization – e.g., service contracts, project by-laws, acceptable use policies – that formalize social relations between the focal artifact, users, and the governing body. These are instrumental for producing the routine everyday practices that allow the focal artifact to persist in stabilized state and for fostering institutionalization of that state. Space considerations prohibit analysis of such design objects.

Cooper, M. N. (Ed.). (2004). *Open Architecture as Communications Policy: Preserving Internet Freedom in the Broadband Era*. Palo Alto, CA: Stanford University Law School.

Coser, L. A. (1982). The notion of control in sociological theory. In J. P. Gibbs (Ed.), *Social Control: Views from the Social Sciences*. Beverly Hills, CA: Sage, 13–22.

Davis, G. F., McAdam, D., Scott, W. R., & Zald, M. N. (2005). *Social Movements and Organizational Theory*. New York, NY: Cambridge University Press.

Fligstein, N. (1999). *Social Skill and the Theory of Fields*. Unpublished manuscript. Department of Sociology, University of California, Berkeley.

Fraser, N. (1999). Rethinking the public sphere: a contribution to the critique of actually existing democracy. In C. Calhoun (Ed.), *Habermas and the Public Sphere*. Cambridge, MA: The MIT Press.

Fraser, N. & Honneth, A. (2003). *Recognition or Redistribution? A Political-Philosophical Exchange*. London, UK: Verso.

Friedland, R. & Alford, R. A. (1991). Bringing society back in: symbols, practices, and institutional contradictions. In W. W. Powell & P. J. DiMaggio (Eds.), *The New Institutionalism in Organizational Analysis*. Chicago, IL: University of Chicago Press.

Galaskiewicz, J. (1991). Making corporate actors accountable: institution-building in Minneapolis-St. Paul. In W. W. Powell & P. J. DiMaggio (Eds.), *The New Institutionalism in Organizational Analysis*. Chicago, IL: University of Chicago Press.

Goodin, R. E. (1996). Institutions and their design. In R. E. Goodin (Ed.), *The Theory of Institutional Design*. Cambridge, UK: Cambridge University Press.

Gualini, E. (2002). Institution capacity building as an issue of collective action and institutionalization: some theoretical remarks. In G. Cars, P. Healey, A. Madanipour, & C. De Megalhaes (Eds.), *Urban Governance, Institutional Capacity and Social Milieux*. Aldershot, UK: Ashgate.

Hargadon, A. B. & Douglas, Y. (2001). When innovations meet institutions: Edison and the design of the electric light. *Administrative Science Quarterly*, 46, 476–501.

Hanseth, O., Monteiro, E., & Hatling, M. (1996). Developing information infrastructure: the tension between standardization and flexibility. *Science, Technology, & Human Values*, 21(4), 407–426.

Horkheimer, M. (1972). *Traditional and Critical Theory (Originally Published 1937). Critical Theory: Selected Essays*. New York, NY: Seabury Press.

Hughes, T. P. (1996). Technological momentum. In M. R. Smith & L. Marx (Eds.), *Does Technology Drive History? The Dilemma of Technological Determinism*. Cambridge, MA: The MIT Press.

International Network of E-Communities. (2006). *The Stockholm Declaration on Open Networks*. Available at http://www.i-nec.com/

Jepperson, R. L. (1991). Institutions, institutional effects, and institutionalism. In W. W. Powell & P. J. DiMaggio (Eds.), *The New Institutionalism in Organizational Analysis*. Chicago, IL: University of Chicago Press.

Kavanaugh, A. L., Isenhour, P. L., Cooper, M., Carroll, J. M., Rosson, M. B., & Schimitz, J. (2005). Information technology in support of public deliberation. In P. van den Besselaar, G. de Michelis, J. Preece, & C. Simone (Eds.), *Communities and Technologies 2005*. Netherlands: Springer, 19–40.

McGarty, T. P. (1992). Alternative networking architectures: pricing, policy, and competition. In B. Kahin (Ed.), *Building Information Infrastructure*. New York: McGraw-Hill.

McGarty, T. P. & Bhagavan, R. (2002). *Municipal Broadband Networks: A Revised Paradigm of Ownership*. The Merton Group.

Mackenzie, D. & Wajcman, J. (1985). *The Social Shaping of Technology: How the Refrigerator Got Its Hum*. London, UK: Open University Press.

Moyers, B. (2006). *The Net at Risk*. Moyers on America. Available at http://www.pbs.org/moyers/moyersonamerica/net/index.html. Accessed October 25, 2006.

New York State Advanced Telecommunications Program. (1996). *First Round Request for Proposals (RFP)*. Albany, NY: State Department of State.

New York State Department of Health. (2005). State Commissioner Novello Coordinates with hospitals to assure access to high quality health care for patients. Press Release available at http://www.health.state.ny.us/press/releases/2005/2005–09–16_translation_services_release.htm. Accessed on September 25, 2006.

Pierson, P. (2000). The limits of design: explaining institutional origins and change. *Governance: An Interdisciplinary Journal of Policy and Administration*, 13(4), 475–499.
Porpora, D. V. (1989). Four concepts of social structure. *Journal for the Theory of Social Behavior*, 19(2), 195–211.
Rao, H. (1998). Caveat emptor: the construction of non-profit consumer watchdog organizations. *American Journal of Sociology*, 103(4), 912–961.
Scott, W. R. & Backman, E. V. (1990). Institutional theory and the medical care sector. In S. S. Mick (Ed.), *Innovation in Health Care Delivery: Insights for Organizational Theory*. San Francisco, CA: Jossey-Bass.
Shin, D. H. (2004). The development of broadband public networks: two case studies. Unpublished doctoral dissertation, Syracuse University, Syracuse, NY.
Star, S. L. & Ruhleder, K. (1996). Steps toward an ecology of infrastructure: design and access for large information spaces. *Information Systems Research*, 7(1), 111–134.
Thelen, K. (2003). How institutions evolve: insights from comparative historical analysis. In J. Mahoney & D. Rueschemeyer (Eds.), *Comparative Historical Analysis in the Social Sciences*. Cambridge, UK: Cambridge University Press.
Tolbert, P. S. & Zucker, L. (1983). Institutional sources of change in organizational structure: the diffusion of civil service reform, 1880–1935. *Administrative Science Quarterly*, 28, 22–39.
Tsoukas, H. (1989). The validity of idiographic research explanations. *Academy of Management Review*, 14(4), 551–561.
Venkatesh, M. & Shin, D. H. (2005). Extending social constructivism with institutional theory: a broadband civic networking case. In P. van den Besselaar, G. de Michelis, J. Preece, & C. Simone (Eds.), *Communities and Technologies 2005*. Netherlands: Springer, 55–74.
Whitt, R. S. (2004). A horizontal leap forward: formulating a new public policy framework based on the network layers model. In M. N. Cooper (Ed.), *Open Architecture as Communications Policy: Preserving Internet Freedom in the Broadband Era*. Palo Alto, CA: Stanford University Law School.
Williams, R. (1997). The *Social Shaping Of Information and Communications Technologies*. Unpublished manuscript.
Williams, R. & Edge, D. (1996). The social shaping of technology. *Research Policy*, 25, 865–899.
Winner, L. (1993). Social constructivism: opening the black box and finding it empty. *Science as Culture*, 3(16), 427–452.
Zucker, L. (1977). Institutionalization and cultural persistence. *American Sociological Review*, 42(5), 726–743.

Chapter 17
Supporting Community Emergency Management Planning Through a Geocollaboration Software Architecture

Wendy A. Schafer, Craig H. Ganoe, and John M. Carroll

Abstract Emergency management is more than just events occurring within an emergency situation. It encompasses a variety of persistent activities such as planning, training, assessment, and organizational change. We are studying emergency management planning practices in which geographic communities (towns and regions) prepare to respond efficiently to significant emergency events. Community emergency management planning is an extensive collaboration involving numerous stakeholders throughout the community and both reflecting and challenging the community's structure and resources. Geocollaboration is one aspect of the effort. Emergency managers, public works directors, first responders, and local transportation managers need to exchange information relating to possible emergency event locations and their surrounding areas. They need to examine geospatial maps together and collaboratively develop emergency plans and procedures. Issues such as emergency vehicle traffic routes and staging areas for command posts, arriving media, and personal first responders' vehicles must be agreed upon prior to an emergency event to ensure an efficient and effective response. This work presents a software architecture that facilitates the development of geocollaboration solutions. The architecture extends prior geocollaboration research and reuses existing geospatial information models. Emergency management planning is one application domain for the architecture. Geocollaboration tools can be developed that support community-wide emergency management planning and preparedness. This chapter describes how the software architecture can be used for the geospatial, emergency management planning activities of one community.

Introduction

Emergencies happen each day such as motorized vehicle accidents, sports injuries, and elderly people falling. None of these events are typically common for the people involved, but to hospitals and first responders, such emergencies are routine. Other emergency events are less frequent and more severe. Natural disasters, such as

J.M. Carroll (ed.), *Learning in Communities*,

tornados, hurricanes, and tsunamis, destroy homes and leave people without power. Terrorist attacks can kill numerous people and disrupt society. Even airplane crashes or extensive motorized vehicle accidents can involve many casualties. These large-scale events, or disasters, are the focus of *emergency management*. Both national agencies and local government emergency management offices are concerned with such events.

Emergency management does not occur in government offices, however. It is a community effort. Local first responders, local hospitals, local businesses, and local public transportation are all involved. They ensure that a community is prepared, and they are on the front lines when an event does occur. This chapter examines this broader perspective of emergency management. It investigates the community aspects of large-scale emergencies, studying community involvement and community preparations.

This work focuses on the planning and preparedness activities of community emergency management rather the actual emergency response. Emergency management planning is an ongoing event in local communities that can benefit from collaboration research. Community preparedness is a constant concern, which equates to a continual process of writing emergency plans, reviewing and discussing emergency plans, and exercising and training. This work adopts a community informatics approach, exploring information and communication technologies to support community emergency management planning (Gurstein, 2002).

Within community emergency management planning, many of the work practices require geocollaboration. Geocollaboration is multiple people working together to solve a geospatial problem. A group of people might look at geographic map together to make a decision or they might engage in a discussion to plan a travel route. Geocollaboration frequently occurs in the planning and preparing phases of emergency management. Emergency planning committees discuss the likely locations for emergency events and they develop coordinated response plans. Different first response agencies need to be able to easily access the emergency scene along with their equipment. The committee works together to make these geospatial decisions.

There are differences among emergency planning committees and their geocollaboration scenarios, though. Communities approach emergency management in different ways, depending on their threats and resources, which correspond to different geocollaboration activities. To address this diversity, our research is developing a geocollaboration software architecture. Such an architecture provides a baseline for developing software solutions for geocollaboration. The resulting software can be uniquely tailored for a specific setting and a set of geocollaboration tasks.

In the following sections, we describe our observations that reinforce the concept of emergency management planning as a community activity. We review some of the current scenarios of geocollaboration in local emergency management planning and we envision collaborative software features that can enhance current work practices. From there, we highlight our geocollaboration software architecture and describe one application of the architecture toward emergency planning. The chapter concludes with a reflection on how geocollaborative software tools, which are available through the software architecture, might impact the field of community emergency management planning.

Studying Local Emergency Management

Even an emergency with immediate world-wide consequences, like the attack on the World Trade Center, is initially a local event. Emergencies occur in small towns and cities within the United States and around the world, and it is the local response teams within these communities who arrive on scene first. The immediate local community deals with the emergency, be it a hurricane, forest fire, or terrorist attack, until their capabilities are overwhelmed and additional assistance arrives. This emphasis on local towns and cities makes emergency management a community-level concern. Local communities need to be prepared for emergency events that might occur in their town. They need to consider the likely threats to their area and evaluate their resources and capacity to respond (Schafer et al., 2008).

Emergency management encompasses more than just emergency response, however. It includes four documented phases of: planning, response, recovery, and mitigation (Haddow & Bullock, 2003). There is not always a clear separation between these phases, but they are iterative and ongoing within towns and cities. For instance, if there has not been an emergency in a specific community recently, the community is very likely planning and preparing for potential events. Communities continually participate in the four phases of emergency management. In the well-known response phase, they call on their first responders, such as the police and fire departments, and their corresponding emergency equipment, such as fire engines and rescue trucks. Less salient, but more widely occurring and the focus of this chapter, is the planning and preparedness phase. Emergency management coordinators work with town managers, public works directors, public schools, public transportation offices, first response agencies, charitable agencies, and local businesses to develop emergency plans and be prepared for any emergency event that might happen. Many of these people are volunteers or volunteer their time for the effort because emergency management is not a part of their day-to-day jobs. For example, according to the National Fire Protection Association (http://www.nfpa.org), 72% of all the firefighters in the United States in 2005 were volunteers.

Community emergency preparedness contrasts with that managed by top-down forces such as the U.S. Department of Homeland Security, Federal Emergency Management Agency (FEMA), or the state-level Pennsylvania Emergency Management Agency (PEMA). The local planning occurs through a collaborative effort of community members with an approach that solicits local area knowledge and relies on local expertise. This emphasis on local geographic communities has been recognized previously. The World Health Organization has published a book on community emergency preparedness that serves as a manual for local emergency managers (1999). This book describes how the early coordination of government, nongovernmental organizations, and private organizations within a community can reduce disaster impact. Also, the field of social science disaster research studies behaviors associated with community disasters, examining individual, organizational, and community-level actions in the preparedness and response phases (Lindell & Perry, 1992; Quarantelli, 2003). Lastly, in the 1990s, FEMA initiated a program called Project Impact: Building Disaster Resistant Communities. It encouraged communities to perform mitigation steps, building partnerships and identifying hazards. Our work follows on from these prior efforts to investigate community emergency preparedness, studying the recent planning and preparing activities of two rural communities.

Our research examines two communities in Central Pennsylvania and their emergency management planning practices. Within Pennsylvania, there is a mandate that each of the 2,600 townships appoint an emergency management coordinator. This legislation recognizes the importance of local towns in emergencies and encourages our focus on community emergency preparedness. Our work investigates the township of Lower Swatara with a population of 8,150 and the Centre Region community, which includes six townships and a total population of approximately 80,000. Five of the six townships in Centre Region border a large university campus, which has about 40,000 students.

The work to study these two communities was conducted by two researchers, one in each community. In Lower Swatara township, the local emergency management coordinator was interviewed on two occasions. Questions were asked about both previous and ongoing emergency management planning activities. Similarly, in Centre Region, we have established a partnership with the local emergency management coordinator and are using long-term participatory techniques (Carroll et al., 2000) to elicit design requirements. This person fulfills multiple roles, acting as the common emergency management coordinator for six townships and as the emergency management coordinator for the university.

In a 9-month period, we conducted eight semi-structured interviews with the coordinator of Centre Region and accompanied him at 14 emergency-related meetings in the community. The primary method of data collection was observation, which was recorded in field notes. Secondary sources of data collection included meeting documents (e.g., agendas, minutes, and other handouts), archival records (e.g., emails and Web sites), and audio recordings of some of the emergency planning meetings. The semi-structured interviews focused on the emergency management coordinator's approach to emergency management and his perception of the local activities in the community. These interviews were not recorded or transcribed to develop a mutual partnership with the coordinator and to not treat him as a subject. To analyze the fieldwork data, we triangulated the multiple sources of data collection. This occurred in monthly research group meetings. The group reflected on the collected data to generate collaborative interpretations. This process of data analysis helped to remove the individual researchers' subjective bias, thus increasing the reliability of data analysis.

Other descriptions of the fieldwork studies are reported elsewhere (Schafer et al., submitted; Lee et al., 2006), while this chapter focuses on the specific geocollaboration activities observed. One of the findings in analyzing the fieldwork was both the prevalence of geospatial representations and the numerous collaboration activities involving locations and spatial relationships. In the observed emergency planning meetings many of the discussions were focused on communication and procedural issues, but local area space was regularly referenced. For example, the locations of fire, police, and EMS stations were considered. Other emergency meetings, on the other hand, concentrated on the geospatial response plans and where first responders should report. To understand these activities, we have documented geo-collaboration scenarios that describe the meeting participants' interactions. These scenarios portray the current work practices of community emergency planning and they reveal ways technology can enhance the process.

Previous work has investigated geocollaboration within emergency response, but our efforts are the first to study emergency planning geocollaboration. We have found that there are issues and negative aspects of current planning activities, which can be addressed through collaborative software. Our work is interested in supporting emergency management planning by developing software-based enhancements, specifically geocollaboration software solutions.

In each of the geocollaboration contexts observed, the emergency planners used paper maps in face-to-face meetings, limiting their abilities to collaborate. Based on these scenarios of existing geocollaboration practices, we have identified a set of software requirements that can enhance this collaboration. These requirements identify some of the important features to include in an emergency planning software solution. For example, there should be capabilities to interact with and explore a geospatial representation as opposed to viewing a static image. The requirements are generic and written at high-level to develop a software architecture that supports a variety of geocollaboration contexts.

Working from these software requirements, we have designed a software architecture for sharing geospatial information. Our geocollaboration architecture recognizes that different communities and even different emergency planning committees engage in unique geocollaboration activities. The architecture design uses a building blocks approach and emphasizes reusing underlying map data, rendering techniques, and existing Web content. This allows emergency planning committees to explore alternative plans as well as enables emergency planning meetings within the same community to share resource-related information.

Local Emergency Management Planning Activities

Through our studies of both Lower Swatara township and Centre Region, the notion of community emergency management planning is exemplified. These towns reveal how emergency planning is a community activity with local area stakeholders, resources, and threats. In these studies, the geographical community comes together to be prepared. Citizens who are involved with emergency-related agencies attend meetings outside of their normal work responsibilities. These people are first response volunteers who participate in emergency planning activities in their spare time, such as volunteer firemen. They are also agency employees who put in extra hours of work to ensure that the actions of their agency are coordinated with others.

In both Centre Region and Lower Swatara township, the emergency management planning meetings are the primary communication place for emergency-related agencies. These agencies do not typically exchange approaches or coordinate efforts outside of the meetings. The first responders will work together during routine emergencies, but these events only involve a handful of agencies and usually their interactions are not analyzed after the event. The emergency planning meetings, on the other hand, bring together all of the emergency-related stakeholders in the region. They provide a forum for the agency leaders to reflect on how to improve their coordination and communication, based on past experiences, to be prepared for a large-scale emergency event in the future.

In observing these meetings, we have a better understanding of emergency management work practices and the domain of emergency management itself. The meetings reveal how the leaders of a community come together to discuss emergency issues. This group is a representation of different agencies and differing expertise, but they work together to address emergency-related concerns. The topics of these meetings are directly relevant to the local town. They might cover a future, potential emergency event or review a past event that already occurred. The discussion focuses on the local resources, including equipment, supplies, local area buildings, and people.

Based on our observations of emergency management meetings, there are different types of emergency planning activities. Some of these activities have a strong geo-collaboration component, while others focus on additional aspects of emergency management, such as communication. We have chosen to categorize these activities around their distinct objectives. Using this approach, we have observed at least five different categories of activities in Centre Region and Lower Swatara township. These categories are exercise planning, post-incident planning, awareness presentations, tabletop exercises, and staging area planning.

Each of these categories is important to consider in a study of emergency management planning. They describe some of the typical group activities that occur. Three of the identified categories are particularly interesting in terms of geocollaboration. Awareness presentations, tabletop exercises, and staging area planning often involve discussions of physical space. The remainder of this section reviews the different categories observed and the follow on section takes a closer look at the specific categories we identified with geocollaboration scenarios (Table 17.1).

Exercise Planning

In Centre Region, there is an ongoing effort to be prepared for an emergency event at the local airport. The commercial portion of the airport is small, offering only short, commuter flights to larger cities, but between the general aviation and commercial terminals a plane crash is possible. The airport management has realized

Table 17.1 Planning activities conducted at emergency management planning meetings

Planning activity	Activity objectives
Exercise planning	Understand which agencies need to work together, how they need to interoperate, and what is needed to ensure a coordinated effort
Post-incident planning	Reflect on previous events and learn from them
Awareness presentations	Disseminate emergency plans; field questions and receive feedback about emergency plans
Tabletop exercises	Investigate response execution using a simulated emergency situation; uncover issues with planned actions
Staging area planning	Determine a spatial, response plan to avoid congestion and chaos among emergency responders

this risk and has formed a group to both discuss the emergency plans in place and conduct exercises to examine their viability.

We observed three meetings of this group where they were planning for an upcoming exercise, or a simulated, practice run of a response situation. The attendees at the meetings represented a variety of local agencies, emphasizing the community-wide, preparedness effort. They included the local first responders, such as nearby fire departments, police departments, and emergency medical services (EMS) organizations, as well as representatives from the county 911 Emergency Communications Center, the township and county-level emergency management offices, the local public information offices, the local Federal Bureau of Investigation (FBI) office, and the local Transportation Security Administration (TSA) office. The airport management specifically invited these agencies because they do not want an airport emergency to turn into a chaotic situation. Many different people are involved in an emergency incident and bringing these agencies together prior to an event allows them to be better prepared. The group was working together to plan an exercise that would practice this multiagency response situation.

In planning for the upcoming exercise, the group focused on coordination and communication issues. Through extensive discussions, the planning committee established how the different agencies should work together. Much of the meetings centered on who will communicate what information when, such as which agency will likely arrive on scene first and give the initial report. This is exemplified in a comment made at one of the meetings by the county-level emergency manager:

> Let's walk through that once. I think we are all saying basically the same thing. The first unit on scene obviously's going to be the two guys standing up there, line services. Where should they go? The second people on scene is probably going to be the police. Where should they go? And how should that transfer happen, if the transfer in fact happens. You're coming in. How should that happen? Let's go through that whole thing step by step.

The exercise planning also dealt with communication mechanics. They discussed the different radio systems and channel frequencies that are used by different local first responders; they discussed who will be in command of different response units and how these commanders will share information; and they went over speech phrases that are understandable and confusing to others when using a radio system.

Each of these issues was discussed in the context of the exercise, but they also directly apply to a real response situation.

Post-Incident Planning

The Lower Swatara township provides another example of community emergency management planning. Recently, this town suffered from heavy rainfall due to a Tropical Depression. In our interviews, the emergency management coordinator recounted how the township had to cope with extensive flooding in two different neighborhoods and a lack of potable water across the township as a result of the storm. The Susquehanna River is a major waterway in Pennsylvania and it flows through Lower Swatara township. This geographic feature makes areas of the township highly susceptible to flooding, a reoccurring emergency threat that is specific to the local area.

The emergency management coordinator recognizes this threat and has initiated a series of post-incident emergency planning meetings. The goal is to be more prepared in the future by bringing together the local agencies involved in the recent response. These agencies will likely be involved in additional response efforts and they need to be able to work together effectively.

The emergency management coordinator is also meeting with the local residents who own houses within the floodplain. He is working with these families and investigating state and federal program to relocate these citizens to homes on higher ground.

Awareness Presentations

Another form of emergency planning we have observed in Centre Region is awareness presentations. In these meetings, the emergency management coordinator presented an emergency plan he had developed and then encouraged a discussion of the plan among the meeting attendees. This type of activity occurred three times in our observations as the emergency management coordinator wanted specific agencies to be aware of the plan for the local university's football stadium. This outdoor stadium is located on the edge of campus and is immense, seating over 107,000 people.

One of these presentations was for the local township managers. These local leaders are concerned about the possibility of a large-scale emergency involving the stadium and the meeting reassured them that a plan was in place. The other two presentations were for the local area fire departments and the local area fire police. Both agencies are expected to be involved in a stadium incident and the goal of the presentation was to make the individual firefighters and fire policemen aware of the plan. The presentation was an agenda item on their regular monthly meeting and it gave them an opportunity to ask questions and give feedback on the proposed plan.

Tabletop Exercises

One of the intentions of multiagency emergency planning meetings is to reveal the different agencies' roles and emphasize their need to work together. A tabletop exercise takes things a step further, engaging the meeting participants in a collaborative activity. This is a common approach in emergency planning which uses a large paper map positioned on a wall and post-its (World Health Organization, 1999). The participants walk through a possible event scenario with each describing their intended actions. The map indicates the emergency event location and the post-its are used to mark the current locations of the emergency equipment and personnel in the scenario. The exercise is called a "tabletop" because the discussions occur in a meeting table setting, as opposed to being in an outdoor environment with emergency response equipment.

In our work, we observed a tabletop exercise conducted at the local airport. The airport's management organized the exercise and the agencies of airport emergency planning committee attended. A leader from the agency and an everyday responder were present, with the everyday responder walking through their likely actions given the scenario. A large paper map of the airport grounds was placed at the front of the room so that everyone could see it. The goal of exercise was to examine the current airport response procedures. The planning committee could then compare this to the documented emergency plan and make refinements to the plan.

Staging Area Planning

The last type of emergency planning activity we observed involved staging areas. Staging areas are the locations first responders are to report to, as opposed to responding directly to the heart of an incident scene. These locations are nearby and planned in advance, allowing for a more organized and coordinated response. In our studies, staging area planning was not a separate meeting unto itself, but rather a major collaborative activity that occurred during exercise planning and post-incident planning. These staging areas were also presented in the awareness presentations and considered in the tabletop exercises.

The goal of staging area planning is to agree, in advance, on where the people and the vehicles responding to an emergency should go during an incident. The airport planning committee, for instance, spent many of their multiagency meetings debating over these decisions. The airport management would organize the meetings, but the agencies in attendance would have differing opinions about the predesignated locations based on their past experiences in emergency response. The committee considered different locations and buildings on the airport grounds as well as the neighboring industrial park areas, as they pictured large numbers of media vehicles and firemen in personal vehicles flocking to the airport. The following transcript is an example of a multiagency discussion about the appropriate location for the media:

Police chief: What is the old admin building being used for?
Airport manager: There's no room this big over there…
Hazardous Materials expert: What about across the street in State-of-the-Art or something? Cause obviously in a major incident they're not going to be here within the first 15 minutes like Centre Daily Times and everybody else. You know if it's a major incident, satellite trucks and everything else will be coming in. Ship them across the street to State-of-the-Art until you come up with a location. Do they have a conference room over there you can use? Something like that.

In this transcript, it is interesting to note that the police chief and the hazardous materials expert are actively involved in a topic not in their expertise. This reemphasizes how emergency planning is a community activity. The local first responders, who are knowledgeable about their town, are offering different location possibilities.

Summary

Each of the types of emergency planning activities, exercise planning, post-incident planning, awareness presentations, tabletop exercises, and staging area planning, demonstrate how a local community works together to be prepared. The discussions at these activities are focused on the likely emergency events in the town and the local people and resources that are available within the community.

Considering these different types of activities, geocollaboration occurs in some activities more than others. Geocollaboration efforts are prevalent in tabletop exercises and staging area planning. Both of these activities involve discussions of physical space, which directly relates to geocollaboration. Other geocollaboration situations occur in awareness presentations. The group considers a proposed emergency plan, including the spatial aspects. They discuss the physical locations and the response routes referenced in the plan. In the next section, specific examples of these geocollaboration activities are discussed.

Geocollaboration Scenarios in Emergency Management Planning

One of the findings in our studies of emergency management planning is the importance of geospatial representations. Geography plays an important role in emergency management and a visual representation makes this information tangible and concrete. For instance, in the emergency offices of Lower Swatara township there are geographic maps outlining the township's roads and birds-eye view imagery that shows the Susquehanna River and the neighboring areas within the floodplain.

Centre Region also has geographical considerations as most of the region is located within a valley. The hills either protect or exacerbate weather effects, which has caused the local university to examine a three-day winter storm scenario.

Geospatial representations also provide information about infrastructure and land use. Emergency management planning requires a visualization of the roadways, bridges, buildings, and even parking lots of a local community. For example, the Centre Region airport emergency planning committee uses maps of the airport grounds and building blueprints for the airport terminals.

In emergency management planning, geospatial representations are neither used by a single person nor left static in time. They are used to share information, coordinate actions, and encourage discussions among stakeholders. For instance, paper maps are on display in tabletop training exercises so that everyone in the room can view and discuss the local area. Documented emergency plans also contain geospatial representations to convey geospatial aspects, such as predesignated emergency response routes and addresses of key emergency response personnel.

In our observations of Centre Region and Lower Swatara township, we observed many instances of geocollaboration. These examples reveal how space plays a role in emergency planning and how various geospatial representations facilitate the planning process. The most interesting geocollaboration scenarios occurred in three types of activities: staging area planning, awareness presentations, and tabletop exercises.

Geocollaboration Scenarios in Staging Area Planning

Some of the most interesting geocollaboration scenarios stem from the observations at the Centre Region airport planning meetings. One question repeatedly debated was the staging area location for the media. Some meeting participants felt that it was important to keep the media as far away as possible and proposed the furthest hangar from the airport terminals. Others felt that this was unnecessary if the emergency event was relatively small and suggested a small conference room within one of the airport's terminals. Different options for the media's staging area location were discussed across multiple meetings, occasionally with different outcomes due to the different agencies in attendance. This resulted in the stakeholders having different beliefs about the agreed-upon location, leading to confusion during an exercise.

The conversation below demonstrates these differing beliefs. The police chief and the public information officer are confused about the agreed-upon location for the media, or PIO, in a post-exercise discussion:

Police chief: "Do we want to have a pre-designated PIO area?"
Public Information Officer: "We had talked at one time about it actually being in this room in a real world scenario."
Police chief: "So we couldn't have incident command in here, if this is for PIO in the real world scenario. I thought this was going to be incident command, pre-designated, or did we not pre-designate were incident command is?"

In the airport planning meetings, deciding on the other staging area choices were more straightforward. For example, the command post with representatives from each of the first response agencies should be located in the large conference room of the airport terminal. Looking at the blueprints for the building, the group decided that this room is the most spacious and includes multiple power outlets, phone lines, and Internet connections. The building is also centrally located on the airport grounds and contains the airport administrative offices and dispatch center. This provides easy access to detailed information about the airport, which could be essential during an emergency.

There was little debate among the participants about where the command post should be located, however we observed no agreement on how the decisions made in the meetings would be disseminated. In the meetings, the group did not discuss how to convey the decisions to those stakeholders not in attendance. They did not review how the local volunteer firemen would learn about the plan or how the paid dispatchers in the 911 Emergency Communications Center would know where to direct first responders. The group also did not identify who would be making the changes to the current emergency plan document and how the revisions would be distributed. This was assumed to be a task for the airport administration, but no details, such as how the paper maps within the document would be modified, were discussed. A comment by the 911 Emergency Communications Center's Assistant Director at one of the planning meetings reflects this lack of organization:

> We should have been taping this! I hope someone is taking good notes!

The airport's emergency plan is only available in hard copy. In the state of Pennsylvania, it is illegal to post emergency plans online verbatim as this presents a security risk. This means that the documented emergency plans exist on a handful of bookshelves across the community. With each new decision made in the airport planning meetings, this paper document was continuously outdated.

Geocollaboration Scenarios in Awareness Presentation

The awareness presentations given by the emergency management coordinator offer different geocollaboration scenarios. In the firemen's meeting about the university stadium plan the presentation reviewed the staging area locations for the local fire equipment, but much of the discussion was focused on the other first responders' involvement. For instance, the group considered the staging area locations for firemen responding outside of the county. They questioned the appropriateness of these locations given the recent changes in land ownership and amount of space required for the large number of responders who could come. The local firemen had a better understanding how much space would be needed in comparison to the emergency management coordinator who wrote the plan.

The firemen were also interested in the parking situation, as the university parks an average of 26,000 cars on a game day. Knowing which parking lots and open spaces will be used for parking is important in organizing a fire response with large equipment. Similarly, the group discussed the roads surrounding the stadium. They talked about which roads experience the biggest traffic problems making them impassible, which roads are pedestrian-only during a game, and which intersections the police control. Many of the local firemen did not know about the university's approach to traffic during an event. These discussions about parking and roadways gave the individual responders detailed information about the likely situation. This background information would be very useful when navigating a large fire truck toward the stadium.

Lastly, the firemen wanted to discuss the role of EMS in the response plan. The university stadium plan includes an extensive medical component. Many people attend sporting events at the stadium and if there is an emergency event, it is possible that many will be injured. The medial component of the plan describes how to configure triage stations, where additional medical supplies are located, and which nearby buildings can act as shelters. The awareness presentation gave the firemen an overview of this aspect of the plan, but they also had questions regarding the people on the sports field. They emergency management coordinator explained the different EMS units available during every game and indicated their physical locations with respect to the stadium. He also described how one unit, staged in a different location from the other EMS units, is dedicated to caring for thc players, coaches, and referees. Again, many of the local firemen did not know about the typical EMS operations during an event. The presentation and follow-up questions provided the individual responders with a better understanding of the EMS units they would likely coordinate with during an emergency.

Geocollaboration Scenarios in Tabletop Exercises

Tabletop exercises present additional geocollaboration scenarios. For example, the airport tabletop exercise facilitated a discussion about the airport facilities. During this exercise, a fireman commented that they would drive a fire truck to the emergency gate. This gate was marked on the large paper map and many questions were raised. Some people in attendance didn't know the gates location, others wondered about the width of the gate and the amount of time that the gate stays open. In a different part of the exercise, the airport manager realized that many of the first responders might not know about the airport's layout and operations. The tabletop exercise simulated a plane crash on runway "RW 6/24." This detail prompted the airport manager to describe how there are two actual runways at the airport and explain the naming conventions, establishing common ground among the attendees.

In walking through the response, different participants also questioned the upcoming changes to the airport. One fireman asked about the plans for the new de-icing facility and the possibilities for a traffic control tower addition. Another person asked if the airport was planning to build a new terminal. Both of these new developments would affect the emergency response at the airport. The airport manager explained the timeline for these changes and that new hangar buildings would also be added. He described the approximate locations of the additions by adding post-its on the large map.

At the end of the airport tabletop exercise, the large map on the wall that had been the talking point of the meeting was discarded and the agency representatives left without a plan for their future activities. The committee agreed to run a more extensive exercise in a year's time, but they did not set a date for the next meeting and no one agreed to pass around a summary of the most recent exercise's results. When the group met again 3 months later, we observed them trying to remember what they learned from the exercise as they planned how the next exercise would be different.

Summary

Emergent management, especially during emergency planning activities, requires geocollaboration. Emergency management coordinators, emergency communication dispatchers, and first responders, need to agree on the geospatial aspects of a response plan. This section has described some of the geocollaboration scenarios from our studies of emergency management practices. These scenarios reveal how staging area decision-making is an extensive process. It lasts over multiple meetings and involves different considerations, such as how many people will likely respond, how far away the location should be, and what resources the responders will require. Once the staging area decisions are made these locations have to be disseminated to both the agencies and individual first responders involved. The agencies that hold a copy of the documented plan need to know the mutually agreed-upon locations, while the first responders need to know the other agencies' planned locations to coordinate. Each agency has information that is specific to their operations, such as the traffic and emergency medical components of the university stadium, but each agency also requires an awareness of other agencies' spatial, response plans. This information enables them to work together effectively as they can anticipate where others will be. The scenarios of this section also show how tabletop exercises cause people to consider additional geospatial features. In walking through a response with geospatial representations, an emphasis is placed on physical space and how this space could change in the future.

Geocollaborative Feature Requirements for Emergency Management Planning

One objective of our fieldwork is to design new software technologies that will enhance geocollaboration in community-based emergency management planning. We have observed numerous uses of paper maps and diagrams, and we are interested in the opportunities available through interactive, online, map software tools. Moving the geocollaboration activities to a computer-based medium has the typical advantages of automation, such as digital files that can be emailed and posted on the Web. This medium also introduces new interaction possibilities as well. The geospatial representation no longer has to be a permanent, static image. It can be available online, can be navigated in real time, can be annotated with drawing sketches, offers additional information through queries, and can be updated as needed.

The concept of using an online map for a community application is not new. The field of participatory GIS, or public participatory GIS (PPGIS), focuses on citizen use of GIS technology to enable community decision-making (Steinmann et al., 2004). Much of this work looks at empowering less-privileged communities by providing them with and teaching them to use existing GIS tools (Rambaldi et al., 2006). Our goal, on the other hand, is to support multiagency collaboration within a community. In designing collaboration software, we consider the ways people communicate and how this can be enhanced through technology.

One of the primary observations from the fieldwork is the emphasis on same-time, same-place emergency planning meetings. These meetings are currently the most effective way for emergency-related agencies to communicate. The leaders of the different agencies might talk on the phone or email occasionally, but the planning meetings provide the place to coordinate and make decisions. To extend their collaboration, our vision is to provide online, collaborative map software that can be used both synchronously and asynchronously. We anticipate that such software can be used for the current, face-to-face meetings as well as for distributed work. For instance, in the emergency planning meetings, one user's interactions could be projected for all to see and discuss. Alternatively, if a couple of people had laptops at the meeting, a set of synchronous features could be used along with a projected view to foster the discussion.

Enabling asynchronous interaction with the map software introduces a new opportunity for collaboration in emergency management. The stakeholders are no longer constrained to the meetings to collaborate. They can discuss and share ideas through the online software, and not be limited to a planning meeting scheduled at a particular place and time. The collaborative map software can provide a common, online environment that persists outside of the meetings. This environment would not be designed to replace the meetings, but augment them because the face-to-face interaction is important in emergency management.

With this vision and an examination of our observations, we have identified needs that could be addressed with technology and translated those into requirements for our architecture design. Table 17.2 presents a summary of the emergency management planning observations and the corresponding software requirements we have identified through these observations. The third column pairs these requirements with the design of our geocollaboration architecture. The observations we address are based on the geocollaboration scenarios described in the previous section. They are observations from staging area planning, awareness presentations, and tabletop exercises that can be enhanced through software-based technology.

Table 17.2 The geocollaboration software architecture design is based on emergency planning fieldwork

Emergency planning observations	Geocollaboration software requirements	Architecture design decisions
Discussions of staging area possibilities consider surrounding area	Capability to collaboratively explore possible locations and determine distances	• Display existing local GIS data • Features for both synchronized and independent navigation
Response staging area alternatives are analyzed	Capability to collaboratively identify locations and associate comments	• Shared, user-created geospatial content • Linking geospatial content with URLs
Staging area decisions need to be documented	Capability to collaboratively label geospatial map locations as part of response plan(s)	• New, shared response plan layered on existing GIS data • Customized, shared styles determine how to render data
Lack of collaboration outside of organized meetings	Support for distributed geocollaboration	• Collaborative, online maps with shared data and rendering techniques • Synchronous features • Information about most recent modifications
Staging area decisions need to be disseminated to volunteers	Geospatial representations available online	• Geospatial software available through a Java application and protected webpages
Agency-specific geospatial plans	Capability to display specialized geospatial representations of an area	• Agency-specific collections of map data and/or rendering styles
Tabletop exercises involve geospatial response walkthroughs using post-it notes	Capability to collaboratively annotate on top of a familiar geospatial representation	• Explore alternatives through multiple, shared, user-created layers
		• Reuse of GIS and shared, user-created data sets
Same geospatial elements considered in different planning contexts	Capability to reuse map data and create specialized applications	• Individual layers of map data • Reuse of map data with customized links

Enhancing Staging Area Planning Activities

The airport's effort to decide on appropriate response staging areas is one aspect of emergency planning that could be enhanced. In this activity, the airport committee members proposed and evaluated different staging area locations across multiple meetings, working toward a mutually agreeable set of locations. Software could enhance this process by providing an interactive, geographic visualization of the area that can be explored. The software could be used to survey the surrounding area and calculate distances, as opposed to guessing how far away a possible staging area is located. To support these interactions, software features are required to allow independent and collective exploration as well as distance calculation.

Our geocollaboration architecture addresses these requirements. It supports explorations of the surrounding area and distance calculations by displaying existing local GIS data. Local government GIS offices create and maintain map data for their local area. These GIS data are in a standard format and it is accessible online. Our architecture supports this format and uses URLs to retrieve the data. GIS offices produce a variety of data that are useful to emergency planning. For example, in Centre Region where we conducted the fieldwork, the county GIS office has geographic map data for the roads, buildings, rivers, floodplains, fire stations, police stations, and hospitals. These data are both accurate and precise, supporting the distance calculations between staging area locations.

The geocollaboration architecture also includes collaboration features so that multiple people can use separate computers and explore a space together. The software design supports multiple collaborators looking at an online map together with both tightly coupled navigation and independent navigation. There are techniques for switching between the two approaches. It also shares mouse cursor locations to display telepointers. These features can be used when the collaborators are in the same room together with multiple computers, as in the emergency planning meetings, or when the collaborators happen to be distributed and online at the same time.

At the airport planning meetings they carefully considered the staging area locations, coming up with a variety of different possibilities within the local area and evaluating each one. Software could facilitate this decision-making by keeping a record of the alternative locations discussed. The user interface could display a geospatial map of the area with markers for the different locations and include the pros and cons considered for each. In terms of software requirements, this means that there is a need for software features that allow the collaborators to identify the geospatial locations and associate them with comments. The software needs to provide appropriate storage for the locations and the corresponding comments so that they can be easily modified and displayed on a map.

Our geocollaboration architecture addresses this requirement for storing locations and corresponding comments through user-created, geospatial content and links. Users can create geospatial elements, such as points, lines, and polygons, and display them on a geographic map. The architecture provides storage for both simple and complex geometric elements and includes reader and writer operations for accessing the content. All user-created elements also can be associated with additional resources through links. Each geospatial element can have a corresponding URL, linking it to a static webpage or another online tool, such as a discussion forum.

In addition to recording the alternative staging areas, the emergency planning committee could benefit from a tool that documents their final decisions. Across meetings, the airport planning group often forgot the staging area decisions they had made. A software package could be used in the face-to-face emergency planning meetings to keep a record of these decisions and provide a geospatial representation of them as documentation. The stakeholders would not have to remember the decisions that were made and they could continue where they left off at the next meeting. To do this, there are additional software requirements. There needs to be support for the generation of geographic maps and labeling of geospatial locations.

The geocollaboration architecture considers this requirement in its design. The user-created content can be layered on top of existing geographic representations for an area. In geographic information systems (GIS), geospatial data are organized through a concept of layers and multiple data sets are layered to produce a combined visualization. Our architecture reuses this concept, allowing user-created elements to be understood with respect to existing map data, as each element is associated with a geographic position. Labeling is also available in the architecture through the rendering approach. Based on a GIS approach, each dataset layer in the map is associated with a rendering style that describes how to draw the geospatial elements. This customized style includes parameters for the fonts, colors, and graphics to use.

Reflecting on the airport emergency planning meetings further, this group lacks a way to collaborate outside of the organized meetings. For instance, if someone misses a meeting they typically must wait until the next meeting to learn about the planning status. With distributed collaboration software, however, the multiple agencies could continue their discussions online in the time between meetings and people not in attendance could be involved. Given the importance of spatial information in emergency response planning, there is a particular need for distributed, geocollaboration solutions.

The geocollaboration architecture provides a way for online geospatial representations to be collaborative. In addition to including geospatial maps in webpages, the architecture shares the map data and rendering techniques, such that similar, interactive, map applications can be used by multiple people in different physical locations. The geocollaboration architecture includes synchronous collaboration features for situations when people are logged in at the same time. It also provides a record about when the map was modified last and by whom, supporting asynchronous interaction. The software constantly maintains the current state of a geospatial discussion and offers a way for contributing ideas outside of traditional meetings.

Enhancing Plan Dissemination and Awareness

Once the emergency response staging area decisions are decided, there is a question of how to disseminate this information. In the airport planning case study, the people not in attendance at the meeting needed a way to learn about the decisions. Some of these people were simply absent from the meeting and others were volunteers who were not involved in the planning process. Making the information available online is one way to address this need, but doing so introduces additional software requirements. The online software needs to make both the geospatial representations and the marked staging areas accessible to the appropriate people.

The geocollaboration architecture addresses this requirement by building on top of an existing collaboration software package. The existing package provides secure access to a suite of collaboration tools and offers two ways to interact with the tools, one that is Web-based and another that is a Java application. Geospatial software developed using the architecture is available as another tool in this suite. It inherits the security and multiple editor features of the existing software package and allows the geospatial representations to be presented within webpages and as separate applications.

Another observation from our fieldwork is that each stakeholder brings different concerns and different informational needs to the emergency planning meetings. For instance, earlier we discussed how the firemen and emergency medical units have different response plans with respect to the university sports stadium. These different roles and responsibilities inherently require different geospatial representations. Software can facilitate this by providing ways to build and display representations that highlight different spatial features. This requires software features that allow users to both identify the data collections that are important and specify how to display them in a representation.

The geocollaboration architecture addresses this requirement for agency-specific representations. It provides a way to group together and organize existing GIS data. For example, a firemen's representation may include fire station locations and hydrant positions displayed on top of roads data. The architecture also provides customized styles for rendering the map data, such that different representations might use the same GIS data but display the contents differently. In the firemen example, the roads data in the display could be colored based on if a road is passable with a large fire engine. The data collections and rendering techniques are reusable. The same data collection can be used in multiple geospatial representations and the same rendering style can be applied in different representations.

Enhancing Tabletop Exercise Activities

The tabletop exercises of emergency planning present additional opportunities for software-based enhancements. These exercises involve geospatial response walkthroughs with a large paper map and post-it notes. Replacing this paper map with a software representation would allow a planning committee to interact with a geospatial representation to a greater extent. Instead of post-it notes that cover up areas of the map, the software could allow the group to annotate and mark directly on the map. It could maintain the annotations associated with alternative paths in a walkthrough. It could also create multiple annotation sets for different walkthroughs. To do this, the software must support a sophisticated approach to annotations.

Each of these scenarios is supported with the geocollaboration architecture. The software allows the same GIS data to be reused in different collaborative representations. These GIS data can be layered with different user-created content to generate alternative annotations. Also, a user-created content layer contains a set of annotations and multiple layers can be used to render multiple annotation sets. This allows an exploration of alternatives as the layers can be toggled off and on to generate unique map views.

Supporting Different Activities with Similar Geographic Locations

Lastly, looking across the different emergency planning meetings, we observed that similar geographic areas are considered in different emergency planning contexts. For example, the university football stadium is adjacent to a large, indoor basketball arena. The roads and the parking lots surrounding these two facilities are the essentially same in terms of emergency response planning, but the emergency preparedness efforts are completely independent of one another. Similar geospatial software that represents the same geospatial element can be used in these two different contexts. This requires software that can create specialized applications for different geocollaboration activities, while reusing map data.

Our geocollaboration software architecture provides this support. It uses the GIS concept of layers to generate a geospatial representation. These individual data layers are reusable and can be combined to produce multiple, unique representations. Some of the layers available to the stadium planning meetings, for example, would be relevant for the neighboring indoor sports arena. The architecture also allows individual geographic features and entire data sets to be linked to other online content. These links can be preserved in reusing map data, which can allow the different planning committees to share resources in a minimal way.

A Comparison to Existing Software

There are commercial software packages with geocollaboration features for supporting emergency management activities. ToucanNavigate (http://www.infopatterns.com/products/toucannavigate.aspx) is a collaborative GIS tool that is available as a plug-in for Microsoft Office Groove (http://office.microsoft.com/en-us/groove/default.aspx). This tool works in the Windows operating system and allows users to share, annotate, and navigate GIS maps together. Disaster Management Interoperability Services, or DMIS (http://www.cmi-services.org/), is a free software tool for first responders provided by the FEMA eGov Disaster Management program. It enables information sharing between organizations at the local, state, and national level, and includes a mapping feature for sharing incident details. Also, Visual Incident Command System, or VizICS (http://gdviz.com/web/solutions/vizics.mtml), is a command and control system that is an extension of a military solution for crisis management. The VizICS software uses shared geographic maps and other visualization tools to organize emergency-related information.

Less specific to geocollaboration, Web mapping services, such as Google Maps or Yahoo! Maps, have made creating Web-based mapping applications more accessible to programmers. Through free, public APIs (http://www.google.com/apis/maps/ or http://developer.yahoo.com/maps/), they make it easier for Web developers to put interactive content (such as clickable icons with a popup information window) on top of map data provided by the service. Such Web applications can then allow many users to asynchronously view or edit custom content layers on top of the server's map data.

Software that can be developed with our architecture has similarities with these commercial solutions. Each of these software packages includes features for user-created content that is associated with GIS data and layers of map content. All of them, except for Google Maps, also include synchronous, collaborative navigation schemes. In addition, ToucanNavigate also has a linking feature that allows map elements to reference other Groove tools and DMIS organizes user-created content in a hierarchy enabling multiple user-created layers.

Our approach of developing a software architecture differs from each of these existing solutions, however. The intent in creating this architecture is to allow for individual geocollaboration solutions to be tailored to emergency management's needs. Software developed using the architecture can be configured with a specialized user interface design and interaction techniques. It is not restricted to a particular screen layout or a specific set of awareness features for knowing who is doing what and where. Customized rendering techniques, agency-specific views, and data reuse across solutions are also possible. Our architecture is also different in that it supports multiplatform software and both application and Web-based clients.

Geocollaborative Software Architecture

Toward a solution of providing appropriate tools for geocollaboration, we must acknowledge that no "one size fits all" tool is likely to exist. Instead, we propose an extensible geocollaborative software architecture that will allow for the construction of these tools. A main function of a software architecture is to document design decisions. Historically, software architectures are grounded in the importance of modularizing software designs, specifically not basing them on the "flowchart" like execution of the system, but instead with an eye to an informed and evolving (i.e., "likely to change") design (Parnas, 1972).

This architecture is primarily based on the detailed analysis of observations and requirements presented in the section "Geocollaboration Scenarios in Emergency Management Planning". In prior work, we have also identified some of the user interface design issues inherent in developing distributed, geocollaboration solutions (Schafer et al., 2005). These issues explore the fundamental ways tools and features provided in geocollaboration software can differ. This geocollaboration architecture also furthers that work. Prior geocollaborative prototyping experience and user studies in this area (Schafer, 2004; Schafer & Bowman, 2006), also guides the architecture work. As a whole, the architecture is designed to provide unified, basic building blocks for any of the systems we have designed, observed, or constructed above. We offer this design as a pattern that can be followed, extended, and improved in the construction of geocollaborative software. The implementation is complete and available as open-source software on SourceForge (http://bridgetools.sourceforge.net/).

Our design takes advantage of existing Java-based collaborative infrastructure: CORK (Content Object Replication Kit) and BRIDGE (Basic Resources for Integrating Distributed Group Environments (http://bridgetools.sourceforge.net) while also building upon GeoTools (http://www.geotools.org/), a toolkit from the GIS community. CORK provides the basic mechanisms for replicating Java objects across multiple clients along with storage and security related to those objects (Isenhour et al., 2001). BRIDGE builds upon CORK providing an application and Web infrastructure, allowing shared objects to be organized in a user accessible fashion (e.g., a file directory type structure). Multiple objects can be viewed at once through multiple windows and a high bandwidth connection. BRIDGE also provides mechanisms for automatic versioning, social awareness, and multiple views for interacting with the same, shared content through either a Java-based application or a Web form. CORK and BRIDGE together provide the building blocks to construct multiplatform, collaborative Web applications. GeoTools is an implementation of Open Geospatial Consortium (OGC) specifications. GeoTools is designed to be a modular architecture so that its features can easily be improved as Open GIS and other relevant standards evolve. These existing software bases provide an ideal starting point as they provide the core collaboration features and GIS functionality around which a geocollaborative system can be built.

Based on the fieldwork observations and design requirements, a number of key features were identified as important for emergency planning activities. These key features were shared annotations and selections (the ability to highlight map data for others); the ability to see as well as lead or follow another's navigation (workspace awareness); and the ability to organize and share existing map data along with specialized views of that data and georeferenced linking of that data to other content (organize and link content).

Geospatial Data

GeoTools provides a design for managing GIS data. We use this model as a foundation to design our own data structures for sharing and storing geospatial data (see Fig. 17.1). Our geospatial data design derives from GeoTools' DataStore interface which is the basis for all collections of geospatial data in GeoTools. We do this in two contexts. First, we provide a SharedMutableDataStore class that is a replicated collection of map features (CORK objects), which is editable and shared across all

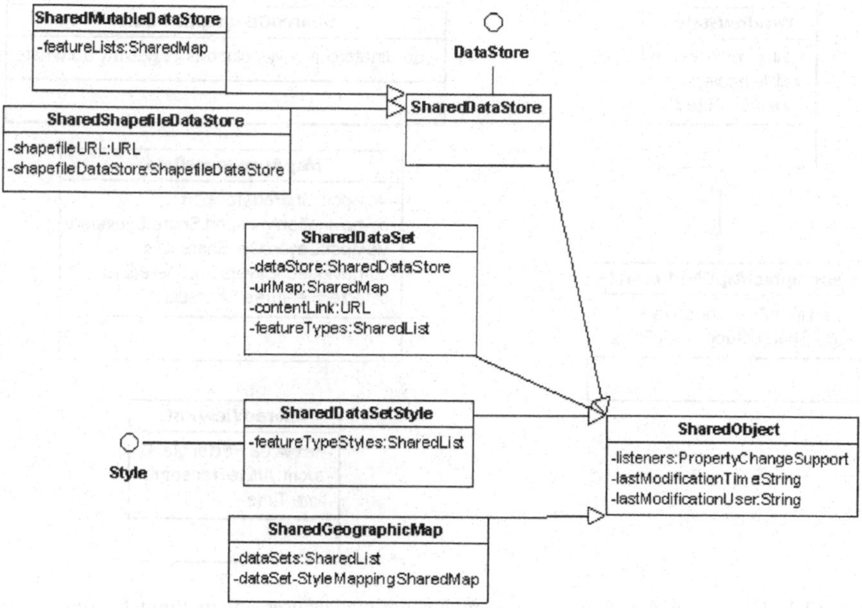

Fig. 17.1 The geocollaboration software architecture reuses classes from the GeoTools toolkit, like DataStore and Style, and provides objects that act as building blocks for development

clients. This allows for the drawing of annotations that can be seen by other users at the same time. In general it allows for other features to be added to the maps. Secondly, we provide a SharedShapefileDataStore class to share one of the most common GIS formats, shapefiles. This allows users to include existing GIS data in maps so that others have access to the same content. Both the SharedMutableDataStore and the SharedShapefileDataStore extend a common SharedDataStore class. Each is an implementation of the existing GeoTools DataStore interface.

Awareness

Part of the existing BRIDGE social awareness mechanisms provides information about who is interacting with the same objects as you (e.g., if you have windows open on the same content). We have extended this structure in BRIDGE to include generic awareness information about each open window (see Fig. 17.2). In the simplest context, we have designed this to broadcast information about whether the opened window is minimized or maximized on the user's screen and whether or not it is in focus and receiving mouse events (WindowState).

This window information can also be specialized to the content type of the open object. In particular, the GeographicMapWindowState object broadcasts telepointer information, a shared latitude and longitude, about where the mouse

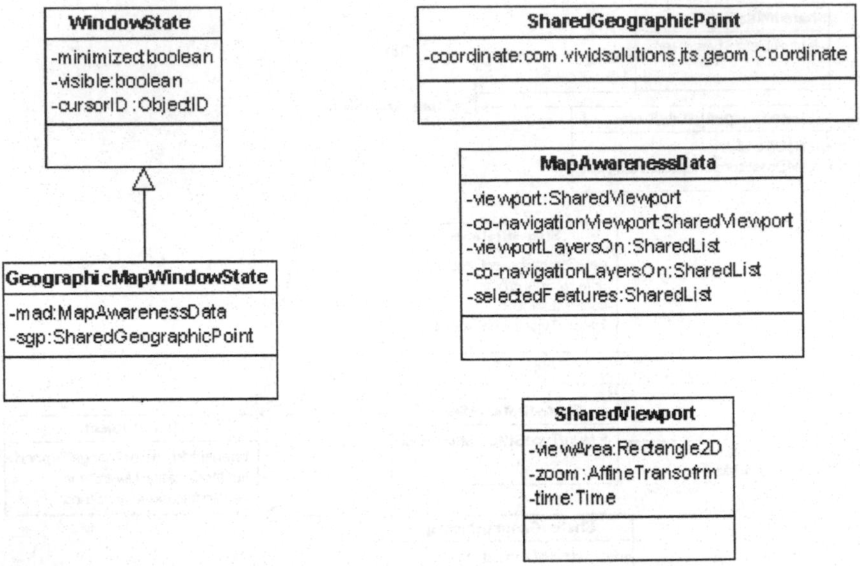

Fig. 17.2 The geocollaboration software architecture models user activity through a separate set of objects that extend the social awareness features of BRIDGE

pointer is over a map for each window (SharedGeographicPoint), and includes information about the area of a map currently being viewed (MapAwarenessData). This viewport information describes: the bounds of the map area being viewed (SharedViewport), the bounds of a previous area viewed (SharedViewport), the map layers currently being viewed, the map layers displayed with the previous area viewed, and the currently selected features. This entire structure is replicated for each map window across all clients viewing that map. Being a replicated object, multiple users can connect their windows to the same shared viewport object and co-navigate the map. They can also disconnect their windows and return to their previous display state.

Our interests in awareness go beyond social and workspace awareness to that of long-term activity awareness. The historical version tracking in BRIDGE provides a foundation to begin examining visualizations for map changes over time. The current design maintains information about the last modifications of all geospatial data though the SharedObject class. These last modification time and last user details will be used to develop the visualizations.

Building Blocks of Geospatial Activities

The rationale behind much of this design was the separation and objectifying of data. Dynamic awareness data are kept separate from geospatial content, hence the two class diagrams. The geospatial data as well as references to and from that data (such as selection and links) are separated in a way to promote reuse, not just by developers but also by users constructing maps. For example, a SharedDataSet object allows users to create URL-type links for individual features within a DataStore. These links can reference other collaborative BRIDGE objects or Web sites. The design intentionally stores the links in a separate object from a DataStore. This allows users to create unique SharedDataSet objects, with links to different content, using the same underlying map data.

The way that BRIDGE manages and encourages separate storage of different shared objects encourages developers and users to plug and play shared content together. Shared style objects (SharedDataSetStyle) that are managed separate from the geospatial data allow users to apply a specific style across multiple map layers or even different maps. A style object is paired with a SharedDataSet object within a geographic map. This allows users to render the same, linked dataset with multiple styles.

Although our implementation is based around CORK/BRIDGE and GeoTools, our intent is also that this provides a pattern, which other geocollaborative systems could model. Any CSCW system that is based on the replication of data across clients, such as GroupKit (Roseman & Greenberg, 1996) or Habanero (Chabert et al., 1998), could replicate these, or derived, structures. Retrospectively, the architecture is also influenced by and designed to operate in a Model-View-Controller (Reenskaug, 1979) like environment, which is the approach taken for managing other shared data in CORK/BRIDGE, separating underlying data models from the visual/widget implementation. Thus, the architecture is designed to model geographic data content and the awareness (shared user state) content. More specifically and somewhat uniquely, it seeks to organize these structures in a way that separates static and dynamic GIS data and also separates different parts of the "view"-related shared data: styles (that define what a map looks like), selection of map features, telepointer, and viewport information. This allows for many alternatives in sharing awareness information, for example, choices of radar views and/or shared navigation between dynamic subsets of users. Splitting more dynamic shared user content from what can be voluminous amounts of fixed geographical data can offer performance improvements over replicating copies of the same data and allows for reuse of that data across multiple maps. Constructed map visualizations can be reused and linked to separate user-specified data sets or associated with different styles.

Applying the Architecture in a Multiple Role Geocollaboration Tool

Our current use of this geocollaborative software architecture is in the development of a prototype tool for emergency planning that features multiple role-specific views (Fig. 17.3). In this tool, emergency planners are given both a public, team map for planning, and a personal, role-specific map (Convertino et al., 2005). So

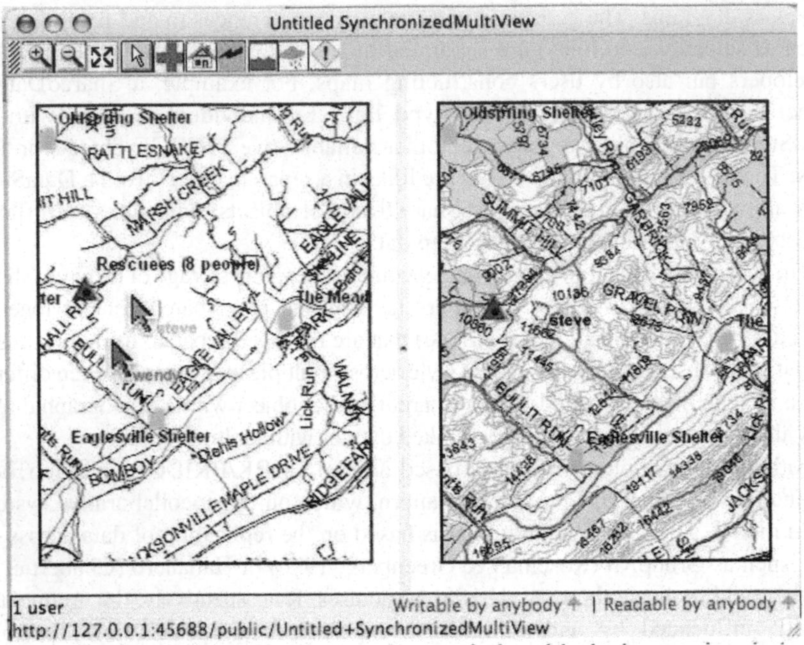

Fig. 17.3 The geocollaboration software architecture facilitated the development of a multiple views, emergency planning tool. The map on the left is the common team view, which displays the mouse cursor locations of others. The map on the right is a role-specific environmental view with floodplains, land contours, and rivers

for example, a planner whose expertise is in public works could have a role-specific map that provides details on community roads and utilities infrastructure while a planner specializing in mass care would have a map that provides rapid access to information about shelters and medical facilities in an affected region along with the resources at those locations. These multiple role views can be more easily constructed within a collaborative software architecture that treats its components as building blocks of a more comprehensive application.

Separate team and role-specific geographic map objects can be constructed from either the same or different existing geospatial data sets (Table 17.3). So the same reference point data, such as major roads and other well-known landmarks are shared across all the views, while personal views include role-specific data sets. A custom style allows the environmental emergency planner to see more details about rivers in his/her role-specific view while a shared style for roads, families to rescue, and shelters provide a common reference.

Shared editable data stores provide a dynamic structure for annotating the map during planning, and are treated just like the data stores used for more static geospatial data. Visibility of these editable data sets within the ream and role-specific views can either be controlled by those components' association with a specific geographic map object (as described above) or through CORK permissions mechanisms (which

Table 17.3 The multiple views geocollaboration tool is composed of two views, a team map and an environmental map. The same underlying data objects are reused in the views with the environmental map visualizing more data objects and rendering the same "rivers" data with a different style

Geographic data and links	Team map view	Environmental map view
Roads	Thin black lines	Thin black lines
Families to rescue	Red bullseye	Red bullseye
Shelter locations	Green building icon	Green building icon
Rivers	*Thin blue line*	*Blue line based on river width*
Floodplains		Blue filled polygons
Contours		Labeled thin brown lines

also apply to other data sets). Through these mechanisms, users can collaboratively edit shared map data within the public team view, immediately seeing each other's additions and changes to the plan. In the private, role-specific view they can take notes and put together ideas that can later be moved or copied into the team space, if or when they become relevant.

Awareness mechanisms in this architecture can then extend across the multiple views of our emergency planning tool. The architecture allows for easy adoption of this as needed (and useful because the user interface design of these mechanisms across multiple map views is still a relatively open research space). Sharing telepointers across both the team and role-specific views extends sharing telepointers with a single map, also keeping track of which window the mouse cursor is over. Navigation of the team view can use a common, shared viewport object for co-navigation or can allow independent navigation with separate viewports and include radar views of those viewports. Allowing users to switch between independent and co-navigation is also possible. Awareness information is shared at the object level, so that opening and configuring two multiview planning tools with different geographic maps is possible.

Related Work

Emergency management can be examined from different perspectives. Our work investigates emergency planning as a community activity. It focuses on the community interactions that lead to preparedness and reflects on the involvement of a community in an emergency situation. Other research has focused on emergency call centers, which receive distress calls and dispatch first responders. These studies consider the cognitive work that occurs by dispatch operators; revealing that scenario-based and nonscenario-based knowledge elicitation provide different types of information (Terrell et al., 2004). Studies of emergency call centers also examine how technology is used. In Swedish call centers, for instance, a listening-in feature of a computer-aided dispatch system is just as valuable as being in the same room and over-hearing (Pettersson et al., 2004). Also, in Norwegian call centers, integrating multiple, specialized systems into a single information system introduces conflicts with the highly reliable teamwork practices (Tjora, 2004). Looking at the existing practices of call centers, there have also been novel designs to support these contexts. For instance, the WaterCalls project used an ambient display with bowls of flowing water to support cooperation across emergency centers (Pettersson, 2004). Likewise, new designs for call center information systems have been suggested that deviate from the traditional, incident-centric model to consider an overall view of responses (Jones, 2004).

Another collection of work related to emergency management examines the coordination issues in providing emergency medical care. In an emergency response situation, the form and extent of medical care provided is typically not well documented. One study has looked at automated speech recognition that allows on-scene medics to easily record their actions (Gröschel et al., 2004). Another extensive study designed and evaluated a combination of a wearable computer and software for maintaining care information at an emergency scene (Holzman, 1999). Other research has studied the applicability of sensor network for medical emergency response. In particular, the CodeBlue architecture allows wireless tracking of both patients and first responders at an emergency scene and addresses issues relating to ad hoc networks and security (Lorincz et al., 2004).

Much prior work has explored how technology can enhance emergency management. For instance, there have been studies of applying computing systems to improve firefighter practices. One paper describes the findings from fieldwork conducted with firefighters and the resulting prototype displays for an incident commander at an emergency (Jian et al., 2004b). Another paper suggests a context-aware messaging system to improve firefighter safety (Jian et al., 2004a), while another proposes a fire communication system that recognizes the different needs of officers and standard firefighters (Camp et al., 2000). Additionally, research has explored the usefulness of software-based simulations. The NeoCITIES simulation uses a scaled world to emulate the decision-making that occurs in emergency (Jones et al., 2004). It provides a controlled, but realistic environment to study team cognition and communication in a crisis. Similarly, simulations are used in studies of emergency evacuation procedures (Johnson, 2005). This software provides a way to assess the risks building occupants might face in an emergency.

While our work focuses on emergency planning, other research investigates the response phase of emergency management. This related work is interested in the design and development of information systems for response operations. Prototypes, such as the interactive, intelligent, spatial information system (IISIS), explore ways to facilitate the interorganizational coordination in response situations (Comfort, 1999). Similarly, design principles have been proposed for the development of a dynamic emergency response management information system (Turoff et al., 2004). These principles identify high-level features of an emergency response system, such as providing open, multidirectional communication and always presenting up-to-date information. Other research has studied the emergency operations centers in charge of a large-scale response effort (Brewer, 2004). One project that is particularly relevant addresses crisis action planning (Jacobs et al., 1998). This work considers humanitarian relief operations and presents a collaborative environment to support the response team's planning. Similar to our architecture, this prior effort uses Java-based collaborative environment that offers data sharing and customized renderings.

Unlike emergency management, geocollaboration is not a widely recognized discipline. Geocollaboration is a new field of research that investigates how technology can support multiple people working together on a geospatial problem. Some of the earlier work in geocollaboration explored novel software solutions for spatial decision-making. This prior research investigated synchronous collaboration settings with collaborators co-located, as well as working asynchronously. For example, the tool called Spatial Group Choice supported collaborative spatial decision-making in face-to-face meetings (Jankowski et al., 1997), while Claus Rinner's work on Argumentation Maps explored asynchronous GIS-based discussions (Rinner, 1999a, b). GroupArc was another early project that demonstrated the possibility for a collaborative geographic information system (GIS) (Churcher & Churcher, 1996, 1999). This prototype integrated a GIS system with a groupware toolkit to allow distributed collaborators to browse and annotate GIS data.

The concept of geocollaboration is particularly interesting to the U.S. military. The military relies on geospatial systems and they are eager for software that allows them to collaborate and share geospatial information. For instance, MayaViz has a product called "Command Post of the Future" that allows military commanders to transfer their perspective to others on the battlefield (http://www.mayaviz.com). Also, the Center for Human-Computer Communication at Oregon Graduate Institute of Science and Technology is investigating an agent-based, collaborative system called QuickSet (http://www.cse.ogi.edu/CHCC/QuickSet/mainProj.html). QuickSet enables the creation of military simulations and explores multimodal user interactions with a geographic map (Corradini et al., 2002; Oviatt, 1997). Both of these projects have geocollaboration features that overlap with our architecture, yet the military setting presents a different work context than community emergency planning. Our fieldwork and scenarios describe citizens and volunteers coming together for the good of their community, while the military has formal structures and processes.

Lastly, there have been prior investigations of geocollaboration situations within emergency response. The GeoVISTA Center at Penn State University is studying the use of speech and gesture recognition with a GIS (Rauschert et al., 2002). Their work considers both same-place collaboration as multiple people interact with a large screen GIS, and distributed collaboration, as emergency personnel communicate between an emergency operations center and a field location (Sharma et al., 2003; Cai et al., 2004). Their work also proposes an initial conceptual framework of geocollaboration (2004). This framework identifies six dimensions of geocollaboration, considering both human aspects, such as collaboration tasks, as well as system aspects, like interaction characteristics.

Conclusions and Opportunities for Geocollaboration in Emergency Planning

This chapter has argued for the community-oriented nature of emergency management planning work. It has described how multiple local agencies come together to prepare for and respond to emergencies. This focus on local agencies and citizen involvement, along with the fact that every emergency occurs in some locale, emphasizes our interest in community emergency management planning. Studying some of the local towns where we, the researchers, live provides examples of the community activities that involve emergency management planning. These local community activities point to the need for geocollaboration in emergency management planning. They reveal how first responders must discuss the geospatial aspects of their community to be prepared. For instance, predesignated staging areas for responders are an important part of an emergency plan, and deciding on those physical locations beforehand is a collaborative effort. Our local communities also motivate new collaboration technology. They evoke an exploration of software technology that will enhance the geocollaboration tasks of emergency management planning. There are definite limitations to using poster-size paper maps and hard copy print outs of geographic information. This work investigates some of the opportunities available through interactive, collaborative geospatial software. It envisions how such technology could be used to enhance community emergency management planning.

The software architecture described in this chapter offers both a design and a toolkit for implementing geocollaboration applications. The architecture allows for the design and development of a variety of geocollaboration software tools. This is particularly well suited for emergency management planning, which has different geocollaboration needs depending on the context. The software architecture allows us, as the researchers, to explore different geocollaboration interactions and features within a specific use context. It also allows the development of unique applications for multiple contexts.

The software architecture, and the corresponding tool development, is also beneficial to community emergency management planning. Through the design and development of collaborative tools for emergency planning work practices, a collaborative, virtual environment for emergency management planning can form. Geocollaboration tools not only directly support collaboration among stakeholders, but they also create an online environment for information exchange. The tools available online allow emergency management planning activities, to occur beyond just the fixed schedule of face-to-face meetings.

Our geocollaboration architecture provides a means to develop tools that allow multiple people to participate in emergency management planning. They do not restrict stakeholders to meet at a particular place and time, in a room where only one person speaks at a time. Rather, they facilitate different levels of participation and different levels of rank. Being collaborative means that the tools are accessible all of the time and people can use them as little or as frequently as they like. For instance, a fire chief now might both attend the meetings and contribute ideas regularly online, while a volunteer fireman might review changes to emergency plans from home and comment on their implications. Both firemen are important to emergency management, but their involvement in emergency management differs. Most likely the chief regularly attends the emergency management meetings and the volunteer does not. Collaborative tools, however, provide the volunteer a way to participate, if only peripherally.

Our geocollaborative architecture can also support the unique roles people play in emergency management and allow tools to be tailored to those specific purposes.

Different agencies can contribute from different perspectives by having access to their detailed GIS data integrated with the plans. The tools can also be tailored for specific purposes by adding features relevant to their specific role. Firemen, for example, have different informational needs than town managers. They need to know not only about staging areas and emergency vehicle routes but also fine details like flow rates from fire hydrants, while town managers need to be aware of the emergency plans overall. Our design allows for the provision of these different pieces of information to the appropriate agency roles, while offering a context for information exchange across the shared management plan.

Emergency management planning will always require face-to-face meetings and in creating collaboration tools our goal is not to replace the meetings but to allow them to carry beyond an individual meeting. The social benefits of face-to-face meetings are unsurpassed, as the stakeholders learn about each other in a natural setting. They see one another's physical expressions and hear one another's attitude and beliefs directly. First responders value this highly. It is important to meet and get to know someone before you have to work together in a crisis situation. Another advantage of collaborative tools is that they allow this social networking to continue outside of the meetings. Personal relationships, which are so important to emergency personnel, can continue to develop online. For instance, a conversation between a police chief and a public works director from neighboring townships does not have to end when the emergency planning meeting concludes. The two could use a geocollaboration tool to continue their discussion of roads susceptible to flooding. One key to this will be providing a means through which the activities at a planning meeting can be captured, either by having members use these geocollaborative technologies synchronously at the meeting or capturing and publishing the results of the meetings.

As mentioned, collaborative tools are not limited to a particular meeting. They can be used for both synchronous and asynchronous communication. People can use them in face-to-face meetings at the same time or they can use them at different times online. There is also the possibility for synchronous online use, if two people happen to be online at the same time. With so many opportunities, emergency management planning can become something more than meetings that happen at a particular day and time. It can evolve into the ongoing process, which it is described as. It can occur at all times, in an online environment. This shift in attention can lead to increased vigilance. As emergency management planning occurs through both face-to-face meetings and collaborative tools, everyone involved, including first responders, may become more cognizant of the emergency plans. We do not expect these changes in practice to take place overnight, but in the long term, these activities can be even more valuable than the documented plans, in terms of vigilance.

References

Brewer, I. Understanding work with geospatial information in emergency management: A cognitive systems engineering approach in GIScience. PhD Dissertation, The Pennsylvania State University, University Park, Pennsylvania, 2004.

Camp, P.J., Hudson, J.M., Keldorph, R.B., Lewis, S., & Mynatt, E.D. Supporting Communication and Collaboration Practices in Safety-Critical Situations. Proceedings of the conference on Computer-Human Interactions, 2000, 249–150.

Cai, G., MacEachren, A.M., & Bolelli, L. GCCM: Map-mediated collaboration among emergency operation centers and mobile teams. Poster presented at GIScience, 2004.

Carroll, J.M., Chin, G., Rosson, M.B., & Neale, D.C. The development of cooperation: Five years of participatory design in the virtual school. Proceedings of Designing Interactive Systems, 2000, 239–251.

Chabert, A., Grossman, E., Jackson, L.S., Pietrowiz, S.R., & Seguin, C. Java object-sharing in Habanero. *Communications of the ACM*, 41(6), 1998, 69–76.

Churcher, N.I. & C.D. Churcher. GroupARC-A collaborative approach to GIS. Proceedings of the eighth Annual Colloquium of the Spatial Information Research Centre, 1996, 156–63.

Churcher, N.I., &Churcher, C.D. Real-time conferencing in GIS. *Transactions in GIS*, 3(1), 1999, 23–30.

Comfort, L. Self organization in disaster mitigation and management: Increasing community capacity for response. Presentation given at The International Emergency Management Society conference, 1999.

Convertino, G., Ganoe, C. H., Schafer, W., Yost, B., & Carroll, J. M. A multiple view approach to support common ground in distributed and synchronous geo-collaboration, Coordinated & Multiple Views in Exploratory Visualization 2005, 5 July 2005, London, UK, 2005, 121–132.

Corradini, A., Wesson, R. M., & Cohen, P. R. A map-based system using speech and 3D gestures for pervasive computing. Presented at the Fourth IEEE International Conference on Multimodal Interfaces, October 14–16, Pittsburgh, PA, 2002

Gröschel, J., Philipp, F., Skonetzki, S., Genzwürker, H., Wetter, T., & Ellinger, K. Automated speech recognition for time recording in out-of-hospital emergency medicine- an experimental approach. *Resuscitation*, 60(2), 2004, 205–212.

Gurstein, M. Community informatics: Current status and future prospects – some thoughts, *Community Technology Review*, Winter-Spring 2002, Available online: http://www.comtechreview.org/winter-spring-2002/000056.html

Haddow, G.D. & Bullock, J.A. *Introduction to Emergency Management*. Butterworth-Heinemann, Amsterdam, 2003.

Holzman, T.G. Computer-human interface solutions for emergency medical care. *Interactions*, 6(3), 1999, 13–24.

Isenhour, P.L., Rosson, M.B., & Carroll, J.M. Supporting interactive collaboration on the Web with CORK. *Interacting with Computers*, 13, 2001, 655–676.

Jacobs, J.L., Dorneich, M.C.P., & Jones, P.M. Activity representation and management for crisis action planning. Proceedings of the 1998 IEEE International Conference on Systems, Man, and Cybernetics, October 1998, 961–966.

Jankowski, P., Nyerges, T.L., Smith, A., Moore, T.J., & Horvath, E. Spatial group choice: A SDSS tool for collaborative spatial decision-making. *International Journal of Geographical Information Science*, 11(6), 1997, 577–602.

Jian, X., Chen, N.C., Hong, J.I., Wang, K., Takayama, L., & Landay, J.A. SIREN: Context-aware computing for firefighting. Proceedings of the Second International Conference on Pervasive Computing, 2004a, 87–105.

Jian, X., Hong, J.I., Takayama, L.A., & Landay, J.A. Ubiquitous computing for firefighters: field studies and prototypes of large displays for incident command. Proceedings of the Conference on Human Factors in Computing Systems, ACM Press, 2004b, 679–686.

Johnson, C.W. Applying the lessons of the attack on the World Trade Center, 11th September 2001, to the design and use of interactive evacuation simulations. Proceedings of the Conference on Human Factors in Computing Systems, ACM Press, 2005, 651–660.

Jones, A.C. The information-technology-people abstraction hierarchy: A tool for complex information system design. Masters Thesis, The Pennsylvania State University, University Park, Pennsylvania, 2004.

Jones, R.E.T., McNeese, M.D., Connors, E.S., Jefferson, T., & Hall, D.L. A distributed cognition simulation involving homeland security and defense: the development of NeoCITIES. Proceedings of the Human Factors and Ergonomics Society 48th Annual Meeting, 2004, 631–634.

Lee, R.L., Schafer, W.A., Knoche, A.J., & Carroll, J.M. The role of social capital in emergency response. Proceedings of the Twelfth Americans Conference on Information Systems (AMCIS 2006), Acapulco, Mexico, August 2006.

Lindell, M.K. & Perry, R.W. *Behavioral Foundations of Community Emergency Planning*. Hemisphere Publishing Corporation, Washington, 1992.

Lorincz, K., Malan, D.J., Fulford-Jones, T.R.F., Nawoj, A., Clavel, A., Shnayder, V., Mainland, G., Welsh, M., & Moulton, S. Sensor networks for emergency response: Challenges and opportunities. *Pervasive Computing*, 3(4), 2004, 16–23.

Oviatt, S. Mulitmodal interactive maps: Designing for human performance. *Human-Computer Interaction*, 12, 1997, 93–129.

Parnas, D.L. On the criteria to be used in decomposing systems into modules. *Communications of the ACM*, 15(10), 1972, 1053–1058.

Pettersson, M., Randall, D., & Helgeson, B. Ambiguities, awareness, and economy: A study of emergency service work. *Computer Supported Cooperative Work*, 13, 2004, 125–154.

Quarantelli, E.L. A half century of social science disaster research: Selected major findings and their applicability. Preliminary Paper# 336, Disaster Research Center, 2003. Available online: http://dspace.udel.edu:8080/dspace/handle/19716/297

Rambaldi, G., Kwaku Kyem, A.P., Mbile, P., McCall, M., & Weiner, D. Participatory spatial information management and communication in developing countries. *Electronic Journal of Information Systems in Developing Countries* (EJISDC) 25(1), 2006, 1–9.

Rauschert, I., Agrawal, P., Fuhrmann, S., Brewer, I., Wang, H., Sharma, R., Cai, G., & MacEachren, A. Designing a human-centered, multimodal GIS interface to support emergency management. Proceedings of ACM Symposium on Advances in Geographic Information Systems, 2002, 119–124.

Reenskaug, T. Models – Views – Controllers, Xerox PARC, 1979. Retrieved from http://heim.ifi.uio.no/~trygver/1979/mvc-2/1979-12-MVC.pdf

Rinner, C. Argumaps for spatial planning. Proceedings of TeleGeo'99, First International Workshop on Telegeoprocessing, 1999a, 95–102.

Rinner, C. Argumentation maps-GIS-based discussion support for online planning. PhD Dissertation, University of Bonn, 1999b. Retrieved from http://www.gmd.de/publications/research/1999/022/

Roseman, M. & Greenberg, S. Building real time groupware with GroupKit, a groupware toolkit. *ACM Transactions on Computer Human Interaction*, 3(1), 1996, 66–106.

Schafer, W.A. Supporting spatial collaboration: An investigation of viewport constraint and awareness techniques. PhD Dissertation, Virginia Polytechnic Institute and State University, Blacksburg, Virginia, 2004. Retrieved from http://scholar.lib.vt.edu/theses/available/etd-04222004-142351/

Schafer, W.A. & Bowman, D.A. Supporting distributed spatial collaboration: An investigation of navigation and radar view techniques. *GeoInformatica*, 10(2), 2006, 123–158.

Schafer, W.A., Ganoe, C.H., Xiao, L., Coch, G., & Carroll, J.M. Designing the next generation of distributed, geocollaborative tools. *Cartography and Geographic Information Science*, 32(2), 2005, 81–100.

Schafer, W.A., Carroll, J.M., Haynes, S.R., & Abrams, S. Emergency Management Planning as Collaborative Community Work. *Journal of Homeland Security and Emergency Management*, 5(1), 2008, Article 10.

Sharma, R., Yeasin, M., Krahnstoever, N., Rauschert, I., Cai, C., Brewer, I., MacEachren, A., & Sengupta, K. Speech-gesture driven multimodal interfaces for crisis management. *Proceedings of the IEEE*, 91(9), 2003, 1327–1354.

Steinmann, R., Krek, A., & Blaschke, T. Analysis of online public participatory GIS applications with respect to the differences between the US and Europe. Urban Data Management Symposium (UDMS 2004), 2004.

Terrell, I.S., McNeese, M.D., & Jefferson, T. Exploring cognitive work within a 911 dispatch center: Using complementary knowledge elicitation techniques. Proceedings of the Human Factors and Ergonomics Society 48th Annual Meeting, 2004, 605–609.

Tjora, A. Maintaining redundancy in the coordination of medical emergencies. Proceedings of the conference on Computer-Supported Cooperative Work, 2004, 132–141.

Turoff, M., Chumer, M., Van de Walle, B., & Yao, X. The design of a dynamic emergency response management information system (DERMIS). *Journal of Information Technology Theory and Application*, 5(4), 2004, 1–35.

World Health Organization. *Community emergency preparedness: a manual for managers and policy-makers*. World Health Organization, Geneva, 1999.

Index